american southwest

Directed and Designed by Hans Johannes Hoefer
Edited by Editors of Apa Productions
Photography by Photographers of Apa Photo Agency
Updated by Katherine Gleason

APA PRODUCTIONS

THE INSIGHT GUIDES SERIES RECEIVED SPECIAL AWARDS FOR EXCELLENCE FROM THE PACIFIC AREA TRAVEL ASSOCIATION.

AMERICAN SOUTHWEST
Second Edition Published by:
© 1987 by APA PRODUCTIONS (HK) LTD.
Published by APA Productions (HK) Ltd.
Printed by APA Press Pte. Ltd.
Colour Separation in Singapore by Colourscan Pte. Ltd.

APA PRODUCTIONS
Publisher and Chairman: Hans Johannes Hoefer
Marketing Director: Yinglock Chan
General Manager: Henry Lee
Administration Manager: Alice Ng
Production Manager: Rafie Sain
Editorial Manager: Vivien Kim
Executive Editor: Adam Liptak

Project Editors

Helen Abbott, Diana Ackland, Mohamed Amin, Ravindralal Anthonis, Roy Bailet, Louisa Cambell, Jon Carroll, Hillary Cunningham, John Eames, Janie Freeburg, Bikram Grewal, Virginia Hopkins, Samuel Israel, Jay Itzkowitz, Phil Jaratt, Tracy Johnson, Ben Kalb, Wilhelm Klein, Saul Lockhart, Sylvia Mayuga, Gordon MaLauchlan, Kal Müller, Eric Oey, Daniel P. Reid, Kim Robinson, Ronn Ronck, Robert Seidenberg, Rolf Steinberg, Sriyani Tidball, Lisa Van Gruisen, Merin Wexler.

Contributing Writers

A.D. Aird, Ruth Armstrong, T. Terence Barrow, F. Lisa Beebe, Bruce Berger, Dor Bahadur Bista, Clinton V. Black, Star Black, Frena Bloomfield, John Borthwick, Roger Boschman, Tom Brosnahan, Jerry Carroll, Tom Chaffin, Nedra Chung, Tom Cole, Orman Day, Kunda Dixit, Richard Erdoes, Guillermo Garcia-Oropeza, Daniel Giannoulas, Barbara Gloudon, Harka Gurung, Sharifah Hamzah, Willard A. Hanna, Elizabeth Hawley, Sir Edmund Hillary, Tony Hillerman, Jerry Hopkins, Peter Hutton, Neil Jameson, Michael King, Michele Kort, Thomas Lucey, Leonard Lueras, Michael E. Macmillan, Derek Maitland, Buddy Mays, Craig McGregor, Reinhold Messner, Julie Michaels, M. R. Priya Rangsit, Al Read, Elizabeth V. Reyes, Victor Stafford Reid, Harry Rolnick, E.R. Sarachchandra, Uli Schmetzer, Ilsa Sharp, Norman Sibley, Peter Spiro, Harold Stephens, Keith Stevens, Michael Stone, Desmond Tate, Colin Taylor, Deanna L. Thompson, Randy Udall, James Wade, Mallika Wanigasundara, William Warren, Cynthia Wee, Tony Wheeler, Linda White, H. Taft Wireback, Alfred A. Yuson, Paul Zach.

Contributing Photographers

Carole Allen, Ping Amarand, Tony Arruza, Marcello Bertinetti, Alberto Cassio, Pat Canova, Alain Compost, Ray Cranbourne, Alain Evrard, Ricardo Ferro, Lee Foster, Manfred Gottschalk, Werner Hahn, Dallas and John Heaton, Brent Hesselyn, Hans Hoefer, Luca Invernizzi, Ingo Jezierski, Wilhelm Klein, Dennis Lane, Max Lawrence, Lyle Lawson, Philip Little, Guy Marche, Antonio Martinelli, David Messent, Ben Nakayama, Vautier de Nanxe, Kal Müller, Günter Pfannmuller, Van Philips, Ronni Pinsler, Fitz Prenzel, G.P. Reichelt, Dan Rocovits, David Ryan, Frank Salmoiraghi, Thomas Schollhammer, Blair Seitz, David Stahl, Bill Wassman, Rendo Yap, Hisham Youssef.

While contributions to Insight Guides are very welcome, the publisher cannot assume responsibility for the care and return of unsolicited manuscripts or photographs. Return postage and/or a self-addressed envelope must accompany unsolicited material if it is to be returned. Please address all editorial contributions to Apa Productions, P. O. Box 219, Orchard Point Post Office, Singapore 9123.

Distributors:

Australia and New Zealand: Prentice Hall of Australia, 7 Grosvenor Place, Brookvale, NSW 2100, Australia. **Benelux:** Uitgeverij Cambium, Naarderstraat 11, 1251 Aw Laren, The Netherlands. **Central and South America; Mexico; Portugal and Spain:** Cedibra Editora Brasileira Ltda, Rua Leonidia, 2-Rio de Janeiro, Brazil. **Denmark:** Copenhagen Book Centre Aps, Roskildeveji 338, DK-2630 Tastrup, Denmark. **Europe (others):** European Book Service, Flevolaan 36-38, P. O. Box 124, 1380 AC Weesp, Holland. **Hawaii:** Pacific Trade Group Inc., P. O. Box 1227, Kailua, Oahu, Hawaii 96734, U.S.A. **Hong Kong:** Far East Media Ltd., Vita Tower, 7th Floor, Block B, 29 Wong Chuk Hang Road, Hong Kong. **India and Nepal:** India Book Distributors, 107/108 Arcadia Building, 195 Narima Point, Bombay-400-021, India. **Indonesia:** PT Java Engineering, Jalan Patiunus 47,

Pekalongan, Jateng, Indonesia. **Israel:** Steimatzky Ltd., P.O. Box 628, Tel Aviv 61006, Israel (Israel title only). **Italy:** Zanfi Editori SRL. Via Ganaceto 121, 41100 Modena, Italy. **Caribbean:** Kingston Publishers, 1-A Norwood Avenue, Kingston 5, Jamaica. **Kenya:** Camerapix Publishers International Ltd., P.O. Box 45048, Nairobi, Kenya. **Korea:** Kyobo Book Centre Co., Ltd., P.O. Box Kwang Hwa Moon 1 658, Seoul, Korea. **Philippines:** National Book Store, 701 Rizal Avenue, Manila, Philippines. **Singapore and Malaysia:** MPH Distributors (S) Pte. Ltd., 601 Sims Drive #03-21 Pan-I Warehouse and Office Complex, S'pore 1438, Singapore. **Switzerland:** M.P.A. Agencies-Import SA, CH. du Croset 9, CH-1024 Ecublens, Switzerland. **Taiwan:** Caves Books Ltd., 103 Chungshan N.Road, Sec. 2, Taipei, Taiwan, Republic of China. **Thailand:** Far East Publications Ltd., 117/3 Soi Samahan, Sukhumvit 4 (South Nana), Bangkok, Thailand. **United Kingdom and Ireland:** Harrap Ltd., 19-23 Ludgate Hill, London EC4M 7PD, England, United Kingdom. **Mainland United States and Canada:** Graphic Arts Center Publishing, 3019 N.W. Yeon, P.O. Box 10306, Portland OR 97210, U.S.A. (The Pacific Northwest title only); Prentice Hall Press, Gulf & Western Building, One Gulf & Western Plaza, New York, NY 10023, U.S.A. (all other titles).

French editions: Editions Gallimard, 5 rue Sébastien-Bottin, F-75007 Paris, France. **German editions:** Nelles Verlag GmbH, Schleissheimer Str. 371b, 8000 Munich 45, West Germany. **Italian editions:** Zanfi Editori SLR, Via Ganaceto 121 41100 Modena, Italy. **Portuguese and Spanish editions:** Cedibra Editora Brasileira Ltda, Rua Leonidia, 2-Rio de Janerio, Brazil.

By Way of Introduction

The resounding success of Apa Productions' first American title, *Hawaii*, published in 1980, and the warm receipt of *Florida* (1982) and *Mexico* (1983) by readers and critics alike, were enough to convince founder-publisher **Hans Hoefer** that American readers were ready for more *Insight Guides*. So 1984 saw the publication of the twin volumes of *Southern* and *Northern California*; and one covering the *New England* states. And *American Southwest*, now in your hand, is by no means Apa Productions' concluding title on the American arena, but is regarded as imminent in its efforts to portray world leading destinations through its highly acclaimed *Insight Guides* series.

Hopkins

J. Anderson

Hoefer

It is surprising, in a way, that *Insight Guide, American Southwest* is Apa's seventh title on America and not its first. So overwhelming is the area's natural beauty and so deep its cultural heritage that anything short of the lush photography and thoughtful commentary found in this book would be unfair treatment to this land. But the task was also a daunting one, not in the least because the area covered is enormous and the native population sometimes a little wary of outsiders.

Apa Productions bided its time until it could assemble the perfect team of experts and insiders. Hoefer, a graduate of printing, book production, design and photography studies in Krefeld, West Germany, is a disciple of the Bauhaus tradition of graphic arts. He established Apa Productions in 1970, and that year published *Bali*, thereby setting a new trend in travel literature. Hoefer continues to be the mastermind behind the *Insight Guide* series, which totals 24 titles at the end of 1984. Hoefer assigned **John Gottberg Anderson** to appoint and supervise the American Southwest project team. Anderson was based in Singapore as a managing editor from 1981 to 1984, during which time, saw the creation of several new titles, including *Burma*, *Nepal*, *Sri Lanka*, *California* and *New England*.

Heading the book's project team in America was **Virginia Hopkins**. Hopkins knew North America well, living down in Aspen, Colorado, and sometimes in New York City, after her graduation from Yale University, Connecticut. But it was her inconceivable love for the American Southwest that won her the role as project editor for the book. She spent months travelling around the Southwest in her van, coordinating writers and photographers, assembling archival material in out-of-the-way museums, collecting information from anyone willing to sit down and tell a story. For Hopkins, it was also a time for renewing old friendships and searching out old haunts. Her experience as editor of *Aspen Magazine* and as writer for publications as varied as *Life* and *Outside* helped her immeasurably.

The array of writers and photographers Hopkins rounded up is formidable—a motley crew of some of the most talented and respected in the land. Each brings a unique style, a special area of interest and long experience to their work.

Tony Hillerman, a professor of journalism at the University of New Mexico in Albuquerque, set the mood right for the book with his introductory piece, "A Beautiful Valley." He also takes the reader on a unique tour to the "Heart of America's Indian Country." An acclaimed mystery writer (his *The Dance Hall of the Dead* won the best mystery novel award in 1973), Hillerman derives great satisfaction when Navajo, Zuni, Apache and others read his books and tell him, "Yes, indeed that's us."

Bruce Berger may have contributed more text than anyone else. He certainly contributed much wit and insight. His pieces on "The Great Land Creation," "Modern Southwest," "The Anglos," "Phoenix City and its Environs" and "Central Arizona" complement his extensive work elsewhere; Berger has written for *New York Times*, *Poetry*, *Aspen Magazine* and *The Yale Review*. He has had two books published on the Southwest besides: *There was a River* (1979) and *Hangin' On : Gordon Snidow portrays the Cowboy Heritage* (1980).

Buddy Mays lives in a town in New Mexico

named after a television game show—Truth or Consequences, it's called. Mays is a well-known sportsman, travel writer and photographer, who manages to do all three with excellence. Bringing his eclectic talents into play, he contributed the chapters on "Indian Prehistory" and "The Great Outdoors." Besides contributions on the literary side, the majority of photographs appearing in this book were gathered from his fine photographic agency.

Santa Fe is another city rich in talents. **Stan Steiner** authored the book's history pieces on "Spanish Explorations" and "Arrival of the Anglos," and has written and edited dozens of other books and articles on the Southwest. His literary background, professional appointments, awards and honors make him a leading authority on the people and history of the Southwest. Four of his books—*The New Indians*, *La Raza*, *The Vanishing White Man*, *The Ranchers*—are filled with Western individuals and their ideas, in relationship to the land.

From one Santa Fean to another; **Richard Erdoes** has nine books to his credit, most of them on the Southwest or its Native Americans, and his contributions to this book—"Early 20th Century," "The Hispanics" and "The Navajo"—are as erudite and charming as he personally is. He spent many years working as an artist for Time-Life Inc., and his vision of the Southwest through photography lends an important aspect to the book.

Living on a small ranch in the Tucson Mountains is novelist **Leslie Marmon Silko**, who contributed "The Indians" and "The Pueblo." Herself a Pueblo Indian raised on the Laguna reservation in New Mexico, and receipient of a prestigious five-year MacArthur Foundation Fellowship, Silko has published two novels, *Ceremony* and *Storyteller*. "Storytelling has always been a part of my life"; the Pueblo people have for thousands of years continued the entire culture through the oral art of storytelling.

Rudolfo Anaya, who wrote about the "Hispanics," is one of the most lyrical and renowned Hispanic writers of the Southwest, as is attested by the popularity of his novels and his long list of honors; which includes a Before Columbus Foundation American Book award for his novel *Tortuga* in 1980 and a national literary award for his first novel, *Bless Me, Ultima* in 1971. He lectures at the University of New Mexico and spends his free time writing and travelling.

Patricia Broder provides her expertise in Southwest painting and sculpture in the book's chapter on "The Anglos." Her award-winning books include *Bronze of The Amer-*

ican West and *Taos: A Painter's Dream*.

Randy Udall, who covered "The Grand Canyon" and "Southern Utah," is an Outward Bound instructor whose great passion is exploring that country by foot, raft and four-wheel-drive vehicle. Randy knows the territory backwards and forwards, and readers of his pieces should take his recommendations and heed his warnings.

Ruth Armstrong gave New Mexico ("Pueblo Country Fares") the rich and varied coverage it well deserves. A travel writer with 40 years of experience in the Southwest, Ruth has been

Hillerman

Berger

Mays

Steiner

Silko

published in major newspapers throughout the United States, as well as in *Reader's Digest* and *Travel and Leisure*. Her husband and travel com-

Armstrong

Barnes

panion, **Ellis Armstrong**, also contributed photographs to the book. **Suzi Barnes**, a freelance photographer and instructor, wrote the sidebar on "Adobe." She also has a few photographic representations in the book. Fittingly, she lives in a passive solar adobe house in Arizona.

Tom Miller whose droll view of "Tucson and the Border County" appears in the book, is an accomplished writer. His recently published book, *On the Border*, has led *Swank* magazine, the great literary arbiter, to declare him "a Southwestern John McPhee." His offbeat stories regularly liven up *New York Times*.

Miller

Barbara Chulick, an avowed freelance writer who lives in Las Vegas, leads readers skillfully through the zany neon world of Las Vegas without missing a beat. She is published in *The Nevada* (the Sunday supplement of *Las Vegas Review/Journal*), and the *Las Vegas Magazine*, among others.

The discussion of the arts and crafts of "The Pueblo" Indians is by **Mary Nelson**, who is also an editor and bookreviewer of *American Artist*.

Bringing readers closer to what many say is the most culturally intact Indian tribe in the country in **Alison Sekaquaptewa**, who penned the piece on "The Hopi." Reporting on the "Apache" was **Ned Anderson**, Tribal Chairman of the San Carlos Apache, while the "Papago/Pima" piece was scribed by **Ofelia Zepeda**, a Papago Indian poet and a Professor of Linguistics at the University of Arizona in Tucson.

The massive task of compiling the book's entire Guide in Brief (except the "Food" essay) and the Info sections was for someone

| Chulick | Nelson | N. Anderson |

| Kurtz | Johnson | Moore |

with a flair for organization as well as a great deal of willpower; **Nancy Kurtz** was the obvious choice. An editor and journalist, Kurtz labored above and beyond the call of duty to create one of the most complete sources of information for travellers to the Southwest. The food of the Southwest is described in loving detail by **Ronald Johnson**, the author of *The Afficionado's Southwestern Cooking*, a classic of its kind.

In addition to those mentioned earlier, several other photographers are represented in this volume. **Mireille Vautier**, who operates the Photothèque Vautier-de Nanxe in Paris, France, travelled extensively through the American Southwest with her photographer colleagues in 1982, shooting 1,000 rolls of film along the way. **Terrence Moore**, whose photographs have appeared in *Newsweek* and *New York Times* contributed some lovely images, as did Tucson resident **Allan**

Morgan and photographer **Kathleen Cook**, whose photographic agency operates out from Laguna Hills, California.

Additional photos were provided by **Donald Young**, **Karl Kernberger**, **Ronnie Pinsler**, **Joseph Viesti**, **Lee Marmon**, **Allen Grazer**, **David Ryan**, **Sam Curtis**, **Tom Tidball**, **Harvey Caplin**, **Ricardo Ferro**, **Maxine Lundberg** and the **Dick Kent Photography**.

Most of the archival illustrations were by courtesy of the **Museum of New Mexico** and the **Colorado Historical Society**.

Associate Publisher **Adam Liptak**, who shared the agonies inherent in the making of a book, deserves special credit for putting the manuscript into final form. A graduate of Yale University, Liptak worked with *Business Week* and *New Yorker* before joining Apa as a consultant on North American and European titles. His writing has appeared in magazines from Connecticut to Alaska. **Nancy Brokaw**, a Brown University graduate, assisted with copyediting.

The maps were produced by cartographers under the direction of **Gunter Nelles** in Munich, West Germany. Assistant Editor **Vivien Loo** saw the book through its final leg at Apa Villa in Singapore. Helping her with last-minute rushes were production coordinator **Mohamed Rafie**, and artists **Salim Jasuni** and **Margaret Chua**.

People who gave behind-the-scene help and who deserves a word of thanks include Dick Shelton, Bret Lundberg, Buzz and Linda Poverman, Fred and Mary Raje, the Nevada Magazine and the Nevada Department of Economic Development, also various members of Apa's staff in Singapore—including marketing director Yuan Van Outrive, production coordinator Nancy Yap, administrative manager Alice Ng, financial controller Henry Lee and editorial secretary June Foong.

When work on a book is complete, the work of getting it to the readers begins. It would be impossible to list all the thousands of individual bookshop owners, travel agents and special sales representatives whose multiple efforts carry this book into private homes and offices in 30 countries around the world. We wish to acknowledge with thanks their individual and collective contributions. In particular, we wish to thank Michael Hunter, head of the general publishing division of Prentice-Hall Inc., and his dynamic sales representatives.

——Apa Productions

TABLE OF CONTENTS

TABLE OF CONTENTS

A BEAUTIFUL VALLEY

Makers of maps like to keep things orderly and tend to define the American Southwest in terms of state boundaries. But those who live in it, and love it, and consider time spent elsewhere as a sort of exile, know another type of boundary must be applied. The Southwest begins where the land rises out of that vast ocean of humid air which covers midland America and makes it the fertile breadbasket of half the world. And it ends along that vague line where winter cold wins out over the sun, and the valleys—as well as the high country—are buried under snow. There is one ever more essential requirement. Wherever you stand in the Southwest there must be somewhere, on one horizon or another, the spirit-healing blue shape of mountains. And thus you have Arizona and New Mexico, a slice of southern Colorado, much of southern Utah, and part of Nevada.

The Southwest is high—an immense tableland broken by the high ridges of the southern Rocky Mountain—and dry, with annual precipitation varying drastically with altitude. Thus Albuquerque, New Mexico, 5,200 feet (1,585 meters) above sea level, measures an arid eight inches (20 centimeters) of rainfall per annum, while the crest of Sandia Mountain only 15 miles (24 km) away but a mile higher, receives more than triple that amount. The few minutes required to go from the Rio Grande in downtown Albuquerque to the top of the Sandia Ski Basin ski run via tramway takes one through five of North America's biological life zones—from the Upper Sonoran Desert to the cool spruce forests of the Arctic-Alpine zone.

This highness and dryness has another effect which endears it to the hearts of Southwesterners. Air loses 1/30th of its density with each 900 feet (274 meters) of altitude gained. Therefore, a resident of Flagstaff, Arizona, or Santa Fe, New Mexico, more than 7,000 feet (2,134 meters) above sea level, looks through air which is not just humidity-free. It has also lost about a quarter of its weight in oxygen and carbon dioxide. Looking through this oddly transpa-

rent air adds a clarity to everything one sees. It makes distant objects seem incredibly close.

But what attracted artist Frederic Remington (and after him scores of other artists) to Taos was not the beauty but the culture. The Southwest is Spanish Colonial country — the very outer limit of the immense empire of King Carlos II. It is also the heartland of America's Indian country. America has been called a melting pot. But in the Southwest, this homogenizing process didn't work efficiently. The dry, inhospitable land didn't attract the first wave of invaders — men like Cortes and Pizarro, who gutted Aztec Mexico and destroyed Inca Peru, or like the English, who eradicated Indians from the Eastern seaboard.

The Spanish who settled the Southwest were milder men, softened by the Papal decision that Indians had souls, and the King's decision that they should, therefore, be treated humanely. The complex culture of the Pueblo Indians has survived in centuries-old adobe villages scattered up and down the Rio Grande and across the mesa country to the west. And so has America's largest tribe, the Navajo. Some 150,000 strong, they occupy a 14-million-acre (5.7-million-hectare) reservation which sprawls, larger than all of New England, across the very heart of the Southwest in Arizona, New Mexico and Utah. These original Americans give the Southwest something totally unique. They make it a Holy Land—a territory of shrines and sacred mountains.

A man tries to explain why he has returned to this empty land after finding loneliness in crowded California cities. He looks down into the immense sink which spreads below the southwest slope of the Chuska Mountains. A wilderness of sun-baked stone stretches into the dim distance—gray caliche, wind-cut clay as red as barn paint, great bluish outcrops of shale, the cracked salt flats where the mud formed by the "male rains" of summer tastes as bitter as alum. Everything here is worn, eroded and tortured. It is axiomatic that the desert teems with life, but there is no life here. Not even creosote brush or cactus survives, not even a lizard, nor an insect for it to feed upon. White mapmakers would call it "Desolation Sink."

"The Navajo name for this," he says, "is Beautiful Valley."

Preceding pages, a rugged old Indian lady shows the marks and wrinkles of a long life in the Southwest desert; and *Carnegiea gigantea* blooms in Tucson Mountain Park. Left, a late winter storm in Grand Canyon.

THE GREAT LAND CREATION

The forces that created the geology of the Southwest have also conspired to lay it bare. The region lies in the latitude of the world's great deserts, where air currents thrown skyward by equatorial heat, drained of their tropic rains, descend in dry, evaporative winds. Moisture-laden Pacific storms slam into the Sierras and the Peninsular ranges in California, rise, cool, drop their rain and snow on the mountains, and continue dry over the same inland basins. The resulting lack of vegetational cover accelerates erosion, gouging out history-revealing canyons, scarps and mesas. Southwestern weather pleases the geologist thoroughly.

One should bear in mind that of the earth's some 4½ billion years of history, only the last half billion is documented in any detail. The first 89 percent of earthly time is known collectively as the Precambrian, and the oldest Southwestern evidence of its events are the dark metamorphic rocks of the Grand Canyon's inner gorge. They began as sediments and igneous rocks deposited 2 billion years ago near the edge of a large continent. Some 1.7 billion years ago, the area underwent a collision between continental plates, lifting the formations into high mountains, heating and buckling the layers, and metamorphosing them into gneiss and schist. Granitic magma infiltrated the cracks, leaving the rocks marbled like beef. Later the sea came in from the west, beveled the mountains flat, and added thick layers of sandstone, limestone, and shale.

The area remained little changed through the Paleozoic Era, which began 570 million years ago. The Southwest bathed in shallow seas that rose gently into land, then sank back into water, so that deposits alternated between marine sediments, deltas and dunes.

The Mesozoic, beginning some 200 million years ago, ushered in a time of upheaval and transformation. Mountains rose in what is now eastern Arizona and western New Mexico. The immense Sierra Nevada burst forth, casting an enormous rain shadow and creating deserts far more severe than those of today. Inland deposits included sandstone and shale from dunes and rivers—rocks that have weathered into the spectacular slickrock country of southern Utah, along with the phantasmagoria of such parks as Arches, Canyonlands, Capitol Reef, Zion, and Mesa Verde. Volcanic ash from the Mesozoic created the painted desert formations of northern Arizona. Toward the end of the Mesozoic, North America broke away from Europe, collided with the Pacific plate, and overrode it, initiating 25 million years of mountain-building known as the Laramide Orogeny. The area was volcanically active, and the Arizona Highlands and Rocky Mountains derive from this time. Hot mineral-bearing magma seeped through the fractures, depositing the copper now extensively mined in Utah and Arizona.

Uplift continued into the Cenozoic, beginning 65 million years ago, elevating the Colorado Plateau—that immense oval of high land that encompasses most of southern Utah, northern Arizona, northwestern New Mexico, and southwestern Colorado. The Colorado River cut into the Plateau as it rose, giving us perfect core samples of the Plateau's interior, and revealing quite a surprise: for all the collisions of plates, volcanism, and assorted calamities, the strata of the Grand Canyon have reposed in calm horizontals, which geologists refer to as "layer-cake geology." It is believed that the crust beneath the Colorado Plateau is unusually thick, and while many layers have been worn away—including almost everything from the Mesozoic and Cenozoic eras—what remains is on solid ground and gives the Grand Canyon a sense of uncanny peace that fills its immensity.

The Cenozoic Era sheared the Colorado Plateau from the Southwest's other major contemporary land form, the basin and range. Beginning at the north in central Oregon and southwest Idaho, basin and range takes in Nevada and western Utah, curls around the Colorado Plateau to include southern Arizona and southwestern New Mexico, and stretches into Mexico. With the Great Plains, it is one of the two major land forms in the United States. The long ranges of fault block mountains, separated by long narrow valleys, are caused by crustal plates slowly pulling apart. As the land widens, the bedrock splits along the faults. The great blocks of stone tip toward their heavier ends in the relatively shallow magma, creating ranges that are often sloped on one side and sliced in dramatic scarps on the other. Valleys, meanwhile, sink into the gaps of stretched land, so that some ranges actually gain more height from dropped valleys than from their own tilting.

Accompanying the gradual fault blocking

was more violent volcanic activity, explosions across southern Arizona that heaved up such ranges as the Superstitions, the Kofa Mountains, and many other jumbles of volcanic ash. Volcanism extended to the Colorado Plateau, with the high volcanoes of the San Francisco Peaks, and such ranges as the Henrys, Abajos, La Sals and Navajo Mountain in southern Utah, all of which are laccoliths—mountains formed by magma that wells up without breaking the surface.

It is, then, primarily the events of the Cenozoic that have shaped the current

soft permeable layer overlies a hard one will hollow caves, and even chip away at the ceiling until the entrance stands as an arch. The Colorado River system, working through the Mesozoic sandstones of southeastern Utah, has created a labyrinth of canyons so high and narrow that some gorges pinch to human width while continuing to soar hundreds of feet overhead. Snowmelt scours the canyon bottoms with its annual burden of silt, until entire mountains and plateaus are reduced to level plains.

Collaborating with erosion to give the

Southwestern landscape, using materials used and reused by previous eras. For the connoisseur of scenery, perhaps more important than all the forces of creation is that slow artist of decay called erosion. The wearing away of stone can be accomplished by blowing sand, seismic shift, and the roots of plants, but the primary force is water. Water, entering cracks and fissures, freezes and expands, chiseling rock apart. Water seeping from a canyon wall where a

Southwest its hold on the human imagination is color. Many factors come into play, but the foremost colorist, surprisingly, is iron. Occurring naturally in volcanic material, iron gradually seeps into sedimentary layers. Highly oxidized iron creates the family of reds, while iron that enters' rock in an oxygen-deprived or reducing environment can create a spectrum of blues and greens one might otherwise associate with coppers and cobalts.

Like the rocks of the Southwest, the materials of the universe get used and reused—so that when we look out at these ruddy landscapes we have travelled so far to see, we are also looking deeply into the history of creation.

Preceding pages, Bryce Canyon National Park; rich and varied cactus growth at Saguaro National Monument; and yellow blossoms in Flagstaff field, Arizona. Above, a horned toad at Gila River Valley.

18

INDIAN PREHISTORY

Most archaeologists agree that *Homo sapiens* did not originate in North America but migrated here from Asia sometime during the final stages of Pleistocene Epoch, a dramatic period in earth's history that most of us know as the Ice Age. During the Pleistocene, nearly one-sixth of the earth's surface was blanketed with ice; it was ice in fact, that made man's arrival in North America possible. As massive glaciers formed from billions of tons of water, oceans receded; in some areas sea level dropped as much as 300 feet (91 meters). In consequence, long-submerged fragments of sea bottom were exposed, and one of these—a 56-mile-long (90-km) strip of rocky earth between northeastern Siberia and northwestern Alaska—was early man's gateway to this continent.

Exact dates of man's New World penetration are simply unobtainable with present technology. We can, however, say that aboriginal Asian man probably arrived upon North American shores about 25,000 B.C. His arrival was not sudden. Late in the Pleistocene, interglacial sub-ages (warming trends) began to occur, causing sea-level ice to melt. As the climate slowly mellowed, grass and low shrubs flourished, even on the newly exposed land bridge. This forage attracted grazing animals from the Asian continent, which in turn attracted the attention of hunting man. Following the mammoth and bison, he came, pursuing the herds from one land mass to another. So began the Paleo-Indian Period in North America.

When did man first reach the Southwest? Archaeological evidence—mostly the datable artifacts found with bones of extinct animals—suggests that he was firmly entrenched in relatively large numbers by 10,000 or 12,000 B.C. This same evidence has allowed scientists to reach some logical conclusions about early man. Paleo-Indians were primarily meat-eaters (although they probably gathered wild plants for food as well). Using flint or bone-tipped weapons of their own creation and design, Paleo-Indians could kill animals 20 times their size. At least in part, early man was a social creature; he hunted in organized groups so as to kill not just a single animal but an entire herd at one time for the good of the community. Because constant expansion of hunting range was necessary, fixed habitations were seldom constructed. Paleo-Indians probably lived in caves.

By 7,000 B.C., human life-styles in the Southwest had changed significantly. The modifications are so noticeable that modern scientists distinguish a separate cultural stage for this more technologically advanced *Homo sapiens*. From about 7,000 B.C. until the time of Christ, man was creeping out of his shell. This span of cultural amplification has been named the Desert Archaic Period. Among the most important changes to occur during the Archaic Period were these: the acquisition of the fire-drill and the grinding stone; utilization of foods other than meat — mainly seeds, wild grains, tubers, and berries; construction of semi-permanent, seasonal habitations — primarily round or rectangular holes in the earth covered with brush and mud called "pithouses;" and the practice of spiritual ceremonies.

The span of the Desert Archaic Period is loosely defined; cultural advancement did not occur at exactly the same moment among all the inhabitants of the Southwest. The development of the Paleo-Indian into the Archaic Indian was a sluggish process at best, dependent upon interaction between groups of people sometimes separated by hundreds of miles. This was not true, however, of the next period of cultural expansion–the Pithouse-Pueblo Period—which began shortly after the time of Christ and ended with the arrival of Europeans in the Southwest in the mid-16th Century. If man had crept out of his shell before, he was now free and running.

Cultural Divisions

Of the many changes occurring during the 1500-year-long Pithouse-Pueblo Period, none exceeded in importance, and indeed all were connected to, the development of widespread, separate, and distinguishable human societies. By A.D. 700, five distinct groups of people had evolved and were inhabiting the Southwest. In the north were the Anasazi—an intelligent, artistic, peaceful society of farmers whose cliff palaces and sprawling canyon-bottom cities were so well constructed that many have survived almost unblemished for a thousand years. To the south, near the San Francisco Peaks area of present-day Arizona, were the Sinagua, an agricultural people whose culture later became a melting pot of building techniques and sociological enlightenment. In the Gila and Salt River valleys near present-day Phoenix, Arizona, were the Hohokam, at their peak perhaps the greatest canal builders in North America. To the east were Hohokam cousins, the Salado; and in the rich mountain country of present-day New Mexico, the Mogollon.

We can only guess how and why these divisions of culture came about. One important factor was probably the introduction and development of agriculture—a totally new concept to primitive man. Because

They were all agricultural societies, heavily dependent for survival upon crops of maize (corns), beans, squash, and melons. In their early stages of development, all lived in underground pithouses or in caves, later moving to aboveground, apartment-style, multistoried homes called pueblos by the Spaniards. By 700 A.D., all used pottery extensively and had acquired the bow and arrow. Three centuries later, cotton and weaving implements were also in use. More important (as far as archaeologists can determine), none cultivated an aristocracy.

agricultural products could be stored for the winter, dependence upon hunting and gathering was drastically reduced. In turn, habitations became more permanent so that farmers could tend their fields. Permanency demanded security from enemies; security required a large and stable population.

Whatever the reason or combination of reasons, these five major cultures (and many minor ones) arose. Geographically they were separated by hundreds of miles, yet each bore striking similarities to the others.

Reminders of Southwest's prehistoric culture, like the newspaper rock (preceding pages) and the stone points (above), are found throughout the region.

such as was common in both the Aztec and Inca civilizations to the south.

Similarities among the cultures occurred also in their people's physical appearance, clothing, and daily activities. From burial evidence, scientists think that most prehistoric Indians were about the same size and build; men averaged five feet, four inches (1.6 meters), the women slightly less. They were muscular, stocky people with sparse body hair. Head hair was thick, however. Men wore it long; women preferred it bobbed or fashioned into elaborate coiffures.

Clothing varied, but variations depended less upon tribal affiliation than upon time of year. In hot weather, most Indians wore nothing but sandals woven from plant fiber or plaited from yucca leaves. As the seasons changed and the days cooled, skirts and aprons made from vegetable material or animal skins were added. In winter, hide cloaks, shirts, and blankets—the latter made from rabbit skin, dog fur, or turkey feathers—were probably sufficient to turn the chill. When cotton was introduced and Indians learned the art of weaving, more elaborate forms of winter clothing—mainly heavy cloaks—came into vogue.

The Golden Age

These similarities were not by coincidence, of course. Throughout the 15-century span of the Pithouse-Pueblo Period, interaction undoubtedly occurred among all prehistoric cultures in the Southwest as well as in northern Mexico, with each contributing something to the cultural pot. So rapidly, in fact, did new ideas and methods spread among the five major cultures that by the mid-11th Century, a Golden Age existed among Southwest Indians. Building techniques and irrigation systems had progressed to a point far ahead of their time. Frivolities—such as ball games and contests with dice—were common. In addition, increased rainfall had mellowed the sometimes harsh environment; natural springs and streams ran full, and game and wild plants flourished. Because of the added moisture and new agricultural techniques, farming increased, and with surplus food available, populations grew. New farming projects were started in areas that could have hardly supported cactus a century before. Existing towns grew more complex.

This new life of relative comfort was only temporary, however, and although many explanations as to why the Golden Age was suddenly cut short are plausible, one of the most feasible is that by the middle of the 12th Century, cyclic weather patterns had once again changed, and the region saw the beginning of drought conditions. In areas where water was permanently available, farmers were little affected; in others, especially in communities where agriculture depended upon rainfall and not irrigation, existence once again became difficult. Many towns and outlying family dwellings were abandoned, the inhabitants migrating to larger centers of population that had been constructed near natural groundwater sources. What possessions could be carried were taken along; all else was left behind. This sudden influx in refugees must have created hardships for the already settled populations, but in most cases, room was found.

Drastic Changes

Then a new threat appeared in the Southwest. Shoshonean raiders (probably the ancestors of present-day Ute) suddenly arrived uninvited from the north, and local Indians found themselves the targets of continual harassment. Few in number, the Shoshone dared not attack a fully protected town, but they easily raided fields, stole harvests, and picked off an occasional farmer or his family. In addition, towns and villages had, probably out of necessity, begun to prey on one another.

Sometime during the late 12th Century, the combination of harassment, thievery, and steadily worsening drought conditions orought about a drastic change in life-styles

for most of the Southwestern cultures. The people began to leave their traditional valleys or mesa-top homes for the security of isolated caves and protected canyon amphitheaters. Whether the move actually ended the Shoshone threat or only prolonged it, we don't know. It did little, however, to ease internal strife or to alleviate the need for water. In the mid and late 13th Century, even as the great cliff cities of Mesa Verde, Mancos Canyon, Betatakin, Keet Seel, and others like them were under

Dioramas give realistic representations of primitive life-style: left, fire-making; and right, a typical Mesa Verde Pueblo of about 850 A.D.

construction, the drought was reaching its peak. Even permanent water sources began to go dry, and life became a matter of day-to-day survival. The soil was worn out and turned to dust; crops failed year after year. Hunting and gathering had never been fully abandoned, but wild food supplies decreased in direct proportion to the decrease in moisture. There was simply not enough food and water for the population. Although we have no idea of its exact nature, some type of social upheaval undoubtedly took place—perhaps a universal uprising against the blameless but available leadership. Migrations began. By 1299, when the drought finally ended, most villages and towns of the Anasazi and Mogollon had been abandoned. Hohokam, Sala-

The Hopi mesas in Arizona, in fact, were perhaps a major refuge for both the Sinagua and Anasazi. Hopi people claim ancestral ownership of many of the great population centers—Mesa Verde, Betatakin, Keet Seel, and Wupatki included. Prehistoric Hopi clan signs found in these ruins give validity to the claims, though many archaeologists argue the point, applying the old riddle: which came first, the Hopi or the sign? Pictographs (prehistoric rock paintings) and petroglyphs (prehistoric rock carvings) similar to those the Hopi claim as clan symbols were once freely used throughout both North and South America. This certainly suggests widespread interaction among early cultures but not necessarily the traditional ownership of the signs that Hopi legends proclaim.

do, and Sinagua communities (most of them near permanent streams) survived longer; however, they met the same fate within a century.

It is here that the real mystery begins. Where did the refugees go? Some probably journeyed east to join or start pueblos on the Rio Grande River in present-day New Mexico. Others went east but not as far, stopping at the pueblos of Zuni and Acoma, also in New Mexico. Some may have gone south to Mexico or west to California, and a good many simply changed their life-styles to meet current requirements for survival and remained nearby, the ancestors of today's Pima and Hopi.

Hopi ancestors were probably an aggregation of several different cultures.

Wherever these early people went, they were gone, for the most part, by A.D. 1400. They abandoned to the wind the homes they had so painstakingly constructed. Many of these prehistoric dwellings, preserved by dry desert air, and in some cases by the stabilization and restoration technology of modern science, still exist and may be easily visited. Remember though, that when viewing these ancient ruins, you are examining a short but important piece of the earth's history. Take nothing when you leave but knowledge, and leave nothing that was not already there. Allow those who come after you the privilege of viewing that history unmarred.

SPANISH EXPLORATIONS

The worst lay in parting little by little with the thoughts that clothe the soul of the European, and most of all the idea that man attains his strength through dirk and dagger and serving in your Majesty's guard. We had to surrender such fantasies until our inward nakedness was the nakedness of an unborn babe, starting life anew in a womb of sensations which in themselves can mysteriously nourish.

—Cabeza de Vaca, *His Relation of the Journey* (1528-1536)
Edited by Haniel Long

On an autumn day late in November, four half-drowned seamen, survivors of the ill-fated Spanish expedition of Pánfilo de Nar-váez in the year 1528, were washed ashore onto the beaches of Texas by the unfriendly sea. Naked, stripped of their clothing by a storm, wet, chilled and starving, they were fortunate to be found alive by the Indians who fed and clothed them.

These naked conquistadors were the first Spaniards to set foot in the Southwest.

The Gods' Messengers

So began one of the most remarkable journeys in American history. The ship-wrecked, led by Nuñez Cabeza de Vaca, walked for thousands of miles through the desert until, eight years later, they reached Mexico City.

On the way, they learned to live and behave like Indians. They adopted not only the clothes but the habits of the tribes they met along the way. The Indians most often feted the men as messengers of the gods, as the Aztecs had Cortés. Especially welcome was one of the four, Estéban, the black Moor, a Christianized slave of the Spaniards who was favored by the Indian women even more than the others. Although no records exist to document the theory, historians conjecture that the first *mestizos*, half Spanish and half Indian, were born of the lost conquistadors and the Indians. In his memoirs, de Vaca mused wryly about "the possibility of life in which to be deprived of Europe was not to be deprived of too much."

On his arrival in Mexico City, de Vaca told tales of walled cities with houses four and five stories tall and Indians who were more civilized than the Spaniards. To the

conquistadors of Cortés, who had conquered most of Mexico and fallen into fighting among themselves over the spoils, the reports meant that new treasures of gold might be found in the desert. The cry went up: *Otro Mexico! Ortro Peru!* Here is another Mexico! Another Peru!

Enticed by de Vaca's tale, the restless and bored conquistadors polished their rusting armor and prepared themselves for battle. They would conquer the entire continent.

The Viceroy, Antonio de Mendoza, sent forth an *entrata*—an expedition—led by

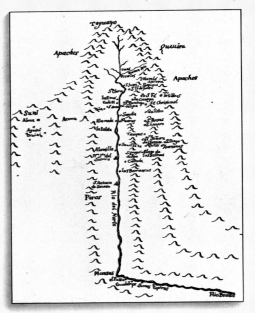

Father Marcos de Niza and guided by the black Moor, Estéban. Its aim was to find the legendary Gran Quivira and the fabled Seven Cities of Cíbola that de Vaca had heard about but never seen.

Cities of Gold

For months, Father Marcos and his men wandered through the desert but found no cities of gold. They returned to Mexico City empty-handed. In the course of their ordeal,

Left, map of New Mexico, 1680. Right, the oldest inscription, other than Indian petroglyphs, was made by Don Juan de Oñate on El Morro Rock in 1605.

Estéban had been killed by the men of Zuni Pueblo, who said he had "assaulted their women." (For reasons no one understands, a statue of Saint Estéban was raised in the nearby pueblo of Acoma, where it still stands today.)

Despite the failure of Father Marcos' expedition, the Spanish were not discouraged. The deaths, the hardships, the dangers challenged their sense of adventure and manhood, and, when that failed, the promise of great riches spurred them on. "To possess silver and gold the greedy Spaniards

dors created a romantic legend.

Coronado was the image of the poor *hidalgo* (gentleman); he was dignified, handsome and so impoverished that he had to borrow the money for the expedition from his wife. His pretension of courtly nobility in the inhospitable wilderness, epitomized by his insistence on wearing armor in the burning desert sun, made him the American Don Quixote; he was one of those rare men who perfectly fit his moment in history.

And, yet, the men of Coronado's army were the riffraff, cutthroats and adventurers

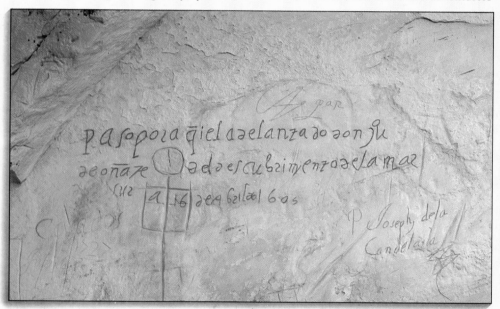

would enter Hell itself," said the Franciscan Father Zarate Salmeron of New Mexico. He could not dissuade them from becoming the Don Quixotes of the New World.

The Knight of El Dorado

Of all the conquistadors who set forth in search of the Seven Cities of Cibola and Gran Quivira, none behaved with more grandeur and nobility than did Francisco Vazquez de Coronado, the Governor of the Kingdom of Nuevo Galicia, the "Knight of El Dorado." With the blessing of the Emperor and the Viceroy, Coronado marshaled a small army and crossed half a continent. He alone among the conquista-

of Mexico City. It was an epic irony. The image of the conquistadors riding forth in resplendent armor of gold, with flags and plumes proudly flying as in a knightly pageant, is largely a myth, created in retrospect. The contemporary description of Coronado's men is not nearly so grand.

Most of Coronado's men wore "American" rather than European clothing, said one observer, and another noted that "many more [wore] buckskin coats than coats of armor." And, while the majority were horsemen, few indeed were high-born. In Spain, only a gentleman was permitted—by Royal decree—to ride a horse, and any knight found on a mule was subject to punishment. But, in Mexico, anyone could ride. In 1554, the Viceroy Velasco complained, "Very few [of the horsemen] are *caballeros* [knights] or *hijosdalgos* [sons of gentlemen]. They are *gente comun* [common people]. In these provinces, the *caballero* is a merchant." The nobleman Don Juan Garay added in disgust, "Even beggars ride horses in Mexico."

According to Francois Chevalie, writing in *Land and Society in Colonial Mexico*, most of these pretenders to knighthood were "rustics who had left their villages [in Spain] under a cloud or children who had left families incapable of supporting them." Whatever their background, de Oñate summed up the general feeling about Coronado's men by saying that those "who were going on the expedition would do more good

And then there were the hundreds of Indians...

No one knows how many Indians marched with Coronado. But it is known the Indians were not simply bearers and carriers. Most of them were hired to be scouts, guides, horse wranglers, herdsmen, *vaqueros* (cowboys) and bridge builders. All of them were well armed with lances, spears and bows and arrows. Were it not for these Mexican Indians and the American Indians who later joined the troops, it is doubtful that there could have been an expedition at all.

The army of Coronado travelled north from Mexico for some 1,500 miles (2,415 km), through the Apache lands of Arizona, into New Mexico. On the Rio Grande, Coronado asked directions from a man he called

than harm by departing, for they were all idle and without means of support."

Coronado's Army

For his *entrata*, Coronado mustered nearly 400 men, almost all of them volunteers. There were officially 235 mounted men and 62 on foot, but unofficially there were many more, ranging from teenagers to old men. It was a motley troop.

Not only were the soldiers not conquistadors, some of them weren't even Spaniards. The company bugler was a German, there were two Italians, five Portuguese, a Frenchman and a Scotsman, Thomas Blake, who had changed his name to Tomas Blaque.

"The Turk," (he was dark-skinned) who explained that his people had no gold—it was all east in Kansas, where the people were so rich that even their canoes were made of glittering gold.

Coronado headed for Kansas. He crossed the Pecos River into West Texas and went northward through Oklahoma. He finally reached Kansas near the present-day town of Abilene, but found no gold canoes there. He ordered "The Turk" executed and, turning back to Mexico, crossed the buffalo

Above, a 19th-Century engraving showing the interior of the Acoma Church; and right, Diego de Vargas Zapata, governor of New Mexico (1688-97, 1703-04).

plains and deserts, having found historical fame, but no treasure.

Neither Coronado nor any of the other conquistadors found the gold and jewels they sought. Most of them returned to Mexico City in disappointment, and, after their discouraging reports, few followed them into the desert in search of fabulous treasure. The conquistadors themselves, weary and aging, had come to that time of life when even old soldiers have to settle down and retire. The conquest was over. Even the mighty Cortés lamented, "I am wasted, and exhausted, by all I have done...."

By themselves, the conquistadors could never have conquered the Southwest. In the rugged mountains and deserts, their mediev-

"peaceful" conquest, the new conquistadors willingly hammered their plowshares into swords and forced their rule on the native tribes.

The Franciscan padres in New Mexico and the Jesuits in Arizona and Texas did more than baptize and make Christians of these Indians (from 1591 to 1631, the Jesuits baptized 151,240 Indians). They tried to transform the Indians into Spanish peasants; to "attract the nomadic tribes to a peaceful, sedentary life." As the Jesuit Father Juan Nentuig wrote in 1763: the Christian Indians were "more inclined to work" and "to till their lands."

The missions of the Jesuits were more than simply churches. Into the hands of the Jesuits was placed the responsibility for the

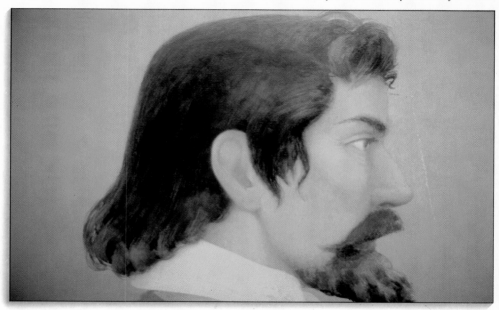

al military tactics and armor were of little use, nor did they have the spirituality to comprehend the deep religiousness of the Indians. So disillusioned were the latter-day conquistadors that they even forgot their discovery of California. Not until more than two centuries after the voyage of Cabrillo did Juan Bautista Anza set forth to settle California in 1777. In the end, it was the Spanish missionaries who accomplished what the conquistadors could not: to conquer the land.

Christian Missionaries

The missionaries came to conquer not by force of arms, but by settlement and religious fervor. Of course, when the Indians rejected

government and the economy. The missions became the centers of farming, commerce and education.

To the suspicious Spanish officials, the Jesuits seemed to be building an ecclesiastical empire within the Spanish provinces. After all, many of the Jesuits—Pfefferkorn, Grashofer, Benz, Keller, Kino, Stiger, Nentuig and others—were not even Spaniards.

Nevertheless, when Jesuits asked for permission to raise their own troops, the Spaniards often agreed. (In one case, prisoners were released from the jails of Mexico City and sent out to protect the missions.) In New Mexico, the mission churches of the Franciscans were more like fortresses than places of worship. The walls were sometimes seven feet (two meters) thick. After the Pueblo revolt of 1680, when the Indians killed 22 Franciscan Fathers, the missionaries protected themselves with Indian slaves and mercenaries.

Even so, in 1792, the Franciscan Juan Domingo Arricivita called for the "protection of troops in order to propagate the faith." It was "impossible without them," he said. And from 1744 to 1745, when the Visitador to Sonora, Juan Antonio Balthasar, had visited the San Xavier de Bac mission of the Papago at Tucson, he requested "soldiers to force these Indians to live in the Pueblo," for "just a hint of soldiering is necessary" to make them go to church.

But not all the missionaries were so eager to take up arms against their parishioners.

Velarde eulogized him, saying that he died like the Indians, as he had lived.

With the missionaries came the settlers, people escaping their lives in Mexico. These settlers, more than the conquistadors, were the true explorers of the land. As soon as they settled, they began detailed surveys of the countryside. As farmers, they had to know the flow and direction of every stream and river, the precise rise and fall of every canyon and valley, the grass and trees of every pasture and forest. The settlers explored the land in ways that soldiers could not; the conquistadors, riding swiftly for their safety in hostile territory, mapped the land on horseback. But the settlers walked the earth, foot by foot, and explored the territory intimately and in detail. Stone by

Father Eusébio Francisco Kino, the Jesuit who founded the San Xavier de Bac mission, would have objected to such a policy. He believed the Indians were to be treated as brothers. One of the most courageous of the missionaries, he was said to have made 40 *entratas* into the deserts and established many missions and the first cattle ranches in Arizona.

The Padre on Horseback

A true folk hero, Kino was known as the Padre on Horseback. At the age of 70, Kino died in the mission of Magdalena in Sonora; his death bed was made of two calf skins, and his pillow was a saddle. Father Luis

stone and tree by tree, they surveyed every inch of land. The old Spanish land grants were measured in just that way, and so were the village deeds.

Many of the settlers were poor farmers and shepherds, Mexican *mestizos* from Sonora and Chihuahua. Few wealthy noblemen or old conquistadors in Mexico or Spain had any desire or need to endure the desert's severe hardships to establish a new life. As always, the immigrants were poor men and women seeking new opportunities, hoping

Santa Fe is the heart of Hispanic New Mexico, and annual fiestas relive the days when "The Spanish came to town"; left, Spanish priests and right, conquistadors.

to escape poverty and ill fate.

But on the poor lands of the desert, the poor settlers became poorer. The dry farming and small mines they established offered a meager existence. "Not only have the settlers of New Mexico not enjoyed riches, but the scourge of God has been upon them always, and they are the most oppressed and enslaved people in the world," the Franciscan Father Zarate de Salermon wrote of them in 1626. "As long as they have a good supply of tobacco to smoke, they are very contented and they do not want riches, for it seems as if they have made a vow of poverty."

To the Spanish and later Mexican authorities, these settlers were the poorest of the poor, the misfits and refugees from civilized

society: they were no better than the heathen, wrote one official. In the palatial mansions in Mexico City, the Southwest was known as the "Land of the *Barbarosos*," the barbarians, and that referred not only to the American Indians but to the "Spanish" settlers as well.

Exodus of the Jews

Few of the settlers who came on the *entrata* of Juan de Oñate into New Mexico were born in Spain. Most were Mexicans and *mestizos*, half-Indians, who, like de Oñate himself, were born in Sonora; he was married to an Indian woman said to be a granddaughter of Montezuma. Typical of the

expeditions of the Southwest, de Oñate's *entrata* included as many as 1,000 Mexican Indians, who outnumbered the "Spanish" settlers by 10 to one. Since these Indians lived on similar land across the invisible borders of Mexico, they knew the terrain and survived more easily than the settlers.

During the height of the Spanish Inquisition, many Jews fled to Mexico to escape persecution. Originally settling on ranches along the coast of Mexico, near Panuco, the Jewish ranchers, led by Don Juan de Caravajal, were given a land grant to the Kingdom of Nuevo Leon by Philip II that extended for 600 to 800 miles (966 to 1,288 km) to the Rio Grande and into West Texas; they established one of the largest cattle ranches in Mexico.

By 1545, more than one quarter of the residents of Mexico City were admitted Jews, and historians estimate that, by the late 16th Century, there were more Jews in Mexico than Catholics. Even the Archbishop de Vitoria of Mexico had been born of Jewish parents.

Alarmed by the great number of Jews posing as Catholics, the Holy Inquisition came to Mexico to ferret them out. The Governor of Nuevo Leon, de Caravajal, was among the many who died. Once more escaping the Inquisition, many Jews fled north. Often in disguise, they joined many of the *entratas* into the Southwest, where they joined the missionaries and poor farmers in settling the desert lands.

So it was that the explorers and settlers of New Mexico and Arizona were Moorish, Spanish, Mexican, Italian, Portuguese, Indian, Jesuit and Jewish—a mixed lot, but one with a decidedly Spanish accent.

A Modern Reenactment

Today, in the foothills of the *Sangre de Cristo* Mountains (the Mountains of the Blood of Christ) high in northern New Mexico, there nestles the village of Chimayo. Poor farmers, the villagers every year reenact the conquest of the Southwest by their ancestors. They dress as conquistadors and Indians, wearing plastic armor and headdresses of polyester plumes. In an open field they perform a ritual battle on horseback, turning the conquest into a pageant.

The fiesta is called *Los Cristianos y Los Indios*, The Christians and The Indians, and it bears a remarkable similarity to a medieval drama known in Spain as *Los Cristianos y Los Moros*, The Christians and The Moors. All that has changed through the centuries is the name.

Cow ixy, going

Geronimo And War Chief Chiricahua Apaches now raiding.

ARRIVAL OF THE ANGLOS

In the East, they were contemptuously known as "Squaw Men" and "White Indians." No one quite like them had ever lived on the American frontier before, and, certainly, no one ever will again. The mountain men who came to New Mexico and Arizona in the early 1800s were "a rare moment in history," the Native American author Vine Deloria has written. These men not only crossed the continent, they crossed from one culture to another.

The first Anglos to settle in the Southwest, they came to hunt beaver and to trade, not to conquer. In the mountain wilderness where they made their homes, they most often lived in peace with the Mexicans and Indians who were there before them, for they became members of native families.

Paradoxically, the mountain men, who went West to escape the civilization of the East, brought it with them in their saddlebags and wagons. The trade goods they offered the native people forever changed the wilderness, and paved the way for the shopkeepers who replaced them. And so, unwittingly, the mountain men made themselves obsolete.

Colorful Figures

By necessity, mountain men were multicultural and multilingual and, by nature, they were invariably colorful figures: the flamboyant Pauline Weaver, a hunter and agent of the Hudson Bay Company, a two-gun-toting adventurer who is sometimes called the "founder of Arizona," and Christopher "Kit" Carson, one of the fathers of Anglo New Mexico. Kit began his career as a grizzled mountain man, then became a U.S. Army scout and officer, a respected citizen of Taos and a civic leader who personally united the three cultures of the territory by marrying, in turn, a Mexican, an Indian and an Anglo wife.

One of the first mountain men in the Southwest, Baptiste Le Land of the Missouri Fur Company came to Santa Fe, New Mexico, in 1804, the same year as the Lewis and Clark expedition. The first Anglo the

Preceding pages, "Cowboys going to dinner," Mora County, New Mexico, ca 1897. Left, Apache chief Geronimo and right, Kit Carson were two great 19th-Century heroes fighting for different causes.

Mexicans and Indians had ever seen, Le Land was, in fact, a French Creole, who married an Indian woman and settled in Santa Fe. He was followed by James Pursell in 1805 and, in 1809, by Zebulon Pike, a mapmaker and government agent who first arrived in Santa Fe as a prisoner on his way to trial in Mexico City. Pike built the first Anglo fort, of cottonwood trees, on the Conejos branch of the *Rio del Norte*, the Rio Grande River.

The Empire of Spain then ruled the land, but just barely. It was sparsely inhabited by the Spaniards, and the Royal authorities

were nervous about the Anglo traders and wanderers who had entered their domain. Between 1812 and 1821, several merchant adventurers were arrested by Spanish soldiers and locked up in the prison dungeons of Chihuahua.

Not until the Mexican War of Independence, in 1822, and the founding of the Mexican Republic in 1824, did the atmosphere change. The Territory of Nuevo Mexico was established, a vast terrain that included New Mexico and Arizona, where the Anglo mountain men and merchants were welcomed in a friendlier manner. In his "Report on Foreigners," in 1825, the Governor of New Mexico, Antonio Narbona, wrote of 20 Anglos arriving in a single month, half of them merchants. By 1827, a similar monthly report listed 36 Anglos, of whom 31 were merchants who "to sell their goods remain for some time in the towns," but who have "no intentions of settling themselves."

With the establishment of the old Santa Fe Trail from Missouri, wagon trains and caravans crowded West. By 1821, the Missouri frontiersman William Becknell led his "company of men destined to the westward" to New Mexico. Of these traders, George Sibley wrote in 1825: "the first adventurers were hardy, enterprising men who, being tired of the dull and profitless pursuits of husbandry, were determined to turn merchants and traders in the true spirit of Western enterprise;" for these men believed the "many strange and marvelous (stories) of inexhaustible wealth" in the West.

Becknell's expedition opened the way West. In Congress, Senator Thomas Benton introduced a bill to maintain a road to New Mexico. Since the distance was much shorter from Missouri than from Mexico City, goods could be brought more easily and sold more cheaply by the Anglo traders than by the Mexican *entratas*. From 1822 to 1844, the value of the merchandise carried across the continent on the Santa Fe Trail increased from an estimated $15,000 yearly to $450,000.

The merchant wagons brought a new way of life into the Southwest. Not merely champagne and beer, whiskey and rum, but oranges, lemons, cherries, whale-oil candles, tobacco, Epsom salts, straw hats, silk handkerchiefs, dried fish and hundreds of other items. In their dusty wake, the merchant wagons also brought settlers. They homesteaded, planted crops, established ranches and built towns—all on Mexican and Indian land grants to which they had no title. For generations afterward, the ownership of the land would be under dispute; it still is.

The settlers were soon followed by soldiers. In 1846, President Polk sent General Stephen Watts Kearny to the West to conquer New Mexico, but the Army found little resistance, and the anticipated War with Mexico became more an occupation than a conquest. In a treaty signed with Mexico in 1848, the United States paid $15 million for 530,000 acres (217,300 hectares)—New Mexico, Arizona, Utah, Nevada, California and part of Colorado.

After the Mexican War, few federal troops besides General Kearny's small detachment were stationed in New Mexico and Arizona.

Left, an 1840 map of the Republic of Mexico. Right, painting shows a Comanche raid for booty and captives on an emigrant train using the Santa Fe Trail.

With so few troops to defend them, the territories were nearly lost to the Confederacy during the Civil War.

Merchandising supplies and food to the troops became the largest and most profitable business in the region. Many an old family fortune was built on government contracts, an irony for people who prided themselves on rugged individualism. "Almost the only paying business the white inhabitants of the territory have is supplying the troops," General Edward Ord wrote to President Johnson after the Civil War. "Hostilities are therefore kept up [against the Apache] with a view of supporting the inhabitants..." Even that irony was compounded by the sending of the 10th Cavalry, composed of black troops, most of whom

strongholds, successfully held back the European invaders. In 1630, Padre Alonzo Benavides called them, "A people fiery and bellicose and very crafty in war." In fact, the Apache were a nomadic people, less interested in conquering places and capturing people than in taking horses and cattle.

By the 1760s, in spite of the efforts of the staunch Jesuit missionaries, the Spaniards had to abandon 48 settlements and 126 ranches in Arizona. By 1775, Padre Bartolomo Ximeno reported that there were only 10 horses and 56 cows left in the territory that the Apache had not stolen.

Those Anglos who did settle in Arizona were mostly Southerners, and, although there were few black slaves in the area, there was a lively slave trade in Apache children.

were former slaves, to subdue and control the Indians.

Arizona presented a dramatic contrast to New Mexico: the settlers who populated the western desert were of a different breed from those in New Mexico. Few people chose to venture into the lands of the Apache, and so, few trading centers, farm towns and ranches were established in Arizona. The main settlements were mining towns, such as Tombstone, Jerome and Prescott, that were to yield billions of dollars in silver and copper ore.

Even in the early centuries of colonization by the Spaniards, few settlers had ventured into Arizona. From the 1600s on, the Apache, fighting from their mountain

During the Civil War, Arizona, unlike New Mexico, sided with the slave states. The citizens of Tucson voted to join the Confederacy and, in 1862, the Confederate Congress proclaimed Arizona a Confederate territory.

Despite their former Rebel sympathies, the Anglo settlers in Arizona were happy to welcome the U.S. Army after the War had ended. The Indian Wars, fought to open more territory for settlement, were largely conflicts between nomads and settlers: the Apache were warriors, not soldiers, and, when faced with Western-style military campaigns, they often chose surrender.

In 1865, the Mescalero headman, Victorio told Lieutenant Colonel N.H. Davis, "I and my people want peace. We are tired of war. We are poor and have little to eat and wear. We want to make peace."

Davis replied, "Death to the Apache, and peace and prosperity to this land, is my motto." To this sentiment, General Edward Ord added his agreement; the Apache, he declared, were "vermin to be killed when met."

Not everyone among the conquering forces agreed in this assessment, however. General George Crook, who led in the capture of Geronimo, said of the Apache, "I wish to say most emphatically that [this] American Indian is the intellectual peer of most, if not all, the various nationalities who have assimilated to our laws...."

During the 1870s, ranching became a new

Brooklyn) the Kid earned his reputation as a gunman. In reality, The Kid worked as a busboy and waiter in a café in the town of Shakespeare; he was no more a cowboy than was Wyatt Earp, Bat Masterson or Doc Holliday, the dentist. Few, if any, cowboys ever fought in the Range Wars.

On the ranches of the Southwest, the cowboy of English-Irish-Scottish-German ancestry inherited the older Western traditions of the Mexican and Indian *vaquero*. Southerner and Easterner, Mexican and Indian, Spaniard and Anglo, all merged into a new and unique quantity known as the Westerner. Perhaps more than anything else, it was the earth and sky that shaped the cowboy culture. The vastness and unbelievable beauty of the land transformed and

way of life. Huge cattle outfits spread over the horizon; the Matador, XIT, King and Lumpkin ranches ran tens of thousands of head of cattle on hundreds of thousands of acres. In their heyday, these ranches were home to the mythic and real cowboys who enjoyed a brief moment of glory in the sun of the Southwest desert.

The Range Wars

Not many years after the Civil War and the Indian Wars had ended, the Range Wars began. These were battles between sheepmen and cattlemen over grazing lands. One of the most famous was the Lincoln County War, in New Mexico, where Billy (born in

overwhelmed newcomers. There was nothing in their experience back East to prepare the Anglos for the awesome vistas of the mountains and deserts that the Mexicans and Indians thought to be holy ground.

In the beginning, the cattle ranches resembled those of Sonora and Chihuahua in northern Mexico, built in the adobe styles of the Southwest. And during the old days of Spanish rule, the ranches were feudal fiefdoms with *haciendas* that were entire towns. But later ranches of the Anglos were rough

Left, early miners and prospectors at Faro game session; and right, four outlaws who went on a trail drive to Dodge, Kansas.

frugal buildings, reflecting the pioneering life of their owners.

In time, with the meeting of divergent cultures under the inhospitable desert sun, a new breed—the buckaroo—was created: he was, as the old saying goes, "Tough as a longhorn cow, and just as dumb."

What the Cowboys and the Cowgirls Say

One of the old cowboy yells of the Southwest says it all. The cowboy yell was a way in which a cowhand proclaimed his manhood:

"Whe-ee-o, I'm a bad man! Whoopeee! Raised in the backwoods, suckled by a polar bear, nine rows of jaw teeth, a double

that of his 19th-Century ancestor. The first cowboys of the Southwest were lusty, ribald, raucous men who lived with a gusto that reflected the Victorian appetites of the era.

With the passing of the open range and the fencing of the New Mexico and Arizona plains the Anglo ranchers and cowboys were doomed. The turn of the century turned their memories into nostalgia. The last of the old-time cowboys, together with the lawmen and outlaws, joined the Buffalo Bill Wild West Shows or the Teddy Roosevelt Rough Riders, who were mostly recruited in New Mexico and Arizona.

When the cattle drives were over and the stagecoach trails faded, the silence of the desert was shattered by the din of the railroads and the motorcars that brought

coat of hair, steel ribs, wire intestines and a barbed wire tail, and I don't give a dang where I dragged it. Whoop-whee-a ha!"

Ranch women of those days were not about to be outdone or outshouted by their men. They thought themselves to be as tough. One proper lady described herself like this in 1887:

"My bonnet is a hornet's nest, garnished with wolves' tails and eagle feathers. I can wade the Mississippi without getting wet, out scream a catamount [mountain lion], jump over my own shadow . . . and cut through the bushes like a pint of whiskey among forty men."

The modest, laid-back, low-key, taciturn style of the 20th-Century cowboy was not

thousands of newcomers into the Southwest. These were the new Anglos from the East, the sick seeking the sun, the land developers and the artists.

As the 19th Century ended, artists discovered the Southwest. Ernest Blumenschein and Bert G. Phillips settled in Taos, New Mexico, in 1898. In 1916, Mabel Dodge Luhan moved her New York salon to Taos, and a few years later, D. H. Lawrence was to proclaim, "There are all kinds of beauty in the world, but for a greatness of beauty I have never experienced anything like New Mexico."

Soon the old-timers were to become a part of the artists' scenery, and the writers' stories.

EARLY 20TH CENTURY

The era between the turn of the century and World War I was an in-between time. The old frontier life was gone—but not quite. The new technological age was as yet a faint outline on the horizon. Gone were the longhorns and the great cattle drives on the Goodnight Trail. Gone were most of the gunslingers and *bandidos*, but by no means all. Gone was the colorful prospector with his burro, pickaxe and pan, though a few unteachable aged optimists still lingered on. Gone were the covered wagons, to be replaced by railroads, which had their own mythology.

Peculiar to the American West was the dizzying speed with which history unfolded and life changed. A man, born in 1820, who came out West in 1840 to be a mountain man and trap the beaver was still essentially a creature from before the Industrial Revolution. He had a strike-a-lite—flint and tinder to light his pipe; an old muzzle-loader and bowie knife to defend himself against marauding Apache. His sole transportation in a roadless empty land was his horse, and, when that died under him, his two legs. In 1890, aged 70, the same man might be sitting with his biographer at Delmonico's, having travelled to New York by train, gone to the restaurant by the elevated rail after having made his appointment via the telephone.

For Indians the change was even more bewildering. Geronimo, born in 1829, for instance, had grown up as a technological stone-age man, his first weapons stone-tipped lances and arrows. Shortly before his death in 1909, as a member of the Dutch Reformed Church, he attended a convention of cattlemen in Tucson, Arizona. In his hotel room he found himself confronted by those newfangled symbols of civilization—electric lights and the flush toilet. He did not know how to use them. As nobody had told him how to turn off the lamp at his bedside, he simply put his boot over it. Later, he was photographed at the wheel of an early Ford automobile.

The Old Frontier Spirit

Even so, there was still a lot of the frontier atmosphere left. Many of the old gun fighters, those who had not died of "lead-poisoning," were still alive. Pat Garrett, the sheriff who killed Billy the Kid, was himself dry-gulched in 1908 with a bullet in his head,

at a time when such goings-on were presumably a thing of the past.

As late as 1911, a classic six-gun shoot-out between two gentlemen who had discovered that they were sharing the favors of the same married lady took place. By some oversight, this lady had invited them "up to her room" on the same afternoon. The battle was fought in—of all places—Denver's Brown Palace, the "Abode of Luxury and Refinement." One of the belligerent Casanovas killed not only his rival, but also two innocent bystanders. He had the good grace to beg their forgiveness for his atrocious shooting before they expired, and they forgave him. They were all gentlemen.

The great gambling saloons of the Southwest closed their doors sometime between 1900 and 1911, outlawed due to an influx of "good women," but in the red-light districts the "soiled doves of the prairie" still did a land-office business. Mexican *bandidos* still strayed across the border to raise havoc on the wrong side of the Rio Grande. And trains were still being robbed until the outbreak of World War I.

The Mexican Revolution

The Mexican Revolution (1910–1923) brought plenty of excitement. It actually started on American soil when, in 1911, Francisco Madero led a few hundred followers across the Rio Grande to start the civil war which would topple the dictator, the "Old Cacique" Porfirio Díaz. A decisive battle was fought at Juarez between the revolutionary army, led by Pancho Villa and Pascual Orozco, and the *Porfiristas* led by Vásquez Gómez. Shouting: "*Viva Madero, Viva la Revolucion!*" the rebels won a brilliant victory, while Americans on the El Paso side across the river had a grandstand view, watching the battle from their roofs and the top of railroad cars.

The Revolution had a way of spilling over onto American soil. In 1912, freshly escaped from jail and fleeing for his life, Villa holed up in a fleabag hotel in El Paso's Chamizal district. Soon, he was back in Mexico to lead his famous Division of the North to meet up with Zapata in Mexico City. Sometimes relations between the revolutionaries and the American Government were good, and sometimes bad. At a time when they were bad, in 1916, Villa made his famous raid on

Columbus, a sleepy New Mexico frontier town where the only excitement heretofore had been caused by a plague of rattlesnakes infesting the streets.

The battle in the streets and houses of Columbus which developed between the *Villistas* and American soldiers and citizens grew into one of the greatest monster shoot-outs the Southwest had ever experienced. It resulted in the death of 16 American citizens and brought on a punitive expedition of the U.S. cavalry under "Black Jack" Pershing in a fruitless pursuit of the

Kansas!" Protestant parsons thundered against statehood which would bring in its wake "Greaser" legislators who would "put the yoke of Romishness and popery upon the morally and mentally superior man from the North." The Arizona Legislature passed the Alien Labor Law stipulating that 80 percent of all workers in the state had to be American born, a measure directed against **the influx of Mexicans and Orientals**. It took a while until **Anglo and Hispanic** learned to live with each other in friendship. In some mountain villages resentment to-

elusive "Centaur of the North."

The time up to the outbreak of World War I and beyond has been described as the "Time of the Gringo." It was a period of racial tension as a flood of Anglo newcomers engulfed the Spanish speaking communities. The Anglos looked down upon the Hispanics. Racial hatred held up the statehood of both Arizona and New Mexico until 1912.

Lawmakers and preachers alike opposed statehood. One congressman argued: "We don't want any more states until we civilize

Advanced telescopes at Kitt Peak National Observatory bring much stunning news about pulsars and quasars.

ward outsiders still persists to this day.

Development proceeded slowly. After all, New Mexico's state motto is *Crescit Eundo*—it grows at it goes. Frontier manners remained rough for a good many years. In the early 1900s it was still necessary to make laws against a man having more than one wife. In Flagstaff, Sandy Donohue, barkeep at the Senate Saloon, greeted President Teddy Roosevelt: "By God, you are a better looking man than your picture, you old son-of-a-bitch." Teddy, the one-time cowboy, took it as the compliment it was.

Modern amenities were slow to arrive. Flagstaff got its first telephone in 1900, with 85 subscribers throughout the county. The first steam-powered automobile arrived in

1902. Electricity came in 1904. Teachers were scarce as their salaries were fixed at $75 a month, while room and board cost $40.

Minerals and Miners

In the mid-19th Century, prospectors had searched for gold. They found some, but gold never really became important. Gold's best year was 1915 when New Mexico produced $1,461,000 worth of what the ancient Indians had called the "Dung of the Gods."

Silver came after gold and was found in some abundance throughout the region, though never rivaling the famed silver lodes of Nevada and Colorado. The most produced in New Mexico was $1,162,200, in 1910. By 1950 this had dwindled to about $100,000 per annum.

Luckily, the Southwest had a wealth of other desirable minerals and copper soon **became king. It is still flourishing now,** though its peak has passed. When American industries began demanding copper, mines and mining towns once again grew up overnight like mushrooms—in New Mexico, 25 copper mines within a decade. Coal also became important, particularly with the ever expanding networks of railroads which needed the black silver for their engines.

The coal and copper miners were a very different breed from the independent spirits who had gone after gold. They were mere proletarians, often imported Mexicans, Germans, Irishmen, Greeks, Hungarians and Slavs who were shamelessly exploited by the mining barons, "who made the laws though nobody had ever elected them to public office." Miners worked under miserable conditions for miserable wages living in miserable shacks for which the company asked outrageous rents. They had to buy their goods at company stores and were little better than slaves. This led to a number of spectacular clashes between management and labor during the early 1900s, culminating in a number of armed battles between the mine workers on one side and company police, supported by National Guardsmen, on the other. Martial law was declared and a substantial number of deaths resulted. Eventually laws protecting the workers were passed and unions were established.

After copper and coal came potash and a number of more exotic minerals such as cobalt, antimony and molybdenum. As one kind of metal gave out to be replaced by another, new communities sprang up and old ones dwindled to ghost towns.

A visitor to the Southwest once exclaimed, "This would be great country if only it had water." "So would hell!" was the native son's answer. The early Anglo settlers had come to till the soil. In 1900, in New Mexico alone, 5 million acres (2 million hectares) were under cultivation, and by 1910 the state had 35,000 farms. Lack of rain during the years from 1906 to 1912 wiped many of these farmers out. In 1911 the first of the big dams—Roosevelt Dam—was built in Arizona, followed in 1916 by Elephant Butte Dam in New Mexico. Irrigation brought farming back, though the smaller **farmer was replaced by agribusiness.**

Some 90 percent of the land in the Southwest is unsuited for cultivation, but is good cattle country. Cattle do not grow fat on southwest ranches. They are raised to be sold to cattle feeders in the Mid-west and

elsewhere. By 1910 there were 40,000 miles (64,374 km) of four-strand barbed wire in Arizona alone. The end of the open range also meant the end of the old-fashioned cowboy. In 1892 a Western writer lamented that "railroads and bobwire spell the demise of that colorful character." After the end of World War I, in 1918, the Southwest was finally ready to become the New West.

Among those affected for the better were the area's oldest inhabitants—the Native Americans. In 1919 Indian men who had

The Indians believe they are an exploited lot; from the historical event of the Long Walk, left, to a commercialization of their cause as seen from tourist kitsch, right.

enlisted in the army to fight the country's enemies became eligible for U.S. citizenship. Oil was discovered on the Navajo reservation, bringing income to the tribe which was wisely invested in education and other projects beneficial to all. In 1922 Pueblo Indians formed the "All Pueblo Council" to fight the so-called Bursum Bill, which was designed to secure the right to Indian land to white squatters. In 1924 American citizenship was conferred upon all Indians born within the borders of the United States.

In 1934 the Indian Reorganization Act gave the right of partial self-government to the tribes. As a result tribal constitutions were framed and tribal presidents and councils democratically elected. This was not an

unmixed blessing. The elected leaders often represented the more assimilated, educated and English-speaking people, while the traditional Indians saw no reason to adopt forms of self-rule patterned after the system of government practiced by whites. They adhered to their old dependence on elders or religious chiefs. This led in some places to a simmering conflict between the "Progressives" and the "Traditionals."

Lagging behind the Anglos in economic gains and the professions, Hispanic Americans of New Mexico concentrated upon politics and effectively ran the state. One author, Francis Stanley, wrote:

"Politics is a religion above the family. It streams into the *nino* from his mother's breasts; it is patted into the tortilla, and ladled with the frijole, masticated with every mouthful of chili, washed down with every glass of beer. Sacred, ingrained, ritualistic, mysterious, it is its race, color, creed – POLITICS."

Prohibition in the Southwest wrought less havoc than elsewhere. The authorities winked at the citizen imbibing his vino and cerveza as they themselves indulged. Hard liquor never played the role it did among the Anglos and gangsterism was never a factor in this relaxed atmosphere.

While gold and silver mining was but a memory, and many coal mines were shut down because they had become unproductive, potash mining started in a big way in 1931. Natural gas became a source of income in the Twenties. Also, in the same period, the Southwest enjoyed a number of moderate oil booms. Large copper mines opened in both Arizona and New Mexico. In 1936 Hoover Dam was completed. Water, or rather the lack of it, was becoming a problem. Old-timers complained that modern industry, farming, ranching, tourists and the increased population were "pumping the West dry."

In 1942 the army took over land belonging to a boy's school at Los Alamos. In the words of Erna Ferguson:

"No secret was ever better kept than that of Los Alamos. The schoolboys had it that they were moving out for the Ethiopian Ski Corps or the Scandinavian Camel Artillery. Santa Feans saw lights against the Jemez peaks, but knew nothing. Only the veteran reporter, Brian Dunne, dared write in the *Santa Fe New Mexican* that 'buses were coming in loaded with Indians, people jabbering Spanish, and Nobel Prize winner."

A town of 8,000 inhabitants was springing up almost overnight in the vicinity of the state capital without anybody being aware of it. On a plateau dotted with hundreds of cave dwelling carved out from the soft tufa rock by prehistoric Pueblo Indians, the atomic bomb was built. It was first exploded at the Trinity site, near Alamogordo, New Mexico, in 1945... "A blind girl saw the flash of light, a rancher thought the end of the world had come," but the country at large did not know that the history of the world had changed. It was a New Mexican officer who "armed" the bomb before it was dropped on Hiroshima, and it was Paddy Martinez, a Navajo Indian who, in 1950, found the first lump of uranium in the Arizona desert. Thus the Nuclear Age was born in the American Southwest.

MODERN SOUTHWEST

Landlocked and chronically thirsty, the Southwest at the end of World War II was remote but hardly unknown. Railroads, highways and scheduled flights made access easy. Inhabitants shipped out iron, T-bones and grapefruit, and got back dude ranchers and tourists doing the national-park circuit. Yet each state seemed in a private trance. Arizona, locus of frantic Air Force activity during the War, returned to its three Cs: cotton, cattle and copper. New Mexico, with its Pueblo and Hispanic agricultural traditions, changed primarily with the seasons.

demanded: water. Reclamation was hardly a new idea. The Southwest had already seen the passage of the Reclamation Act in 1902, the completion of Hoover Dam on the Colorado River in 1935 and the construction of countless lesser dams by Federal, state and private concerns. But with the war effort over, the Bureau of Reclamation could direct its attention westward in a major way, and it made proposals for virtually every watercourse. Its grandest single monument was Glen Canyon Dam, completed in 1963 and backing water 180 river miles into some

Southeastern Nevada, in decline since the silver boom of the 1880s, was a polity of sand and collapsing buildings. And southern Utah deliberately stayed out of the postwar mainstream to preserve the isolation and purity of its Mormon culture. The Southwest in 1945 resembled the Great Basin of Utah and Nevada, whose rivers dead-end in separate valleys instead of reaching out to the sea. Like the Great Basin it encompassed, the Southwest faced inward, fixed on its several selves.

Great and Mighty Dams

The Federal role was crucial in developing what Southwesterners of all persuasions

of the Colorado's least known and most spectacular canyons; and its most ambitious scheme is the ongoing Central Arizona Project, to hoist Colorado River water to Phoenix and Tucson at cost-estimates that have quadrupled from the original billion dollars.

Federal stimulation of the Southwestern economy developed a wide spectrum of activities, while shifting balances of power within the Southwest itself. Contracts for reclamation projects went primarily to regional companies, allowing them at last to

Among the works of men towards development is modern Las Vegas city, the nation's major center of live entertainment.

escape Eastern domination. Agriculture benefited from reclamation and crop subsidies, but the most benefits went to the largest operations and to agribusiness, often squeezing out the small farmer. Cheap leasing on public lands favored expansive ranching operations, and often led to overgrazing. Oil and gas industries were subsidized through depletion allowances. Conservative politicians rallied against Federal intrusion and Washington bureaucrats—and snared all the public works money they could. Such support made the commercial development of the Southwest possible, but often at the expense of the homegrown independent operator.

Much of the openest, driest and least productive land had been allotted to the military during World War II, and the military kept it. During the Fifties, the salt and alkali basins of Nevada became the site of hundreds of underground nuclear tests, and Hill Air Force Base in Utah became the West's leading missile center. Towns like Yuma and Sierra Vista, in southern Arizona, are virtual adjuncts to the military, and many of the Southwest's emptiest reaches are off-limits to civilians.

Ironically, much of the land in the hands of the military—scarred by tanks, pounded by artillery, glittering with shrapnel—has remained relatively intact, while the drive for minerals, timber and cheap energy has caused the more lasting devastation. Mining on Federal land was encouraged by minimal fees and scant regulation, while timber contracts didn't—and still don't—make that most basic requirement that a new tree be planted for each cut down. In the early Fifties, uranium prospectors gouged roads at random across southern Utah, leaving permanent scars. Uranium was developed more systematically in northwestern New Mexico in the Seventies, leaving behind carcinogenic mill tailings for the Indian inhabitants.

'Black Gold': A Source of Energy

But it was coal, abundant and often lying near the surface, that became the most coveted resource. In 1957 a Utah company made the first contract with the Navajo Tribal Council for coal on the Navajo Reservation. The major oil companies, sensing that the coal beds of the Colorado Plateau would become a vital energy source, began acquiring coal companies and turning them into subsidiaries. The future of coal was given a further boost with President Nixon's Project Independence speech in 1973, which argued that the United States could no longer rely on undependable foreign companies for its energy needs and had to develop its own resources to become energy self-sufficient.

A far-reaching plan, with great potential profits, was conceived for the Colorado Plateau. Cities like Los Angeles and Phoenix badly needed new energy but had to generate it elsewhere because their pollution levels were already intolerable. Coal that abounded in southern Utah and northern Arizona could be burned on the spot, sending fly ash over a sparsely populated area. Power would surge through transmission lines to cities hundreds of miles away. A consortium of 21 utilities, representing seven states, banded together in 1974 and proposed a mesh of strip mines, power plants and transmission lines of unprecedented complexity. Not all of the proposed grid came into being, but major coal-fired power plants went up at Farmington, New Mexico, and Page, Arizona. The Page plant, near Glen Canyon Dam, was linked by a company railroad to a strip mine 70 miles (113 km) east on Black Mesa, a formation sacred to the Hopi.

By the time of the assault on the Colorado Plateau, large-scale development was no longer wholly popular. Many of the Southwest's new residents had fled industrial devastation elsewhere. In the late Sixties, environmentalists were strong enough to kill a proposal to build two hydroelectric dams in the Grand Canyon.

The fight came to a head over a plan to strip-mine coal on the Kaiparowits Plateau and combust it in a plant that would scatter ash across southern Utah's national parks. Feelings on both sides ran high. Lawsuits and lobbying delayed the project until California, realizing it had overestimated its need for energy in the first place, pulled out; the Kaiparowits scheme collapsed.

Retirees and Real Estate

While energy battles were being fought on the Colorado Plateau, the warmer lands to the south were filling with humanity. With the advent of air-conditioning during World War II, no desert was too hot for colonization. Snowbelt retirees settled in vast retirement communities like Sun City, Green Valley and Youngtown, in tracts and trailer parks along the Colorado River from Boulder City, Nevada to Yuma, Arizona, and even in the small towns of southern New Mexico. While traditional industries like copper mining and small-scale ranching fell into decline, high-technology industries in Albuquerque, Phoenix and Tucson drew ambitious young people to the area, balancing the demographics and inflating the population.

The real-estate industry was the prime beneficiary, and development exploded

from the cities. Mesquite gave way to mobile home communities, to pseudo-adobe duplex compounds, to townhouse labyrinths around artificial lakes that obliterated the desert. One developer brought the London Bridge to the Colorado River and ran the world's tallest fountain on subsiding groundwater merely to promote his ventures. Easier on the terrain was outright land fraud, wherein development took place on paper and the land, if any, was spared. During the Seventies, Phoenix, Albuquerque and El Paso all grew by more than 30 percent. By the Eighties, Phoenix was swelling by more than 100,000 people a year, Las Vegas was America's fastest growing city under half a million and Santa Fe—that museum piece of Hispanic

tradition — became too expensive for the people born there.

President Carter came up with a proposal to place MX missiles on a railroad maze through 4,600 shelters in vast reaches of western Utah and eastern Nevada. Those from Southern Utah, who formerly would have welcomed the jobs, were less willing to embrace the latest defense scheme — especially as many of them had started showing up with cancer attributed to underground nuclear testing in Nevada 20 years back. Local politicians who routinely supported construction and national defense sensed new qualms among their constituents, stalled for time, then turned against the project after it was attacked by the Mormon Church. The MX racetrack plan collapsed.

While recent changes in the Southwestern landscape represent the works of man, what most visitors still come for are the works of nature. The tourist industry is thus torn between the need to accommodate the visitor and the need to preserve those features the visitor came to see. Efforts on behalf of the Southwestern terrain have been a holding action. What has been protected in parks is well-known enough to be threatened by overvisitation. A few corners are surprisingly intact: relatively unvisited are the area north of the Grand Canyon known as the Arizona Strip, southern New Mexico, and the restful Texas hill country north of Big Bend National Park— full of little towns, unmechanized ranches and lava-crowned mesas. Those trying to escape unpleasant change, and avoid their fellow visitors, may be best off just aiming for some curious blank spot on the map.

But not all the novelties of man need be avoided, even in the Southwest. The art enclaves of Santa Fe, Taos and Scottsdale, the Flagstaff Summer Festival of the Arts, the Santa Fe Opera, the dense-pack experimental communities of Paola Soleri and the superb buildings of Frank Lloyd Wright scattered through Phoenix—all prove that good weather has not entirely numbed the artistic spirit. Probably the most significant artistic work currently being produced is that of Native Americans, who are reviving and extending such traditions as weaving and ceramics and in sculpture and painting, combining traditional motifs with the latest innovations from New York.

Farther reaching if less visible are ad-

Left, Hoover Dam, Nevada, was a boost to the state's transition to a modern economy during the 1930s. Right, landing of *Columbia 3* at White Sands Missile Range.

vances in the sciences. Los Alamos, which continues to hone weaponry in top secret, has branched into such life-oriented pursuits as solar and geothermal energy, cancer research, laser surgery and astrophysics. Kitt Peak National Observatory, west of Tucson, has the world's foremost concentration of advanced telescopes, and has brought much of our stunning news about pulsars, quasars, black holes and storms on the sun. The Very Large Array, a collection of radio telescopes in an empty stretch of western New Mexico, is probing the very edge of the universe and peering backward in time to the Big Bang itself. The White Sands Missile Range, near Alamogordo, New Mexico, has been the site of many of NASA's experiments, and plays alternate host to the Space Shuttle. In

catered to the common man in down-town's Glitter Gulch. However hard to take seriously, Las Vegas has become a major convention center, and is an important Southwestern crossroads of economic and political power. Las Vegas is an object of pilgrimage for connoisseurs of the surreal as well as those with loose change. If neon signs are an art form, as some folklorists claim, Las Vegas is their Louvre.

Such various assaults upon a formerly remote landscape make recent Southwestern history seem a whirlwind of population sprawl and resource development. But new factors could radically alter its course. Nature, for instance, could foreclose on the increasing defiance of heat and drought.

Alamogordo itself is the International Space Hall of Fame, whose displays of moon memorabilia and John Glenn's space suit prove that even the cutting edge of science needn't preclude a little kitsch.

Finally, among the works of man, there is Las Vegas. Nevada legalized gambling in 1931, in time to welcome the construction workers for Hoover Dam, and the little Mormon town of Las Vegas enjoyed a fleeting boom as the cement was poured. But Las Vegas only became *Vegas* in 1946 with the opening of the Flamingo, first of the clubs to feature heroically bad architecture and superstar entertainment. Clubs on the Strip reached new summits of commercial flamboyance, while merely gaudy casinos

Culturally, the deluge of legal and illegal immigrants from Latin America, seeking jobs and political asylum, has encouraged speculation that the Southwest may face a Spanish-speaking separatist movement similar to that of the Quebecois in Canada. Rather than being at risk of losing its regional flavor, the Southwest may be about to witness its flowering.

Anyone rooted in the Southwest knows that much of its fascination lies in the change of scene around the next bend. From geology to biological adaptation, those changes are falling within the mental compass of the Southwesterners. It is their own history, in headless acceleration, that is now careening too fast to decipher.

PEOPLE

The people of the Southwest have been fashioned by its history and landscape. They came in waves and adjusted to one another sometimes with hostility, sometimes with patience and sympathy. All of them were burnished by the heat and horizons. All of them felt the spiritual force of this special land.

The Indians were here first, of course. Whether they came from Asia or through a series of other worlds is a matter of opinion, but no later arrivals could escape their influence. This is their land.

There are many tribes and many cultures, many languages and many traditions, and assuming that all Indians are the same was only one way European settlers showed their ignorance. They devised more brutal ways as well. But the Indians of the Southwest take the long view. Other peoples have come and gone more than once during their long stay here.

The Spanish influence is everywhere in the Southwest, too, and it is the mingling of Hispanic and Indian cultures that gives the Southwest its special flavor. Spanish is spoken all over the Southwest, and Hispanics have traditionally dominated the political scene. Their food, their religion and strong family ties complement well the Indian ways.

The vague and not always affectionate term "Anglos" covers everyone else who came to the Southwest, almost always later than the Indians and Hispanics. They brought with them commerce, for the most part, and a culture that does not always fit in with the more indigenous ones. These days the Southwest is home to corporations and health spas, and to the people who come to spend their last few years someplace warm and dry. It is mostly the Anglos who migrate here; the Indians and Hispanics have roots that go much deeper.

The peoples of the Southwest are living in a transitional time, and no one can say with any certainty whether the clash of the old and new that the overlay of the various cultures seems to represent will be resolved. There are vast amounts of space in the Southwest, and all of that space makes one feel there are vast amounts of time, too. None of these conflicts needs to be resolved tomorrow. The Southwest is an object lesson in the merits of the long view.

THE INDIANS

Whether they are called "American Indians" or "Native Americans" matters less to most individuals than their tribal identity. Native American people tend to think of themselves first as members of a particular tribe, and many tribes further differentiate according to specific locales. Even tribal names such as Navajo, Ute or Pueblo are mere labels attached to the tribes by Europeans who were unable to pronounce or did not bother to discover the name each tribe has to identify itself.

The myth that all "Indians" are alike still persists, but nowhere is this falsehood more clearly disproven than in the Southwest. For here, often within a few miles of each other, are Native American communities whose cultural and linguistic differences are as different from each other as England's are from Turkey's. Seeing one Indian community is, most emphatically, not seeing them all.

Climate and Land

Whatever the tribe, the determining factors in the life-patterns that were followed, and in many cases still practiced, have always been the weather and the terrain. The Native American people of the Southwest, no matter what their linguistic or philosophical differences are, have always seen themselves in relation to the landscape around them. Survival, until very recently, has always depended upon powers of adaptation, not change, and upon intimate knowledge of weather patterns, clouds, animals and plants.

In places where annual rainfall and drainage patterns allowed farming, and where nearby hills and mountains offered small game or deer, groups like the Pueblo people of New Mexico and the Hopi of northern Arizona, established permanent villages with massive stone-and-mortar walls to ward off the rigors of winter. The Pima and Papago of southern Arizona settled in villages near desert springs, since water was of primary concern in their locale. Their villages, while permanent, did not require elaborate masonry walls but, rather, cool,

People of the Southwest make a fascinating ethnic mosaic. Preceding pages, cowgirls at Santa Fe; county sheriff poses in front of car; and left, handsome Mr. Mitchell, Navajo elder and teacher.

airy thatching woven from local cane to provide protection from the sun and to allow the wind to circulate throughout. Although vast cultural and linguistic differences existed between them, these communities, who farmed and supplemented with hunting and gathering, shared the similar concerns of clouds and rainfall. In religious ceremonies, the focus was always, and continues to be, on adequate precipitation throughout the year. Prayers for rain and careful surveillance of the sky are activities understood by all human cultures engaged in farming without benefit of modern technology.

Because the terrain and climate of the Southwest are so unpredictable and the consequences of long droughts irreparable, all Native American tribes of the Southwest have survived here, as one Hopi Pueblo elder put it, "by prayer. We live by our prayers." Thus, the figure of the Rainbow Woman arching over the Great Seal of the Navajo Tribe (displayed prominently on tribal motor-pool vehicles) symbolizes, literally, the sustenance that the Rainbow Woman is believed to provide the Navajo people when she brings rain.

Creation or Migration?

All tribes in the Southwest have religious beliefs connecting their creation and the creation of the Universe with a higher force or being. Each tribe has its own particular story of Creation, but anthropological theories about Native Americans originating in Asia or the South Seas are firmly rejected by Native American people.

Regardless of how the Native Americans came to the Southwest, when the Spanish arrived in 1540, Native American people had already been living there for some 9,500 years. It is within this immense span of time that the tribes of the Southwest have come to understand their intimate relationship with Earth, the Mother Creator for many Pueblo tribes. Mountains and hills are sacred, streams and springs are sacred, and the Native American people feel a kinship with even the most humble living beings.

It is difficult to gauge the impact of the arrival of the Spaniards and later European settlers upon the tribal cultures of the Southwest. The difficulty lies in the fact that any attempt to evaluate or compare the "before" of Native American cultures with the "after" is impossible. Furthermore, implicit in such an assessment are Western European assumptions about "change" or "loss of cultural purity," which are appropriate only when applied to Western European cultures. Western European views of life and culture tend to place an inordinate emphasis on material evidence, while the Native American cultures of the Southwest are spiritual, not materialistic, cultures. No outsider, no anthropological "expert" can truly comprehend what lies at the heart of the Navajo or Pueblo or Apache cultures.

What is visible is evidence that deep within these Native American cultures is the profound philosophical belief in coexistence with all living things, including human beings of other races and cultures. The Native American cultures of the Southwest have continually demonstrated their belief in and respect for many alternative ways and beliefs. This adaptability and intellectual breadth enabled these cultures to survive and even thrive in the harsh Southwestern climate. Within the world view of these Southwestern Indian cultures, the fact that a medicine man has a color television in his house does not necessarily mean that he has rejected ancient beliefs and traditions; what it means is that his curiosity and belief in knowledge about all humanity have prompted him to include within his world this peculiar artifact of contemporary high-tech culture. His view is that what he might see, or learn by seeing, can add to and strengthen his traditional healing powers.

While many of the sacred dances and ceremonies are closed to outside visitors (due to 150 years of boorish behavior), a great many are performed for the renewal of all human beings and all the world, and these ceremonies do include outside visitors. In fact, the Zuni Pueblo people of western New Mexico believe that, if they were to bar outside visitors from their impressive Winter Solstice Shalako Ceremony, the ritual would have no effect, and the world would not be renewed. Consequently, the giant carved wooden masks of Shalako Dancers who appear at sundown and cross the Zuni river are witnessed every year by many hundreds of visitors.

No-Nonense Patriotism

At the same time, it is important to remember that nearly all Native American people, no matter which tribe they come from, are intensely conscious of being Americans, of being not only the original Americans but Americans who have fought

and died for this land in every major war. The overwhelming richness and intensity of tribal identity may occasionally obscure the plain no-nonsense patriotism which is also a key ingredient in the individual identity of a White Mountain Apache or an Isleta Pueblo. The special "trusteeship" of the U.S. Government over tribal lands is not a Native American scheme. The Founding Fathers conferred this unique (and some Indians add "paternalistic") legal status upon Indian Tribes in the Commerce Clause of the U.S. Constitution.

The unusual legal status of communities located on the Federal Indian reservations often brings strange or interesting results. For example, in Arizona, the New Pascua Tribe of Yaqui Indians can conduct million-

dollar bingo games 10 miles (16 km) west of Tucson because Arizona state laws limiting the size of bingo jackpots do not apply to the New Pascua Yaqui Reservation, which lies under the Federal jurisdiction of the United States Department of the Interior. The special legal status means that the Jicarilla Apache Tribe in northern New Mexico may manage their trophy-size elk and mule deer as they see fit, without state intervention. The result is a paradise for big game hunters and for trout fishermen at the Jicarilla's

The Indian way of life is a rythmic one; the cloud dancer at San Juan, left, could well be dancing to the beat of drums by musicians at the San Ildefonso pueblo, right.

Stone Lake Resort.

On the minus side, Native American communities do not have direct control over the leasing or development of their tribal lands. Before tribes can do *anything*, they must secure the approval of the Secretary of the Department of the Interior and the Commissioner of the Bureau of Indian Affairs. The results of this 200-year-old policy toward Indian tribes is readily apparent: Native American communities are notoriously lacking in many of the modern amenities other American communities take for granted. Because neither individual tribal members nor the Tribe itself has "ownership" of the land, financing for housing, sewage treatment and solid-waste disposal were in past years impossible for Native

American communities to obtain.

Very few of the businesses located on reservations are controlled by Native Americans. Again, until recently, it has been extremely difficult for enterprising Native American businessmen to obtain bank financing since reservation lands cannot be used as collateral. Because of these complexities, in past years tribes in the Southwest had little control over land use and development of natural resources on tribal lands. Large mining corporations, aided by apathetic bureaucrats in the Department of the Interior, obtained vast mineral and petroleum leases on tribal lands without paying more than token sums for these lease privileges. Although these unfortunate leases

were made in the mid-1950s, many have a 40- or 50-year duration. Equally unfortunate was the past policy of the Department of the Interior allowing mining operations to strip-mine coal and uranium without requiring reclamation of the land. Evidence of these past abuses are readily visible on many reservations.

For people who trace their origins to Mother Earth, the natural-resource policies of the Department of the Interior have been particularly painful. But in the past 10 years a gradual shift has been taking place, in which young Indian lawyers and PhDs have aided their tribes in asserting more control over their lands and natural resources. But always there remains a deep conflict between the traditional reverence for Mother Earth and the critical need for jobs and housing in communities where unemployment may run as high as 75 percent, and the woefully scarce housing is often without electricity or indoor plumbing.

Because the tribes of the Southwest remained relatively untouched by Western European influences for so many years after the arrival of the first Spaniards, the evidence of recent arrivals of the modern technological age have a far greater shock effect on the eye. High-tech sewage treatment plants are juxtaposed with weathered sandstone walls built in 1000 A.D.

This juxtaposition of the ancient and non-European with the contemporary high-technological world is disturbing because it raises many questions—and provides no answers—about the multiplicity of cultural identities. Clearly, the tribal people living in the Southwest are very much part of the present, with its attendant material culture.

But time and again, outsiders have seriously misjudged the visible and superficial evidence. In 1900, Franz Boas, the giant of cultural anthropology, announced that the Pueblo tribes faced cultural extinction within a matter of 10 years. Eighty years later, cultural anthropologists are just beginning to realize that as outsiders to Native American cultures they are unable to understand that ineffable core of tribal identity which lies intact beneath layers and layers of debris left behind by successive waves of invaders. But as one old Pueblo woman said, "How much could you expect Franz Boas to know? The United States of America hasn't even existed 250 years yet. But we have been around nine or 10 thousand years at least. We've seen them come and we've seen them go. We watched the Spaniards come and then go. We watched it happen to the Mexicans. I wonder if it surprised them?"

THE HISPANICS

In 1598 Governor Don Juan de Oñate led 130 families and 270 single men, the first colonists, from Mexico into New Mexico to settle just north of present-day Santa Fe. The Pueblo Indian world which existed along the Rio Grande was linked, from that time on to the destiny of the new colonists. For over a century the Hispanic villages, surrounded by towering green and enchanting mountains, clung to the Rio Grande. To the first Hispanic colonists making their living from the fields in the valley and from their flocks, Mexico and its urban centers were far away. The settlers were Hispanos and Mexicanos who had come in search of a new life, the Catholic friars for souls to convert to Christianity. El Paso was the resting point, the link between Old Mexico and New Mexico, as it and Júarez are today. Heading north from El Paso through the stretch of desert called *La Jornada del Muerto* (The Journey of Death), the colonists were rewarded with the high plateaus and mountains of the *Sangre de Cristo* (Blood of Christ), a land which reminded some of their native southern Spain and others of Mexico.

From the initial villages the settlers began to extend their influence. Groups of families petitioned the Spanish authorities in Mexico for land grants, and communities spread along the river and into the mountains. After the independence of Mexico from Spain in 1821, the land grant system continued, so that when Anglo America came into the Southwest it found a communal system it did not understand.

This system of allotting land grants played a crucial part in the formation of the culture. The original land grants provided space for homes, fields, irrigation water, firewood and the grazing of animals. The communal land helped shape the character of the Hispanos, but with the coming of the Anglo Americans in 1846, a new system of land ownership came to the Hispanic Southwest and many of the land grants were lost or greatly diminished in size. Now, those that are left struggle for survival, and as the Hispanic population moves further away from its origins in the villages and into the larger urban centers, a transformation of cultural

Hispanic woman at doorway in El Rancho De Las Golondrinas, an 18th-Century Spanish working ranch.

character is underway. Perhaps the dominant theme in the Southwest today when one looks at the Hispanic culture is the rapid sense of transformation which is brought about by assimilation into the mainstream Anglo culture.

For centuries the neighbors of the Hispanos of the Southwest were the native Indian Pueblo. A sharing of the cultures continued until 1680, when the Pueblo Indians of New Mexico, incensed about their subservient role in relation to the Hispanic colonists and enraged because the Catholic friars insisted they give up their native religion, finally took up arms against the Hispanos and drove them out of New Mexico in a bloody revolution. The Spanish colonists returned in 1692; led by Don Diego de Vargas they reconquered Santa Fe and re-established Spanish rule. Thereafter the cultures survived side by side, not always in harmony, but certainly historically linked.

Earth, Water and Sky

Three elements seem to form the character of the individual, the communities and the Southwest as a whole: earth, water and sky. The Hispanos discovered that the Pueblo Indians' relationship to the earth was a sacred partnership; the earth and her creatures nurtured the community. The relationship was fragile, one to be closely attended. In Spanish the earth is *la tierra*, and the land which belongs to the community of the land grant or village is to be guarded for the well-being of all. The Hispanic loves his village, his sense of place is strong. He is honor-bound and loyal to family and community, and this long history of attachment to the lands of the village evolved into a close relationship with *la sagrada tierra*, the sacred earth. Like the Pueblo Indians before them, the Hispanos learned to live in close harmony with their native land. Now that the Hispanic population is primarily an urban population, the attachment takes new forms. A garden, a few trees, a flower patch or just the geraniums in an old coffee can express this love for the land.

Two rivers dominate the Hispanic Southwest. The Colorado cuts down from Colorado to form the Grand Canyon in Arizona and empties into the Gulf of Baja California. The Rio Grande originates in southern

Colorado and flows through New Mexico on its way to the Gulf of Mexico. Historically, the Hispanic population has clung to the life-giving Rio Grande. To look at the river is not only to look at the important resource of water, it is to see the corridor of Hispanic culture which strides the borders of Mexico and the United States. The Rio Grande is to Hispanic culture in this region what the Mississippi is to the United States.

The third element added to the fragile desert, to the grand mesas, the *arroyos* and the canyons completes the picture of attraction. Sky. The sky and the light determine the tone, the color and the mood. The sky is clear, the air is crisp, the colors sharp, sunrise and sunset are definite times, the cloud formations of summer are unrivaled in beauty.

The Hispano has lent his unique character and industry to the land. He gave rise to the first mining industry in the Southwest. He was the original horseman, the *vaquero* who introduced the lore and trappings of the cowboy. He learned from the Pueblo Indians how to build humble mansions of *adobe*, the sun-dried mud bricks, and he learned how to use the system of *acequias* to water his fields. The Spanish language is spoken all over the Southwest. One has but to listen to the place names to become aware of the centuries of Hispanic influence: from San Francisco to San Antonio, the corridor of the border region bears a real Hispanic stamp, Santa Fe, Española, Albuquerque, Belen, Socorro, Las Cruces, El Paso—all along the Rio Grande, all original Hispanic settlements.

The roots of Hispanic culture were nurtured in a tradition which included the Catholic religion, the ceremonies of family and community, oral storytelling and other folk arts. The Spanish language continues to be at the core of the culture, although as more and more activities take place in an English-speaking world, the loss of the language is felt. However, ethnic consciousness and pride are rallying to make the language more available in schools and in the marketplace, and the same consciousness, although it may express itself in English, still identifies with Hispanic values.

Family and home are at the center of the value system, as is strong identification with family name. Within the family unit, relationships are extended by use of the *compadrazco* network. *Compadres* and *comadres*, godfathers and godmothers, serve to extend the family ties. For the baptism of a baby, for confirmation in the Catholic church or for a wedding, godparents are selected. This cultural tradition helps to extend the nuclear family into the larger community. A New Mexican family may have *compadres* as far away as California, Texas or the Midwest, and they are all included in the family. This vast network of communication also helps keep the cultural ways alive.

Likewise, the migrations of Mexican workers northward into the United States serve to reinforce the culture. As the workers move north, so does their music, lifestyle, social needs and, most important, their language. There are probably 20 million Hispanics living in the United States, with a major portion residing along the border region.

Chicano Pride

In all the border states the Hispano has been actively involved in the historical development of the Southwest. The contemporary social and political movement began with the "Chicano Movement" in the 1960s. Like the Black Civil Rights movement, the Mexican American population of the Southwest demanded access to equal schooling, health care, and acceptable working and living conditions. The movement was a resurgence of ethnic pride, and the word "Chicano" was a reflection of that pride.

In searching for their roots, Mexican American leaders and artists returned to the mother country, Mexico. By asserting their heritage, they reinforced their pride. The history of political leaders, folk heroes, the role of Chicanos in mining, ranching and the railroad industry revealed an active community. Folk arts, oral storytelling, religious music and the presentation of morality plays during the Christmas season all display a creative imagination which has been kept alive and well by the old ones. In effect, the contemporary Chicano had but to look at his own history in the Southwest to discover the wealth of his heritage.

The Southwest today does not represent a melting pot, it is a "sharing pot." The various cultural groups give and take, share and learn to grow with each other. Mexican foods are enjoyed by all groups. For Christmas, native people and world travellers attend the festive lighting of the *luminarias*, the lights which illuminate churches and homes. These candles, burning in brown bags, have become a staple item for Christmas, as have the foods. Everyone eats *posole, chile, carne adovada, natillas, biscochitos* and *enpanaditas*—all traditional Christmas foods. The rest of the year, beans, *chili, enchiladas, burritos* and *tacos* are the fare for those who like Mexican food. The kitchen is still the heart of the house.

The Chicano Movement inspired a renaissance of artistic expression. Art groups sprang up in every community. A resurgence of ethnic pride carried the Chicano into new fields: cinema, mural artworks, and innovations in music.

Hispanic Art: An Expression of Tradition

But traditional art and ritual are at the root of this renaissance, and Hispanic artists work within a great tradition. Picture, for instance, this example:

A solemn procession winds its way down the *arroyo*, meanders like a long, colorful

ribbon through fields and chapparal, finally coming to a halt on top of a hill crowned by an ancient adobe chapel. There is a ringing of bells, the sound of fiddles, of voices singing. At the head of the procession stands a man holding aloft a gilded cross, by his side the village priest. Behind them four men carry a wooden image representing San Isidro, patron saint of all who till the soil, with his yoke of oxen, his plow and his helper, a diminutive angel—a fine example of traditional wood carving. Behind them follows the crowd of worshipers—men in

Chile harvest at New Mexico. The vegetable is not just a taste preference; it is an addiction for true New Mexican Hispanics.

old costumes, devout women in black shawls beneath black umbrellas shading them from the bright rays of the Southwestern sun, children, tourists, everyone who cares to join.

Twice a year this procession can be witnessed—in spring when the fields are being blessed, and in fall when thanks is given for a plentiful harvest. It takes place at El Rancho De Las Golondrinas, an 18th Century Spanish working ranch and, at the same time, a living museum. The procession always heralds a two-day fiesta of music and dance as well as a gathering of Hispanic craftsmen—*santeros*, or carvers of holy images; painters of religious *retablos*; smiths making beautiful handwrought objects; women at their looms weaving colorful Chimayo blankets; basket makers; women doing embroidery or ladling out superb, but devilish hot chile dishes. All this takes place against a backdrop of ancient chapels and buildings which underscore the historical roots of the traditional artists and *artesanos* of today.

Traditional Hispanic art was, and is, homemade, rustic and original, fashioned by simple farmers who, from necessity, also became artists. One of the chief aspects of this art is that it was created with little outside influence. For centuries, the Southwest was virtually cut off from the rest of the world. The populous cities of Mexico were more than a thousand inhospitable desert miles away. Maybe two or three times a year a mule train, or a caravan of *carretas*, clumsy, lumbering oxcarts, prone to breakdowns and agonizingly slow, made their way to Santa Fe. In the years when the Apache were on the warpath no caravans arrived at all. From the 1820s onward, Yankee goods arrived via the long and perilous Santa Fe Trail, but until the coming of railways, the country remained slumbering in isolation. Works of art or elegant European furniture, which could have served as models for the local craftsman, were rarely seen.

Hispanic artists were thrown upon their own resources, making do with whatever materials their environment had to offer. Even the homes of the *ricos*, the *gente fina*, or fine folks were simple, with only the most essential furnishings. Finery was the status symbol of the rich.

The main piece of furniture in the Hispanic house was the *trastero*, or cupboard, often richly carved and painted. Chests, in which a family's possessions were kept, also served as tables or benches. Fancy chests and boxes had elaborate hand-forged locks and were richly decorated with carved lions and scalloped wheels, less often with designs of Moorish origin. Chairs were sturdy, rough-hewn, and thick-legged. Hanging in the corners of rooms were ornate painted *nichos*, to hold the images of saints and other religious objects. Lithographs of saints or biblical figures were displayed in punched tin frames. There were also usually a number of *retablos*, pictures of saints painted on wooden boards. Many churches held naive paintings on tin, showing the person who ordered them on his or her knees, giving thanks to some saint for having cured him of an illness. Other such *retablos* might show a fire or fall from a horse which someone had survived, thanks to the intercession of a patron saint.

Santos: Religious Art

Santeros were the men who carved *santos*—that is figures of the Savior, the Virgin, saints and angels. Such images made no effort to be anatomically correct. Works of faith rather than of art, angels were typically short-legged; saints were elongated, narrow-waisted and big-footed. Anglos, used to the realistic, formal art of white America at first called these *santos* "fearful artistic abominations." Today, these abominations are highly prized works of art eagerly sought by museums and serious collectors who value them for their peculiar charm and individuality. One also often encounters tragic figures of the suffering Christ, hollow-cheeked and emaciated, the body chalk-white, hair and beard coal-black, the bright blood trickling from many wounds.

Death and suffering have always played a large part in Hispanic art, possibly as a reminder of centuries of oppression of Spanish Christians by the Moors. They are uppermost in the mind of the mysterious sect called *Penitentes* who will scourge themselves until the blood flows and whose prayer is, "Lord, give us a good death." This preoccupation with the inevitability of dying, with damnation and salvation, shows itself in the most impressive of Southwestern sculpture, the large death cart with its skeleton which admonishes the viewer, "As I am now, so you will be, repent!" Typical also are statues of *La Conquista*, patroness of Santa Fe; of *Nuestra Senora de Guadalupe*, the Indian Virgin; and of the Holy Trinity. The more ambitious sculptures in the round are known as *bultos*.

Material used for *santos* is usually cottonwood and plaster made from locally found gypsum. Colors came out of the native

earth — the red and orange from pulverized iron ocher; white and yellow from the abundant clay; black from finely ground charcoal; green from boiled herbs. Blue had to be imported and was not much used before the 1850s. *Santos* were and still are an integral part of every household, particularly patron saints after whom family members have been named. Crosses made from wood and combined with straw mosaics covered with resin are also popular.

Women excel in embroidering coverlets called *colchas*, using designs of humans, birds and flowers, usually on a white background. Sheep had been brought to New Mexico by the earliest Spanish settlers and provided cheap and super-abundant wool. Women wove, and still weave, their richly colored thick blankets described as "made in the pattern of a maze of concentric diamonds." Chimayo and Truchas weavers also create strikingly modern blankets, woolen carrying bags and pillowcases or miniature rugs.

Silver and Clay

Silversmithing is done by the *platero* who sometimes still fashions his wares with the help of a homemade mud oven, charcoal, bellows of goatskin and a blow pipe. Often also doubling as blacksmith, the *platero* melted down silver pesos to make crosses, necklaces of hollow beads, rosaries, bracelets, earrings, tobacco and powder flasks, silver buttons, head stalls for horses and spurs for the rider. It was the Spanish *plateros* who taught the craft to Navajo Indians in the 1850s.

Pottery was simple, made for every day use, though nowadays some ceramicists make charmingly painted and fired clay figures of Mary, Joseph and the Holy Child in his manger, the three wise kings and praying shepherds, all of them typical Hispanic farmers surrounded by their animals— burros and lambs, oxen and goats. These things may be admired and bought in museum and antique shops throughout the Southwest, particularly in Taos and Santa Fe. In spite of a flood of plastic saints made in Taiwan, or of biblical figures (and nude blondes) painted on black velvetine from Mexico, traditional *bultos*, *santos* and *retablos* are still being carved, Chimayo blankets still woven, the ancient crafts still practiced.

Woman in Truchas, one of the old Spanish villages, where the Hispanic way of life is still evident.

THE ANGLOS

So diffuse is the Southwestern cultural majority known as Anglos that it is difficult to say who is included, except that very few actually descend from the Angles, a small German tribe that invaded England in the Fifth Century, A.D. Given currency by Spanish-speaking Southwesterners, the label generally includes all pale-skinned Americans of European descent who do not have Spanish surnames.

The first Anglos to reach the Southwest were explorers, fur trappers, and traders who brought long-coveted goods along the Santa Fe Trail and introduced a dominant Anglo cultural strain: commerce. That small breach through the formerly self-enclosed New Spain soon became a flood. The American military presence began with forts and garrisons to protect trade routes from outlaws and raiding Apache, but it was soon engaged in the largely trumped-up war with Mexico that resulted in Arizona and New Mexico being ceded to the United States by a treaty in 1848. Before long the Southern Pacific and Santa Fe railroads had opened the Southwest to the American public.

The Great Move

The enterprising Yankees who built the railroads also built the first grand hotels, and the pleasure-seeking self-indulgent Southwesterner of the future was imported. Within decades paved highways, plane service, and national promotion opened the Southwest to tourism. Respiratory patients discovered the clean dry air, and Northerners found an ideal place to resettle. A national migration was launched by the 1960s, that organized Southwestern retirement into vast planned communities. By the 1970s, resorts had passed through the grand-hotel and dude-ranch phases, to emerge as lavish resort complexes with golf and tennis, restaurants, discos and national convention facilities. Mobile home communities and trailer parks staked out mile after mile, trail bikes and dune buggies roared across the open desert, and motorboats plied the reservoir. Organized leisure became the

Typical Anglo faces; young girl on ranchland in Artesia, New Mexico (left) with her roping horse, while working cowboy on fence (right) looks on.

Southwest's most visible industry.

Traditional agriculture and manufacturing, meanwhile, went into relative decline. Mining, subject to falling demand, foreign competition, shrinking deposits and labor disputes, suffered the most, and many smelters and open pit mines have closed. Ranches, faced with expensive mechanization, have further consolidated into large spreads; cattle are fattened more in feedlots than on the open range, and cowboys work machines or they don't work. Water-intensive surplus crops like cotton no longer make economic

sense, and municipalities are clamoring for water. Ranches, citrus groves, and cotton fields increasingly have been bought out by agribusiness or have given way to the walled-in multiplex developments now radiating from most Southwestern cities.

The industrial slack has been taken up by the leisure boom, and by aerospace and electronics. Arizona now ranks third in the nation for high-tech industries, which employ 38 percent of its manufacturing workforce, and defense-oriented research into microbiology and particle physics are major employers at Los Alamos and Sandia Laboratories in New Mexico. While those who work in the high technologies cannot—yet—be called a leisure class, the so-called silicon desert has resulted in the upwardly mobile career-oriented subculture represented by singles bars and clublike apartment complexes, all epitomized by "lifestyle" magazines that are named for towns but glamorize a rootless mix of dating, updated eating, airborne sports like ballooning and hang gliding, and elaborate new ways to look casual.

Such a fast-moving, fun-centered culture has had a drastic impact on stable minorities. Indians have the deepest ties to place, yet more than half have left their jobless homelands for disorienting cities. Even reservation communities are divided between those favoring development and those trying to shore up traditional ways. Reservation boundaries, originally drawn by Anglos around presumably worthless land, are now invaded by Anglo corporations mining newly-discovered coal, oil, and uranium—often in areas traditional Indians hold to be sacred, and under contracts that reflect tribal ignorance of Anglo law. Strange cultural alliances have developed: Kitt Peak, sacred to the Papago god I'itoy, was available to astronomers only after assurances that telescope-wielding Anglos were practicing their own form of skyworship; Navajo, worried that the new generation is learning only English, are planning to teach Navajo by computer. Less appropriately, ceremonial dances are mobbed by Anglo tourists who treat them as camera fodder, and a band of 300 Prescott businessmen calling themselves the Smokis dress up annually as Hopi, present the sacred snake dance as a tourist pageant, and shrug off protests from Hopi elders. Most humiliated of all is the Papago Reservation in southern Arizona, which has been rendered nearly uninhabitable by hundreds of sonic booms a day from military aircraft that perform war games at nearly ground level, and ignore complaints.

Problems experienced by Hispanics are less severe, as a result of a partly shared culture, differences that are largely linguistic, and bilingual education. Tensions run deepest in New Mexico, where 25 percent of the population have Spanish surnames, and resentment dates from the transfer of the Southwest from Mexican to American control, when many Hispanics were cheated out of their Spanish and Mexican land grants. Hispanics complain of Anglo bigotry, while Anglos allege political corruption in which contracts and appointments are made over the three-martini lunch. Anglo-Hispanic relations are more peaceful in Arizona, where illegal immigration from Mexico is the severest problem — and where a promising example is being set by south Phoenix, in which Anglos, Hispanics, and blacks in nearly equal numbers live in admirable harmony.

The trend toward consumerism and resource exploitation finds its strongest opposition within the Anglo community itself. Mormons, powerful in Arizona as well as Utah, have held out for conservative, family-oriented values, though even they have had to strike compromises that allow them, for instance, to own or manage gambling casinos, but not to deal cards or gamble themselves. Environmentalism, which grows increasingly passionate as the landscape disappears, is a primarily Anglo movement that runs counter to Anglo materialism. Curiously, environmentalists look to traditional Indians, particularly the Hopi elders, as philosophical allies, and often join tribal councils in suing Anglo corporations.

Even as it is fought from without and within, the Anglo assault of resource extraction and organized leisure seems to knock down everything in its path. The landscape has been wasted by strip mines, deforestation, overgrazing, fly ash, transportation grids, sprawl, and above all by the redistribution of water. Water has been impounded behind dams, sluiced through canals, hauled out of aquifers, and tunneled from basin to basin until rivers as fierce as the Colorado have been turned into careless plumbing. Fast travel, franchise marketing, and the mania to sell are leveling cultural differences just as radically.

Southwestern Retirees

The phrase "retired to the Southwest" invariably conjures up images of the swimming pool and deck chairs, the golf and hot sun of a Snow-Belter's afterlife. The reality, while including those items, is fortunately far livelier and far more reflective of the American spectrum.

The terrain itself does not permit uniformity. Much of the Southwest is higher in elevation than outsiders realize and suffers classic northern winters. A few individuals settle in such mountainous small towns as St. George, Utah, and Flagstaff, Arizona, knowing that they will enjoy temperate summers while their contemporaries are holed up with their air-conditioning. A few more will strike some compromise like Santa Fe and Taos, in New Mexico, or Sedona and Prescott, in Arizona, where the summers are slightly too warm and the winters just overchilled. But most incoming retirees have spent their previous Januaries numb to the marrow and go to the opposite extreme, demanding perfect winters and the summer be damned. Given the sunward tilt of the Southwest—high in the north and falling as the Rio Grande and Colorado River Basins drain southward—retirement country thickens in southern New Mexico and reaches peak density in the Sonoran Desert of central and southern Arizona, where the winters might be called celestial.

Most responsible for the popular image of Southwestern retirement is Sun City, west of Phoenix, invented by the Del Webb Corporation in 1960 and the granddaddy of American planned retirement communities. Some 46,000 people now inhabit its walled-in labyrinth of curving streets, single-story

Valley, and the uncomfortably-named Youngtown. Arizona's hyper-planned communities offer a bewildering range of activities, yet on streets where nearly identical houses are tinted complementary pastels, and graveled yards are sprayed minutely divergent shades of green, one can't help feeling that individuality is being held onto only lightly.

Uniformity hardly threatens those with the means to design their own oases. Aging jet-setters have discovered the old adobes of Santa Fe, where they can dabble in the arts, entertain, and unwind from trips to the Continent. Less sophisticated is Carefree, in the Sonoran Desert north of Scottsdale, where architecturally flamboyant homes pose between giant granite boulders. Zoning

dwellings, golf courses, artificial lakes, recreational centers, churches, medical facilities, and subdued commercial areas. All home-owners must be at least 50 years old. Residents gather in travel clubs, bicycle clubs, alumni clubs, even a club for retired union members, and a giant Sundome hosts a symphony of Sun Citians plus visiting celebrities. So calm and safe is the environment that circulation is largely by bicycle and golf cart. With a long waiting list for potential residents, Sun City has spawned such kinsmen as Sun City West, Green

Generous farmer's wife offers handful of fresh squash, fruits of her labor at Lovina farm, New Mexico.

defends the surrounding cacti, greens fees are a major investment, and addresses include East Street, Landuid Lane, and Ho Street—the latter so named as to cross with Hum Street, where candle shops flourish.

Coffee Klatsch, Cocktail Parties, and Everything Nice

Far more numerous are the mobile-home communities found outside El Paso and Albuquerque, along the Colorado River from Boulder City, Nevada, to Yuma, Arizona, and in diminishing perspectives from Tempe through Mesa to Apache Junction, east of Phoenix. Due to the population density, social life is intense, with evenings of bingo and cards, community meals and dances, and the floating coffee klatsch that slides into a cocktail party as the day matures. Forays outside the community are often by recreational vehicle: dune buggies for the hills, motorboats on the reservoir. To give each residence a personal stamp, care is lavished on gardening and decor, but the turnover is far greater than in communities like Sun city or Carefree. Strangers overcome the sense of impermanence by an immediate exchange of life stories and a communal watch over each others' comings and goings.

Most evanescent and fascinating of all retirement groups are those which converge on the Southwest each winter in campers, trailers, even trucks with homemade cabins, to improvise life wherever they pull up. Some retain roots where they spend the summer, but many are too nomadic even for the tax collector. They range throughout southern New Mexico and the Sonoran Desert, but can be found in greatest concentration at Quartzsite, a two-café desert crossroads in Arizona, near the California border. During the winter Quartzsite swells from a few hundred residents to tens of thousands of Snow-Belt refugees. A few hook up to utilities in compounds, but most just stake out a spot in the surrounding hard sand. The town's one thoroughfare is lined with acres of open space waiting for their winter-long flea market. Up go the tables of glassware, antiques, tools, old bottles and campaign buttons collected the previous summer, or jewelry, ceramics, leatherwork, wood carvings, and clothing the retirees have made themselves. The season climaxes with February's Powwow—a "rock festival" that features minerals raw and tumbled, gems rough and set—a visitor-sponsored event that now draws over a million other visitors annually.

If the Southwest's more settled retirement meccas tend to conformity, here individuality is flaunted, with the men often bearded and creaking with leather, the women resplendent in homemade clothing, and both genders flashing with silver, feathers and turquoise. For all their independence, the Quartzsite transients have banded together, raised a $200,000 civic center and a medical center, held dances and dinners open to the public, and, without a single local policeman, maintained order through sheer mutual respect. To become a gypsy seems an odd fulfillment of the American dream, but the nation can take pride in a place like Quartzsite, Arizona.

20th Century Art: A Fidelity to Reality

Almost the first Anglo-European artists to depict the land and people of the American Southwest were the explorer painters, the expeditionary artists. But the earliest images of the Southwest are found in *The Conquest of America*, a pictorial fantasy of the land and inhabitants of New Mexico painted in about 1545 by Jan Mostaert, a Netherlandish painter. Based on reports of the Coronado Expedition to the Zuni Pueblo, this painting includes images of stone mountains, hills, forests, animals and naked aboriginals.

John Mix Stanley, the official recorder of the W.H.Emory Survey Expedition of 1846-1847, was among the earliest painters to actually see the area. Stanley's 1855 painting, *Chain of Spires Along the Hila River* is one of the first heroic landscapes of Arizona.

During the next three decades, many of America's most distinguished artists travelled to the Southwest. In 1872, Thomas Moran, after completing his monumental series of watercolors of the Yellowstone, visited the Grand Canyon and painted a wide range of watercolor sketches which served as preliminary studies for a series of heroic landscapes. *The Chasm of the Colorado*, was purchased by the United States Congress (for $10,000) for display in the center of the lobby. During his lifetime, Moran often returned to paint the geological wonders of the Southwest.

By the last quarter of the 19th Century, only the Apache offered even a limited resistance to the American reservation system, and artists began chronicling what they perceived as the last days of a defeated race, romanticizing a noble, primitive world destined for extinction. This new generation of artists was motivated by different goals and ideals than the expeditionary artists. They were determined to record for posterity a world which they believed they were among the last to witness.

During the early years of the 20th Century, Frederic Remington and Charles M. Russell won world renown as master painters and sculptors of the romantic West. Remington's work extols the beauty of the land, dramatizes the heroic lives of the first white settlers and soldiers, and glorifies the superhero of the West, the American cowboy. The work of Remington and Russell became the primary model for narrative paintings of the West, their choice of subject and style setting the standards for traditional Western art.

In the course of the 20th Century, the

artist colonies of Taos and Santa Fe have become a major feature of the Southwest, attracting both conservative and avant-garde artists. In 1898, Bert Phillips' decision to establish permanent residence in Taos marked the beginning of Taos as an artists' colony. In 1915, Taos painters founded the famous Taos Society of Artists. Although the primary function of the organization was to encourage excellence in the arts and to provide marketing and exhibition opportunities for its members, by the time the society dissolved in 1927, the members had achieved critical and financial success and Taos had become an established art center.

The artists' colony in Santa Fe developed later than in Taos and followed a different direction. Santa Fe was a more cosmopolitan

and encouraged many of his friends, disciples, and students to travel to the Southwest.

Old Arts Die Hard

Although the new realist and abstract art is slowly gaining acceptance in the Southwest, representational narrative paintings are favored by the majority of dealers and collectors—paintings which illustrate incidents in history, traditional ranch life, the heroic feats of the rodeo, and vingettes of an Indian world which has remained untouched by time. The Southwest has become the center of a traditional art that confirms basic American values and celebrates heroes and idols of the West—past and present.

A host of organizations hold annual ex-

area and the keystone of the colony was the Museum of New Mexico, which opened in 1917, and offered visitors and newcomers community studio facilities, exhibition space, and financial assistance. The arrival of Robert Henri in the summer of 1914 marked the beginning of a new direction for art in the community. His insistence that art must be a record of life, focusing on the daily life of average people, set the focus of the realist vision in America. Henri spent three summers in Santa Fe, painted an outstanding series of portraits of the Indian people,

Old Anglo water tender of Avalon Dam, near Carlsbad, flashes toothless grin.

hibitions and sales that feature seminars, juries and prizes. At a series of special auctions, collectors and gallery-owners compete for the opportunity to pay record prices. Olaf Wieghurst, Tom Lovell, John Clymer and Clark Hulings are a few of the stars of these events.

Sculpture of the Southwest has the same basic history as painting. Traditional sculpture is characterized by a similar fusion of idealism and realism, a romantic subject depicted with precision of detail, particularly in the costumes, weapons, and artifacts. Today, the working cowboy and the rodeo cowboy are among the favorite subjects of most contemporary sculptors, along with Indian portraits, and ceremonial figures. -

PLACES

After spending time in the American Southwest, most other places will seem cramped. This is a land of endless horizons and big skies. At the same time, usually hidden in the landscape and discovered off the beaten track, are lush green canyons and valleys that rest the eye and provide shelter from the sun. These unexpected pleasures are as much a part of the Southwest as the great masses of red rock and open stretches of desert, but ones which a traveller rushing from national monument to natural spectacle can easily miss.

The geographical parameters of the Southwest have been defined in dozens of ways, and sometimes include areas as far east as Oklahoma, as far west as Southern California, and as far north as Salt Lake City, Utah and Reno, Nevada. This book defines the Southwest according to the following map on the basis of cultural and geographical similarities, and because the area can be reasonably explored by car without long detours.

This tour of the Southwest begins at the Grand Canyon—one of the most frequently visited natural spots in the world. From there it's on to Southern Utah, as spectacular in many ways as the Grand Canyon, but less accessible, less crowded and on a more human scale. Heading south from Utah is Indian Land, which spills over from Arizona into New Mexico, but as the home of the Navajo and Hopi Indians it is an entity unto itself. Next comes Pueblo Country, which includes Albuquerque, Santa Fe and Taos, New Mexico. This area represents a mixture of Indian Pueblo and Hispanic villages existing side by side with the cities. It is culturally and geographically so rich and diverse that one could literally spend years exploring it. Here is the place to satisfy a fascination for old Spanish churches and adobe architecture; to look for Indian and Hispanic arts and crafts in the plazas, pueblos and villages; and the place with the best red chiles to be had anywhere. Eastern and southern New Mexico are more spread out, but the deserts, mountains and plains offer equal rewards of a different quality for those who stop and explore.

Southern Arizona is border country—the line between the United States and Mexico creating what is almost a separate country, offering the most interesting desert flora and fauna, as well as the laid back ambience of Tucson.

Phoenix seems to dominate central Arizona on the map, but the mountains surrounding it to the south, east and north are an outdoorsman's paradise, and the home of the largest Apache Indian tribes.

Las Vegas is an anomaly in the Southwest—a big, garish non-stop neon city dedicated to entertainment of every imaginable variety. Try it out and you'll probably end up going back for more.

The writers of this section have lived in the Southwest and written about it for most or all of their adult lives. Rather than trying to do the impossible and cover everything, they concentrated on their favorite spots.

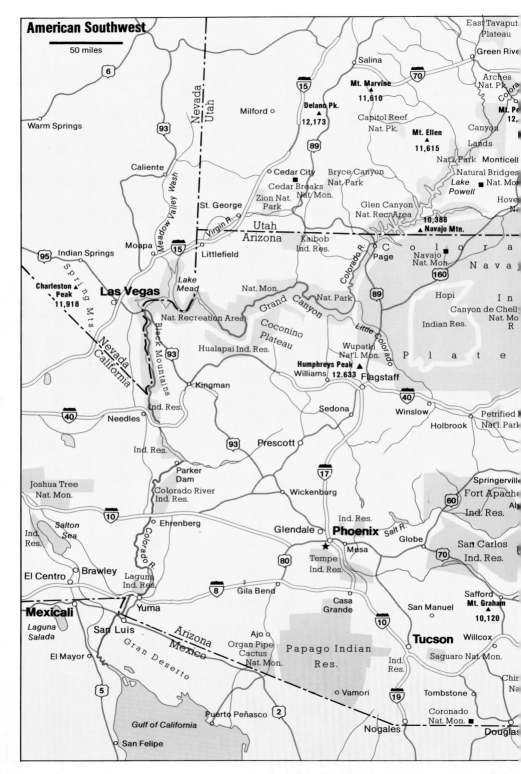

American Southwest

50 miles

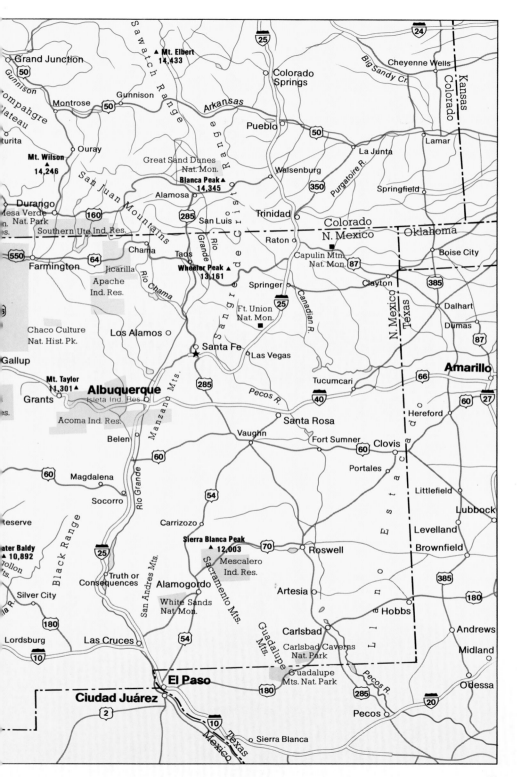

Grand Junction

50

Gunnison

Montrose

50

Gunnison

▲ Mt. Elbert
14,433

Sawatch Range

Arkansas

25

Colorado
Springs

Big Sandy Cr.

Cheyenne Wells

Kansas
Colorado

Umcompahgre
Plateau

Gunnison

urita

Pueblo

Sange

50

La Junta

Lamar

Ouray

Mt. Wilson
▲ 14,246

Great Sand Dunes
Nat. Mon.

Blanca Peak ▲
14,345

Walsenburg

350

Purgatoire R.

Springfield

Durango

Mesa Verde
n. Nat. Park
es.

San Juan Mountains

Alamosa

285

San Luis

Trinidad

Raton

Colorado
N. Mexico

Oklahoma

Boise City

Southern Ute Ind. Res.

550

Farmington

64

Chama

Jicarilla
Apache
Ind. Res.

Taos

Wheeler Peak ▲
13,161

Rio Grande

Capulin Mtn
Nat. Mon.

87

385

Clayton

Dalhart

Springer

Canadian R.

Rio Chama

Sangre de Cristo

Ft. Union
Nat. Mon.

25

N. Mexico
Texas

Dumas

87

Chaco Culture
Nat. Hist. Pk.

Los Alamos

Santa Fe

★

Las Vegas

Amarillo

Gallup

Mt. Taylor
11,301 ▲

Albuquerque

Manzano Mts.

285

Pecos R.

Tucumcari

66

60

27

Grants

Isleta Ind. Res.

es.

Acoma Ind. Res.

Belen

Santa Rosa

Vaughn

Fort Sumner

Clovis

40

Hereford

60

60

Magdalena

Rio Grande

Socorro

60

Portales

Littlefield

Lubbock

Reserve

Black Range

ater Baldy
▲ 10,892

ollon
ts.

Silver City

25

Truth or
Consequences

San Andres Mts.

Carrizozo

Sierra Blanca Peak
▲ 12,003

Sacramento Mts.

Mescalero
Ind. Res.

54

70

Roswell

Levelland

Brownfield

Llano

Estacado

385

180

a R.

180

Lordsburg

10

Las Cruces

Alamogordo

White Sands
Nat. Mon.

54

Artesia

Hobbs

Andrews

Midland

Guadalupe Mts.

Carlsbad

Carlsbad Caverns
Nat. Park

Pecos R.

Odessa

El Paso

Ciudad Juárez

2

Guadalupe
Mts. Nat. Park

180

10

Mexico

Texas

Sierra Blanca

285

20

Pecos

THE GREAT
OUTDOORS

The vast and varied world of outdoor recreation awaiting visitors to the Southwest cannot be easily described. You'll find a unique blend of enticing, year-round activities, many of which are unavailable in other regions of the continental United States. Where else, for example, can you ski two miles high in the morning, then play afternoon tennis or golf in 75°F (24°C) sunshine? Where else can you, wearing only shorts and a T-shirt, cast streamer flies for huge rainbow trout in January? Where else can you drive a herd of longhorn cattle across an open prairie, accompanied by a chuckwagon (circa 1870) complete with banging pots and a cowgirl cook? Where else can you ride a bucking raft through the white water of an isolated desert canyon and then later that evening dine on *steak tartare* in the comfort of an urban restaurant?

These questions have a simple answer: only in the Southwest! Bicycling to bass-fishing, hiking to hot-air ballooning, trail-riding to turkey-hunting, whatever your particular craving in outdoor fun, you'll find this heterogeneous land to be an eager and willing host. "When your spirit cries for peace," wrote August Frugé, "come to a world of canyons deep in an old land; feel the exultation of high plateaus, the strength of moving waters, the simplicity of sand and grass, the silence of growth." Take a single sojourn into the great outdoors of the American Southwest, and you'll know exactly what Frugé meant.

To help you along, a selected potpourri of outdoor adventures appears in the following pages. There are many more, hundreds more; the stewpot of outdoor recreation is filled to the brim with goodies—far too many to consume in a single bite.

Ride The Big Water

We have an unknown distance yet to run; an unknown river yet to explore. What falls there are, we know not; what rocks beset the channel, we know not; what walls rise over the river, we know not.

Amateur naturalist John Wesley Powell scribbled that diary notation on August 13, 1869, and a few hours later set forth with nine companions in three flimsy wooden boats to explore the Grand Canyon on the Colorado River in Arizona. Sixteen days later, half starved and totally exhausted, Powell and his party emerged from the chasm's lower end, the first men in history to negotiate the full 277 river miles (366 km) of the Grand Canyon successfully.

The termination of Powell's historic voyage marked the beginning of an era. Within a century, white-water boating— as sport, not transportation—would be one of America's favorite pastimes. And not surprisingly, thousands of participants have discovered in recent years that nowhere is the scenery more breathtaking or the rapids more exciting than where it all began—the remote canyons and untameable waterways of the desert Southwest. Whether you're alone with your thoughts in a one-man kayak, or accompanied by a dozen companions in a high-riding "baloney" boat, floating the white water of a Southwestern river is an unforgettable experience.

The prevailing monarch of all desert streams is the Colorado River, a 1,600-mile (2,576-km) ribbon of watery turmoil that heads in the Rocky Mountains and terminates in the silty waters of the Gulf of California in Mexico. You can float this magnificent river along most of its length, but a raft or dory trip through Arizona's Grand Canyon is by far the most visually overwhelming. All float trip adventures on the Grand begin at Lee's Ferry, a tiny desert community located a few miles below Glen Canyon Dam on Lake Powell. Depending on whether your boats are oar- or motor-powered, you'll need eight to 15 days to run all 277 miles (446 km) of the canyon, but you can arrange to float to the half-way point at Phantom Ranch and then catch a helicopter to the rim. Reservations far in advance of your trip are necessary since a Grand Canyon voyage is the most popular river-running adventure in America.

The upper Colorado River in southern Utah offers a couple of fine whitewater escapades as well. Float trips through 26-mile (42-km) Westwater Canyon and 47-mile (76-km) Cataract Canyon begin in the town of Moab, Utah, just east of Canyonlands National Park on U.S. Highway 163. Here, nu-

ceding
jes,
nper
ds down
n National
k; neon
rquees at
Vegas
npete for
ntion; and
se trailing
Iryce
nyon. Left,
k packer
templates
rified
est
ional
num ent.

merous expedition companies offer full-length excursions through both canyons as well as single-day junkets on less demanding sections of the Colorado. Most river companies furnish everything you'll need for your trip, except sleeping bags and personal clothing.

The Colorado River and its exquisitely carved canyons may have the market cornered on float trips, but plenty of other Southwest waterways exist to carry you into the wilderness. For instance, you might want to float the mighty Green River through Desolation Canyon or The Canyon Of Lodore, both extraordinarily beautiful chasms carved from the Utah red rock north of Moab. You can also explore the inscrutable backcountry of Dinosaur National Monument on the Colorado-Utah border, via the Yampa River, a wide, turbulent stream that tumbles, like its cousin the Colorado, from the Rocky Mountains.

If you're looking for something short but sassy, take a kayak or paddle-boat tour of the Rio Grande River Gorge west of Taos, New Mexico. Fifty miles (81 km) long, 800 feet (244 meters) deep and generally less than a mile in width,

this slab-sided gouge in the earth's crust is known locally as "The Box." Only the lower 25 miles are navigable, but nowhere will you find a more exciting one-day trip. Rapids like Powerline Falls and Ski-Jump give plenty of whitewater thrills, but long quiet eddies and meandering currents allow time to enjoy the spectacle of vertical, lava-rock walls that seem to grow literally from the water's edge. The most favorable season in which to float the Rio Grande and other Southwestern rivers is from early May to late June when streams are gorged with spring runoff.

The Wild West Revisited

Less than a century ago, horseback travel was the only available transportation on the Western frontier. A man's horse was precious; horse thieves were summarily hanged while murderers, bank robbers, cattle rustlers and other "owlhoots" often went unpunished for their crimes. "Pity the scoundrel who pilfers a horse," said one frontier judge as he passed sentence, "his boots will kick air before sundown."

Motorbikers at Winter Park, Colorado.

The era of inflexible, Wild West justice is gone, but horseback travel is not. Recently this ancient mode of transportation has undergone a rebirth of sorts as more and more "dudes" seek adventurous vacations away from the madding crowd. In the Southwest, backcountry pack trips have become so popular that rare is a slice of wilderness that cannot boast a dozen outfitters ready and willing to guide you into the boonies.

If you don't mind thornbush, cactus and wide-open vistas, try a horseback camping trip into Arizona's 125,000-acre (51,250-hectare) Superstition Mountain Wilderness, 30 miles (48 km) northeast of Phoenix. Of all America's mountain ranges, the Superstitions are the most legendary—steeped in mystery, surrounded by tales of misplaced treasure and miscreant men. The most famous tale is that of the Lost Dutchman Mine, an enormously rich vein of gold worked for years by prospector Jacob Waltz (known to his friends as The Dutchman), its location lost from knowledge in 1892 when Waltz died.

Today, astride surefooted horses, you can visit Dutchman's Valley, supposed-

ly the site of the old mine, and view breathtaking sights like the ancient Sinagua Indian dwellings at Roger's Canyon Cliff Ruin and Weaver's Needle, a shark's tooth desert peak that for two centuries has been a landmark for westbound travellers. Evenings you'll camp beneath towering saguaro cactus, eat such desert delicacies as fried rattlesnake (not mandatory) and watch glorious sunsets. Most pack trips vary in length from two to seven days. Outfitters usually furnish everything but riding clothes and toothbrushes.

Another memorable desert trail ride is a 25-mile (40-km) trip from Navajo Mountain Trading Post, Arizona, to Rainbow Bridge National Monument on the north shore of Utah's Lake Powell, along the old Rainbow Trail. Used probably from the time of Christ by nomadic Indians, this ancient pathway winds its way through a land of giant sandstone monoliths and deep, sandstone canyons, both carved by eons of unhindered erosion. You'll generally spend one full day exploring the Indian ruins of Surprise Valley, a remote box canyon made famous by novelist Zane Grey in *Riders Of The Purple Sage*. At

most ready
r dinner;
ttle drive,
ew Mexico.

trip's end, you can leave your horse with the guides and for the next few days leisurely investigate the magical slickrock canyons of Lake Powell aboard a fully-equipped houseboat.

If you prefer pine-covered ridges and murmuring brooks to cactus gardens, you'll find plenty of both on a pack trip into one of New Mexico's sprawling wilderness areas. Near Taos, for instance, lies Wheeler Peak Wilderness, 21,000 acres (8,610 hectares) of alpine landscape girdled by half a dozen of the state's loftiest peaks. Here, you might see bighorn sheep, black bear and even mountain lions, but more impressive are the unbelievable panoramas viewable from the higher ridges; some of them encompass 11,000 square miles (28,490 sq km) of terrain. Two hours' drive south near Santa Fe is the 220,000-acre (90,200-hectare) Pecos Wilderness, once a favorite beaver-trapping area for 17th-Century mountain men. Take your fishing rod if you make a trail ride here; most lakes and streams in the high country abound with hungry brook and cutthroat trout. In the southern part of the state near Silver City are the Gila and Aldo Leopold Wilderness areas, two adjacent hinterlands that together offer 800,000 acres (328,000 hectares) of virtually unexplored high-desert terrain to trail-riders. You could easily spend weeks riding there and never negotiate the same trail twice.

If you want to try America's most unique horseback adventure, sign up for an old-time cattle drive. Simulating as closely as possible the strenuous Texas trail drives of the 1870s, these modern-day junkets offer guests an opportunity to relive a bit of Western history. You'll work alongside real cowhands, branding, herding cattle and shoeing horses. Sleeping on the ground and eating traditional cowboy grub, like mountain oysters (fried calf testicles), beans and beef, sourdough biscuits and spotted-pup pudding, are part of the experience. Several of these drives are available in the Southwest, most of them offered by working cattle ranches and lasting from three to seven days. Previous riding experience isn't necessary, and most organizations furnish everything you'll need except your personal gear.

Early winter and spring are the best times to explore the desert trails of the Southwest. By mid-October the merci-less heat of summer has abated, desert springs are usually brimming, and wildlife is more active. The most favorable season for mountain trips is late June through September. You'll experience warm, pleasant days, crisp nights, few biting insects and the widest and most colorful selection of wildflowers in the Rocky Mountains.

In Pursuit of the Furred, the Feathered and the Finned

Have you ever dreamed of going on safari in Africa? Try New Mexico instead, where sportsmen stalk exotic species of African and Asian game animals through terrain closely resembling the veldt of Kenya. Two decades ago, selected breeding pairs of kudu, oryx (both African antelope) and Barbary sheep, were imported and released in protected New Mexico reserves. The programs were so successful that limited hunting seasons are held annually on White Sands Missile Range near Alamogordo and in the Canadian River Canyon near Wagon Mound.

If you've no desire to parrot Frank Buck or Jungle Jim, but still enjoy the

Skiing, near Durango, southern Colorado.

shooting sports, conventional big-game hunting opportunities in the Southwest are numerous. Mule deer, elk, black bear and wild turkey seasons begin in November and last through Christmas. Permits for mountain lion and javelina—a pig-like member of the hippopotamus family native to South America—are also available in limited quantity. For waterfowl hunters, the golden days of autumn bring with them enormous flights of ducks and geese into the Rio Grande and Colorado basins. Skies turn black as flocks of mallards, pintails, Canada and snow geese are coaxed from the central flyway to rest and feed in quiet river sloughs. In these same areas, you'll find healthy populations of upland game birds like quail, dove, and chukar grouse.

Trout fishing in the Southwest boasts many aficionados because of year-round seasons and countless miles of uncrowded shorelines. You'll find rainbow and German brown trout inhabiting most mountain streams, while high lakes usually contain cutthroat and brook trout. Two noteworthy areas that for decades have drawn anglers from all over the world are New Mexico's San Juan River east of Farmington, New Mexico, and the Colorado River below Glen Canyon Dam in Arizona. Both of these streams contain rainbow trout that reach weights of 15 pounds (seven kg). In Arizona, you'll be fishing in shorts and a T-shirt, even in January.

Warm-water angling on man-made reservoirs like Arizona's Lake Mead, Lake Roosevelt and Lake Powell and New Mexico's Navajo Lake and Elephant Butte Lake draws its share of rod-and-reel addicts as well. Largemouth-bass fishing is superb in these lakes, but you'll find crappie, smallmouth bass, channel, blue and yellow catfish, too. And the striped bass, a rangy battler native to the Atlantic Ocean, has found a new home here. Quite often, Southwest stripers attain weights of 70 pounds (32 kg).

"I sho-nuff figgered it was all desert outcheer," a winter visitor from Georgia once drawled, "but there shore is lots of that white stuff!"

Surprise! Snow is no stranger to the Southwest. More than 50 percent of the region, in fact, lies above 7,000 feet (2,134 meters) in elevation, and winter

Duck hunters Caballo ake, New exico.

sports of all kinds are in good supply from mid-November through Easter.

Alpine skiers find New Mexico best equipped to satiate their downhill desires. The state contains 12 major ski areas, most of them within easy reach of Albuquerque. The most famous names in Southwest skiing are Taos Ski Valley, located northeast of the town of Taos, and Santa Fe Ski Basin, "up mountain" from the capital city. Reasonable prices, short lift lines and magnificent winter scenery make both of these resorts a must if you like a Swiss-Alps environment. On the outskirts of Albuquerque, atop 10,447-foot (3,166-meter) Sandia Crest lies Sandia Peak Winter Recreation Area. You can, if you wish, drive to this ski area, but most visitors load their equipment aboard the Sandia Peak Tramway and take an 18-minute skyride to the top. The slopes are within a snowball's throw of the tram's upper terminal. Because Albuquerque's winter climate is so moderate, many visitors ski in the morning, then enjoy a sunny afternoon of tennis or golf in the city.

Arizona has only two major downhill ski areas, the Snow Bowl, north of Flagstaff, and Mt. Lemmon, 40 miles (64 km) northeast of Tucson in the Catalina Mountains. Cross-country skiing is superb, however, in the state's numerous national forests. Two unique cross-country areas are along the rims of the Grand Canyon and atop the famed Mogollon Rim near the town of Payson. The vistas are extraordinary, and the snow conditions excellent.

Southern Colorado's best-known ski resort is Purgatory, north of Durango. Hellish in name only, this large, well-groomed basin offers fine views of the southern Rocky Mountains and an average snowpack of 100 inches (254 cm) at the base. Reasonably priced accommodations are available in nearby Durango. Another noteworthy resort is Wolf Creek Ski Basin, located northeast of Pagosa Springs atop 10,850-foot (3,307 meter) Wolf Creek Pass. This ski area boasts the longest season of all Southwest resorts; if you don't mind toting your gear uphill, you can ski here into July.

The Southwest offers several unusual outdoor activities that are available in few other regions in the United States. If, for instance, you find yourself in Albuquerque, New Mexico, during the first weeks of October, you'll notice lots of hot air in the atmosphere, and it won't be coming from a boastful companion. The International Hot Air Balloon Festival comes to town in October, and for nine days the Albuquerque skies are filled with these lighter-than-air craft, drifting where they will on the desert breezes. On the first and last weekends of the festival, pilots take part in a mass ascension. The sight of more than 400 balloons lifting as one in the crisp morning light is unforgettable. This is mostly a spectator sport, but if you would like to ride one of these colorful behemoths many pilots—for a fee—will carry hitchhikers.

Not as death-defying as ballooning, llama trekking is a relatively new outdoor activity in the Southwest. If you're a backpacker but hate to carry all that weight up the mountain, then this sport is for you. Long-eared, bulbous-nosed cud-chewers with the front end of a camel and the caboose of an ostrich, llamas will patiently haul your camping equipment into the wilderness. You lead, they follow—it's as simple as that.

Llama treks are available in both the Pecos and Gila Wilderness areas of New Mexico and in the San Juan National Forest of southern Colorado. More and more outfitters are using them instead of horses or mules on pack trips because llamas eat very little, drink almost no water and have an almost negligible effect on forest trails and meadows. If you're on a tight budget, you'll find llama trekking at $30 to $50 a day, cheaper than standard horse and mule pack trips.

Ever had a hankering to captain your own yacht? The opportunity awaits on Utah's Lake Powell and Arizona's Lake Mead. Here, you can rent a fully equipped houseboat for two or 20 people, then spend up to two weeks exploring the thousands of remote backwaters that few speedboaters or fishermen ever reach. Most rental boats are large—30 to 70 feet (nine to 21 meters) in length, but you'll need no previous boating experience. All hands are given a crash course in navigation, marine mechanics and the rules of the road before leaving the marina dock. Each craft is equipped with a complete set of navigational charts, plus linens and kitchen utensils. All you need is food, clothing and an appetite for adventure. Houseboating excursions are excellent multiple family vacations.

80

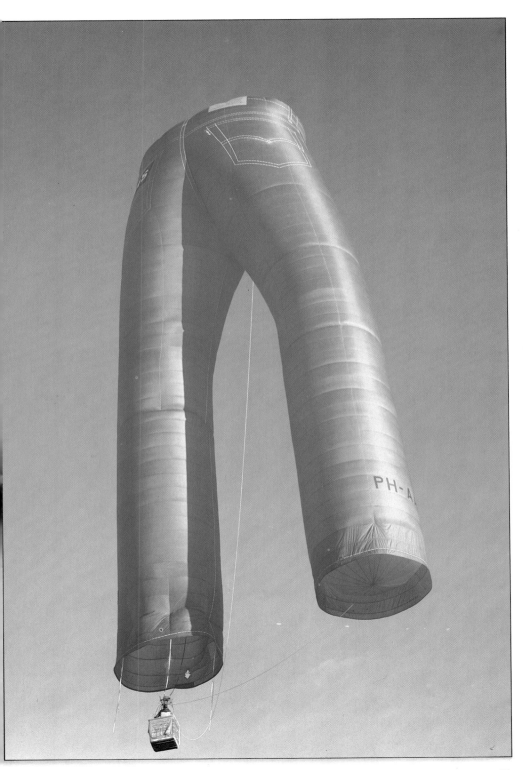

info

SKIING
ARIZONA

Excellent cross-country skiing areas include Fairfield Snow Bowl, Mt. Lemmon Ski Area, Sunrise Mountain, Bill Williams Mountain Ski Area and Mormon Lake Ski Touring Center.

For further information on winter recreation, contact the Arizona national forest areas offering winter sports, **Apache-Sitgreaves, Coconino, Caronado** and **Kaibab**.

NEW MEXICO

For more information about these ski areas, contact the areas themselves or local chambers of commerce for information on accommodations and restaurants. For booklet, *Winter Enchantment in New Mexico*, free and full of information, contact the Tourism and Travel Division, New Mexico Commerce & Industry Department, Bataan Memorial Building, Santa Fe, NM 87503; 800/1545-2040.

Generally, most beginner/some intermediate runs are open by Thanksgiving; upper intermediate and advanced by mid-December. Elevations are approximate. For current rates, please call ski areas.

For information on snow conditions, events and races, contact **Mountains and Rivers**, 2320 Central SE, Albuquerque 87110, 268-4876; or **Base Camp**, 121 West San Francisco, Santa Fe 87501, 982-9707.

There are ski rental shops in Albuquerque, Angel Fire, Chama, Los Alamos, Red River, Ruidoso, Santa Fe and Taos. Early January through early March, races are held at Angel Fire and Sandia Peak. Chama Chili Chase X-C Ski Race, on Sunday, Presidents Weekend, February. For more information, contact the Norski Racing Club, 8512 Osuna NE, Albuquerque 87111; 299-2873.

UTAH

For astonishingly complete information on transportation, lodging, as well as data on individual area, send for booklet,

Ski Utah, at 307 West 2nd South, Suite 5005, Salt Lake City 84101; 801/534-1779.

For **daily snow conditions**, call 801/521-8102 or 800/824-UTAH. Information on handicapped skiing, write Utah Handicapped Skiers Association Inc., P.O. Box 108, Roy 84067.
Utah's foremost (and formidable) ski areas are located in the north, with a dense cluster in the general vicinity of Salt Lake City. Two less well-known, and for that reason, also less crowded, areas are located in the southern section; Brian Head Ski Lifts and Mt. Holly (see page 113).

COLORADO

The lion's share of Colorado's better-known ski areas are located north of Mesa Verde and the Great Sand Dunes. However, worthy of note is **Purgatory Ski Area and Alpine Slide**, 25 miles north of Durango off U.S. 550 in the San Juan National Forest, a popular resort with seven chairlifts and a tow, open daily 9-4. Day care available. Family-oriented area, experiencing a current buildup including nearby accommodations, condos, etc. Phone 303/247-9000 or contact the Durango Chamber of Commerce for information.

If you are an avid skier and it's winter, you may wish to go a bit out of your way and check out **Telluride**, a funky old Western mining town/cum growing ski area with a variety of ski terrain

ranging from easy to difficult (with the aptly-named "Plunge" a favorite challenge), definitely worth a visit for serious skiers of all abilities. 303/728-3856.

LAS VEGAS

Lee Canyon Ski Area. 45 miles northeast of Las Vegas at Mount Charleston, 80% intermediate, two lifts and a 1,000-foot vertical range. Call 702/872-5462 for information.

Cross-country skiers will find a good beginner's area a mile down Nevada State 156 at Lee Canyon Meadows, while experienced ski tourers can explore Old Mill Picnic Area and Macks Canyon Road. For more information on these, call the U.S. Forest Service, 702/385-6255.

RIVER RUNNING

To perhaps overstate the obvious, it is not advisable to try to run rapids yourself, unless you are trained in the art. Professional river runners are plentiful wherever the rapids warrant river trips. However, there are also easy cruises for experienced kayakers, sportyaks and private boats. Permits for private users can be obtained from the nearest park rangers.

HORSEBACK

For information on specific areas contact National Forest offices, ranger stations, national and state parks, and Chambers of Commerce.

Superstition Mountains, Arizona: Gold Canyon Stable, Box 867, Apache Junction, AZ 85220; 602/982-7822.
Perralta Riding Stable, 1527 S. Meridian, Apache Junction 85226; 892-5488.
Superstition Mountain Stables, 5349 East Charter Oak Rd., Scottsdale, AZ 85254; 982-6353.
Dave Wiggins, American Wilderness Experience, Box 1486, Boulder, CO 80306; 303/444-2632.

Tucson: El Conquistador Stables, at the Sheraton Tucson, El Conquistador Resort. 10,000 North Oracle, Tucson 85704; 742-1164.

Westward Look Resort Stables, 245 E. Ina Road, Tucson 85704; 742-1889; 6283.

New Mexico: Bitter Creek Guest Ranch, Red River.
Chippeway Stables, Cloudcroft.
Doc and Petey's Santa Fe; Double Arrow, Santa Fe.
Flemming Stables, Ruidoso.
Horse Country Club Stables, Sandia Peak Stables, Spear Cross Country Ranch; Albuquerque.
Taos Equestrian Center, Taos Indian Horse Ranch.

PACK TRIPS, CATTLE DRIVES, LLAMA TREKKING

Ranger stations are good sources for information on **pack trips**. For example, in Arizona contact: Mesa Ranger District, 26 N. MacDonald St., Mesa, AZ 85201; 602/261-6466, and Tonto Basin Ranger District, Box 647, Roosevelt, AZ 85545; phone 602/467-2236.
For general information about pack trips in New Mexico, contact the **New Mexico Council of Outfitters and Guides**, P.O. Box 952, Albuquerque 87103; 505/344-4143. Many council members offer day and overnight trips throughout the state.

Colorado Back Country Pack Trips, Box 110-E, La Jara, Colorado 81140; 303/274-5655.
Price Canyon Ranch, P.O. Box 1065, Douglas, AZ 85607; 602/558-2283.
Wilderness Pack Trips-Pecos Wilderness, Rte. 3, Box 8, Tererro, NM 87573; 505/757-6213.

Cattle Drives: Bob and Bea Frisch, Canyon Ranch, 9820 Transfer Rd, Olathe, Colorado 81425; 303/323-5288.
Rudy and Virgina Rudibaugh, 711 Ranch, Parlin, A, Colorado 81231; 303/641-0666.
Running M Ranch, Box 498, Ojo Caliente, NM 87549; 505/583-2452.

Llama Trekking: Arch Arnold, Paiute Creek Outfitters, Rte. 1A, Camas, UT 84036; 801/783-4317.
Columbine Llamas, 589 High Llama Line, Durango, Colorado 81301; 303/259-2251.
Bobra Goldsmith, Rocky Mountain Llama Treks, 5893 Baseline Rd., Boulder, Colorado 80303.
Travel Works, 109-1 E. Palace Ave., Santa Fe 87501; 505/983-6356. Attention: Sunny Bynum.

HUNTING AND FISHING

Licenses are necessary, except, in some cases, for children under 12. Fishing licenses are generally available at local marinas, bait shops, sporting goods stores, and trading posts. There are minimum ages for hunting big game, e.g., in Utah. Because regulations are variable and subject to change, we encourage you to contact the proper state authorities for the most comprehensive information:

New Mexico Department of Game and Fish, State Capitol, Villagra Building, Santa Fe 87503; 505/827-7882. Free brochure.
Arizona Game and Fish Department, 2222 W. Greenway Rd., Phoenix 85023, 602/942-3000.
Colorado Wildlife Division, 6060 Broadway, Denver 80216; 303/297-1192. Fishing: 292-3474; Hunting: 292-4868.
Utah Division of Wildlife Resources, 1596 West North Temple, Salt Lake City, UT 84116; hunting 533-9333; fishing 533-5681; call 532-2473 or 530-1298 for recorded hunting and fishing news. This department also has information on bird refuges.
Nevada Department of Wildlife, Southern Nevada Office, 4747 West Vegas Dr., Las Vegas 89108; 702/385-0285.

Chambers of Commerce centered in major fishing and hunting areas will also provide extensive information, as will pertinent parks. Those fishing and hunting on Indian lands usually need to obtain licenses there; fees and seasons will vary. For example, state fish and game licenses are not required on the Navajo Nation, but sportsmen must have a permit from the Navajo Fish & Wildlife Dept.

BALLOON TRIPS

Early morning flights above Albuquerque and Santa Fe are available by the hour or by the package. Costs vary; a one-hour flight currently costs in the neighborhood of $100 per person. For more information, free brochures, etc., in Albuquerque, contact Adventures Aloft, 5300 Pan Am Highway, Albuquerque 87125, 892-5550; J.P. Ballooning, 3217 Valencia NE, Albuquerque 87110, 881-2637; or World Balloon Corp., 4800 Eubank NE, Albuquerque 87111, 293-6800. Wind River Balloons, P.O. Box 983, Santa Fe 87501, 983-8714 is currently touted as the only company between Albuquerque and Colorado to offer a full line of balloon services and will arrange for special champagne flights and lessons. In Arizona, the Pegasus Hot-Air Balloon Company offers champagne flights above Phoenix: 4606 S. Fair Lane, Tempe 85282, 968-4705; also Arizona Balloon Company, 1808 N. 7th Ave., Phoenix 85007, 254-5017; and Golden Eagle Balloon, P.O. Box 9533, Phoenix 85068, 944-1022. Advance booking for personal flights, especially for large groups, is recommended.

GOLF AND TENNIS

Central Arizona is a mecca for golf and tennis fanatics of all ages and persuasions. The Phoenix area and, to a somewhat lesser extent, Tucson, provide not only public and private facilities, but lists of hotels and guest ranches with golf and/or tennis offered in the package. For a direct line to such information, contact:
Metropolitan Tucson Convention and Visitors Bureau, P.O. Box 3028, Tucson, AZ 85702; 602/624-1817.
Phoenix & Valley of the Sun Convention & Visitors Bureau, 4455 East Camelback Road, Suite D-146, Phoenix, AZ 85018; 602/952-8687; toll-free reservations, 800/528-6149.

Las Vegas: Several hotels have championship golf courses, some open to the public. Tennis can be found at hotels, private clubs and the city's parks. Contact Las Vegas Recreation and Leisure Activities Department (702/386-6296) or Clark County Parks and Recreation (702/386-4384). During the summer, nearly all of the public courts are lighted in the evening.

THE GRAND CANYON: A GREAT ABYSS

Although the Grand Canyon lies a 90-minute drive over the horizon, to the locals in Flagstaff it is an elemental part of the landscape. They call it, with a blend of awe, affection and understatement, "the big ditch."

A few miles north of Flagstaff on U.S. Highway 180 is the **Museum of Northern Arizona**, which sponsors much of the scientific research taking place in the Grand Canyon. One popular misconception is that the Canyon is, geologically speaking, an open book. The geologists know better. For more than a century they have carried on their investigations and yet many of the most basic questions about the great abyss still lack definitive answers. For instance, there is a lively debate among geologists over how (and how long ago) Colorado River came to be established in its current course. It's worth stopping at the museum to view its geological exhibits and admire a splendid collection of Indian rugs and pottery.

Then, full of anticipation, continue north through the ponderosa pine forests and broad meadows that dress the flanks of the San Francisco Peaks, the highest mountains in Arizona, sacred to both the Navajo and Hopi Indian tribes. From the approach to the **South Rim** the Canyon is hidden from view by a gentle incline. Not until you've entered **Grand Canyon National Park** and driven another 2½ miles (four km) is there a glimpse of the abyss from **Mather Point**. Mather Point is generally crowded; to savor your first impressions in a more tranquil setting drive another mile to **Yavapai Point**.

Park your car. Leave **Yavapai Museum** and its explanations of the Canyon's geology for later. For now walk along the **Rim Trail** to a quiet spot from which to gaze at what 19-Century geologist Clarence Dutton called, "the most sublime of the earthly spectacles."

Grand Canyon Gestalt

Having heard so much about the Grand Canyon most visitors are prepared to find it breathtaking. Another typical response, however, is unanticipated. The inhuman scale of the chasm can be profoundly disconcerting: what should one make of this gulf of space, which reeks of an unfathomable span of time? To put it more graphically,. how does a human being, cradling a small black rock from the Inner Gorge, come to grips with the fact that it is two billion years old? So old that it dates from a time when life, in any of its miraculous forms, had not yet appeared on the planet Earth.

Of course the Canyon's ability to humble us and its ability to amaze us are inextricably intertwined. When we stand on the rim we face a quandary: only by accepting that the Canyon belittles us can we fully appreciate its grandeur. As Yevtushenko, the Russian poet, writes,

Into the Canyon
with all who are sick with megalomania!
As a guest in the abyss
the dwarf will quickly understand
that he is a dwarf.

There is nothing new about this quandary. The various Indians who have lived in the canyon for at least 2,000 years must have struggled with it. As did

Lieutenant Joseph Ives in 1857. After reluctantly acknowledging that the landscape promotes a "wondering delight," Ives evades the visitor's predicament by protesting, "The region is, of course, altogether valueless. It can be approached only from the south, and after entering it there is nothing to do but leave. Ours has been the first, and will doubtless be the last, party of whites to visit this profitless locality."

He was wrong. Two million people—a third of them from overseas—come each year. The Grand Canyon is the most universally celebrated of America's natural features. It is, says a Colorado River boatman, "the first church of the Earth."

The South Rim

After a moment's communion at Yavapai Point, walk through the piñon and juniper trees a few hundred yards or meters west to an intersecting trail that leads south to the visitors center. Take some time to tour the exhibits, see the slide show, browse through the fine selection of books and admire the ancient boats in the courtyard, resting

on their laurels after the perilous journey down the rapids of the Colorado.

Across the road from the visitors center are Mather Campground and Babbitt's General Store as well as a gas station, post office, bank, public showers and laundromat. Three-fourths of a mile west is **Grand Canyon Village** where most of the lodges and hotels are located, including the **El Tovar Hotel** and the **Bright Angel Lodge**, built at the turn of the century when most visitors arrived by train. But times change and especially during the summer you may want to avoid the congested traffic by walking between all these places along the Rim Trail. (The section between the visitors center and Grand Canyon Village is a self-guided **Nature Trail**).

Immediately adjacent to the Bright Angel Lodge is the **Bright Angel Trailhead**. Since the Bright Angel and the **Kaibab** are the only maintained trails descending into the Canyon, the Park Service recommends hiking one of them before venturing onto any of the unmaintained trails. There is no water on the Kaibab, so most visitors choose to take their introductory hike on the Bright Angel, which has water in three

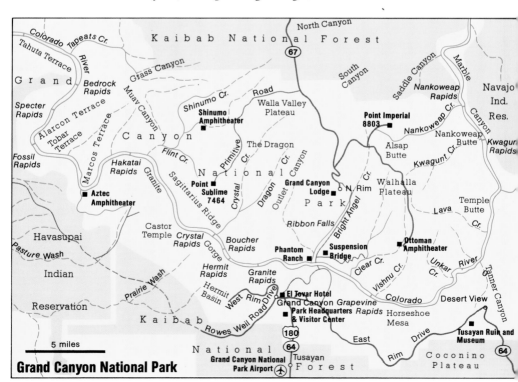

Grand Canyon National Park

places. Because of the heat—temperatures routinely exceed 105°F (41°C)—hikers should still carry water, at least a liter per person.

Stepping below the rim of the Canyon changes your experience of it. Suddenly, away from human distractions, you can hear the quiet and measure the grandeur of the landscape against the length of a footstep. You need not go far to sample these pleasures and everyone should spend at least an hour or two doing so.

A logical destination for an all-day hike is **Indian Gardens**, a verdant oasis 4½ miles (seven km) and 3,100 vertical feet (945 meters) below the rim. Follow the cue of avid hikers and photographers by rising early; the colors are most radiant and the heat most merciful shortly after dawn. This prospect is made more palatable if you plan on watching the sunrise while eating a leisurely breakfast at the El Tovar.

Day hikes will satisfy most people, but others will want to stay out overnight, perhaps on a hike to the Colorado River and back. Backpacking in the Grand Canyon is hard, though rewarding, work. An option for the elderly,

parents of young children and others who are reluctant to tackle such toil: ride a mule. To stay overnight below the rim you must have a reservation at either Phantom Ranch or a designated campground. Unfortunately, it's sometimes necessary to have made these arrangements as much as six months in advance. For more information, check at the Backcountry Reservations Office in the visitors center.

The West Rim

Two roads, one going east and one west, extend along the rim from Grand Canyon Village. During the summer the **West Rim Drive** is closed to private vehicles and a free shuttle bus is provided in their place. You can get on or off the bus at a half dozen viewpoints; this makes it possible to take the 10-minute hike between **Pima Point**, which offers one of the best views of the Canyon and the Colorado River, and **Hermit's Rest**, the terminus of the West Rim Drive.

The hermit was Louis Boucher, one of many prospectors who arrived in the late 1800s, and one of the South Rim's

les on bab Trail ing winter.

first white inhabitants. Deposits of copper, asbestos, lead and silver were found, but the costs of transporting ore by mule train were so astronomical that none of the ventures proved profitable. We do, however, have the miners to thank for most of the unmaintained trails that descend into the Canyon, including the **Hermit Trail**, west of Hermit's Rest. There are two good day hikes on the Hermit: a five-mile (eight km) round trip to **Santa Maria Springs** and a six-mile (nine-km) round trip to the less frequently visited **Dripping Springs**.

Although the paved road ends at Hermit's Rest, it is possible, via the **Rowe's Well** road, to drive from Grand Canyon Village further west along the rim. For safety's sake obtain a topographic map and a few gallons of water at the visitors center before setting forth. The **Bass Trailhead**, beautifully situated on a narrow peninsula jutting into the Canyon, is one possible destination. Backpackers find the Bass one of the most scenic and easy-to-follow of the unmaintained trails, and the trailhead itself makes a fine picnic or camping site for anyone anxious to escape the hustle and bustle of Grand Canyon Village.

Even farther west is the **Topocoba Hilltop Trail** that leads to **Havasu Canyon**, home, since 1300 A.D., of the Havasupai Indians.

Until this century the Havasupai, in addition to tilling their fields, spent part of each year roaming widely throughout the Canyon in search of game and edible plants. Once a rarely visited Stone Age Shangri-La, **Havasu Canyon** has recently become a popular vacation spot for boy scouts and college students. The attraction is **Havasu Creek**, a blue-green stream that plunges over three stunning waterfalls, one of which, **Mooney Falls**, is almost 200 feet (60 meters) high.

Havasu is the most spectacular of the side canyons that drain into the Colorado, and, despite the crowds, is still worth visiting—particularly during the off season, late September through early April. Access is difficult. Most visitors walk or ride horseback along the eight-mile (13-km) trail from **Hualapai Hilltop**, 67 miles (108 km) north of **Peach Springs** on U.S. 66. You can also hike in via the 12-mile (19-km) Topocoba Hilltop Trail or from the Colorado river; most raft trips spend a day doing just this.

Havasu Fa
Grand
Canyon.

There is a small motel in Havasu, but most visitors stay at a campground. Boil your drinking water and make reservations in advance.

The East Rim

Driving east from Grand Canyon Village through fragrant forests of ponderosa pine on the **East Rim Drive** you pass the Kaibab Trailhead near **Yaki Point** and after 20 miles (32 km) arrive at **Tusayan Ruin & Museum**. Anthropologists believe that the Anasazi Indians who built this small pueblo came to the Canyon around 500 A.D. The Anasazi were not the ancestors of the Havasupai, but lived a similar life—raising corn, squash and beans on the rim during the summer, moving down to the warmer canyon floor in the winter. Around 1150 A.D. a lengthy drought forced the Anasazi to abandon Tusayan and a number of other sites throughout the Southwest.

But even the Anasazi were not the first Indians to inhabit the Canyon. Anthropologists have discovered split-twig willow figurines pierced by small spears that date man's presence here to 2000 B.C. What, one wonders, did these Indians think of the Grand Canyon? A clue is found in Hopi Indian myth. The Hopi, descendents of the Anasazi who left 800 years ago, return on an annual pilgrimage and continue to believe that mankind entered the Earth through a spring in the Grand Canyon!

The last viewpoint on the East Rim Drive is **Desert View**. Here the **Watchtower**, a beautiful stone tower that rises 67 feet (20 meters) high, offers excellent views of the Colorado River 4,000 feet (1,200 meters) below. There is a campground at Desert View, as well as a little-known road which soon deteriorates to a trail leading five miles to **Comanche Point**. This secluded and rarely visited spot with its marvelous views is ideal for lovers, gazers, and seekers of solitude.

From Desert View, continue east on State Highway 64 to the **Cameron Trading Post**. Stop for gas and what connoisseurs report is a "respectable Navajo taco," a local dish that is a cultural hybrid featuring Indian frybread smothered with refried beans, lettuce and cheese.

Here the road forks. South to Flag-

Sitting on the edge of time at Nankoweap Ruins for a view of the Colorado.

staff; north to Page and the North Rim. The Grand Canyon is sandwiched by two immense, man-made lakes. **Lake Powell**, upstream of the Canyon, is formed by **Glen Canyon Dam**, near Page. **Lake Mead**, downstream, is formed by **Hoover Dam**, near **Boulder City**. Both of these dams are engineering wonders and are worth exploring on a free guided tour.

Rafting the Canyon

The departure point for all raft trips, as the boatmen say, "down the Grand" is 15 miles (24 km) below Glen Canyon Dam at **Lee's Ferry**. John D. Lee founded the ferry in 1871 while on the lam for his part in the massacre of a wagon train of California-bound emigrants by members of the Mormon church. Like many Mormons, Lee was a polygamist. His years in hiding were shared with one of his wives, Emma, who called their isolated home, Lonely Dell. Eventually, the fugitive was captured by federal officials and shot—at which moment Emma, along with Lee's 16 other wives, became widows.

The ferry is located just upstream of the mouth of the Paria River. An increasingly popular and spectacular four-day hike goes upstream through the **Paria Canyon Narrows**, where sheer sandstone walls, only 50 feet (15 meters) apart, rise 1,000 feet (300 meters) high. This hike should be avoided during the thunderstorm season due to the danger of flash floods. For more information contact the rangers at the ferry or the Bureau of Land Management (BLM) in Kanab, Utah.

Two years before Lee arrived at the ferry, nine gaunt men in three battered boats drifted out of Glen Canyon. Ten weeks earlier they had left Green River, Wyoming, 500 miles (805 km) away, with four boats and 10 months of supplies. After repeated upsets they were down to rancid bacon, musty flour, dried apples and coffee. The men were getting mutinous, but the man in charge, Major John Wesley Powell, seemed unperturbed. "If he can only study geology," grumbled one of the hands, George Bradley, "he will be happy without food or shelter, but the rest of us are not afflicted with it to an alarming extent."

At the time, Powell was unknown.

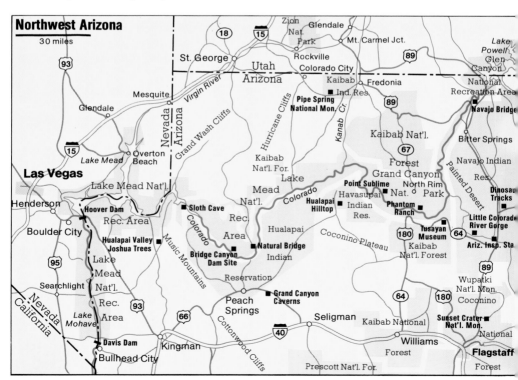

Years later, as the head of the Geological Survey and the Bureaus of Ethnology, he would be one of the most influential men in Washington, D.C. But for now he was simply a one-armed Civil War veteran, a self-taught amateur scientist who, on the strength of curiosity, intuition and discipline, would make fundamental contributions to the budding sciences of geology and anthropology. The Major was also a gifted writer, as this passage, often quoted by modern boatmen, reveals: "August 13th 1869—We are now ready to start on our way down the Great Unknown. We are three quarters of a mile in the depths of the earth, and the great river shrinks into insignificance as it dashes its angry waves against the walls and cliffs that rise to the world above; the waves are but puny ripples and we but pigmies running up and down the sands or lost amongst the boulders.

"We have an unknown distance yet to run, an unknown river to explore. What falls there are, we know not; what rocks beset the channel, we know not; what walls rise over the river, we know not. Ah, well! we may conjecture many things. The men talk as cheerfully as ever; jests are banded freely this morning; but to me the cheer is somber and the jests are ghastly."

Rythms of a River

Two weeks after he wrote that passage Powell and five of his nine men safely completed the exploration of the Colorado. Another three men, unwilling to risk their lives at a final, unusually nasty rapid, had abandoned the expedition two days earlier and were killed by Indians while struggling overland towards Mormon settlements in Utah.

Commercial river trips began in 1938 when Norm Nevills shoved off from shore with a boat built of planks scavenged from an outhouse and a horse trough. Nevills' boat was so small that his two passengers were forced to ride through 160 rapids sprawled flat on the deck—sacrifical spread eagles. A decade later the white-water industry was revolutionized by the introduction of Army-surplus rafts. Today, Powell and Nevills would be astonished to learn that more than 10,000 people float through the Canyon each year.

otor trip on
e Colorado.

A river trip has its own rhythm built of a series of small unexpected delights: the evocative, trilling song of a canyon wren; bighorn sheep grazing at the water's edge; a sudden thunderstorm which runs down the sheer cliffs in hundreds of glistening waterfalls. . .

Floating downriver you pass through successive layers of rock, each older than the one above, all of them fluted and polished by the river's ceaseless caress. It is the raft as time machine—in the first 30 miles (48 km) of this 225-mile (368 km) voyage, 350 million years of history drift past at arm's length. It is no wonder that one passenger has said, "The river offers a look at the soul of the Canyon." Or that Buzz Holstrom, who made the first solo descent, said, "It seems like I actually lived more in a few hours out there on the river than I have in a year in the city."

The North Rim

An hour's drive west of Lee's Ferry is **Jacob Lake**, the turnoff point for the **North Rim**. Because the North Rim is 1,000 feet (305 meters) higher than the

South Rim it is closed from late October to late May by snow. But during the summer and fall it is open as a cooler, less crowded alternative to the South Rim.

Buy whatever groceries you need in Jacob Lake and then drive south through lush forests of ponderosa pine, spruce, fir and aspen trees, interspersed with wide meadows that are edged by lingering snowbanks and dotted with duck-filled ponds. After 45 miles (73 km) you arrive at the **North Rim Village** whose centerpiece is the **Grand Canyon Lodge**. This handsome structure, a masterpiece of beam and stonework, was built by hand in 1928 and is best appraised while eating a piece of pie in the lodge restaurant, perched on the edge of the abyss.

During your stay at the North Rim you will want to drive to **Point Imperial**, offering views of the eastern Grand Canyon and the **Painted Desert**, and to **Cape Royal**. Favorite day hikes along the rim include the **Widforss Trail** and the **Ken Patrick Trail**. The only maintained trail into the Canyon is the **North Kaibab Trail**. Allow a full day to hike to **Roaring Springs** and back, a nine-mile

White water rafters in action.

94

(15 km) round trip. More experienced hikers might want to backpack the **Thunder River Trail** to **Deer** and **Tapeats Creeks**, gorgeous trout streams that plunge full born from springs at the base of the Redwall Limestone.

West of the North Rim is the least visited section of Grand Canyon National Park—the **Tuweep** area. Tuweep is reached over 60 miles (97 km) of dirt roads from either **Fredonia** or **Colorado City**. Be sure to heed the Park Service's advice: "A trip into this area, one of the most remote in northern Arizona, should not be attempted without ample gasoline, water, and food."

Molten Rocks and Melted Snow

Despite the difficult access, it's surprising that Tuweep is so rarely visited. "Because what we have there," says Dr. Ken Hamblin, "is one of the planet's most spectacular conjunctions of volcanic and erosional phenomena." Hamblin's research suggests that within the last million years the Colorado has been dammed 11 times by molten lava. The largest dam was 550 feet (165 meters) high and backed water 180 miles (290 km) upstream to Lee's Ferry. "What a conflict of water and fire there must have been here!" wrote John Wesley Powell on his pioneering voyage. "Just imagine a river of molten rock running down into a river of melted snow. What a seething and boiling of the waters; what clouds of steam rolled into the heavens!"

There are two points of interest at Tuweep: **Toroweap Overlook** offers unexcelled views of the lava flows which cascaded into the Canyon. Secondly, there's a short, but extraordinarily rugged trail to **Lava Falls**, the most violent rapid in the entire Canyon, and the standard by which boatmen compare other rapids in North America. (Check at the Tuweep Ranger Station for more information on this trail.) If you want to photograph rafts running the rapid, leave the rim at dawn to arrive by 10 a.m. For stability's sake, boatmen love heavy boats at Lava, so if after looking at the rapid you want to ride through it, ask. For if the Grand Canyon is a church and we are all pilgrims, there is no better place to get baptized than Lava Falls.

Antelope Canyon, Arizona.

NATIONAL PARKS AND MONUMENTS

Glen Canyon National Recreation Area Extends from north-central Arizona into Utah. Central feature is Lake Powell, formed by the Glen Canyon Dam. All kinds of lake sports available. Boat trips on Lake Powell can be arranged at Wahweap, nine miles west of Page. One-day raft trips may be arranged at the John Wesley Powell Museum in Page. Facilities at Wahweap and at Marble Canyon, 5 miles from Lee's Ferry. Boat excursions at Wahweap: phone 602/645-2433. Trips to Rainbow Bridge National Monument, in Utah, 50 miles from Wahweap, are available. Float trips on Colorado River through the Grand Canyon depart Lee's Ferry, reservations must be made six months to one year in advance. For contact addresses, see page 111, Info—Southern Utah.

Grand Canyon National Park Year-round magnet, except for the North Rim, which closed by snow from about late October to mid-May. Different views, tours, lodging available. Mule rides, scenic air trips, river-running boat trips. Indian ruins, museums and camping. Admission to the park area is by one-day or annual permit. Muleback trips should be undertaken only by those in good physical condition. Confirmed reservations strongly recommended, especially from May to October. Since around 2 million people visit the Canyon in a year, during spring, summer and fall you need a reservation to do just about anything, whether it's ride a mule, spend a night, find a campsite or take a hike. In some cases, reservations must be made up to a **year** in advance. For a smooth trip make reservations as soon as plans are definite. For reservations at one of the seven lodges on the South Rim or at Phantom Ranch on the Canyon floor, or for mule trips into the South Rim, contact Reservations Office, Fred Harvey, Inc., Grand Canyon, AZ 86023; 602/638-2631 or 638-2401. For reservations on the North Rim, write TWA Services, Box TWA, Cedar City, UT 84720; 801/586-7686. For mule trips on the North Rim, write Grand Can-

yon Scenic Rides, Kanab, UT 84741. For information and reservations in Havasu, write to Havasupai Tourist Enterprise, Supai, AZ 86425; 602/448-2121. Most campgrounds on both rims are on a first-come, first-served basis. From May through September they usually fill by 10 a.m. Campers are advised to spend the previous night as close to the park as possible in order to arrive early the next morning. The Mather Campground, on the South Rim, is an exception. From May 15 through September 30 reservations can be made by writing Mather Camp-

grounds, Box 129, Grand Canyon, AZ 86023. If you don't mind sleeping under a ponderosa pine rather than on asphalt, the best camping might lie on one of the many dirt roads that lead away from the rims into adjacent national forests. For instance, on the South Rim, just west of the Bright Angel Lodge, is a dirt road called the Rowe Wells Road that offers splendid camping for anyone with a sleeping bag, a water jug and a poorly developed herd instinct. Backpackers must obtain permits from the Backcountry Reservations Office, Box 129, Grand Canyon, AZ 86023. Or call 602/

638-2474 to request an application form. No permit is needed for day hiking. Hiking equipment can be purchased at Babbitt's General Store on the South Rim, or rented from Grand Canyon Trail Guides, who offer guided trips into the Canyon.

Hiking the Canyon As everywhere else in the Southwest, bring plenty of water, don't bite off more than you can chew, and swim in the Colorado River at your own risk; more hikers drown than die of heat stroke.

If you want to take an overnight hike the Park Service design is to herd visitors safely down the Kaibab or Bright Angel. And for the timid or inexperienced, this is a good idea. The rub is that often you can't get reservations for one of these trails, and even if you can, they tend to be inhabited by a cast of thousands. Experienced hikers may want to take an unmaintained trail like the Hermit, Grandview or Bass. Excellent jogging is available on both rims. The Rowe Wells Road west of the Bright Angel Lodge (see above) is one example. For further information write Grand Canyon National Park, Box 129, Grand Canyon, AZ 86023.

Lake Mead National Recreation Area Extends along the Colorado River from the Grand Canyon to below Hoover Dam—Arizona's most heavily visited section. Two large lakes (Mead and Mojave) for fishing, boating and other sports in rugged desert-canyon terrain. Good shoreside facilities. Licenses required for fishing. Major recreational center about 80 miles north of Kingman at Temole Bar—other centers on the Nevada side (see also Nevada). For information: Headquarters, 601 Nevada Highway, Boulder City. Twenty-four hour emergency telephone number 702/293-4041.

Pipe Spring National Monument On the Kaibab-Paiute Indian Reservation on AZ 389, 14 miles west of Fredonia. A tribute to Mormon pioneers, protects the Mormon-built 1870s fort and other structures that show the history of the outpost. Visitors center and daily tours.

ATTRACTIONS

Desert View Watch Tower, Tusayan Ruin and Museum On AZ 64 north of Flagstaff between Cameron and the Grand Canyon. The Watch Tower offers vistas of Arizona's panoramas; the Ruin, a former Pueblo Indian Settlement, offers a glimpse of history.

Glen Canyon Dam Lake Powell area, on the Utah border, due north of Flagstaff. A curved gravity structure on the Colorado River, the 700-foot high dam contains 210 miles of water. See also Glen Canyon National Recreation Area.

Grand Canyon Caverns Northwest of Flagstaff on U.S. 66. A hideaway known only to the Hualapai Indians until 1927, these caverns were once used as a burial ground. A modern elevator takes you 21 stories into the earth for a guided tour along lighted walkways. 602/422-3223.

Hoover Dam Is 72 miles northwest of Kingman, near Nevada border. Largest of all Federal

Navajo Bridge Seven miles below historic Lee's Ferry, due north of Flagstaff. The bridge floor is 467 feet above the water level of the Colorado River.

White Hills (Ghost Town) Is 50 miles north of Kingman off U.S. 93. In the 1890s it was the rowdiest silver camp between Globe and Virginia City. In a brief six years, the 15 mines which surround it gave up $12 million in silver bullion. Mostly old diggings.

River Rafting; Colorado River: trips ranging from three days to three weeks are offered by around 21 companies. The park (see under Grand Canyon region) will have a list of concessionaires, as should the Bureau of Land Management, which maintains jurisdiction over such activities as river running. Most companies offer both large and small rafts. Large ones are motor-driven; the small ones manned by oars.

Costs: Rates average roughly 85 dollars, per person, per day. This includes transportation to and from the river, three wonderful outdoor meals and

reclamation projects and a feat of engineering, the 727-foot structure is the highest concrete dam in the United States. Tours available.

Lake Powell/Wahweap Lodge and Marina Is 138 miles north of Flagstaff. A family vacation resort, with attractions on land and lake. Guided cruises, jeeps, boat rentals, water sports, warm all year.

"lodging."
Arizona Raft Adventures, Inc., Box 697, Flagstaff, AZ 86002; 602/526-8200.
American River Touring Association, 445 High Street, Oakland, CA 94601; 415/465-9355.
Canyoneers, Inc., P.O. Box 2997, Flagstaff, AZ 86003; 602/526-0924.
Georgie's Royal River Rats, Box 12057, Las Vegas, NV 89112; 702/451-5588.

Grand Canyon Dories, Box 3029, Stanford, CA 94305, 415/851-0411.
Grand Canyon Expeditions, Dept. AG, Box 0, Kanab, UT 84741; 801/644-2691.
Don Hatch River Expeditions, Dept. B, Box C, Vernal, UT 84078; 801/789-4316.
Tag-a-Long Tours, Box 1206, 452 N. Main Street, Moab, UT 84532; 801/259-8946.

INDIAN RESERVATIONS

Fort Mojave Reservation Is 236 miles northwest of Phoenix. This reservation borders three states, Arizona, Nevada and California, with tribal headquarters in California. Noted for basketry and beadwork, the tribe operates a Smoke Shop. Fishing, hunting (dove and quail), camping, water sports. Fort Mojave Tribal Council, P.O. Box 888 — 500 Merriman Avenue, Needles, CA 92363; 714/326-4591.

Havasupai Reservation Is 438 miles northwest of Phoenix. The "People of the Blue-Green Waters" are located at the bottom of Havasupai Canyon, a tributary of the Grand Canyon. To reach Supai, take an 8-mile trail from Hilltop by pack mules or hike. Campgrounds are limited. The tribe is noted for basketry and beadwork and hosts the Annual Peach Festival in August. Havasupai Tribal Council, P.O. Box 10, Supai, AZ 86435; 448-2961.

Hualapai Reservation Is 252 miles northwest of Phoenix. This large reservation includes within it the western 100 miles of the Grand Canyon. The tribe is noted for basketry and doll-making. Attractions: camping, hiking, hunting, fishing, white water Colorado River trips. Hualapai Tribal Council, P.O. Box 168, Peach Springs, AZ 86434; 769-2216.

Kaibab-Paiute Reservation Is 398 miles north of Phoenix. The tribe is noted for "Wedding Basket"; attractions include the Pipe Springs National Monument, a camper and trailer park with museum, store, laundromat and campsites. Kaibab-Paiute Tribal Council, Tribal Affairs Building, Pipe Springs Rte., Fredonia, AZ 86022; 643-5545.

SOUTHERN UTAH: HIKERS' PARADISE

In 1869, after a two-month journey down the Green River, an expedition led by Major John Wesley Powell reached the confluence of the Green and Colorado rivers, one of the most inaccessible spots on the North American continent. The voyage was not an easy one; there had been more rapids than the men cared to count, and in one of them, Disaster Falls, they had lost a boat and much of their food.

Here at the confluence, in the heart of what Powell called "the Great Unknown," both rivers lay deep within the earth imprisoned by sheer cliffs of their own making. Anxious to determine where, exactly, the confluence was relative to the rest of the world, the Major climbed to the rim. "What a world of grandeur is spread before us!" he wrote. "Wherever we look there is but a wilderness of rocks; deep gorges, where the rivers are lost below cliffs and towers and pinnacles; and ten thousand strangely carved forms in every direction; and beyond them, mountains blending with the clouds."

It is now possible to drive across southern Utah in a couple of days, but to do justice to the geography Powell described, you need more time—anywhere from a week to a year or two. Ironically, part of the area's appeal lies in what it lacks: there are no great cities here, no famous museums or soaring cathedrals. There is simply a landscape whose predominant feature is bare rock sculpted by the ages. On first glance, this slickrock topography may seem desolate, odd or even grotesque. Only later, as one's discernment grows, does it become apparent that the inconceivably bizarre is a transparent mask for the astonishingly beautiful. It is no fluke that so much of the region has been preserved in five national parks, four national monuments, three national forests and three primitive areas.

Moab: Beauty and the Bomb

Since every tour must start somewhere, let's begin in eastern Utah, in **Moab**. Moab was settled by members of the Church of Jesus Christ of Latter-day Saints, a religious sect founded on the East Coast of the United States during the early 1800s. In 1847, having endured decades of frequently violent persecution, the Saints (as they called themselves, although they practiced polygamy and were more widely known as Mormons) fled across the Great Plains to Utah—at the time an uninhabited wilderness owned by Mexico.

Thereafter, the theocratically organized, methodical and courageous Mormons overcame great obstacles to pioneer Salt Lake City, followed by a series of small settlements throughout Utah, including, in 1855, Moab. For almost a century, Moab was a sleepy town, 100 miles from nowhere. And it might have stayed that way, except for the Bomb.

As it became clear, following Hiroshima, that the Soviet Union was building nuclear weapons, the U.S. Atomic Energy Commission (AEC), as part of a nationwide search for uranium, established a generous fixed price for the ore as an incentive to miners. The first big strike was Charlie Steen's. In an area south of Moab that the AEC had deemed "barren of possibilities," Steen discovered his *Mi Vida* (my life) mine, from which he shipped $100 million worth of U235. Overnight, Moab became the "Uranium Capital of the World." Due to recent difficulties in the U.S. nuclear energy industry, most of the bloom is now off the uranium rose, but Moab remains the largest city in southern Utah, as well as the departure point for a visit to Arches or Canyonlands national parks.

The Truth about Arches

Superlatives quickly get blisters in southern Utah. Let's stick to the facts: **Arches National Park** has the largest cluster of, that's right, arches in the world. The arches—there are more than one hundred—have been carved by wind and water in a 300-foot layer of red sandstone deposited 150 million years ago during the age of dinosaurs. All of the arches are visible along a paved road that begins at the visitors center, five miles (eight km) north of Moab, or within easy walking distance along well-maintained trails.

If you're pressed for time, visit the **Windows Section** to view **Double Arch, Parade of the Elephants** and **Balanced Rock**. Then take the short guided hike

Preceding pages, Monument Valley. Left, Delicate Arch," Arches National Park.

through the **Fiery Furnace**. This mile-long trail snakes its way through a spectacular maze of rust-colored sandstone cliffs separated by dry streambeds. So many people have gotten lost within the maze that you must accompany a ranger on this hike; check at the visitors center for scheduled departures.

Travellers equipped for camping may spend a night at **Devil's Garden Campground**, 18 miles (29 km) north of the visitors center. From the campground a six-mile (10-km) loop trail takes you to seven different arches, including **Landscape Arch**. This slender arch, the longest in the world, is nowhere more than a few feet thick yet spans 291 feet (89 meters) or nearly the length of a football field. Mid-summer temperatures often exceed 105°F (41°C) throughout southern Utah. On this, and any other hike that takes longer than an hour, carry at least one quart of water per person.

From Arches head back to Moab. Pause here, prior to visiting **Canyonlands National Park**, to buy gas, groceries, and perhaps a meal. (Be fore-warned: You'll find filling fare at local restaurants, but nothing that wins rave reviews.)

The challenge of Canyonlands is picking and choosing. At more than 500 square miles (800 sq km), this fabulous park is so huge that it's unlikely you'll see more than a portion on any one visit—particularly since the Colorado and Green rivers divide the park into three "districts" which, though tangent to one another, are isolated by the tortured topography. In Canyonlands, it's generally the case, as the locals say, that "you can't get there from here."

The closest district to Moab is the **Island in the Sky**, 40 miles (67 km) away. The hurried traveller headed north toward Interstate 70 might spend a night at one of the two campgrounds on the Island, perhaps after touring Arches. The Island is a sheer-sided plateau that towers 2,000 vertical feet (600 meters) above the surrounding terrain and consequently offers panoramic views of the rest of Canyonlands from **Grand View Point**, the **Green River Overlook** and **Dead Horse Point State Park**. Immediately below the Island is the best jeep tour in southern Utah, the **White Rim Trail**. (Tours can be

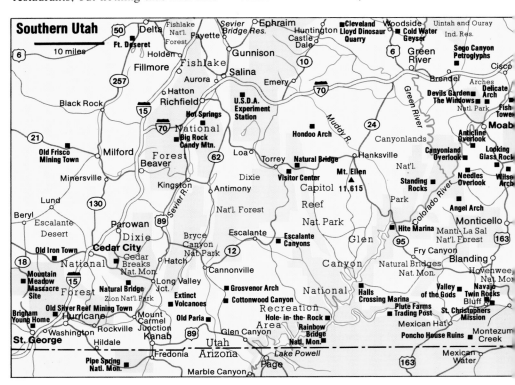

102

arranged in Moab.)

If you have at least a day—preferably two—and are headed south from Moab visit the **Needles District**. There is a campground within the district at **Squaw Flat**, but no grocery stores, gas stations or motels. These services can only be found 53 miles (85 km) away in **Monticello**. Thus, it is most convenient to buy food in advance and come prepared to car camp.

The attractions of the Needles are myriad and include prehistoric Indian ruins and pictographs, or paintings; a number of arches, one of which, **Angel Arch**, is perhaps the most sublime in Canyonlands; and the Needles themselves, massive fins of sandstone eroded into buff, red, and cream colored pinnacles, 500 feet (150 meters) high. For a quick introduction to the Needles, hike the **Peekaboo Springs Trail** that begins at Squaw Flat Campground. After wandering up the floor of a lovely canyon, this trail traverses a long expanse of bar slickrock where it is marked only by *cairns*—small piles of rocks for which one must be alert.

A four-wheel-drive vehicle allows quick access to another attraction in the

Needles, the downfaulted valleys, shaped like shoe boxes, that geologists call "grabens," reached via what many people regard as the final exam in jeep roads, **Elephant Hill**. In surmounting the hill, the driver must at one point turn completely around while perched on a flat rock teetering on the edge of a cliff, while later he must negotiate one 30-degree switchback...in reverse. Not surprisingly, passengers often forsake the jeep in favor of their feet.

On the eastern edge of the Needles, four canyons—**Davis**, **Lavender**, **Salt** and **Horse**—contain Indian ruins, arches, intermittent water and splendid scenery. Although the lower sections of these canyons can be explored on day hikes or by jeep, the magnificent upper reaches are best seen on a multi-day backpacking trip. Check with the rangers at the visitors center for more information. Finally, to share the view of the Green and Colorado rivers which so inspired Powell, visit the **Confluence Overlook** either by jeep or by walking a 10-mile (16-km) round-trip trail beginning at **Big Spring Canyon**.

Although the **Maze District** is directly across the Colorado from the Needles,

one must have a yearning for adventure to drive the 250 miles (400 km) between the two. To get to the Maze, backtrack to Moab and drive north to **Green River**. Since you're going into the "back of beyond," stop here to fill water jugs and the gas tank, and buy three or four days' worth of groceries. (Anyone going through the hassle of getting there will want to stay at least that long.)

Leaving Green River, drive west on I-70, then turn south toward **Hanksville**. After 24 miles (39 km) you'll see a sign warning that you're about to take your life in your hands. Turn left and drive 60 dusty miles (97 km) to **Han's Flat Ranger Station**. Shortly before you get there you'll pass the **Robber's Roost Ranch**. A century ago, this was the hideout of two of the West's most famous outlaws, Butch Cassidy and the Sundance Kid, along with the rest of their gang, the Wild Bunch.

From Han's Flat, it takes a day to hike or a half day to drive to the **Maze Overlook**, which offers an enticing view of the **Land of Standing Rocks** and the Maze itself, a labyrinthine snarl of six sinuous canyons. A trail beginning here takes you into the Maze; there are only a handful of other places in this 30 square-mile (49 sq km) fortress of stone where one can get in or out. First-time visitors should buy a map from the rangers at Han's Flat and have them mark these routes as well as the scattered Indian ruins and springs to be found.

Although backpacking into the Maze is arduous and riding a jeep may be worse, there is, happily, an alternative. Raft companies located in Green River and Moab offer four-to-seven-day white-water trips through **Cataract Canyon**; on most trips time is set aside for hiking into the Maze.

Goin' South

After Canyonlands, you may want to visit Capitol Reef, Bryce and Zion national parks. If so, you must first head for Hanksville—either by driving north through Green River (as if you're going to the Maze) or south via **Blanding**. If you have time, take the southern route—it's twice as long, but three times as interesting.

Driving south from Moab, you reach

Fall colors a
Zion Nation
Park, Utah.

104

the small town of Monticello on the flanks of the snow-clad **Abajo Mountains**. The Abajos provide a pleasing counterpoint to the slickrock country—and an escape from the summer heat. Between Monticello and Blanding there's a refreshingly cool campground located at **Devil's Canyon**. Take a walk through the aspen trees on the canyon floor.

Backpackers wishing to explore **Grand Gulch Primitive Area** should obtain hiking permits and further information from the Bureau of Land Management (BLM) in Monticello. The Anasazi Indians who once lived in Grand Gulch departed 800 years ago. But hundreds of their buildings, typically shielded from the weather under south-facing overhangs, remain in mint condition. So much so that the BLM must patrol Grand Gulch by helicopter to prevent illegal excavation of the ruins by pothunters dealing in the lucrative black market for pre-Columbian potter.

A few miles south of Blanding is a highway junction. If you're bound for **Monument Valley** and **Arizona** or can afford a short detour to see the world-class entrenched meanders of **Goose-** necks State Park, continue south to **Bluff** and **Mexican Hat**. You can double back on scenic State Highway 261 across Cedar Mesa. From Blanding, a right turn on State 95 (which figures so prominently in Ed Abbey's novel, *The Monkey Wrench Gang*) leads directly to **Natural Bridges National Monument**, a logical place to break the journey between Moab and Capitol Reef. There is a campground in Bridges, but no gasoline, groceries or other services. Buy your food beforehand in Blanding or Hanksville.

Bridges is to bridges what Arches is to arches: the world's largest cluster of natural bridges. (Although bridges and arches are similar in appearance, only the former have been carved by a stream.) Each of the three bridges in the monument can be seen from a paved loop road that departs from the visitors center. But don't just gawk at the bridges from the canyon rim. A 10-minute hike will take you to the base of any of the three. If you must choose, **Sipapu** is perhaps the most spectacular. For a longer hike, stroll downstream from Sipapu or **Owachomo** to **Kachina Bridge**. A good swimming hole at the

base of a waterfall is situated between the latter two. If you're really feeling adventurous, you can go on an overnight past Kachina down into **White Canyon** and explore the rarely visited canyons of **Hideout** and **Cheesebox**.

"The Place No One Knew"

Just west of Natural Bridges is another junction: State 263 goes to **Hall's Crossing Marina** on **Lake Powell**, while State 95 continues northward to Hanksville. The 180-mile-long (290-km) Lake Powell is the second largest, and most spectacular, manmade lake in the United States. The lake is formed by 710-foot-high (215-meter) **Glen Canyon Dam**, which generates 1,200 megawatts of hydroelectricity and ample controversy.

When it was begun in 1956, the dam had the blessing of everyone concerned. By the time it was finished in 1963, conservationists had belatedly recognized that Glen Canyon, "the place no one knew," was comparable in grandeur to anything—including the Grand Canyon—on the Colorado Plateau. Today, many people believe that the drowning of Glen Canyon was an unspeakable tragedy. Because so much of southern Utah is a *de facto* wilderness rich in uranium, coal, and other natural resources, there have been many such controversies. The most recent concerns a proposal to store nuclear waste next to Canyonlands National Park.

Nevertheless, Lake Powell is a stunning place to waterski, fish or explore. Consider visiting 290-foot-high (188-meter) **Rainbow Bridge**, the tallest natural bridge on the planet. You can buy gas and groceries, rent fishing tackle, powerboats or houseboats at any of the five marinas on the lake. If possible, make reservations in advance.

The mountains to the south of Hanksville are the **Henrys**, the last discovered, named and explored mountain range in the continental United States. Forty miles (64 km) west of Hanksville **Capitol Reef National Park**, whose central attraction is the **Waterpocket Fold**, a 100-mile-long (160-km) uplifted ridge of rock, dubbed a "reef" by uranium prospectors who found it a barrier to travel. After it was uplifted the reef was eroded into narrow canyons, interspersed with giant domes of white sandstone which

Bryce Canyon National Park, a ros colored palace carved in limestone.

resemble the domes found on capitol buildings throughout the United States.

Because the reef is nowhere more than 15 miles (25 km) wide, most of the hikes in the park are short, two-to-four-mile (three-to-six-km) round trips are most common. For instance, stroll through the **Grand Wash Narrows**, where 500-foot-high (150-meter) canyon walls loom less than 20 feet (6½ meters) apart. A more difficult hike takes you to the base of the **Golden Throne**, which offers tremendous views of the rest of the park. Another excellent day hike is along the **Chimney Rock Trail**; be sure to walk a mile or two into the upper reaches of marvelous **Spring Canyon**.

The Roads to Bryce Canyon

Backpackers should be advised that all of Capitol Reef provides rewarding backcountry hiking. However, since the terrain is extremely rugged and water is only found in a few places, it is best to ask at the visitors center for more information on hiking **Spring Canyon**, **Deep Creek**, **Hall's Creek** or **Muley Twist Canyon**.

From Capitol Reef, there are a number of ways to get to **Bryce Canyon National Park**. Some are more civilized than others. If you're in a rush or don't have a spare tire, keep to State 24, 62 and 89. On the other hand, if you don't mind moseying along dirt roads, fill your gas tank and water jugs and drive south to **Boulder** and **Escalante**, either across the **Aquarius Plateau** or south along the east edge of Capitol Reef to the **Burr Trail**.

Each route has its advantages. During the summer, go the cool way over the top of Plateau. In the spring and fall, when that road is not open, drive the Burr Trail. On both routes, there are two established campgrounds and any number of other suitable campsites. In either case, you'll be traversing the rugged, lonely heart of the Colorado Plateau. In 1861, the *Deseret News* described this area as "one vast contiguity of waste and measurably valueless, excepting for nomadic purposes, hunting grounds for Indians and to hold the world together."

But that description neglects the scenery. Clarence Dutton, a member of Powell's Geological Survey, described the view from the Aquarius Plateau as

One of the many "goosenecks" of San Juan River, Utah.

"a sublime panorama—a maze of cliffs and terraces lined off with stratification, of crumbling buttes, red and white domes, rock platforms gashed with profound canyons, burning plains barren even of sage—all glowing with bright color and flooded with blazing sunlight. It is the extreme of desolation, the blandest solitude, a superlative desert." Until 1929, the town of Boulder got its mail by pack mule. Today, the mail is delivered on what is easily the most beautiful paved road in Utah.

At the BLM office in Escalante, backpackers can get more information on hiking into **Escalante Primitive Area**. Most hikers enter Escalante by walking past the two stone arches in **Coyote Gulch**. An enjoyable alternative is **Harris Wash**.

From Escalante it's a few hours' drive to Bryce Canyon National Park. The Paiute Indians called Bryce the place where "red rocks stand like men in a bowl-shaped canyon." Mormon settler Ebeneezer Bryce, who gave his name to the canyon, had a more prosaic term. He called it "a hell of a place to lose a cow!"

Bryce is a fantasy land, a colorful fairy tale, a rose-colored palace carved in limestone. Technically, it's not a canyon at all, but rather a series of 12 amphitheaters eroded into an escarpment. The beauty of this gutted badland can be appreciated from overlooks along 20 miles (32 km) of paved roads, but it's best to take at least one hike below the rim for a more intimate look at the details of the place—a patch of wildflowers, a shady glen, a wind-sculpted tree.

Some hikes to consider: a guided walk along the short, easy **Navajo Loop Trail**, the more strenuous **Fairyland Loop Trail**, or a horseback trip on the **Peekaboo Loop**. Or walk the **Rim Trail** between any two of the viewing points and then ride the Inter-park Tram back to the car.

Before leaving Bryce, drive south to **Rainbow Point**. You'll climb slowly out of the ubiquitous forest of piñon and jumper until you're surrounded by spruce, aspen and fir. In early summer, the flowers along this road—Indian paintbrush, scarlet gilia and sego lilies—are gorgeous. On a clear day from **Yovimpa Point**, you can gaze over 100 miles (160 km) to the North Rim of the Grand Canyon, where the rocks are 160 million years older than those on which you stand. If that time scale overwhelms you, ease your way back across the ages by contemplating one of the 4,000-year-old bristlecone pines on the **Bristlecone Loop Trail**.

One of the classic trails in the entire national park system is the thrilling route up **Angel's Landing** in **Zion National Park**. Safely perched on the landing—after climbing 1,500 vertical feet (460 meters), the last few hundred along a narrow hogback ridge where you safeguard your progress by holding onto a chain—one can savor the sheer cliffs of this sandstone Yosemite. More than the other parks, Zion is truly wild, large sections of it accessible only to mountain lions.

Perhaps the two most popular trails on the flat floor of the canyon are the **Gateway to the Narrows** and **Emerald Pools**. But as is so often the case in southern Utah, it is hard to go wrong in Zion: all of the maintained trails are worth hiking. Again, since this is a wilderness, explore a bit, perhaps by poking your way up one of the side canyons between the Mt. Carmel Tunnel and the East Entrance to the park.

Left, pretty *Opuntia phaeacanth* at Arches National Park; and right, a close up of "Thor: Hammer," Bryce Canyon.

NATIONAL PARKS AND MONUMENTS

Within the south region, the Utah Travel Council lists two main visitor information centers: **Thompson Information Center**, 45 miles west of Utah-Colorado border on I-70, Thompson, UT. 84540; and **St. George Information Centre**, four miles south of St. George on I-15, St. George, UT 84770. Other information centers listed are included below **Some tips**: The state levies fines for any excavation, appropriation, injury or destruction of prehistoric ruins, monuments or objects of antiquity; allows no hunting in national parks; fires only at designated campsites.

Fishing is allowed in all parks with a valid Utah fishing license. However, spring runoffs cause few park streams to have good consistent fishing, with the exception of the Fremont River through Capitol Reef.

The most important precaution for hikers is to sign in with the park ranger and inform him of your plans. Back-country permits are necessary, free, and available at ranger stations. Rock climbing is tempting but can be extremely dangerous. You need a permit from the park ranger and preferably a guide. The soft sandstone is a different ball game from hard rock.

Four-wheel-drive vehicles are excellent for seeing Arches, Canyonlands and Capitol Reef, while Bryce and Zion are primarily for hikers. Vehicles must stay on established roads; rentals are available in major towns near the parks and guides are available.

For current information on camping in Utah's national parks or for further information, contact **National Park Service**, 125 South State, Salt Lake City, UT 84138; 801/524-4165.

For information on backpacking, river running, rockhounding, camping, primitive and wilderness, contact **Bureau of Land Management**, Office of Public Affairs, University Club Building, Room 1500, 136 South Temple, Salt Lake City 84111; 524-4227. For information on hunting and fishing regulations

and bird refuges, contact **Utah Division of Wildlife Resources**, 1596 West North Temple, Salt Lake City 84116; 533-9333.

Arches National Park 5 miles north of Moab on U.S. 163 and 191, open all year. About 90 structures in the park are considered to be true arches. Animals include deer, coyotes, foxes; small birds, squirrels, kangaroo rats, rabbits. Paved road runs the length of the park, with good foot trails en route to many impressive sights. Avoid soft sand and inform ranger of destination and return time: Visitors Center, located 5 miles north of Moab, just off U.S. 191, with exhibits

and slide program, opens daily. Several campgrounds within and nearby the park. Accommodations in Moab or Green River. For more information, write Superintendent, Arches, c/o Canyonlands, 446 South Main, Moab, UT 84532; 801-259-8161.

Bryce Canyon National Park Southwest Utah, east of Cedar City. Some roads closed in winter, check with ranger. Roads paved, some closed in winter. Main features of park easily seen from roadside viewing areas. Best way to see park is on foot or horseback (riding available in park). Trails from 1/2 to 23 miles, mostly self-guiding. Visitors center at north end, off U-12, open year round. Camping year round in the park; water available only during the summer months. High altitude, as park is

on an 8,000 to 9,000-foot plateau. For information, write Superintendent, Bryce Canyon National Park, Bryce Canyon, UT 84717, 801/834-5322. For information on accommodations inside the park, write TWA Services, Inc., P.O. Box TWA. Cedar City 84720. 801/586-7686. Accommodations are available in the park, just outside the park and in Cedar City, Escalante, Hatch, Panguitch. Campgrounds in the park and surrounding area. Visitor Information Centers: Cedar City Chamber of Commerce and Information Center, 286 N. Main; I-15 Information Center, see above; Kanab Information Center, junction highways 89 and 89A, 25 S. 100 E; Garfield County, U.S. 89 at Panguitch and Hatch; St. George, Chamber of Commerce, 97 E. St. George Blvd; St. George Temple and Visitors Center, 440 S. 300 E.

Canyonlands National Park In southeast Utah, 11 miles south of Moab. Open all year. Spectacular canyons formed by the Green and Colorado rivers. Paved state roads into park, some interior roads graded, check at ranger station for road conditions. Ranger stations at northern and southern ends of the park. Best ways to explore: hiking, river running, jeeping, horseback, scenic flights. Guides available in Moab or Monticello for jeep, air, or river trips in the interior. Accommodations and guest ranches at Moab, Green River, Monticello. Primitive campsites in four-wheel-drive areas of the park. Water available near campground in Needles district; everywhere else, water must be carried in. Visitor Information centers in Moab, N. Main Street on Highway 191; Crescent Junction Rest Stop, just off I-70 west of Crescent Junction (summer only); Monticello Courthouse, 117 South Main; I-70 Information Center, Thompson (see above); Green River, off I-70 in center of town. For information write Superintendent, Canyonlands, 446 South Main, Moab 84532, 801/259-7146.

Capitol Reef National Park In south-central Utah, entrance 4 miles east of Torrey on U-24, open all year, though park is cold in winter. Visitors Center at the northern end of the park 7 miles from the entrance. Massive gorges, scarps, and artifacts of the Columbian Indians of the Fremont culture. U-24 crosses the park, but most spectacular attractions are off the main highway on graded or dirt roads. Marked trails lead to ancient petroglyphs, water pockets and overlooks. Two campgrounds within park. Main campground, 1 mile south of Visitors Center, has 53 sites with fireplaces. Accommodations and services in Torrey, Bicknell and Loa. For more information, contact Superintendent, Capitol Reef National Park, Torrey, UT 84775. 801/425-3871.

Cedar Breaks National Monument Between Bryce Canyon and Cedar City, 23 miles east of Cedar City on U-14, a natural, multicolored amphitheater created by water, frost and wind erosion. Open late May through mid-November. All other times, check road conditions. Six-mile paved rim road through fields and forests for views of the breaks. Visitors center, picnic area and campground at the monument. Center opens early July through mid-October campground opens late June through mid-September. Accommodations at Brian Head, Cedar City and Parowan. Contact: Superintendent, Cedar Breaks National Monument, P.O. Box 749, Cedar City 84720; 801/586-9451.

Glen Canyon National Recreation Area Includes Lake Powell, most of which is situated in south-central Utah. Area includes Indian ruins, rock formations, islands, pictographs and petroglyphs. Mid-May through October provides ideal conditions for waterskiing, scuba diving, parasailing, canoeing, kayaking, houseboating and fishing. Regularly scheduled boat tours to Rainbow Bridge National Monument are available. Four marinas and facilities are on the lake—one in Arizona, three in Utah. Wahweap Lodge & Marina, P.O. Box 1597, Page, AZ 86040, 602/645-2433; Bullfrog Resort & Marina, Hanksville, UT 84734; 801/684-2233; Hall's Crossing Resort & Marina, Blanding, UT 84511, 801/684-2261; Hite Resort & Marina, Hanksville, UT 84734, 801-

684-2278. Fishing especially for largemouth bass and crappie; check marinas for information on licensing within respective state. Marinas have auto service stations, groceries, licenses, supplies, etc. Visitors are advised to reserve boats, houseboats, accommodations and trailer parks well in advance; call toll-free for reservations, information, fishing guide services and the like, 1-800/528-6154. Or contact Superintendent, Box 1507, Page, AZ 86040; 602/745-2471.

Hovenweep National Monument Between Blanding and Bluff Junction on U.S. 191 and U-262, then graded road to park entrance (see Indian land).

Natural Bridges National Monument Is 42 miles west of Blanding on U-95. Open all year, weather permitting. Visitors center at entrance with exhibits, slide presentations. A photovoltaic solar system, world's largest at the time of its construction in 1980, provides electricity for park facilities. Campground near visitors center; nearest accommodations and services in Blanding. Contact Superintendent, Canyonlands National Park, 446 South Main Street, Moab 84532; 801/259-7164.

Rainbow Bridge National Monument One of the seven natural wonders of the world. Can be reached on foot or horseback from Navajo Trading Post or on foot from abandoned Rainbow Lodge. Most common approach, by boat on Lake Powell. No designated campground or picnic area within monument area. Nearest services in Page, Arizona. Contact Superintendent, Glen Canyon National Recreation Area, Box 1507, Page, AZ 86040, 602/745-2471.

Zion National Park South of Cedar City, access from I-15 and U-9 from the west and U.S. 89 and U-9 from the east. One of the nation's oldest parks, spectacular canyons, colorful gorges, sheer rock walls, unique formations in southern Utah's plateau country, formed by a combination of the Virgin River and weathering of sandstone rock. Visitors center (museum, auditorium, information) at the south entrance, one mile north

of Springdale, open all year. Paved road cuts through park, better views on foot and horseback, with well-marked trails. Guided horseback trips available; inquire at Zion Lodge. Park contains three campgrounds, one open year round. For accommodations in park, contact TWA Services, Inc. (mid-May to mid-October); see address under Bryce Canyon. Accommodations also available Springdale, Mt. Carmel Junction, Orderville, Cedar City. For information: Superintendent, Zion National Park, Springdale, UT 84767; 801/772-3256.

NATIONAL FORESTS

For maps ($1 each), recreation and campground directory, trail information, information on backpacking, skiing, mountaineering and snowmobiling, primitive and wilderness areas, etc., in national forestlands, contact **U.S. Forest Service**, Intermountain Region Office, 324 25th Street, Ogden, UT 84401; 801/625-5182.

Dixie National Forest Includes 1.9 million acres in southwestern Utah, divided into four sections, ponderosa pine and spruce in abundance. The forest contains or is adjacent to Bryce Canyon, Capitol Reef and Zion national parks and Cedar Breaks National Monument. Hunting for deer, turkey, cougar. Ample recreational opportunities include skiing (Brian Head) and other winter sports; horseback riding; water sports; fishing at Duck Creek, Cascade Falls, Panguitch Lake, streams renowned for brook trout; boat rentals, cabins and camping facilities from late May through early October.

Fishlake National Forest Encompasses 1.424 million acres in south-central Utah, four sections. Includes Thousand Lake Mountain and Fish Lake in the southeast; Fish Lake is six miles long in the high country, offers excellent fishing June through October; three resorts, several campgrounds and trails are adjacent to the lake. Beaver Mountain, in the southwest portion, is a spot for fishing and scenic drives. Also available are hunting; skiing (Mt. Holly) and other

info

winter sports; camping; hiking; boating; water sports. For information, contact Forest Supervisor, 115 E. 900 N., Richfield. UT 84701.

Manti-LaSal National Forest 1.338 acres in southeastern Utah. LaSal portion, divided in two sections, is within prescribed area, east of the Canyonlands region. Forest headquarters are located in Price, Utah. The mountains are the LaSals, east of Moab, and the Abajos, near Monticello. Scenic drives, skiing and snowmobiling in the Fisher Towers takes you through spectacular mountain scenery on paved road. Redrock towers rise above valley floor; follow U-128 from Moab along the Colorado River, return via Castle Valley and the Scenic Loop Road, which goes through the LaSal Mountains.

STATE PARKS

For further information on state parks and boating, contact the **Utah Division of Parks and Recreation**, 1636 West North Temple, Salt Lake City 84116. 533-6011; 801/532-2473 for recorded fishing and hunting news. The UDPR sells a "Fun Tag" (1987 price $45) that serves as a yearly pass to all Utah State Parks.

Coral Pink Sand Dunes State Park Sits south of Mt. Carmel Junction on U.S. 89, 20 miles northwest of Kanab. Drifting dunes are really pink; park contains an RV campground. Popular area for dune buggies or four-wheelers. Camping information, call 801/874-2408 or call Kanab Chamber of Commerce visitor information, 801/644-5229.

Dead Horse Point State Park Is nine miles north of Moab on U.S. 191, then southwest to the park entrance. Great views of Canyonlands and 2,000 feet down to the Colorado River. Paved road to Visitors Center which is open daily. Popular for hang-gliding, camping, open all year; 801/259-6511.

Kodachrome Basin State Reserve Is 6 miles south of Cannonville off U-12 on dirt road, high-toned red rock formations frequently photographed. Ten miles further

on a dirt road is the Grosvenor Arch natural bridge. Camping, hiking, picnicking; 801-679-8562.

Minersville Reservoir State Recreational Area Is 14 miles west of Beaver on U-12. Trout fishing, boating, water skiing, modern camping facilities; 801/438-5472.

Newspaper Rock State Historical Monument Is between Monticello and Moab, 12 miles off U.S. 191. En route to Canyonlands. A large cliff mural of ancient Indian petroglyphs and pictographs. Primitive camping and picnicking are allowed. Open year-round.

Otter Creek Lake State Beach. Southeast of Marysvale at junction of U-62 and U-22. Locale for boating, fishing, hiking, camping, 801/624-3267.

Palisade Lake State Park Is south of Manti off U.S. 89. Lake closed to motorized boats, outstanding for swimming, canoeing, fishing. Nine-hole golf course directly adjacent; 24-unit campground within park.

Paria Ghost Town Is 36 miles east of Kanab, off U.S. 89, a 19th Century ghost town surrounded by vast rock formations. Dirt road; check conditions locally. Administered by the Bureau of Land Management 801/524-5348.

Piute Lake State Beach Is north of Mt. Carmel Junction on U.S. 89. Spot for rockhounding,

waterfowl hunting, camping, boating, fishing, swimming.

Edge of the Cedars State Historical Monument In Blanding. Ancient Anasazi ruins within the city limits. Museum, visitor information center, 801/678-2238

Escalante Petrified Forest State Reserve Is one mile west of Escalante on U-12, then short stretch on county road. Fossilized wood and dinosaur bones, freshwater lakes for fishing and other water sports. Boating, hiking, camping; 801/826-4466.

Goblin Valley State Park Is situated 68 miles southwest of Green River off U-24, first 10 miles paved, then seven miles of dirt road. Picnicking, camping (no fires allowed, no water) hiking, thousands of multihued rock formations stir the imagination. Bring camera.

Goosenecks State Reserve Is north of Mexican Hat on junction of U.S. 163 and U-261. Five-mile drive overlooks "gooseneck" canyons of the San Juan River.

Green River State Recreation Area South of Green River, on a graded road; offers camping, fishing, boating, picnicking on 53 acres. Green River is a noted headquarters for river running; check for guided trips.

Gunlock Lake State Park Is 17 miles northwest of St. George off U-97. Lake offers excellent year-round fishing and boating (boat ramp); camping, swimming, waterskiing.

112

Snow Canyon State Park Is 7 miles northwest of St. George off U-18, wonderland of desert trails, colorful canyons good for summer exploring. Extinct volcanic cones near the head of the canyon. Picnic areas, camping and boating. 801/628-2255

ATTRACTIONS

Beaver: National Historic District With over 200 historical homes of different periods and architectural styles. **Old Courthouse Museum, Art Gallery and Summer Theater**, 100 East Center Street.

Kanab: Navajo Bridge, Seven miles below historic Lee's Ferry, due north of Flagstaff. The bridge floor is 467 feet above Colorado River's water level.

Panguitch: Panguitch-Escalante-Boulder Scenic Drive 121 miles traversing Bryce Canyon, borders one of the largest unsurveyed wilderness areas in the country.

Parowan "Old Rock Church" Today the Museum of Pioneer Living. The Parowan Gap is known for Petroglyphs. Cowan's Honey Extraction Plant is world-famous for its methods of removing honey from beehives.

St. George: Brigham Young Winter Home 89 W. 2nd North. Tours daily. 801/673-5181.

Daughters of Pioneers Museum 143 N. 100 East in the McQuarrie Memorial Building, memorabilia from the pioneer days. Open Monday to Saturday. 2-5 p.m.

Jacob Hamblin Home Open every day, former residence of a Mormon Missionary with furnishings from the 1880s.

Springdale (Gateway to Zion National Park): **O.C. Tanner Amphiteater** Concerts and laser light shows outdoors, light show May 15-Labor Day. For concert schedules and information, call 801/673-4811.

ENTERTAINMENT

Repertory Theater The Pioneer Courthouse Players in the historic St. George Old Pioneer Courthouse concentrate on a series of productions produced in the round; the Old Courthouse in Beaver is also the scene of summer repertory events.

The Utah Shakespearean Festival Played in an outdoor theater patterned after the famed Globe Theater, this festival has acquired a reputation as one of the country's best. Located on the campus of Southern Utah State College in Cedar City, the festival performs three plays in nightly rotation during summer months. Tickets should be purchased by mail in advance.

ROCK HOUNDING

The state of Utah urges visitors to "take nothing but pictures, leave nothing but footprints." With this caveat in mind, travellers are encouraged to enjoy rocks and gemstones in their natural habitat, with topaz, agate, flowering or snowflake obsidian, golden labradorite, jasper, chalcedony, black agate, red agate, chert, geodes and pyrope garnets part of Utah's mother lode of gems. In the area this guide covers, you find mostly:

Jasper, chalcedony: About five miles south of Woodside on U.S. 6/50, take dirt road north and west, 4 to 6 miles.

Red agate: Along Colorado River, approximately 10.4 miles southwest of Cisco on U-128. Agate on hill to right.

Pyrope garnets: In the Four Corners area you can sometimes trade with the Indians for fine stones.

For additional information contact **Information Division, Utah Geological and Mineral Survey, 606 Blackhawk Way, Salt Lake City, 84108, 581-6831.**

SKIING, TRAIL RIDES, RAFTING

Brian Head Ski Lifts Three and one-half hours north of Las Vegas or five hours south of Brian Head Enterprises, P.O. Box F, Cedar city 84720; 677-2035.
Brian Head is also a center for other winter sports in the Dixie National Forest. Cross-country skiers are permitted to ride the alpine lifts. Snowmobile and cross-country ski tours, guided horseback tours are available. **Brian Head Nordic Ski Touring Center** has complete shop, marked and packed trails, races, ski dorms and cabins available; group discounts. Touring in nearby Cedar Breaks National Monument. 586-4010.

Mt. Holly Four hours north of Las Vegas or three and one-half hours south of Salt Lake on I-15 at the Beaver City exit. 67 miles from airport in Cedar City, paved runway in Beaver, 17 miles. Elevation 9200/10,200. Varied terrain and powder runs, uncrowded. Season from Thanksgiving, daily through Easter. A family-oriented resort with lodging and facilities within walking distance of the slopes. Ski rentals (alpine and nordic), convenience store, state liquor store, cafeteria, bar, game room. Restaurant at the hill. Varied terrain, lots of snow. Low lift rates. Ski touring and snowmobiling available. P.O. Box 1059, Beaver; 435-2488.

In addition to the above areas, Utah's wilderness areas abound with opportunities for ski touring. Please contact the U.S. Forest Service or individual forest areas — Dixie, Fishlake, and Manti-LaSal — for more complete information.
Usually **Trail Rides** can be arranged at Bryce, Zion and elsewhere. As one brochure says, "No experience necessary. We'll have you riding with the confidence of any cowboy in a short time . . . on trails first blazed by ancient Indian tribesmen in search of food and game." Prices start at $15. In Bryce or Zion, contact Bryce/Zion Trail Rides, P.O. Box 58, Tropic, UT 84776 or call after May 1. 801/834-5219.

Rafting: Most popular are one to seven day white-water trips on the Green River, the Colorado River and the San Juan River. Generally, the season runs from May through September. Outfitters are located in Moab, Green River, Grand Junction, Colorado (for the one-day trip down Westwater Canyon on the Colorado) and at Recapture Lodge in Bluff (for the San Juan). Cost is typically around $80 per person, per day. For a directory of professional outfitters and river runners, contact **Western River Guides Association, Inc.**, 994 Denver Street, Salt Lake City 84111; 355-3388.

HEART OF AMERICA'S INDIAN COUNTRY

First, a glance at two scenes. One at Bosque Redondo in New Mexico, May 28, 1868; the other in mythological time, the dark night when Hopi emerged from the underworld in what is now Northern Arizona. Myth tells us the people who had just emerged from the womb of Earth were greeted by Maasaw, deity of this Fourth World. "You are welcome," Maasaw said. "But know this land offers scant food or water. Living here will not be easy." The Hopi chose to stay.

The other scene is from the record of the Peace Commission named to establish a reservation for the Navajo. General William Tecumseh Sherman offered three options: the tribe could remain at Bosque Redondo where the Army held it; move to fertile river bottom land in Oklahoma, or return to their homeland—in the arid canyon country on the Arizona-New Mexico border. Sherman said he doubted this wasteland could support the tribe, but since it was worthless the Navajo should be safe there from the greed of white men. It was, Sherman told President Andrew Johnson, "far from our possible future wants."

It was the same choice the Hopi faced in their myth. The Navajo spokesman that day was Barboncito, a man noted as a fighter and not as orator. But listen to his words to Sherman:

"If we are taken back to our own country we will call you our father and mother. If there was only a single goat there, we would all live off of it...I hope to God you will not ask us to go to any other country but our own. When the Navajo were first created, four mountains and four rivers were pointed out to us, outside of which we not should live...Changing Woman gave us this land. Our God created it for us."

The 7,304 Navajo held at Bosque Redondo voted, without a dissent, to turn down the lush Oklahoma reservation and return to their desert. It was, as Barboncito told Sherman, "the very heart of our country."

It is still the very heart of America's Indian country, this high, dry southwestern side of the Colorado Plateau. Thus it seems appropriate when visiting it to follow the advice of Changing Woman, the great teacher of the Navajo Way, who said all things should begin from the East. Thus we begin at Gallup.

Bureaucrats and Sacred Places

Gallup, New Mexico, calls itself "Indian Capital of the World," and is America's most Indian off-reservation town. It's the trading center for the eastern Navajo and the Zuni Reservation and you're not likely to stroll down Railroad Avenue without meeting Hopi, Laguna, Acoma and possibly Jicarilla Apache. It's a ramshackle, unkempt, lively and interesting town, a good place to prowl the pawnshops for Zuni jewelry, Navajo sandcast silver, rugs, kachina dolls and other artifacts of Southwestern Indian cultures.

From Gallup head into the **Checkerboard Reservation**, so named because the tribe once owned only alternate square miles—an oddity now partially corrected. Interstate 40 takes you 38 miles (61 km) east to Thoreau. (The great red cliffs to the left were the background for uncounted cowboy movies, and the earthen humps to the

eceding
ges, a
eo at Hopi
d,
zona. Left,
Indian
y heavily
decked in
ns; and
nt, Pueblo
nito,
aco
nyon.

right are bunkers of Fort Wingate Ammunition Depot.) A left turn on State Highway 57 leads through Satan Pass 23 miles (27 km) to Crownpoint.

Crownpoint has a school, a medical center, a Navajo tribal police station and the offices of the Navajo bureaucrats who administer three or four million acres (about 1.5 million hectares) of the tribe's eastern territory. Like all Navajo communities, it has a temporary, government-built look as if tomorrow the tumbleweeds will reclaim it. Crownpoint is the site of a special event—a rug auction which six times a year attracts scores of Navajo weavers and hundreds of buyers for the sale of the fruit of Navajo looms.

From Crownpoint, State 57 jogs northeast 37 miles (60 km) to **Chaco Canyon National Historical Park** and its mysteries. In the shallow canyon a great civilization flourished and fell during the 12th and 13th centuries, leaving the ruins of its multistoried houses and myriad unsolved anthropological puzzles. New techniques in satellite photography have confirmed that Chaco Canyon was the center of a network of at least 250 miles (400 km) of improved roads and have aroused speculation that the great Chaco pueblos housed a sort of religious/administrative base. The visitors center and the ruins offer a rare look into America's past.

Thirty miles (48 km) north, State 57 joins State 44 at Blanco Trading Post. Two miles up the highway toward Farmington is Dzilth Na O Dith Hle Navajo Boarding School and beyond it rises **El Huerfano**. This great mesa is the center of an area as rich in sacred places for the Navajo as Palestine is for Muslim, Jew and Christian. The mesa was the home of First Man and First Woman and other Navajo Holy People. From it you can see other landmarks of Navajo Genesis. The blue shape of **Mount Taylor** looms on the horizon 50 miles (80 km) to the south. It is Tsoodzil, the Turquoise Mountain, one of the four sacred peaks First Man built as cornerposts of the Navajo universe. Northeast of Mount Taylor, the basalt thumb jutting into the sky is Cabezon Knob. In a cloud covering its crest one mythical day, First Man and First Woman found the infant White Shell Girl. According to the traditions of the Eastern Navajo clans, it was somewhere on the rolling

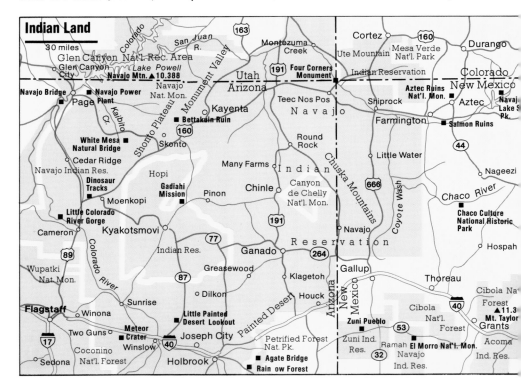

sagebrush hills north of Huerfano where Talking God, Black God and the other Holy People held the first puberty ceremonial, converting White Shell Girl into Changing Woman.

The Holy Birthplace

Eight miles northeast of El Huerfano, a right turn leads to the **Angel Peak Scenic Overlook**, offering a spectacular view across the wilderness formed by the Blanco Wash and Canyon Largo. Here the Holy People hung out the stars, the Changing Woman, made pregnant by sunbeams and mist from the San Juan River, bore Monster Slayer and Born for Water, the Hero Twins who were to purge this "Glittering World" of its monsters.

Just before State 44 drops into the San Juan Valley, it passes one of the West's most spectacular examples of man's power to modify nature. The endless silver-gray of sage and rabbit brush abruptly gives way to the dark green of corn, potatoes and alfalfa— 44,000 acres (18,000 hectares) of the Navajo Irrigation Project, lush circles formed by computer controlled over-

head irrigation pipes. The "capital" of this San Juan River country is **Farmington**—an Indian border town quite different from Gallup. It's economy is based on oil, gas, farming and coal—with tourism and Indian trading secondary. But it's a convenient base for recreational trips.

About 35 miles (56 km) up the river is the **Navajo Dam**, which forms a blue-water lake in a network of drowned canyons backed across the Colorado border. The lake is popular with trout and Coho salmon fishermen, and on several miles of the river below the dam is the best fly fishing in New Mexico. Aztec, just 13 miles (21 km) east of Farmington, is the site of the **Aztec Ruins National Monument**, a wonderfully-preserved example of how people lived in the Golden Age of the Pueblo. Visitors can walk into the living quarters of these vanished people and into a huge *kiva*—the underground "church" of one of the pueblo's religious societies. An hour and a half drive north of Farmington takes you to **Mesa Verde National Park**. The cliff dwellings here are deservedly among the West's most popular tourist attractions. Most

liff Palace
uins, Mesa
erde
ational
ark.

visitors tend to focus on Cliff Palace, a 200-room apartment house high on the wall of a cliff, or the Spruce Tree House, a 114-room structure under a massive stone overhang. But you may find yourself staring at the myriad smaller houses in cracks and crevices—wondering at the dangers motivating people to make homes in such dizzy places, and how they raised children where a toddler's misstep meant death.

A Navajo Doughnut

Farmington is also the gate to the "**Big Reservation**," a term which requires explanation. The Navajo Tribe, the nation's largest, with some 150,000 members, controls some 16 million acres (6.5 million hectares)—an expanse larger than New England. Most of this is in a West Virginia-sized area on the New Mexico/Arizona/Utah borders. But also covered is the "Checkerboard Reservation," the Alamo, the Ramah and the Canoncito. On this Navajo Nation, an elected tribal council operates its own courts, police force, and other services. More than 1,100 miles (1,770 km) of paved road, and another thousand which range from quality gravel to tracks impassible in wet weather, tie the reservation together. Its climate ranges from less than five inches of rainfall annually in its lowest deserts to 25 inches (161 cm) on the forested slopes of the Chuska Mountains, where elevation reaches 10,416 feet (3,174 meters). Surrounded by all this is the 600,000-acre (250,000 hectare) Hopi Reservation, like a Pueblo Indian hole in a Navajo doughnut.

It's a huge place, and one of the best ways to visit its interior is by driving west out of Farmington to **Shiprock**, which, like Crownpoint, is a Navajo bureaucrats' town. As you drive west on U.S. Highway 550, you see the sky over the San Juan smudged with plumes of whitish smoke. The pollution (sharply reduced by millions of dollars worth of soot precipitators in the towering stacks) is from the Four Corners Generating Plant. Coal from the adjoining Navajo Mine, the nation's largest open pit operation, rolls directly into the furnaces, and thence over electrical transmission lines to warm California swimming pools. Only the ashes and pollution are left behind. A six-mile

Tourists snapping at Shiprock, New Mexico

120

side trip through the farming town of Kirtland gives you a look at this mind-boggling operation.

Take State 504, the **Navajo Trail** west from Shiprock—but first take U.S. 666 16 miles (26 km) south to The Rock With Wings. You have been seeing the ragged blue shape of Shiprock for miles but as you climb the long hill south of the town you finally realize its size. It is the core of a volcano, the cinder cone cut away by 15 millions years of wind and rain. This core towers 1,450 feet (440 meters) above the grassy prairie— 20 stories taller than the Empire State Building—suggesting an immense black Gothic cathedral. In Navajo mythology, it was the home of the Winged Monster, slain by the Hero Twins with the help of Spider Woman. Chinese Walls of basalt radiate for miles from its base, 20 or 30 feet (six to nine meters) high in places but only three or four feet (one meter) thick. They formed when volcanic pressures cracked the earth and molten lava squeezed upward like toothpaste. Eons of erosion have left lava standing exposed in great black walls, with the wind whistling through the holes time has created.

West from Shiprock the Navajo Trail takes you past the tiny trading post communities of Teec Nos Pos, Red Mesa, Mexican Water, Tec Nez Iah and Dennehotso to Kayenta, gateway to **Monument Valley Navajo Tribal Park**— that odd vertical landscape made famil-iar by a million calendar photographs and a hundred Western movies. Ero-sion is the subject here. All of the Colorado Plateau was ocean bottom in an earlier era and this portion of the Arizona-Utah borderland was repeat-edly buried under sediment as the sea rose and receded. What the visitor sees now is the product of millions of years of weather cutting through soft sand-stone and shale, leaving wind-sculpted spires and monoliths where harder stone endured. The area north of Kayenta offers the most dramatic of these weird and wonderful forms, but the entire borderland country gives a look at what time can do to stone.

Bewildering Ruins

Another not-to-be-missed sight is **Be-tatakin Ruin**, a drive of about 30 mi-nutes from Kayenta. A mile walk from

ading
sts, such
this at Fort
fiance,
zona,
ve as
ses for
vellers to
arsely
tled areas.

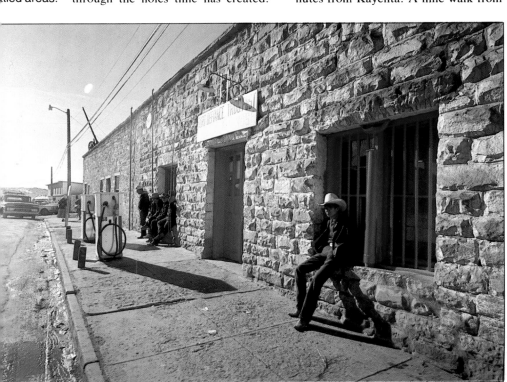

the visitors center takes you to the 13th-Century cliff houses. The nearby **Keet Seel Ruins** are more impressive but reaching them takes half a day. Under the overhanging stone roof which has protected them for 700 years they look as if they were abandoned yesterday.

From Navajo National Monument, a 13- mile (20 km) detour/shortcut down Navajo Route 221 connects with State 98 and a 60-mile (96 km) drive west and north across the dramatic landscape of ,**Kaibito Plateau** to Page, Lake Powell and the Glen Canyon National Recreation Area. There's a visitors center near the dam, and the lake itself is famous throughout the West as the best possible place to take a houseboat vacation. Blue water and a shoreline of carved cliff makes the lake a photographer's dream. It also provides access to some of Utah's most spectacular canyon country, including the Rainbow Bridge National Monument.

If you follow U.S. 89 southward from Page, a turn on 89A at Bitter Springs takes you to **Marble Canyon** and then under the incredible **Vermillion Cliffs** formation to **Jacobs Lake** and the **North Rim of the Grand Canyon**. The drive across the Kaibab Plateau is beautiful and this approach to the Grand Canyon offers a special thrill. When you walk into the lobby of the Grand Canyon Lodge you are confronted with what seems to be an immense mural of the canyon. It takes a moment to realize you are seeing reality through a great glass wall. The effect is memorable.

If you decide to skip the North Rim, the route from Page leads southward through the narrow Cornfields Valley with the Echo Cliffs towering east of the highway and Limestone Ridge walling off the west. Fifteen miles (25 km) south of the Tuba City turnoff, there's Cameron, with a **Navajo Information Center**. From Cameron, it's 53 miles (85 km) west on State 64 to the South Rim Center of the Grand Canyon National Park, and the best views of what is probably the planet's most spectacular chasm. But just 15 miles (24 km) west of Cameron the gorge of the **Little Colorado** bends to within a few hundred yards of the highway. There's an overlook into the incredibly deep, incredibly narrow slice that river has cut into the crust of the earth. Even with more colorful and spectacular views

Two divers Indian lifestyles in perspective left, rug weaving ar right, enjoying a rodeo special. (right).

ahead, it's worth the time.

Somewhere west of this spot, according to Hopi myth, the people who were to occupy the surface of the world emerged from the womb of earth and began this, their fourth existence. From this point, the clans who were to form the Hopi People began the epic migrations to the four corners of the world and returned, eventually, to Black Mesa. The ruins at Mesa Verde, Chaco Canyon, Aztec, Keet Seel and the others are the "footsteps" left by the Hopi ancestors in their travels toward the stone villages on First, Second and Third Mesa, where they now live out their destinies.

At **Wupatki National Monument**, 20 miles (32 km) south of Cameron, more than 800 ruins still exist. Archaeologists say the eruption of **Sunset Crater** covered the Painted Desert with a fertile black ash. The year was 1065, and the result was a land rush. But about 200 years later a 23-year drought forced evacuation.

The cone of Sunset Crater juts a thousand feet above its surrounding lava beds and meadows just four miles (six km) from U.S. 89, which is linked to Wupatki by a 34-mile (55-km) route through the Painted Desert. The crater is interesting and offers a self-guided trail through the blowholes and ice caves of its lava beds.

This entire area is overshadowed by one of America's most sacred landmarks—the **San Francisco Peaks**. They rise to 12,633 feet (3,850 meters) just north of Flagstaff—the highest point in Arizona. For the Navajo, they are Evening Twilight Mountain, First Man's Mountain of the West. For the Hopi, they represent something like Mount Sinai and Islam's Dome of the Rock combined. Here the kachina spirits live during that half of the year when they are not with their people on the Hopi mesas. Humphrey Peak is the doorway through which these supernaturals pass between the worlds of men and of spirits.

The area around **Flagstaff** is rich in the unusual. Only about 50 miles (80 km) southeast of the volcanic Sunset Crater and just five miles (eight km) from I-40 there's **Meteor Crater** with its adjoining museum explaining the 570-foot deep, 4,150-foot wide (175 and 1,260 meters) hole punched out by a rock

fragment visiting from space. **Walnut Canyon National Monument**, with one of the most beautiful cliff house sites, is even closer to I-40 and practically a Flagstaff suburb. But for natural oddities don't miss **Grand Falls**, 20 miles (32 km) north of I-40, where a "waterfall" higher than Niagara has formed giant stairsteps into the Little Colorado gorge. The few times each year when runoff water roars down it stirs up a cloud of red dust. If you continue east on I-40 to New Mexico, the route also takes you through the heart of the Painted Desert and past Petrified Forest National Park, with its fallen forests of broken stone trees. Whichever route you choose, be sure not to miss the Hopi villages.

Hopi Home

Visit **Hopi Country** by turning east on State 264 at Tuba City. The road drops into Moenkopi Wash past the red stone Hopi village of Moenkopi. The little fields of corn, bean and squash you'll see here provide an idea of how people have survived in this desert country for thousands of years. The route takes you through some 50 miles (80 km) of empty country and into the oldest continually occupied area of America.

Most of the Hopi villages are built on or near three lofty fingers of stone which jut from Black Mesa. You reach **Third Mesa** first, and the little stone towns of Hotevilla, Bacobi and Oraibi. **Oraibi** dating back to about 1100, is partly deserted ruins but is an impressive place to visit. On **Second Mesa** the **Hopi Cultural Center**, provides insight into the complex culture of this ancient civilization. The center operates a motel and dining room as well as the tribe's museum. Shungopovi and Mishongnovi on Second Mesa are interesting, but most memorable of all are the **First Mesa** communities of Hano, Sichomovi and (especially) Walpi, which perches on its lofty mesa cliff and offers a spectacular view of the desert landscape.

State 264 takes you back to Gallup via the old Hopi government town of Keams Canyon and through Ganado, where John Hubbell, known to the Navajo as "Double Glasses" opened his historic **Hubbell Trading Post** in 1870. It's maintained as a National Historic Monument and shouldn't be missed by anyone interested in how the frontier was. **Window Rock**, the capitol of the Navajo Nation, is also on this route and deserves a look.

But first there's an essential side trip. North of Ganado 30 miles (50 km) is **Canyon de Chelly National Monument** where three great gorges have sliced through the plateau under the Chuska Mountains. Generations of cliff dwellers, Hopi and Navajo have lived along the sandy bottoms of these washes, under cliffs which in places tower a thousand feet (300 meters). There's access by vehicle tours from Thunderbird Lodge, or by foot trails down the cliff.

In a way these canyons sum up this heartland of America's Indian Country. They offer spectacular sculptured stone. (Spider Rock, for example, rises as tall as the Empire State Building from the sand of De Chelly Wash.) They offer White House, Antelope House, Standing Cow and other cliff dwellings. And they offer a sense of the silence, the space and the great beauty which caused Navajo, Hopi and their ancestors to choose this hard inhospitable land as the heart of their country.

Views of Canyon de Chelly; left the Spider Rocks and right, near White House Ruins.

NATIONAL PARKS AND MONUMENTS

Aztec Ruins National Monument 6 miles northeast of Farmington on U.S. 550. A surprising small site which is a fine example of a pre-Columbia pueblo and contains the only full restored *kiva* on the continent. Open 8 a.m. to 5 p.m. daily. P.O. Box U, Aztec, NM 87410.

Canyon de Chelly National Monument On the Navajo Reservation 3 miles east of Chinle, enter from Gallup or Shiprock, NM; Holbrook or Tuba City, AZ. Enormous monument combining cliff dwellings in sheer canyon walls with skyscraper-like formations and modern Navajo peach orchards. Principal ruins: White House, Antelope House, Standing Cow, Mummy Cave. Four-wheel-drive vehicle trips conducted by Justin's Thunderbird Lodge, near monument headquarters, daily early April through October 31; 602-674-5443 or 674-5265. Authorized Navajo Indian guides also available, park rangers on duty 8 to 5. Except for one trail, all visitors within canyons must be accompanied by park ranger or authorized guide; plans to drive four-wheel-drive through must be made one day in advance to arrange for guide. Thunderbird Lodge is the only overnight accommodation within the park, with a good restaurant. Other accommodations in Chinle. For information write Canyon de Chelly National Monument, Box 588, Chinle, AZ 86503; 602/674-5436.

Chaco Canyon National Historic Park Fascinating ruins 67 miles south of Farmington via U.S. 64, NM 44 and 57. NM 57 is 20-plus miles of desolate dirt road impassible during flash summer storms. Check tires, gas, oil and road conditions at the Nageezi Trading Post on 44. Sites open mid-April through mid-October. Tours of Pueblo Bonito, principal pueblo ruin, are available. Visitors Center, open daily, houses displays, books, snacks. Star Route 4, Box 6500, Bloomfield, NM 87413. 505/786-5384.

El Morro National Monument 43 miles southwest of Grants on NM 53. 56 miles southeast of Gallup on NM 32 and 53. The 200-foot high sandstone butte dubbed "Inscription Rock" contains graffiti from early Indians, Spanish explorers, U.S. settlers and military units, and two pre-Columbian pueblo ruins perch on top of the rock. Nine RV sites for camping. 505/783-5132.

Hovenweep National Monument The monument lies west of Cortez, a "deserted valley" of mesas and canyons containing the remains of prehistoric pueblos and small cliff dwellings. Best access is through Utah. In Colorado, turn off U.S. 666 18 miles north of Cortez. Information station and modern campground at monument headquarters, and a park ranger on duty. McElmo Route, Cortez, Colorado 81321.

Hubbell Trading Post National Historic Site On the Navajo Indian Reservation. 1 mile west of Ganado and 55 miles northwest of Gallup, NM. Century-old store that is a museum of Indian arts and crafts. Open daily from 8-5, 8-6 in summer. Box 150, Ganado, 86505.

Mesa Verde National Park One of the country's prime national attractions; proclaimed America's first world Heritage Cultural Park in 1978. Extensive, beautifully preserved Indian ruins in a stunning natural setting; ruins date back to the 6th Century. Mesa Verde is open all year, on a limited basis in winter; in general, accommodations, facilities, services, most tours, bus from Cortez, are available early May through mid-October. Far View Visitors Center is 15 miles from the Park entrance, adjacent to the 150-room Far View Motor Lodge. with dining room, cocktail lounge, gift shop, and theater for evening programs. Cuisine features Indian and Hispanic entrées and accents, and the lodge offers some interesting packages. Cafeteria also on the premises. Advance reservations highly recommended; call Mesa Verde Company, 303/529-4421; P.O. Box 277, Mancos, CO 81328. Mesa Verde Company also provides bus information. **Wetherill Mesa** ruins (by bus tour from Far View Center) are open only in summer. **Chapin Mesa**, six miles from Far View, contains a mu-seum, information center and park's administrative headquarters. Many ruins are approached from this center, including **Spruce Tree Ruin** right nearby, which is always open if the weather allows.

Navajo National Monument Within the Navajo Reservation. Take U.S. 160 to a nine-mile paved road (564) leading to monument headquarters. Largest and most imposing of Arizon's clif dwellings. Visitors center a headquarters with exhibits slides. Navajo arts and craft shop, open daily.

The Betatakin Area Contains monument headquarters. Access to the ruin is via a good but difficult trail. Ranger-guided tour daily mid-May through September. **Keet Seel Area** reached on foot or horseback from headquarters via rough 8-mile trail. Reservations taken up to 60 days in advance from Memorial Day through Labor Day. For information and re servations, telephone headquarters, 602/672-2366. Or write Tonalea, AZ 86044.

Petrified Forest National Park 20 miles east of Holbrook. Eigh major sections, best viewed from main park road that passes chie sights. One section includes a spectacular part of the Painted Desert. No overnight accom modations. Permit required fo camping in Painted Desert and Rainbow Forest Wilderness areas. Park open daily. Some major park attractions: Agate Bridge; Newspaper Rock Painted Desert Inn Museum, mile north of I-40, hours vary Rainbow Forest Museum, nea the south entrance, open daily.

Sunset Crater National Monument North of Flagstaff off U.S 89, boasts a rose-tinted volcani cone that rises above pine forests. A self-guiding trail lead over Bonito lava flow. Monu ment connects with Wupatk by paved road. Camping permit ted April to mid-November Visitors center open daily. I winter monument may be occa sionally closed because of snow 602/526-0586.

Wupatki National Monument 25 miles north of Flagstaff o U.S. 89. 800 prehistoric Puebl Ruins on more than 35,00 acres. The Big House, The Citadel, Wupatki Ruin Visitors Center open daily. Write: Tuba Star Route. Flagstaff, 86001. AZ. 602/774-7000.

NATIONAL FORESTS

Kaibab National Forest In three-parts, all in north-central Arizona, Flagstaff-Grand Canyon area. North portion is especially known for variety of trees, beautiful meadow, deer herd, rare Kaibab squirrel, one of the state's few buffalo herds. On and south of the Grand Canyon South Rim lie recreational lakes like Whitehorse and Kaibab; Sycamoare Canyon; Indian ruins and a full range of outdoor activities including skiing in the winter months.

STATE PARKS

Bluewater Lake 29 miles west of Grants on I-40 and MN 12. Boating, camping, waterskiing, swimming, fishing for rainbow trout and channel catfish in the reservoir.

Red Rock East of Gallup on I-40, NM 566. Site of the Gallup Inter-Tribal Indian Ceremonial held annually in August. Park has an 8,000-seat arena for rodeos and other events.

ATTRACTIONS

Holbrook East of Flagstaff on I-40. Gateway to the Petrified Forest and Painted Desert and county seat of Navajo County. Museum at the Old County Courthouse is in the center of town.

Hopi Villages Northeast of Flagstaff, Walpi, Oraibi, Hotevilla, Shonagopovi, etc. Annual Snake Dance held in late August. Oraibi is considered the oldest continuously inhabited village in North America, dating back to 1200 A.D.

Ice Caves/Bandera Crater 26 miles south of Grants, NM 53. Caves of perpetual ice, along with crater, which was volcanically active 5,000 years ago.

Monument Valley Navajo Tribal Park 160 miles northeast of Flagstaff on the Arizona-Utah border. Monolithic rock formations rise hundreds of feet into the air from the sand-covered prairie. Guided four-wheel drive is recommended. Visitors Center open daily. Reservations advised for accommodations.

Painted Desert Part of the Petrified Forest, may be seen from I-40 east of Flagstaff. One of the state's most spectacular attractions, with every hue of the rainbow featured in ribbons of sand.

Salmon Ruins County-owned; one of the two largest pre-Columbian colonies of the 12th Century. Ongoing archaeological excavations may be visited in summer. Nearby museum. 9 to 5 daily. 13 miles east of Farmington on U.S. 64. Rte. 3, Box 858, Farmington 87401; 632-2013.

ENTERTAINMENT

Four Corners Opera Association San Juan Symphony Orchestra. For a quarterly calendar of events, contact the San Juan Arts Council. Farmington, NM 87401, 325-4545.

INDIAN RESERVATIONS

Hopi Reservation A large reservation situated within the Navajo boundaries. The Hopi are uniquely noted for kachinas; also basketry, plaques, silver and pottery. Attractions: the Cultural Center, ceremonials throughout the year, with Snake Dances now open to the general public. Hopi Tribal Council, P.O. Box 123, Kyakotsmovi, AZ 86039; 734-2445.

The reservation encompasses Monument Valley, Canyon De Chelly, Little Colorado River Gorge, Grand Falls, Rainbow Bridge, Betatakin and Window Rock, the so-called "Seven Wonders of the Navajo Nation." Also within it is part of the Four Corners region, where four states, Arizona, New Mexico, Utah and Colorado, meet. Ceremonials, three-day rodeo and fair, arts and crafts shops, camping, hunting, fishing and hiking. The tribe weaves blankets and tapestries, silver crafts, some basketry. For more information, contact the Navajo Nation, Window Rock, AZ 86515, 871-4941; or the New Mexico Office of Indian Affairs, Bataan Building, Santa Fe 87503; 505/827-6440.

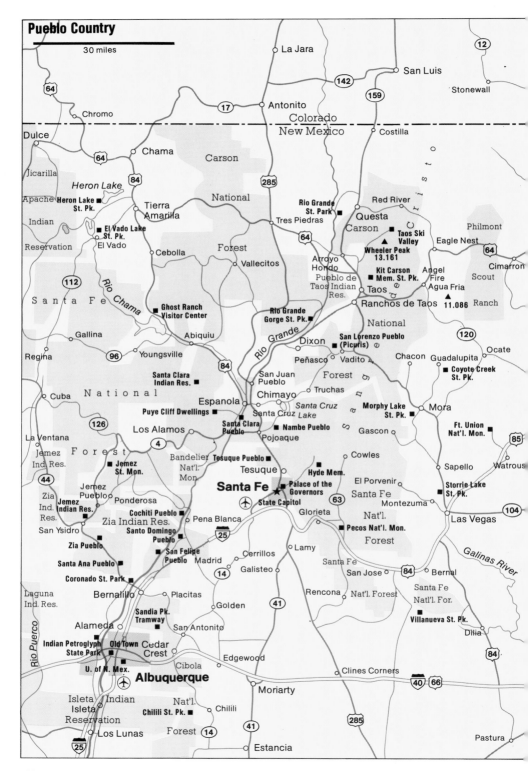

Pueblo Country

30 miles

La Jara

⑫

San Luis

⑭²

Stonewall

㉖

Chromo

⑰

Antonito

⑲⁵⁹

Colorado

New Mexico

Costilla

Dulce

㉖

Chama

Carson

②⁸⁵

Jicarilla

⑭

Heron Lake

Heron Lake

Apache   Heron Lake St. Pk. ■

Tierra Amarilla

National

Rio Grande St. Park ■

Red River

Questa

Indian

⑧⁴

El Vado Lake St. Pk. ■

El Vado

Tres Piedras

Carson

Taos Ski Valley

Philmont

Reservation

Cebolla

Forest

Vallecitos

⑥⁴

▲ Wheeler Peak 13.161

Eagle Nest

⑥⁴

Santa   Rio Chama

⑪²

Arroyo Hondo

Kit Carson Mem. St. Pk. ■

Angel Fire

Cimarron

Fe

Ghost Ranch Visitor Center ■

Pueblo de Taos Indian Res.

Taos

Agua Fria

Scout

▲ 11.086 Ranch

Gallina

Abiquiu

Rio Grande Gorge St. Pk. ■

Ranchos de Taos

National

⑫⁰

Regina

⑨⁶

Youngsville

Dixon

San Lorenzo Pueblo (Picuris) ☞

Chacon

Guadalupita

Ocate

Santa Clara Indian Res. ■

⑧⁴

Peñasco

Vadito

Coyote Creek St. Pk. ■

National

Cuba

San Juan Pueblo

Chimayo

Santa Cruz Lake

Forest

Truchas

Morphy Lake St. Pk. ■

Mora

Puye Cliff Dwellings ■

Espanola

Santa Cruz

Nambe Pueblo ■

Gascon

⑫⁶

Los Alamos

Santa Clara Pueblo

Pojoaque

Cowles

Ft. Union Nat'l. Mon. ■

⑧⁵

La Ventana

④

Bandelier Nat'l. Mon.

Tesuque Pueblo ■

Sapello

Watrous

Jemez Ind. Res.

Forest

Tesuque

Hyde Mem.

El Porvenir

Storrie Lake St. Pk. ■

㊹

Jemez St. Mon. ■

Santa Fe ★

Palace of the Governors

Montezuma

⑩⁴

Zia Ind. Res.

Jemez Pueblo

Ponderosa

✈ State Capitol

⑥³

Santa Fe

Las Vegas

Jemez Indian Res. ■

Glorieta

Nat'l.

San Ysidro

Zia Indian Res.

Cochiti Pueblo ■

Pena Blanca

Pecos Nat'l. Mon. ■

Zia Pueblo ■

Santo Domingo Pueblo

㉕

Forest

Lamy

Santa Ana Pueblo ■

San Felipe Pueblo ■

Madrid

Cerrillos

Santa Fe

Coronado St. Park

Galisteo

San Jose

⑧⁴

Bernal

Laguna Ind. Res.

Bernalillo

Placitas

Rencona

Nat'l. Forest

Santa Fe Nat'l. For.

Sandia Pk. Tramway

Golden

㊶

Villanueva St. Pk. ■

Alameda

San Antonito

Dilia

Indian Petroglyph State Park

Old Town Cedar Crest

Edgewood

⑧⁴

U. of N. Mex. ■

Cibola

Clines Corners

㊵㊅

✈ Albuquerque

Moriarty

Isleta   Indian

Nat'l.

Isleta Reservation

Chilili St. Pk. ■

Chilili

Pastura

Los Lunas

Forest ⑭

㊶

②⁸⁵

Estancia

㉕

130

A Look At Pueblo Country Fares

Thousands of years ago the odyssey of prehistoric man took him through the misty migrations of the Ice Age to the peak of his Stone Age civilization around 1100 A.D. in the Four Corners states: New Mexico, Arizona, Colorado and Utah. By the time the Spaniards came north from Mexico in 1540 the descendants of the Anasazi, the Ancient Ones, were well settled in their communal villages along the Rio Grande and its tributaries, from Isleta in the south to Taos in the north. A few tribes had moved west. The Spaniards called them Pueblo Indians because they lived in villages, to distinguish them from the nomadic, war-like tribes such as the Navajo, Apache and Ute who had come into the Southwest from the northern plains.

Today more than 80,000 Indians live in the 19 Pueblo groups in New Mexico. For the most part, they live where they lived when the Spaniards came. Each pueblo has its own governor and coun-

Preceding pages, north edge of town of Taos gets its share of winter. Below, Acoma Church Tower.

cil, is subject to federal and most state laws, but is autonomous in many ways. Elaborate ceremonial dances are performed as they have been for thousands of years. They may appear to be social events (they are), but they are also prayers for rain, good harvests, fertility, peace and a thanksgiving for all the good things of life. Outsiders are permitted to attend most dances in Indian pueblos, but one should never forget he is a guest. Never take photographs, tape or sketch unless you have obtained permission at the tribal office and have paid the fee if there is one. Some pueblos do not permit photography under any circumstances, for any amount of money. Others permit it part of the time. In all pueblos there are certain ceremonies to which outsiders will not be admitted, but in those cases there will be a sign or a guard at the entrance to the Pueblo.

Anyone visiting New Mexico should visit some of the pueblos, preferably on a feast day. All the pueblos except Zuni are close to, or within driving distance of, Albuquerque, Santa Fe or Taos.

Ancient Architecture at Acoma

Acoma, often called Sky City, is 65 miles (105 km) west of Albuquerque off Interstate 40. Perched on a 400-foot (125-meter) high rock mesa, the old pueblo had a strong defensive position. Most Acomans live in two newer villages below, raise cattle and sheep, operate highway businesses, or work in nearby towns. Some are chosen each year to live on top of the rock and keep the old village and church in repair, and the tribe returns there for special feast days. An overwhelming sense of history pervades the church, which was built around 1630 of flagstone and adobe mud. Every timber had to be carried from the distant mountains, and water and mud for the adobe was carried up the steep trail of the mesa. The high ceiling, hand-hewn beams, 10-foot-thick walls, square towers, and adjoining priests' quarters are a masterpiece in primitive architecture.

A visitors center is located near the base of the mesa, and visitors may drive up the steep, winding road. Guides will conduct them through the pueblo. Photography is permitted for a fee.

Acoma pottery is thin, well-fired and

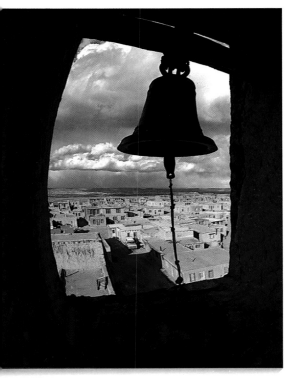

watertight. It is usually white and painted with black geometric designs; a newer style is all white with fingernail marks pressed into the wet clay.

Cochiti is 36 miles (58 km) southwest of Santa Fe or 45 miles (22 km) north of Albuquerque. Cochiti potters are famous for their drab, earth-tone pots in the shape of or decorated with animal figures and painted with black designs. The most sought after designs are of storytellers, pueblo mothers or sometimes fathers, with anywhere from one to 30 children crawling all over. The variation are endless, and are copied by other tribes now, but Cochiti women originated them.

Cochiti people farm and work in town. The resort community of Cochiti Lake, a few miles north, is on reservation land. The Indians sit on decision-making boards, and many of them work at the lake, where water sports are available. They also operate a campground there. The annual feast day is July 14. when they do a corn dance.

Isleta, only 13 miles (21 km) south of Albuquerque, manages to retain a strong identity nevertheless. They farm the good bottomlands along the river, and hold jobs in Albuquerque. Most of the Isletans remained friendly to the Spaniards in the revolt of 1680 and fled south with them, returning with de Vargas in 1692–1694. Their magnificent mission church, built around 1615, was gutted during the rebellion and restored on their return. It is still in use, one of the most venerable in New Mexico. San Agustín, their patron saint, is honored on September 4, but they perform many other dances during the fall and summer. For many years Isleta potters produced only a ''tourist pottery,'' but the art has been revived, and they now produce an attractive brown ware.

Cliff Dwelling Craftsmen

Jemez, 48 miles (77 km) northwest of Albuquerque, is set among the red and ocher cliffs of the Jemez Mountains. One of the last tribes to submit to Spanish rule after the re-conquest, many of them went west to live with the Navajo. Even today, at any feast day in Jemez, a surprising number of Navajo will be there. A craft cooperative on the highway sells Jemez pottery, usually reddish-brown and tan, painted black.

A place of worship for Indians in Cochiti, New Mexico.

When the Spaniards first came to New Mexico there were several Jemez pueblos farther up the canyon and in the mountains, but now all live in the one pueblo. About 12 miles (19 km) up the canyon, just beyond the resort village of Jemez Springs, Jemez State Monument preserves the ruins of a mission church built by and for the Jemez people around 1617. It too was gutted in the rebellion, and never re-built. Jemez celebrates their patron San Diego on November 12, and in August they perform the Pecos Bull Dance to honor the Pecos people who moved in with them in 1838.

Laguna is along I-40 about 45 miles (75 km) west of Albuquerque. A turnout gives travellers a good view of the pueblo—a church and squat, square adobe homes on a low hill a few hundred yards away. For a better view, drive into the pueblo. This is one of the largest pueblo groups, with almost 5,000 members living in seven villages on the reservation. Uranium mines on the reservation provided much employment until recently. Once again, cattle ranching and jobs in Albuquerque provide a livelihood for most families.

Nambe, 21 miles (34 km) north of Santa Fe, has been largely Hispanicized, but their impressive mission church is well-maintained and dominates the area. They celebrate San Francisco on October 4, and on July 4 they stage a popular festival at the foot of Nambe Falls, where many dances are performed and photography is permitted. A campground has recently been built near the falls. (Route 1, Box 117-BB, Santa Fe, NM, 87501, 505/455-7692.)

Picurís, 20 miles (32 km) southwest of Taos, was once much larger than it is today. Being on the eastern edge of the pueblo world, they were subject to attacks from the Plains Indians more than any other pueblo. This pueblo is believed to have been founded around 1250 by a group of Taos Indians, and the two tribes speak the same language. (The 19 pueblos speak six distinct languages.) Their annual feast day and corn dance is August 10 in honor of San Lorenzo. Women potters produce utilitarian cooking pottery, reddish brown with highlights of mica, not decorated, but serviceable. (P.O. Box 228, Penasco, NM 87553. 505/587-2519.)

Pojoaque, 16 miles (26 km) north of

coma
dian
ueblo, one
f the oldest
ontinuously
habited
illages in
orth
merica.

Santa Fe, dwindled almost to extinction a few years ago. It was reorganized and now has a tribal structure. On December 12 they honor Our Lady of Guadalupe, patron saint of New Mexico and Mexico. (Route 1, Box 71, Santa Fe, 87501. 505/455-2278.)

Sandia, 14 miles (22 km) north of Albuquerque, has fertile river bottomland for farming, and has capitalized on its nearness to Albuquerque by encouraging tourist-related industries. The reservation extends to the top of the Sandia Mountains. On the road to the Sandia Peak Tram, they have built a large arts and crafts center where the work of many tribes is sold. On June 13 they honor San Antonio with a corn dance. (P.O. Box 608, Bernalillo, NM 87004. 505/867-2876 or 5021.)

Dancing Deer and Jiving Buffalo

San Felipe, 28 miles (45 km) north of Albuquerque, is one of the most conservative pueblos, never permitting photography under any circumstances. The lovely 18th-Century mission church is open only during religious services.

On Christmas Eve, the spirits of the animal kingdom pay homage to the Christ Child as dancers representing deer or buffalo. Elaborately dressed women dancers enter the church after midnight mass. In hushed closeness, onlookers await the arrival of the procession. No one is supposed to be abroad to see the dancers come from their kiva. Buffalo dancers wear the dark fur and horned headdress of the buffalo, with their exposed skin darkened, and stomp on the floor. Deer dancers, headdresses bedecked with antlers, move more lightly. One by one, the dancers move to the altar to greet the figure of the holy baby.

San Ildefonso, 20 miles (32 km) northwest of Santa Fe, is best known as the home of the famous potter, Maria Martinez. She and her husband Julian developed the process for making black pottery burnished to a coppery sheen. It is now made in several other pueblos. Their son, Popovi Da and *his* son, Tony Da, continue making the burnished and matte black ware, simple and classic in form and design. Tony Da has developed his own style of inlaid turquoise and shell. It brings some of the highest

Making mud bricks for the construction of adobes.

THE ADOBE: AN INTRIGUING ART

Adobe has long been the traditional building material of the Southwest. Structures made from it are undulating and sculptural in nature, yet their mass gives them a sense of permanence and timelessness. The word "adobe" originated in the Arabic language and was brought to this country by Spanish colonists at the end of the 15th Century. It is used to refer to the earth from which structures are built, the structures themselves and the unbaked clay bricks made from earth.

In New Mexico, archaeologists have discovered remnants of adobe walls built by the Pueblo Indians that date back to 1200 A. D., 400 years before the arrival of the Spanish. From that time through the 15th Century there is evidence of two types of earthen walls. One was coursed adobe, which started with a stiff mixture of mud and was blended with anything from stones to pot shards. The mud was applied by the handful, course on top of course, until the desired wall height had been reached. A more sophisticated method made use of hand-formed, unbaked clay bricks. When the bricks were dry mud mortar was used to hold the bricks in place on the wall.

The Spanish colonists not only brought the word adobe with them, but they also brought a new method of making them. Wooden forms the size of the needed adobe were made, with a handle on each end. They could generally hold from one to eight bricks. These forms were set on the ground; mud mixed with straw was shoveled in. The straw was added to aid in drying by conducting moisture from the center of the adobe and to help keep the bricks from cracking as they dried. The excess mud was scraped off the top. When the bricks were dry enough not to sag, the forms were lifted up, moved to a new spot and filled again.

These were the two primary methods of building with adobe until the coming of the railroad in the 1880s, which almost eliminated the use of adobe for several decades. American settlers brought new technology as well as prejudice against the long established culture of the native populations. Red fired brick, board and batten, concrete block and frame-stucco are just a few of the construction materials and methods that dominated the Southwest landscape. The coming of the railroad also had tremendous impact on the already existing architecture. Elaborate ornamentation and new rooflines gave the simple, flat-roofed buildings a radical face-lift.

Not until after World War I was there any significant reemergence of adobe architecture. An awareness of decreasing natural resources turned builders' and architects' eyes toward a building material of infinite supply, which also had excellent passive solar properties. Adobe has the ability, when properly oriented to the sun, to retain its temperature for long periods of time. In an age of high utility bills this becomes an attractive feature.

With the reemergence of adobe came commercial adobe yards, which are now producing a stabilized adobe block. As the word implies, a stabilizer is an additive, such as an asphalt emulsion, that when mixed with mud produces an unbaked clay brick that resists moisture penetration, adobe's worst enemy.

But building adobe structures with brick is only one method of construction. *Pise' de terre*, better known as rammed earth, is a process developed in France during the 16th Century. Wooden wall forms are set in place and filled with a blend of moist soils. The soil is compressed with a hand or pneumatic tamper. The forms are moved to another section of wall and filled again.

Unfortunately the amount of labor required in adobe construction often makes it too expensive for the average home-buyer, though its use by owner-builders is steadily increasing. Solutions are slowly being found. Recently architects and builders have been looking for more innovative methods that will increase productivity and decrease the dollar margin between adobe and conventional building materials.

prices of any Indian pottery. The family operates a shop on the plaza, and their work can be bought at museums and shops around the world.

San Ildefonso has a large, clean plaza where they perform their most exciting dance on January 23, an animal or hunting dance. It begins at daylight and continues all day. (Route 5, Box 315-A, Santa Fe, NM 87501. 505/455-2273.)

San Juan, 29 miles (47 km) north of Santa Fe, is across the river from the place chosen by Juan de Oñate as the first capital of New Mexico in 1598. Only a cross on the mound of an unexcavated pueblo marks the spot today, but the modern pueblo is large and active. Their feast day is celebrated on June 24, and on Christmas Day they perform the Matachines Dance, an adaptation of a Spanish morality play.

San Juan pottery is traditionally black, brown or red, with symbols on the surfaces. (P.O. Box 1099, San Juan Pueblo, NM 87566. 505/852-4400.)

Santa Ana, 30 miles (48 km) northwest of Albuquerque, keeps the entrance to the pueblo chained except on special feast days, when visitors are permitted to come in. Most of the people live in three smaller villages down by the river near Bernalillo and return to the old pueblo only on feast days. Photography is not permitted. Traditional polychrome pottery almost became a lost art, except for Endora Montoya, who undertook to teach the younger women, and has revived the art. Coronado State Monument, near Bernalillo, preserves the ruins of an ancient pueblo said by the Santa Ana Indians to be their ancestral home.

Santa Clara, 30 miles (48 km) northwest of Santa Fe, has several outstanding potters. Among the best known are Lonewolf and Medicine Flower, members of the Naranjo family. It is red or black ware, polished and incised with intricately carved designs.

In Santa Clara Canyon each July, the Puye Cliff Ceremonial, a thrilling weekend event, takes place high atop the mesa. A modest craft show accompanies traditional dances performed against a backdrop of stone and adobe ruins. Puye, which is part of the Pajarito Plateau, is a majestic place to see a pair of Eagle dancers, wearing white feathered headdresses, with feather wings strapped to their arms, swooping and

Race Day at San Juan Pueblo Church.

gliding in solemn mimicry of the eagles whose aeries are on the clifftops.

Santo Domingo, 31 miles (50 km) southwest of Santa Fe or 39 miles (63 km) north of Albuquerque, is best known for its jewelry, particularly *heishi*, small shells polished to a silky smoothness. These Indians are born traders and most of the artisans you see selling on the portals of public buildings in Santa Fe and Albuquerque are from Santo Domingo. Theirs is a large pueblo, and the people are active in Indian affairs and conservative about pueblo life, strictly forbidding photography. Santo Domingo holds its Corn Dance on August 4th, the feast of Saint Dominic, in an open-air extravaganza involving 500 dancers from age two to age 80. Each barefoot woman dancer has a blue stepped *tablita* painted to symbolize a mountain with an indication of rain. She wears a one-shouldered *manta*—a woven sash—the best family jewelry, and holds a pine bough in each hand. The men wear short white embroidered kilts with long bold sashes, armbands and moccasins, and they too carry pine boughs. The entry of two long files of dancers into the plaza is pageantry at its finest, but the purpose is sacred—to raise the spirits of rain and fertility, to stamp the earth, to beat the drum and chant and raise the vibrations of the earth to insure a fine harvest. On Christmas and Easter they have dances lasting several days.

Taos, two miles (three km) north of the city of Taos, is the most photographed and familiar of all Indian pueblos, with its large, multi-storied pueblos facing each other across the plaza. Taos marked the northern frontier of the Spanish province, and it was here the Comanche and other Plains Indians came to trade with the Spaniards and Pueblo Indians. All year long they might raid and plunder, but during the trade fair a truce prevailed. Even today, Taos Indians show traits of their Plains brothers: long braids, beaded moccasins, aquiline noses, high cheekbones. The Plains war dances sometimes performed at Taos are unlike the traditionally quieter dances of the pueblos. Taos potters produce a good red-brown micaceous pottery, like that at Picurís, not ornamental, but useful. On September 29 and 30 they pay homage to San Geronimo with dances.

e Santa
ara Dance
a colorful
nual event.

At dawn, male members of North House race against those of South House; at the end of the race the teams are showered with Crackerjacks and oranges by Taosenos from the stepped roofs of North House. The Chifonetti are male clowns, their bodies painted with black and white stripes, cornhusks in their hair, who cavort through the onlookers, carting off children and teasing the crowd. (In other pueblos a similar clan is known as Koshares.) Their joking has a moral purpose—to chastise those who have misbehaved, and to warn others to be good.

Immediately after the races, an inter-tribal trade fair begins. Selected artisans show their wares in booths set up on the wide dirt plaza between North House and the stream that divides the pueblo. Except for a few special feast days, photography is permitted in Taos. A visitors center is at the entrance to the plaza to collect fees and issue permits. (P.O. Box 1846, Taos Pueblo, NM 87571. 505/758-8626.)

Tesuque, 10 miles (16 km) north of Santa Fe, is a small pueblo, but has some excellent potters, usually working with earth colored clay in animal fi-

gures. Their patron saint day, November 12, celebrates San Diego. They perform turtle, deer and other animal dances in the winter. (Route 5, Box 1, Santa Fe, NM 87501. 505/988-5075.)

Zia, 36 miles (58 km) northwest of Albuquerque, sits on a volcanic mesa, its mud-plastered houses blending so well with the landscape that they are easily missed. Zia pottery, usually earth tones painted with stylized figures of birds and flowers, and well-fired, is sought by collectors; especially prized are the pots made by Candelaria Gauchpin. It is a small pueblo and quite conservative, never allowing photography. Zia watercolor paintings are also prized. The Zia ancient sun symbol appears on New Mexico's state flag as a symbol of "perfect friendship." The feast day is August 15, with a corn dance. (General Delivery, San Ysidro, NM 87053. 505/867-3304.)

Zuni, in the far western part of New Mexico, 40 miles (64 km) south of Gallup, was the first New Mexican pueblo seen by Spaniards. In 1539 soldiers and priests leading an advance party for Coronado's expedition saw the cluster of flat-roofed adobe buildings, the straw in the mud glinting in the afternoon sun, and immediately went back to report that they had seen the "Seven Cities of Gold." Zunis are superb jewelry and pottery craftsmen. The silver inlay jewelry is usually made with small pieces of turquoise, jet, coral, mother-of-pearl and tortoise shell set in intricate patterns. Their crafts are available at a cooperative store in the pueblo. The most famous Indian dance in the Southwest is Shalako at Zuni, held in late November or early December each year. Beginning at sundown grotesque figures, 10 and 12 feet tall, come into the village where they dance and sing all night at designated homes.

The extremely costly costumes are draped over a wooden framework, which includes pulleys to move parts like a puppeteer. A covering is created of feathers, paint, animal skins and other materials. The head seems birdlike, the body is conical. To be chosen as a Shalako is an honor, and the man who assumes the role must train for it physically and spiritually.

Zuni is at over 7,000 feet (2,100 meter) elevation, and the night of the Shalako is almost always bitterly cold and snowy.

Left, San Felipe de Neri Church in Old Town Albuquerque where the city was founded in 1706. Right concha belt and bracelet are common ornaments among Indians.

141

AESTHETES' ALBUQUERQUE

Albuquerque began in 1706, a cluster of mud huts near a simple mud chapel in a place where the Rio Grande makes a wide bend, leaving rich bottomlands where settlers could plant corn and orchards. For a century and a half it was a Spanish farming community on El Camino Real, the road from Santa Fe to Mexico City. When the railroad came in 1880 New Albuquerque moved two miles east, leaving Old Town to enjoy a long *siesta*—without losing its identity at all.

Albuquerque is the largest city in the state of New Mexico, with almost a half-million people in the metropolitan area. It is the trade center of the state, headquarters for regional governmental agencies, a medical center of some renown, home of the state university and one private college and since World War II, a center for Space Age research and development. Slightly more than a mile above sea level, it has a dry, crisp climate, and a relaxed life-style.

Any visit to Albuquerque begins with **Old Town**. Galleries there and in other parts of town represent some of the most prestigious artists in the state. Jewelry, pottery, rugs and weavings are good buys of dependable quality.

Most activity in Old Town revolves around **San Felipe de Neri Church**, which hasn't missed a Sunday service in 278 years. In May it is the scene of *The Blessing of the Animals*, and in June the *Old Town Fiesta*. For nine days before Christmas *Las Posadas* processions circle the plaza in candlelight reverence, reminding the faithful how Mary and Joseph sought shelter for the birth of baby Jesus. On Christmas Eve the plaza glows with thousands of *luminaria*, an old Spanish custom to light the pilgrim's way to the Christ Child. Originally a small bonfire of crossed sticks called *farolitos*, today's version is a small brown paper bag with a votive candle burning inside, held steady by an inch or two of sand in the bottom.

Albuquerque Museum in Old Town is a modernistic, solar-heated adobe building with changing exhibits in art, history and science. The major permanent exhibit covers 400 years of New Mexican history. A new natural history museum across the street is scheduled to open in 1985, the first such museum built in this country in over 100 years. New Mexico is rich in paleontological material which has gone to museums in the east for years; now it will remain where it should be.

Culture and Creatures

The **Indian Pueblo Cultural Center**, a few blocks from Old Town, is owned by the 19 pueblos of New Mexico, each of which has an exhibit area showing its own unique arts and crafts. It is a good place, for example, to see the difference between a Zuni and an Acoma pot. One floor is devoted to the history of the Pueblo Indians, and there is a sales room and small restaurant. On weekends during the summer different tribes perform dances on the patio where photography is permitted at no charge.

The **Rio Grande Zoo**, to the south of Old Town, rates among the best in the country. A rain forest, reptile house, and great ape house are some visitor favorites.

Downtown Albuquerque has made a

ceding
es, the
rnational
oon
tival at
uquerque.
, Laguna
all
ssed for a
ival; and
t, hiking
he of the
ny trails in
Sandia
untains,
t of
uquerque.

successful comeback in recent years after almost succumbing to that common illness, suburbia exodium. The new civic plaza sparkles with flowers and a fountain, serving the same purpose as the plaza in any Spanish town, that of a communal gathering spot. The old buildings on Central Avenue are becoming a center for art galleries and studios, and the **KiMo Theater**, a marvel of ornate Indian art of the 1930s, was restored by the city for use as a performing arts theater.

The architecture at the **University of New Mexico** farther east along Central Avenue, shows how adaptable the basic Pueblo style is. Traditional buttressed walls with protruding *vigas* (rafters) sit happily beside modern angular lines with lots of glass. In the center of the campus the seven-story library and the president's home are outstanding examples of Pueblo architecture. Also on campus are the **Maxwell Museum of Anthropology**, the **Fine Arts Museum** and **Popejoy Hall**, which has a full schedule of symphony, light opera, Broadway shows and many other forms of live entertainment.

The **Sandia Mountains**, hard against the east side of the city, dominate Albuquerque—aesthetically, recreationally and in climate. The side that faces the city is rugged and steep; the other side is gentler, with forested slopes. Both sides offer miles of hiking trails. **Sandia Peak Tram**, the longest in North America, goes up the west (city) side in about 15 minutes.

The tram ride is a must. By day you can see mountain ranges a hundred miles away to the north, west and south. At night you can eat at a restaurant at the top while the lights of Albuquerque, Santa Fe and Los Alamos twinkle like stars below you. In winter skiers take the tram to the top of Sandia Peak Ski Area, or drive up the other side.

Mountains and Monuments just outside Albuquerque

Of special interest geologically and historically is a drive through the **Jemez Mountains** northwest of Albuquerque. The sights on this tour range from red and saffron cliffs to mountain streams, from forested slopes and alpine meadows to Indian pueblos, abandoned prehistoric pueblos and cliff dwellings.

Luminarias on Christm Eve at Old Town, Albuquerqu

It covers 200 miles (320 km) and can be done in a day, but two are better.

The first stop is **Coronado State Monument**, 20 miles (32 km) north of town where you leave Interstate 25 and turn northwest on State Highway 44. These are the ruins of a large prehistoric Indian pueblo, thought to be the spot where Coronado's expedition headquartered during the winter of 1540–1541. The Indians never re-occupied it. Of special interest is a *kiva* (underground ceremonial chamber) with rare restored murals. This is probably the only chance you will ever have to enter a *kiva*. All Pueblo still use them, but they are off-limits to visitors.

Just beyond the village of **Jemez Springs** are the ruins of a Spanish mission built around 1617, preserved as **Jemez State Monument**, with a visitors center and walking trails. The highway follows the Jemez River past the camping and picnic sites and the hiking trails of the Santa Fe National Forest.

Where the road turns east you'll see **Valle Grande**, a valley 12 miles (19 km) across, cupped in high mountains, lush with grass. A few million years ago this was the innards of a seething volcano which, layer by layer, gradually built up the entire 50-mile-long (80-km) Mountain Range. Finally the volcano collapsed, creating Valle Grande. The volcanic ash and dust from this cataclysmic event added another 1,500 feet (450 meters) to the basalt plateau. Erosion cut the plateau into deep canyons, and where layers of volcanic ash were exposed, natural caves were hollowed out by the wind. Eons later Indians used the caves for homes. **Bandelier National Monument** preserves these cliff dwellings and a large circular pueblo on the floor of the canyon, probably occupied by the Pueblo Indians before they moved into the Rio Grande Valley, where they are today.

A few miles from Bandelier is **Los Alamos**, a city built in secrecy during World War II, so scientists could work on the atomic bomb. It is now an open city with attractive residential and business areas. Inside huge laboratories scientists go quietly about their business which today includes research in cancer treatment, geothermal and other forms of energy, in addition to weaponry. The road comes quickly down the mountains to Santa Fe.

andelier
ational
onument,
ew Mexico.

The Cities that Died of Fear

This tour goes to the ruins of three Spanish missions, built 150 years before those in California, Arizona and Texas. Head east from Albuquerque on I-40 and turn south on State 14, which follows the east side of the **Manzano Mountains**. In the early 1600s the Spaniards built the missions to serve the Pueblo Indians on the eastern face of the mountains, but within 50 years raids from the fierce Plains Indians became unbearable and the peaceful Pueblo abandoned their mountain homes for the Rio Grande Valley. Together the three missions make up **Salinas National Monument**, headquartered at Mountainair, on U.S. Highway 60.

At **Quarai** and **Abo** stand high walls of red sandstone, like primitive cathedrals open to the sky. Farther south along State 14, **Gran Quivira**, built of gray limestone, stands lonely on a high, windswept hill, brooding over the plains from whence came destruction. Most of the pueblo has been excavated, as have the ruins of two large mission churches, one of which was abandoned before it was finished. There is a visitors center with picnic sites at Gran Quivira and Quarai. You can turn to Albuquerque by going west on U.S. 60 to I-25, then north to Albuquerque, about 200 miles (320 km) total.

The Turquoise Trail

This scenic road from Albuquerque to Santa Fe goes around the east side of the Sandia Mountains, through ghost towns and Hispanic villages. The Turquoise Trail is State 14, beginning at the Tijeras-Cedar Crest exit from I-40, east of Albuquerque.

At the village of San Antonio, State 44 bears left to **Sandia Peak Ski Area** and on to **Sandia Crest**, at 10,447 feet (3,166 meters) the highest part of these mountains. Many picnic areas and hiking trails are marked as the highway gradually climbs through **Cibola National Forest.** In fall aspen glades turn golden, and scrub oak lights red flares on the mountain sides. In winter cross-country skiers seek out these trails. A few miles farther is the base of the ski area where the chair lifts operate.

To continue on the Turquoise Trail, return to State 14 at San Antonio and

Caretaker a[t] Salinas National Monument, New Mexico

turn north again to **Golden**, an inhabited "ghost town." But it's a ghost of what it used to be. Nearby the first gold strike west of the Mississippi was made in 1826. Look sharply and you will see rubble foundations in the narrow canyon. At the north end of Golden, on a hill beside the road, stands **St. Francis**, a mission church built in the 1830s and restored in 1958. The church and cemetery still serve the parish. The gate is usually locked, but you can drive up to the gate to photograph it. This is one of the most photographed mission churches in New Mexico, and if you are there on one of those days of cobalt skies and whipped cream clouds you will understand why.

Eleven miles (18 km) beyond Golden is **Madrid**, once a coal mining town of thousands. It died in 1952 when diesel fuel replaced coal on the Santa Fe Railroad. Many of the cottages have been restored, but on entering the town you look down a desolate street of abandoned houses in all stages of decay, screens flapping, broken windows like empty eyes staring at the cold slag piles.

Lively ghosts inhabit Madrid now and operate the **Mine Shaft Tavern**, the **Old Coal Mine Museum**, a melodrama theater, a dress shop which uses handcrafted materials, art galleries and several stores. Bluegrass, jazz or country and western bands belt out thigh-slapping, foot-stomping music on Wednesday through Sunday evenings at the Tavern, and, during the summer on Sunday afternoons, at the baseball diamond of the abandoned school. In winter things slow down at Madrid, but the Tavern always has a fire in the stove and a spot of grog on the bar.

The turquoise mines of Cerrillos, the last town on the Turquoise Trail gave the name to this back road to Santa Fe. In the early 1600s the Spaniards found Indians already working turquoise mines here, but when the veins played out, the Indians left. Cerrillos turquoise is a rare and expensive collector's item today. Hobby-miners still find enough lead, gold, zinc or silver in the dry hills and arroyos near here to keep them in chewing tobacco. A good Indian jewelry and antique store and several smaller shops are clustered around the plaza. Movies and TV series have been filmed in this colorful little village at the end of the Turquoise Trail.

round the
ld Wood
tove, San
ose.

NATIONAL PARKS AND MONUMENTS

Salinas National Monument 97 miles southeast of Albuquerque's Old Town on I-40 and NM 14. Remarkably well-preserved pueblo ruins side by side with 17th Century Franciscan missions at Abo, Gran Quivira and Quarai. Guided group tours by prior arrangement. P.O. Box 496, Mountainair, NM 87036, 505/847-2770.

NATIONAL FORESTS

Cibola National Forest 10308 Candelaria NE, Albuquerque 87112; 505/766-2185. Includes the Sandia Mountains of Albuquerque, Apache Kid, Manzano Mountain, Withington Wildernesses. Camping, hiking, fishing, horseback riding, skiing. Ranger stations at Grants: 287-8833; Magdalena: 854-2381; Mountainair: 847-2990; Tijeras: 281-3304.

STATE PARKS

Coronado State Monument/State Park 32 miles north of Albuquerque's Old Town on I-40, I-25, NM 44. Camping, picnicking, utility hookups. The site of the prehistoric Indian pueblo of Kuaua, which has an excellent museum and interpretive trail. P.O. Box 95, Bernalillo, NM 87004; 505/867-5351.

Manzano Mountains, 13 miles northwest of Mountainair on NM 14. Hiking, camping and picnicking in the foothills of the Manzanos near the Spanish mission and Indian pueblo ruins of Abo and Quarai of Salinas National Monument.

Indian Petroglyph State Park Near Albuquerque. Rock carvings, hiking, picnic areas.

Rio Bravo Near Albuquerque. Preserves a stretch of the bosque, a cottonwood forest that flanks the Rio Grande. Nature trails along the riverbank, day-use facility including outdoor amphitheater, playgrounds and playing fields.

San Gabriel Albuquerque, near Old Town section. Day-use urban park with picnic areas, playgrounds, baseball diamond, scenic loop drive through the bosque cottonwoods.

BALLOONING

The early-morning wind patterns, the weather, wide open spaces, history, and pure chance conspired to make Albuquerque the "Hot Air Balloon Capital of the World." The city's nine-day Balloon extravaganza, held every fall, is by far the most ambitious of its kind, playing host to hundreds of the vivacious, multicolored seven-story Titans, as well as international audience bent on witnessing the spectacular sunrise mass ascensions.

Held in 1972 with 14 entries, the Inaugural Fiesta reportedly occurred when a local resident named Sid Cutter used a hot air balloon as a centerpiece for his mother's birthday party and subsequently challenged balloon enthusiasts from other corners of the world to a race. Today's festival is an extraordinary hodgepodge embracing square dancing and a chile cook-off, puppets, a symphony orchestra, a costume ball and high school bands, in addition to the standard and not-so-standard flying events. For information write Albuquerque International Balloon Fiesta, Inc., 3300 Princeton NE, Albuquerque 87107, 505/883-0932.

ATTRACTIONS

Albuquerque Museum, 2000 Mountain Road NW. Extensive collection of area art, history and science dating from 1800s. Free. Tuesday through Friday 10 a.m. to 5 p.m., Saturday and Sunday 1 to 5 p.m. 766-7392.

Bien Mur Indian Market Center, Tramway Road and I-25. A unique Indian store on Sandia Pueblo featuring only authentic Indian made wares. 821-5400.

Cochiti Lake Recreation Center, north on I-25. Fishing and seasonal boating. 242-8302.

Ernie Pyler Memorial Branch Library 900 Girard SW near U. of New Mexico Museums. The former home of the famed war correspondent, complete with memorabilia. Free. 12:30 to 5:30, Tuesday to Thursday; 9 to 5:30 Friday and Saturday.

Indian Pueblo Cultural Center Just east of historic Old Town. Indian-owned and operated museum, restaurant and arts and crafts center. Monday through Saturday, 9 to 5. Sunday, 12 noon to 5

Jemez Springs Monument, NM 4 into the Jemez Mountains. Ruins of a 13th Century Indian pueblo and early 16th Century Franciscan mission. The hot springs at Soda Dam are popular, a bit off the road and uphill. Allow plenty of time for this drive and check on snow conditions.

Los Alamos Driving in and out of the Atomic City can be confusing. But even if you are not interested in atomic energy past and future, the surrounding area is worth the trip in itself for its justly praised natural beauty.

Bradbury Science Hall On Diamond Drive. Exhibits include WWII history as well as energy, weapons and life science research of Los Alamos National Laboratory. Open 9 to 5. Tuesday to Friday, 1 to 5, Saturday to Monday, 505/667-4444.

Los Alamos Historical Museum Social and natural history. Inquire about walking tours of Ice House Area and Bathtub Row, where prominent nuclear scientists lived. 662-6272.

Los Alamos National Laboratory Does research on nuclear power, laser technology, geothermal energy, cancer therapy. Exhibits open to the public.

Museum of National History Old Town area. Scheduled to open 1984.

National Atomic Museum Kirtland Air Force Base East. Enter by the Wyoming Boulevard gate. Most complete nuclear weapons collection and exhibits on nuclear science, medicine and power. Free. 9 to 5 daily. 844-8443.

Old Town Off Rio Grande Boulevard, NW. Historic plaza. San Felipe de Neri Mission, built 1706. The original Albuquerque with numerous shops, galleries and gift shops; three restaurants; Albuquerque Museum.

Rio Grande Nature Center On the east bank of the Rio Grande at Candeleria Road. History, ecology and geology of the Rio Grande Valley. Open 9 to 5 daily. 377-7240.

Rio Grande Zoological Park, 903 10th St., SW. New Mexico's largest zoo, lush tropical forest, aviary, reptile house. Open daily 10 to 5. 843-7413.

Sandia Peak Crest I-40 to NM North. The mountains offer a scenic drive to the crest with a lookout point and restaurant. 243-0605.

Sandia Peak Tramway I-25 north to Tramway Exit, Tramway East road to the longest aerial tramway in North America. 2.7-mile ascent. Dining at base and at the top. Year-round. Call for schedule. 298-8518.

HORSE RACING

New Mexico State Fair Albuquerque. Held mid through late September, features horse racing every afternoon for more than two weeks, with extensive horse shows in various categories and other attractions. For information and tickets write New Mexico State Fair, P.O. Box 8546, Albuquerque 87198 or call 265-1791.

The Downs at Albuquerque Meet lasts January-April in the glass-enclosed track at The State Fair Grounds. Thoroughbreds and some Quarterhorses.

CAMPGROUNDS

In New Mexico, public/private campgrounds are located in or near all National Forests/parks, monuments/recreation, wildlife areas; in some, near most state parks/monuments; near all communities with chambers of commerce. Lists of private campgrounds are available at state welcome centers in Anthony (24 miles south of Las Cruces), Carlsbad, Gallup, Glendrio (41 miles east of Tucumcari), Hobbs, La Bajada (17 miles southwest of Santa Fe), Lordsburg and Raton.

Also, check local libraries for privately published campground directories. For regulatory information, on RVs and otherwise, contact the **New Mexico Highway Department**, 1120 Cerrillos Road, Santa Fe 87503; 983-0452.

WINTER SPORTS

New Mexico is an all-around center for winter sports, offering not only variety, but downhill challenges and ample powder as well as smaller, family-oriented resorts. The state has 14 downhill areas and devotes some energy to marketing and augmenting them. Direct-Dial NM Ski Report is available 24 hours a day, seven days a week from Thanksgiving through March 31 with tape-recorded ski conditions which are updated twice a week. Call 505/984-0606. In-state road conditions report available toll-free, 800/432-4269. In-state regional reports available, call information for phone numbers. Angel Fire, Eagle Creek, Santa Fe, Sierra Blanca, Pajarito and Taos put out their own reports.

SHOPPING

The Plaza in Old Town is one of the best in the state, with several dozen shops carrying the work of top New Mexico artisans. The R.C. Gorman studio and the Gallerie del Sol, which hang the work of four outstanding Southwestern artists, are among the better galleries in the city.

EVENTS

Old Town Fiesta Held in June. Sandia Pueblo San Antonio Feast Day, June 13. Annual corn dance. 867-2876.

Albuquerque Arts & Crafts Fair Late June. Annual show is currently the largest in New Mexico with more than 200 artisans. State Fairgrounds, 884-9043.

New Mexico Arts and Crafts Fair Late June. State Fairgrounds.

Annual Feria Artesana Mid to late August. A celebration of more than 400 years of Hispanic heritage. Arts and crafts, tradi-

tional and modern; continuous entertainment; folk Mass highlight of the fair. Tiguex Park in Old Town. 243-3696.

Annual Southwest Arts and Crafts Festival Early November. Juried show and competition. 243-3696.

Annual Indian National Finals Rodeo Mid to late November. American Indian rodeo riders from the U.S. and Canada compete for $80,000 in prize money and the title of World Champion Indian Cowboy. Indian National Finals Rodeo, Inc., P.O. Box 1725, Albuquerque, 87103.

Las Posadas In Old Town. For nine days before Christmas, processions circle the plaza in candle-lit reverence, reminding the faithful how Mary and Joseph sought shelter for the birth of Jesus.

Luminaria Tours, December 24. Albuquerque's Christmas lights are famous. 766-7972.

Albuquerque Gymnastics Invitational Early January. Champion athletes from the United States, Russia, Romania, Japan, France, Germany and other countries compete and demonstrate their magnificent strength and grace. University of New Mexico Arena.

Blessing of the Animals, May. In Old Town, near San Felipe de Neri Church.

ENTERTAINMENT

New Mexico Symphony Orchestra Performs from January through June at Popejoy Hall, University of New Mexico, with well-known guest artists. All performances 8:15 p.m. Tickets, information: 843-7657.

Also: the **Albuquerque Opera Theater**, the **Albuquerque Civic Light Opera**, the **Albuquerque Little Theater**, the **Albuquerque Ballet**, the **Chamber Orchestra of Albuquerque**; various visiting artists. For further information, the Albuquerque Visitors and Convention Bureau publishes a bi-monthly calendar of events.

TIMELESS SANTA FE

Santa Fe is "in" now, but fads come and go, and if it becomes too faddish, the faddists will tire of it and leave, and *voila!* There's old Santa Fe, timeless and mellow, calmly waiting.

Santa Fe was founded in 1610, capital of the Spanish province of New Mexico. The governor's residence and official buildings were on the north side of the plaza. They are the heart of the state's museum system today. In the early days there was much internal bickering between secular and civic officials, with the Indians caught in the middle. In 1680 the Indians rebelled against heavy-handed missionaries and taxes, gleefully burned all records, books and churches, smashed bells and religious accoutrements, and tortured and killed every Spaniard who didn't get away. Governor Diego de Vargas reconquered the province in 1692 without firing a shot, but the Spaniards had learned an important lesson. No longer did they forbid the Indians to practice their ancient ceremonies, so long as they went to Mass first.

Santa Fe continued to be the capital during the Mexican period (1821–1846) and after Americans took over the territory. It has seen people of many nationalities and religious and political persuasions come and go, and will see more. Today Santa Fe has a population of about 50,000. During the winter it swells with politicians and skiers; during the summer it explodes with vacationers. Narrow and crooked old burro trails have been paved to become streets, and have a rough time handling traffic, so you're better off walking the downtown areas. You'll get the feel of Santa Fe better, anyway.

The city sits at 7,000 feet (2,100 meters) at the base of the *Sangre de Cristo* (Blood of Christ) Mountains, the southernmost part of the Rockies. The sun is bright and warm, the air cool. If you get warm walking, find a shady spot and sit down. Clothes don't stick because the air is dry and crisp. Blankets feel good at night, and never go out without a light wrap.

The Palace of the Governors extends the length of the north side of the plaza. Indians spread their jewelry and pottery on blankets along the portal (covered walkway). Exhibits in the museum relate to the history of New Mexico's Indian, Spanish, Mexican and Territorial periods. In one area the original walls are exposed under glass, showing adobe almost 400 years old.

Museums Galore

Across the street to the west is the **Museum of Fine Arts**. Built in 1917, this branch of the state museum is a classic example of pueblo architecture. The permanent collection has works by names that have made art synonymous with New Mexico for the past 60 years. Other exhibits are changed frequently, as a showcase for outstanding New Mexico artists—but playing no favorites in periods, styles or media.

On piñon-dotted Museum Hill at the southeast edge of town, too far to walk, is a complex of three eminently worthwhile museums. The **Museum of International Folk Art**, a state museum, contains exhibits of religious and other folk art, highlighted by the **Girard Exhibit**. Alexander Girard, a world-renowned architect who has lived in

Preceding pages, San Jose de Gracia Church boasts the best Pueblo architecture in the state. Left, Doorway, Santa Fe. Right, Santa Fe, 1880s.

Santa Fe for about 30 years, gave the state his collection of 120,000 pieces of folk art from around the world, which promptly added a new wing to house it. Three years in preparation, the Girard Exhibit must not be missed.

Also on Museum Hill is the **Wheelwright Museum**, a privately endowed museum which was once devoted exclusively to Navajo ceremonial art but now includes Indian culture and art from other tribes as well. The state-owned **Museum of Anthropology** is the third museum here, and it has excellent displays of pottery, kachinas and other Indian artifacts.

A Cathedral and a Chapel, in Memory of a Bishop

Back downtown, the **Cathedral of St. Francis of Assisi**, a block east of the plaza, stands in Romanesque plainness, a monument to Jean Baptiste Lamy, Archbishop of Santa Fe. Willa Cather's novel, *Death Comes for the Archbishop*, immortalizes Lamy's work in the Southwest. Five minutes north of town on Bishop Lodge Road is the **Bishop's Lodge**, one of Santa Fe's nicest resorts.

Here Bishop Lamy's private chapel is open to the public. The lodge closes in winter.

Our Lady of Light Chapel, now on the property of the Inn at Loretto, one of the bigger and better downtown hotels, houses the **Miraculous Staircase**, constructed without nails or visible support. Legend says an itinerant carpenter appeared at the door of the convent of the Sisters of Loretto in 1878 in answer to a novena, and built the circular, freestanding stairway. The carpenter disappeared, but the sisters believed he was St. Joseph.

"The Oldest Church" and "The Oldest House" in America

Mission San Miguel, on Old Santa Fe Trail, two blocks east of the plaza, is sometimes called "the oldest church in America." It isn't, but it stands over the foundations of one built around 1636 and burned during the rebellion of 1680. It has been rebuilt and remodeled five times since then. Across the street is **The Oldest House in America**, housing a gift and souvenir shop. There are many Pueblo houses that are older, but

it nevertheless serves as a good example of ancient construction.

El Cristo Rey Church, at the east end of Canyon Road, was built in 1940 and holds the most remarkable piece of Spanish colonial art in the United States: a huge stone altarpiece—*reredos*—carved with many saints and intricate designs. Forty feet wide, 18 feet high (12 meters by five) and weighing many tons (thousands of kilos), the piece was originally made in 1760 for an older church on the plaza. It was kept in storage for over 200 years before this church, large enough to house it, was built.

A Pre-War Hotel

La Fonda Hotel on the plaza is the 'best place for people-watching in town. Sit in the lobby a while and you'll see movie stars, politicians, Indians, artists, poets and maybe your next door neighbor. There has always been some kind of a hostelry here at the end of the Santa Fe Trail. The present one, dating back to well before World War II, is built like a multistoried Indian pueblo with protruding *vigas*, smooth, flowing lines, flagstone floors, interior patios, colored glass, carved corbels and furniture. The lounge is the kind of place where you sit in comfortable dimness, listen to classical guitar, sip margaritas, and crunch nachos. When the guy at the next table finishes his drink, he takes his glass and sets it on the bar like any good New Mexican cowboy.

There are too many shops and galleries in Santa Fe to mention them all, but two general areas are outstanding: **the plaza** and **Canyon Road**. In the block east of the plaza, **Sena** and **Prince plazas** open off Palace Avenue and have some of the most interesting shops in Santa Fe. One shop in particular, called Rare Things, at the end of the block, halfway up the alley, is a treasure trove for collectors of Indian and Spanish art. Several of Santa Fe's best art galleries can be found on Washington and San Francisco streets, either facing the plaza or within one block of it.

Canyon Road, once a crooked trail for wood-hauling where artists could rent adobe houses for $10 a month, is now Santa Fe's other great shopping area. Those huts have been converted to pricey condominiums or house some of

The Harves Procession Las Golond nas heralds gathering c Hispanics.

the finest shops, galleries and restaurants in Santa Fe.

Season Skiing

Outdoor recreation is important in Santa Fe. The season at **Santa Fe Ski Basin** is one of the best in the state. Only 16 miles (26 km) from downtown, it gets 160 inches (406 cm) of powder snow a year, and the runs are mostly expert to intermediate. A day lodge and cafeteria are located at the base, but overnight lodging is not available. The road to the ski basin, State Highway 475, passes through **Hyde Park State Park** in **Santa Fe National Forest**, a favorite place for hiking and picnicking in the summer and admiring beauteous colors in the fall.

Music is as much a part of the ambience of Santa Fe as art is. In 25 years, the **Santa Fe Opera** has built a world-wide reputation for excellence. The season runs through July and August, and performances are almost always sold out. Those who haven't made reservations ahead of time might try at the gate for standing room. The Opera house is in the hills north of town, and with the sides and part of the roof open to the stars, the setting becomes part of the performances.

El Rancho de las Golondrinas (Ranch of the Swallows), 10 miles (16 km) south of town, is a reconstructed Spanish colonial village, once a stopping place on El Camino Real. It is open on the first Sunday of each month from mid-April through October. There is a moderate admission fee. Fiestas are held on the first weekends in May and October, with demonstrations in colonial folk arts and activities. The village of **La Cienega** grew up around the hacienda.

The High Road To Taos

The High Road to Taos, State 76, winds through mountain villages whose names roll like poetry from the tongue—*Chimayo*, *Truchas*, *Las Trampas*, *Penasco*. This is colonial New Mexico. During the 1700s a blanket of isolation covered New Mexico. Gone were the swashbuckling days of the conquistadors. Small villages away from the capital lived unto themselves, customs and beliefs becoming so deeply

ft, El ntuario in nimayo, ew Mexico; d right, the ar inside an Jose de acia.

ingrained that they linger today, a relic of New Mexico 300 years ago.

From Santa Fe go north on U.S. Highway 84/285 to **Santa Cruz** and then onto State 76. **Holy Cross Church** in Santa Cruz was built in the 1740s, one of the largest of the old mission churches. Its buttressed walls are three feet thick and served as a shelter for the villagers many times when Plains Indians came through the mountains to steal crops, women and children.

El Santuario in **Chimayo** is called the Lourdes of America. During Holy Week (the week before Easter) pilgrims from miles around drive, walk and even crawl toward it. The altar screen and Stations of the Cross are fine examples of religious folk art. To the left of the altar a room is hung with crutches, braces, photographs, poems and letters from the devout. In an adjoining room about 10 feet square is a hole in the dirt floor where pilgrims get a pinch of the holy mud of Chimayo.

Several families of Chimayo weavers have achieved fame for their tightly woven, brightly colored blankets. The **Chimayo Weavers Showroom** is open to the public.

Village with a View

The village of **Truchas** sits high on a timbered plateau beneath the snow-covered Truchas Peaks. On the main street are a *morada*, a church of the Penitente sect, and a plastic-roofed Pentecostal church. Truchas is not known for its hospitality, but the setting is superb.

A few miles farther is **Las Trampas**, best known for its church, which architects claim is the best example of Pueblo architecture in the state. The village was founded in 1760 to act as a buffer for Santa Cruz and Santa Fe against marauding Comanches. The church, **San Jose de Gracia**, is on the State and National Historic registers. Find the kindly neighbor who keeps the key, and he will let you inside.

At **Peñasco**, the next village, the route divides. Jogging right six miles (10 km) to State 3, the traveller drives through the mountains into Taos. Or turning left onto State 75, he reaches the intersection with State 68, the main road to Taos. Those who choose the second route should stop at the Picurís pueblo for a visit.

Snowshoe at Sandia Peak Ski Area, where many skier take to in winter.

Pecos National Monument

Earliest Spanish records mention a large Indian pueblo in the mountains east of where Santa Fe is today. Lying in a high green valley, watered by the Pecos River, the pueblo consisted of two great communal dwellings, each four stories high, with a thousand rooms. There were five separate plazas and 16 *kivas*, attesting to the size and importance of the pueblo. The Spaniards built a large mission church there around 1617 to 1620. The thick walls were red sandstone, carefully mortared and solidly buttressed, the corbels handsomely carved. The Pecos Indians took an active part in the revolt of 1680, and burned the church. Pecos was resettled after the reconquest, and, in the 1700s, a smaller adobe church was built inside the foundations of the earlier one, but Pecos was never an important pueblo again. In 1838 about two dozen survivors walked away from the once great pueblo and went west to live with the Jemez Indians, the only other tribe that spoke their language. The ruins of both churches and the unexcavated pueblo are preserved at **Pecos National Monument**.

The drive to Pecos heading east from Santa Fe on Interstate 25 follows the route of the old Santa Fe Trail. State 63 goes north from the monument for 20 miles (32 km) where it deadends at Cowles, a summer home area and trail head for horse- and backpacking trips into Santa Fe National Forest and Pecos Wilderness.

You can continue east on I-25 past the Pecos turn-off for another 15 miles (24 km) to State 3 which goes to several villages as pastoral and quiet as they were a hundred years ago. At San Miguel, three miles (five km) south of I-25, you can still see where the Santa Fe Trail forded the Pecos River. During the Mexican Period, 1821-1846, San Miguel was the port of entry into New Mexico, where all the wagon trains had to stop and pay duty on the goods they brought in.

Villanueva State Park, nine miles (14 km) south of San Miguel has picnic and camping facilities on the Pecos River. The drive down this narrow valley where the stream is bordered with small fields and villages is the heart of rural Hispanic New Mexico.

sons roam
eadows of
ew Mexico.

NATIONAL PARKS AND MONUMENTS

Bandelier National Monument
Outside of Los Alamos. Popular site with cliff dwellings, the ruins of a 250-room pre-Columbian pueblo and extensive back country trails, plus summer moonlight tours and weekend Indian arts and crafts demonstrations. Camping at RV sites from April through September. Los Alamos, NM 87544, 505/672-3861.

Pecos National Monument Small Santa Fe Trail landmark two miles south of Pecos on NM 63. Contains the ruins of a 660-room pre-Columbian pueblo and two early Franciscan missions. On summer weekends, Indian artisans bake and sell bread and make pottery in outdoor ovens. Drawer 11, Pecos, NM 87552. 757-6414.

NATIONAL FORESTS

Carson National Forest Broken into several parts, one of which surrounds Taos; Pecos, Cruces Basin, Latir Peak, Wheeler Peak Wildernesses; boasts elevations up to 13,000 feet, skiing, riding, water sports, camping, fishing, seven ranger stations at Blanco: 325-0508; Canjilon: 684-2489; El Rito: 581-4555; Penasco: 587-2255; Taos: 758-2911; Tres Piedras: 758-3243; Questa: 586-0520. Write Forest Service Building, Taos 87571; 758-2238.

Santa Fe National Forest Pinon Building, Santa Fe 87501; 988-6940. Surrounds Santa Fe, Los Alamos, encompasses Bandelier National Monument, Jemez, ski areas, cliff dwellings and more: offers picnicking, hiking, camping, fishing. Ranger stations at Coyote: 638-5526; Cuba: 289-3265; Espanola: 753-7331; Jemez Springs: 829-3535; Las Vegas: 425-3534; Los Alamos: 667-5120; Pecos: 757-6121; Tesuque at 1155 Siler Road, Santa Fe 87501. 988-6938.

STATE PARKS

Hyde Memorial Northeast of Santa Fe on NM 475, near the Santa Fe Ski Basin. Used as base camp for trips into the Santa Fe National Forest. Skating pond, sledding area, camping, utility hookups, lodge.

Santa Fe River Urban park in Santa Fe. Tree-lined walkways and shaded picnic benches flank the Santa Fe River.

ATTRACTIONS

Armory for the Arts 1050 Old Pecos Trail. Mon. – Fri. 9–5, Sat., Sun. 12–5. Art exhibits, in the same building as Santa Fe Festival Theater. 988-1886.

Chapel of Our Lady of Light (Loretto Chapel), 200 block of Old Santa Fe Trail, on Inn of Loretto grounds. Lovely Gothic chapel houses the "miraculous staircase" built by a mysterious carpenter who is supposed to be St. Joseph. 9–5 daily. 982-3376.

Chimayo An old Spanish village on the high road to Taos, 6 miles east on NM 76, creates an abrupt change of scenery from the modern car strip to the bucolic. El Santuario de Chimayo, built in 1816 above a now-dry spring said to have miraculous healing powers, is known as the "Lourdes of America." Free, open 8 to 5 every day.

Christo Rey Church Canyon Road at Cristo Rey, daily 8–6, mass Sun. at 8, 10, 12 noon. Beautiful thick-walled adobe with world-famous handcarved stone. 983-8528.

El Rancho de las Golondrinas At La Cienega, south of Santa Fe, west of I-25, open summers. Restored old Spanish village and colonial estate. Tours Wed. and Sat. 10 a.m. by reservation; open house first Sunday of the month, 10–4. 471-2261.

Jemez Springs Monument NM 4 in the Jemez Mountains. Ruins of a 13th-century Indian pueblo and early 16th-century Franciscan Mission. The hot springs at Soda Dam are popular, albeit a bit off the road and uphill. Allow plenty of time for this drive and check on snow conditions. Monument open Thurs. – Mon., 9–5.

Museum of New Mexico's (Three branches in Santa Fe): **Museum of Fine Arts** Just off the Plaza at the corner of E. Palace and Lincoln. Prominent New Mexico artists, Western painting, sculpture photography. Daily, 9 to 4:45. 982-6400.
Palace of the Governors On the Plaza. The oldest Anglo public building in the States, historic seat of Spanish government. Archaeological and historic exhibits. 10 to 4:45. Closed Mondays in winter. 827-6483.
Museum of International Folk Art 704 Camino Lejo. Folk art from all over the world, with the Girard Foundation collection. The largest of its kind anywhere. 827-8350.

Ortega's Weavers. Chimayo, a sixth-generation family of famed weavers, still create blankets, coats, serapes. Self-guided tours. 9 to 4, Monday through Saturday.

St. Francis Cathedral One block east of the plaza on San Francisco St. Built by Archbishop Jean Lamy, who established the diocese of New Mexico. 6 a.m.-6:30 p.m., daily mass at 5:30 p.m. 982-5619.

San Miguel Mission 401 Old Santa Fe Trail, three blocks from the plaza. Oldest mission church in the U.S. 9 to 11:30 and 1 to 4:30 daily, Sun. mass 5 p.m. 983-3974.

Santuario de Nuestra Senora de Guadalupe Corner Guadalupe and Agua Fria. Former mission now a gallery of contemporary Indo-Hispanic art in traditional styles. Mon. – Sat., 10 to 4, Sun 1 to 4. 988-2027.

State Capitol Building Old Santa Fe Trail and Paseo de Peralta. Tours Mon. – Sat. 9 to 12 and 1 to 5. 827-4011.

Valle Grande 18 miles southwest on NM 4. A giant 176-square-mile volcanic caldera, largest in the world. Created by a number of volcanoes that collapsed on one another. Buffalo Tours provides a tour of Valle Grande 505/662-3965.

Wheelwright Museum of the American Indian 704 Camino Lejo. Indian arts and crafts

Mon. – Sat. 11 to 5, Sun. 1 to 5. 982-4636.

Rio Grande: The Rio Grande's lower gorge and Rio Grande Gorge State Park offer full-day and half-day river rides. Please check for river conditions, as the river depends on snow runoff. In high snow years, trips should be available through the greater part of September, as are trips on the nearby River Chama, full day or overnight through mesa country. The Taos "Box," runs either a full day or overnight. The following list of firms is approved by the Bureau of Land Mangement:

Artemis Wilderness Tours, Box 1178, Taos, NM 87571; 505/-758-9524 or 758-1774.
Far Flung Adventures, Box 31, Terligua, TX 79852, 915/371-2489 or 505/758-2628. NM 87529; 758-2628. Los Rios, Learning Services, PO Box 2840, Santa Fe 87501 505-982-3126. Los Rios, PO Box 398, Red River 87555; 754-6630.
New Wave Rafting, Route 5. Box 302A, Santa Fe 87501; 455-2633 or 988-6565.
Rio Grande Rapid Transit, Box A, Pilar, NM 87571; 505/758-9700. Toll free in New Mexico 800/222-7238, outside NM 800/545-4020. Or 505/758-9700.
Rocky Mountain Tours, Inc. (handles reservations for Southwest Wilderness Center and Sierra Outfitters & Guides), 102 W. San Francisco, Suite 5, Santa Fe 87501; 984-1684 in-state, toll-free elsewhere, 800/457-9223.
Santa Fe Mountain Center, Route 4, Box 34C, Santa Fe 87501; 983-6158.
Santa Fe Rafting, 520 Franklin St., Santa Fe 87501 505/988-4914.
Sierra Outfitters and Guides, Box 2756, Taos, NM 87571; 505/758-9556 (reservations), 758-1247 (office). Reservations available through Rocky Mountain Tours, see above.

HORSE RACING

The Downs at Santa Fe 5 miles southwest of Santa Fe on I-25; first weekend in May through Labor Day weekend. Route 14, Box 199-RT, Santa Fe 87505. 505/471-3311. General admission $2.00. Round trip bus service from Albuquerque direct to The Downs available each day from the Sheraton Old Town and Hilton Inn hotels. For reservations, call Sanchez Southwest Coaches, Ltd., 345-7821. Round trip taxi available from Santa Fe's Hilton Inn. Inn at Loretto, La Posada, Ramada Inn and Plaza Ore House. For pick-up elsewhere call Capitol City Cab. They run London taxis as well as the local variety, at 982-9990.

EVENTS

Annual Rodeo de Santa Fe Early July. Parade, entertainment. 983-7317.

Spanish Market End of July. More than 30 artisans display such uniquely New Mexican crafts as colcha embroidery, along with wooden bultos, retablos, furniture and filigree jewelry under the portal of the Palace of the Governors. 983-7317.

Annual Indian Market Mid to late August. More than 500 artisans, juried competition for $20,000 in prize money. Indian dances under the portal of the Palace of the Governors, arts and crafts on the plaza. 983-5220.

Fiesta de Santa Fe Early to mid-September. Oldest community celebration of its kind in the country. Commemorates the 1692–93 resettlement of New Mexico by General Don Diego de Vargas. Santa Fe Convention & Visitors Bureau, 983-7317.

Santa Fe Annual Harvest Festival Early October. Held at El Rancho de las Golondrinas, an authentic Spanish colonial village and living museum. Ideal for sketching and photography. 471-2261.

Santa Fe Annual Festival of the Arts Late October. More than 150 exhibitors, juried competition in fine arts, contemporary crafts photography. 982-4923.

Santa Fe Spring Festival Late April through early May. The annual El Rancho de las Golondrinas Spring Festival features traditional Spanish colonial crafts, food, entertainment, old-fashioned farming demonstrations. 471-2661.

Pilar White Water Races Early May. Annual Rio Grande event—75 canoe-kayak-raft experts challenge 14 miles of fury below Pilar. James Fretwell, 758 47th St., Los Alamos, NM 87544.

ENTERTAINMENT

Santa Fe Bach Festival Early February. An annual event spearheaded by the Orchestra of Santa Fe. P.O. Box 2091, Santa Fe 87501. 988-4640.

Santa Fe Festival Theater July and August. Most performances Thursday through Saturday 8 p.m., Sunday matinees 2 p.m. Armory for the Arts, 1050 Old Pecos Trail. 983-9400.

Santa Fe Film Festival Late April. An annual event, with appearances and discussions with actors, writers and directors. 827-2889.

Santa Fe Chamber Music Festival Mid-July through mid-August. Internationally acclaimed musicians. St. Francis Auditorium and Santuario Guadalupe. 983-2075.

Santa Fe Opera The city's summer focus, the opera performs throughout July and August. For information write P.O. Box 2408, Santa Fe 87501. 982-3851.

ACCOMMODATIONS

Bishop's Lodge P.O. Box 2367, Santa Fe 87504. 983-6377. Situated at the head of the Tesuque Valley, five minutes north of Santa Fe on Bishop's Lodge Road, NM 22.

La Posada de Santa Fe 330 E. Palace Avenue, 87501. 983-6351. Old-time Southwestern charm with modern comforts. Rooms with fireplaces.

Rancho Encantado Rte. 4, Box 57 C, Santa Fe 87501. 982-3537. A beautiful mountain spot 8 miles north of Santa Fe at Tesuque. Riding, hiking, cookouts, escorted trail rides. Lodging in casitas; fine dining. Open March through January.

Sunrise Springs Inn Box 203, Rural Rte 14, La Cienega, Santa Fe 87501. 471-3600 Astrology, massage, alpha chambers.

TAOS AND ITS MAGIC

Taos glows with a physical radiance, white sunlight and lavender shadows, blue distance and golden earth. In 1912 the quality of this light drew eight young artists from the East who formed the Taos Society of Artists, the beginning of a legacy. Whether the spell lies in the physical beauty, the legends or the history, few people visit Taos without feeling its magic.

Taos was settled by the Spaniards in the early 1600s, close to Taos Indian Pueblo. Taos plaza has seen a lot of history go by—Indians, Spanish conquistadors, mountain men and merchants. The American flag flies 24 hours a day in the plaza, a special honor commemorating the bravery of Kit Carson and other frontiersmen during the Civil War. When Confederate sympathizers tried to replace the American flag with the Confederate flag, Carson and friends nailed the stars and stripes to the tallest pine tree they could find, and stood armed guard day and night until the Confederates had been driven back to Texas.

Taos has more than 80 art galleries, its major industry, and you will be missing the meaning of Taos if you don't explore them. Walk up **Ledoux Street**, a couple of blocks west of the plaza. Mellow adobe walls crowd the winding street, and turquoise-colored gates stand ajar, inviting you in.

Legacy of a Murdered Governor

Governor Bent Museum preserves the historic home where the first American governor of New Mexico was murdered in 1847, a few months after the American occupation. Kit Carson, famous scout and soldier, lived in Taos with his Spanish wife during his later years, and their house is now the **Kit Carson Home and Museum**. The cemetery where he and other Taos personalities are buried is part of **Kit Carson State Park** off the main street of Taos.

During the 1920s, the flamboyant Mabel Dodge Luhan brought many artists, including D. H. Lawrence, to Taos. She married a Taos Indian and built a rambling adobe home (now a bed-and-breakfast inn) on the edge of the reservation where she entertained talented and famous people in great style. She gave the Lawrences a ranch in the Sangre de Cristo Mountains about 15 miles (24 km) north of town. After his death in Europe Lawrence's wife brought his ashes back and built a shrine for him on the ranch, which she willed to the University of New Mexico. Visitors may visit the **D. H. Lawrence Shrine**, see the adobe house where he lived, and admire the view which influenced him so much.

The **Church at Ranchos de Taos** (1722) on the south edge of town, though not one of the oldest in New Mexico is probably the best-known and most-photographed because of its classic pueblo style architecture. Georgia O'Keeffe and other artists have captured the flowing lines that seem to be part of the earth.

The **Rio Grande** river runs a few miles west of Taos through a deep gorge. Along its first 50 miles (80 km) south of the Colorado border is the first officially designated Wilderness River Area in the nation. The Rio Grande Gorge is accessible by hiking down from the rim of the steep volcanic mesas which con-

ceding
ges,
man
nts
umn of the
ngre de
stos. Left,
Grande
rge,
ally known
"The
x." Right,
le deer
ar Raton is
camera-
.

fine it. In May and June white water rafters find this part of the Rio Grande a real challenge with some rapids classed Grade VI, the most suicidal kind of white water. Nine miles (14 km) west of Taos on U.S. Highway 64 a dramatic bridge spans the green and white ribbon flowing between black basaltic walls 650 feet (200 meters) below. South of town at **Pilar** a road leads down to the river to **Rio Grande State Park** with camping and picnic shelters—a favorite spot for trout fishermen.

Taos Ski Valley, 20 miles (32 km) northeast of town, is the best known of New Mexico's 12 ski areas. The runs are on the slopes of Wheeler Peak, over 13,000 feet (4,000 meters) high, and the ski area has dozens of powder bowls, glades and chutes. The season usually lasts from at least early November into April. Ernie Blake, a Swiss transplant known as The Godfather of the Slopes, has developed Taos Ski Valley over many years, earning a reputation for high standards. Miles of hiking trails lead from the ski valley into the national forests and wilderness areas fringing Taos.

Sipapu Ski Area is 25 miles (40 km)

southeast of Taos, its gentle slopes popular with young families and beginners. Twenty-six miles (42 km) east of Taos, on the other side of the mountains is **Angel Fire**, a new year-round resort. The ski runs are long and challenging, and facilities include condos, lodges, restaurants and a private airport. The drive from Taos over **Palo Flechado Pass**, U.S. 64, is a beauty, especially in the fall.

Trips out of Taos

Red River, a town 34 miles (55 km) north of Taos, affords two developed ski areas. One has expert and intermediate runs, the other mostly beginner and intermediate runs. Other winter sports, including snowmobiling and cross-country skiing, are popular at Red River, and all equipment can be rented. Summer guests can fish, hike, camp and visit ghost towns. Reservations are almost always necessary for lodging, and the Chamber of Commerce acts as a central reservations system. The merchants operate a daily shuttle bus, year-round, from the airport in Albuquerque.

The west end of the church at Ranchos de Taos (Saint Francis Assisi Mission).

Chama is the New Mexico terminal for the **Cumbres & Toltec Scenic Railroad** which runs to Antonito, Colorado, and is about 60 miles (95 km) west of Taos on U.S. 64. The sturdy little train has authentically restored old cars that chugged over this route carrying ore and timber a hundred years ago. The ride takes you through alpine meadows, over passes and deep gorges, and across sagebrush flats. The route zigzags across the state line, and is jointly owned and operated by both states. Reservations may be made at and the trip taken from either terminal. It is a long day's trip, returning by bus to the point of departure. Or a half trip may be taken from either terminal, returning by train. In winter Cumbres Pass is buried under many feet of snow, so the train only runs from mid-June into October. The New Mexico portion is very scenic.

Chama lies in the Sangre de Cristo Mountains at an elevation of around 7,680 feet (2,340 meters). Fishing is good in the Chama River, as it is at two lakes south of town, El Vado and Heron Lakes. Elk and deer hunting parties are headquartered here, and snowmobiling is popular in winter.

Alamosa is in the San Luis Valley of Colorado, a productive farmland 50 miles (80 km) wide, between the San Juan Mountain to the west and the Sangre de Cristos to the east. **Great Sand Dunes National Monument** lies 35 miles (56 km) northeast of Alamosa against the base of the Sangre de Cristos like piles of soft brown velvet. Prevailing winds blow across the valley from the west, picking up particles of sand and dust, and dropping them when they reach the solid barrier of the mountains. The dunes are over 700 feet (215 meters) high and 10 miles (16 km) long. A visitors center has exhibits describing the plants and animals that have adapted to the dunes, as well as the human history of the area. There are no trails on the dunes, and you may walk where you please. When storms sweep down from the northeast, winds reverse the pattern of ridges, creating a constantly shifting pattern.

Santa Fe Trail Country

From 1821 on, the Santa Fe Trail was the channel of commerce and communication between the Spanish Rio

ellow
dobe
ansions at
aos Indian
ueblo.

Grande and the United States. Because of the social and business relationships established, commerce made victory easy when the United States took the Southwest in the War with Mexico (1846–1848). Forts were established to protect settlers, pioneers and miners as they acted out "manifest destiny."

The main branch of the Trail came across southeast Colorado into New Mexico, over Raton Pass, through Cimarron, Las Vegas, and around the southern end of the Rocky Mountains to Santa Fe. Strangers sometimes doubt it, but you can still see parts of the Santa Fe Trail in northeastern New Mexico. Wherever the ground has never been plowed, as in the areas north of Las Vegas and Fort Union, the grass-grown ruts are plainly visible from the train or from Interstate 25 in Apache Canyon.

Bent's Fort, eight miles (13 km) east of La Junta in Colorado on U.S. 350 was built by the four Bent brothers in 1833 and became one of the most famous forts and trading posts in the West. It has been authentically reconstructed and is a National Historic Landmark, open year-round except for Christmas and Thanksgiving. To walk within the thick adobe walls, climb ladders to the roof, see the goods in the company store, examine the wooden contraption where trappers stretched their beaver pelts, and talk with costumed Park Service employees, is an experience in American history.

Bent's Fort was the meeting place for fur trappers from all over the Rockies, the most famous of whom was scout Kit Carson. Military and government surveying parties, wagon freighters and stagecoaches stopped for supplies, food and rest. Indians came to trade buffalo hides and furs for food and tobacco. Charles Bent became the first American governor of New Mexico Territory, which at that time included southern Colorado. He was murdered in Taos in 1847.

Another stopping place on the Santa Fe Trail was on *El Rio de las Animas Perdidas en Purgatorio* (River of Lost Souls in Purgatory)—generally shortened to Purgatory or Purgatoire—just before it crossed over the mountains into New Mexico. Today the town of **Trinidad** is on that spot, a coal mining and trade center with many brick buildings dating back to the last century. One

Early morning breakfast, New Mexic cattle drive

block of the historic downtown has been set aside to preserve two mansions and a museum. The **Baca House**, built of adobe in 1869, was the home of a prominent rancher and merchant of Spanish ancestry. The **Bloom Mansion**, a three-story brick Victorian house, was built in 1882 by a pioneer merchant, cattleman and banker. The **Pioneer Museum** is in a 12-room adobe building behind the Baca House.

A Town by the Spring

Across the mountains from Trinidad, a good spring provided another stopping place on the trail, and here the town of **Raton** grew. A historic district on First Street preserves several old buildings which now house specialty shops, a theater, museum, and the **Palace Hotel** which does not rent rooms but has a fine restaurant.

Raton Ski Basin is really in Colorado, but the only way to get to it is through Raton. It is a small, family-oriented ski area, especially suitable for beginners and intermediates.

One of the colorful men in Raton's past, Uncle Dick Wootton, trapped

beavers, hunted and scouted for the Fermont Expedition with his close friend Kit Carson. He is best remembered for his toll road over Raton Pass. He moved boulders and trees from 27 miles (43 km) of extremely rough terrain to make what was, for the time, a fair wagon road. He built a home and way station at the summit, and not many people argued with this 6'6" (198 cm) frontiersman, rifle in hand, when he stood at his toll gate and asked $1.50 a wagon, or a nickel or dime a head for livestock. Anyone who chose not to pay could go around the mountains, a detour of over a hundred miles. He never charged Indians. He sold his road to the railroad, and the site is marked today. The main line of the Santa Fe Railroad still follows the same route, and I-25 is on the hillside just above it.

Capulin Mountain National Monument, 34 miles (55 km) east of Raton on U.S. 64/87, is a perfectly shaped volcanic cone that served as a landmark on one branch of the Santa Fe Trail. At the base is a visitors center with picnic area, and a road circles the cone to the top where the view reaches into Colorado, Oklahoma, Texas and Kansas. Trails

ross-
ountry
kiers try
eir hand at
elemarking
n a New
lexico peak.

lead into the crater.

Cimarron, 35 miles (56 km) southwest of Raton, was another stop on the Santa Fe Trail. Cimarron was started by Lucien Maxwell, another trapper-trader-scout-freighter friend of Kit Carson. Through inheritance and purchase he became sole owner of the 1,714,765-acre (694,480-hectare) Maxwell Land Grant which covered most of northeastern New Mexico and some of southern Colorado. Maxwell became a legend of the Santa Fe Trail, entertaining lavishly in his baronial adobe mansion in Cimarron. Weary stagecoach travellers were drawn into gambling at cards or on the horses when they stopped at Cimarron. Maxwell paid his losses—when he lost—from a chest of gold coins. He sold the grant in 1870, and it was broken into many large ranches and several townsites.

A Sanctuary for the Boy Scouts

The **Mill Museum** is the four-story grist mill Maxwell built in Cimarron in 1865. The **St. James Hotel** (sometimes called the Don Diego) was built around 1872 by a French chef from Lincoln's White House, and has been well-restored as a museum. The tin ceiling of the original bar, now a gift shop, is pierced by 30 bullet holes, reminders of Cimarron's wild past.

Four miles (six km) south of Cimarron on State Highway 21 is **Philmont Scout Ranch** where as many as 17,000 Boy Scouts and their leaders come every summer. The 127,000-acre (51,000-hectare) ranch was given to the Scouts by the wealthy oil baron, Waite Phillips. It contains grassy valleys, timbered mountains, streams and a mansion with 14-room guest house.

Visitors are welcome at Philmont, especially to visit its two museums. One is the **Kit Carson home**, rebuilt and enlarged, where he lived briefly in the 1850s. The other houses a library and art collection which contains much of the work of the famous naturalist, Ernest Thompson Seton, one of the founders of scouting. The museums are open to the public daily in the summer at no charge.

Fort Union, nine miles (14 km) off I-25, 19 miles (30 km) north of Las Vegas, used to be one of the largest and most important forts in the West. Built in 1851 (two replacements were built during the next 30 years), it was a supply depot for other forts throughout the Southwest. It was almost at the end of the Santa Fe Trail, and many a conestoga wagon thundered into its protecting walls barely ahead of the Comanche. Fort Union was closed in 1891, and is a national monument today. A walk around the parade grounds, past ghostly chimneys on Officer's Row, past the jail and supply buildings, brings to life the soldiers and pioneers who once walked here.

Las Vegas (not to be confused with the Nevada gambling center) was the capital of New Mexico for two months during the Civil War when the Confederates held Santa Fe, and is still a major trade center for the big cattle and sheep ranches in the area. Most of the older part of town around the plaza has been designated a historic district. Las Vegas began as a land grant village during the Mexican period and was an important stop on the Santa Fe Trail, as well as a division point on the railroad. When the railroad bypassed the old plaza by two miles (three km), a new Las Vegas quickly grew up there. Houses, churches and public buildings show the rich architectural heritage of all the periods of Las Vegas.

Left, interior of St. James Hotel, Cimarron. Right, National Park Service staff at Bent's Fort dresses up as a Mountain Man.

NATIONAL PARKS AND MONUMENTS

Capulin Mountain National Monument 30 miles east of Raton on U.S. 64/87 and 3 to 4 miles north of Capulin on NM 325. A perfectly symmetrical volcanic cinder cone formed more than 7000 years ago, 1,000 feet tall with panoramic views of Great Plains. 278-2781.

Fort Union National Monument 29 miles northeast of Las Vegas on I-25, NM 477. This isolated military outpost guarded the Santa Fe Trail in the late 19th Century. Also remnants of a star fort constructed during the Civil War to ward off attack that never came. See the ruts of the wagons that trekked across the fabled trail. Costumed soldiers and settlers mill around during summer weekends. 425-8025.

Great Sand Dunes National Monument 38,000 acres, 34 miles northeast of Alamosa on CO 150. A desert valley ringed by mountains, a 50-square mile ever-shifting "sandscape" with 700-foot high dunes. Visitors center with exhibits open every day. Phone: 303/378-2312. There is an RV campground and picnic area with water and tables; other services are available in Alamosa and other nearby towns. Provisions, snacks, gasoline available during the season at the Dunes Outpost, one mile south of the monument. Summer programs include guided nature walks and evening campfire discussions. No hiking trails on the dunes; most visitors begin walks at the picnic area. Midday in summer, sand may be hot. Best times are early morning and late afternoon. Pets must be kept under control on account of the many forms of protected plants and animals. Campfires may be built only in constructed fireplaces. Hunting is prohibited, as is driving on the dunes. For further information, contact Superintendent, Box 60, Alamosa, CO 81101.

STATE PARKS

Chicosa Lake Near Roy. Fishing, camping, hiking.

Cimarron Canyon East of Eagle Nest on U.S. 64. Part of a state wildlife area. Campers must possess current New Mexico fishing or hunting licenses. Troutfishing in the Cimarron river, backcountry hiking, wildlife viewing.

Clayton Lake North of Clayton on NM 370. Lake is stocked with rainbow trout, channel catfish, bass.

Conchas Lake West of Tucumcari on NM 104. 25-mile long reservoir with full range of water sports, boating, waterskiing, fishing, two marinas. Waterfowl hunting in winter. Cabins, trailer park with hookups, golf.

Coyote Creek In the northeast near Mora, 45 miles north of Las Vegas on NM 3, 38. Hiking, fishing for rainbow and cutthroat trout, campsites.

El Vado Lake Southwest of Chama on NM 17; U.S. 84, NM 112. Boating, waterskiing, fishing (ice fishing in winter, salmon and trout year-round), hiking, campsites, marina.

Heron Lake Southwest of Chama on U.S. 64/84, NM 95. Trout and salmon, ice fishing, visitors center, camping sites, hiking trails, utility hookups, boat ramps and boat slips.

Kit Carson Memorial State Park In Taos. Centers upon graves of Kit and family. Museum with historical displays, picnic areas, bike path, skating pond, playground. No camping.

Morphy Lake 29 miles northwest of Las Vegas on NM 3, 94, and 105. 15-acre-high mountain lake amid towering ponderosa pines. Designated as a primitive use area, this park is accessible to backpackers or via four-wheel-drive, truck or horse.

Navajo Lake State Park(s) East of Aztec and Farmington on NM 173, 511. Two distinct areas horseshoe the largest lake in northwestern New Mexico. Pine River Site: camping/picnicking, utility hookups, showers, visitors center, boat ramp.

Oasis Southwest of Clovis, near Portales. An oasis in the desert, with drinking water, showers, small fishing lake, picnicking facilities, campground

Rio Grande Gorge South of Taos near Pilar. Along the banks of the Rio Grande, some of the finest public fishing in the state. From the park north to the Colorado border, fine white-water boating on the river: area administered by the Bureau of Land Management. See Info—Santa Fe, page 159.

Santa Rosa Lake North of Santa Rosa on access road. Pronghorn antelope graze near this reservoir on the Pecos River. Water sports, camping/picnicking sites, utility hookups, boat ramp, showers.

Storrie Lake North of Las Vegas off NM 3. Favorite fishing hole with boating, swimming, waterskiing, camping/picnicking sites, showers, utility hookups, boat ramp, playground.

Sumner Lake Northwest of Fort Sumner on U.S. 84, NM 203. Boating, waterskiing and fishing (pike, bass, bluegill and channel catfish); camping; boat ramp, drinking water, showers, utility hookups and playground. Fort Sumner State Monument, 23 miles to the southeast, is the site of U.S. military post established 1862 to guard Apache and Navajo prisoners. Billy the Kid is buried near the fort entrance.

Ute Lake 27 miles northeast of Tucumcari on U.S. 54, NM 540.

Villanueva 31 miles southwest of Las Vegas on I-25, NM 3, near the picturesque Spanish colonial village of Villanueva.

ATTRACTIONS

Chama: Home of the famous **Cumbres & Toltec Scenic Railroad,** a narrow-gauge steam locomotive that chugs 64 miles to Antonito, and back from mid June through mid October. The run ascends Cumbres Pass, for a 10,000-plus foot climb. Other trips, too. Call or write for brochure. Box 789, Chama 87520, 756-2151.

Cimarron: This old Western town was settled in 1841. Nearby are the wagon ruts of the fabled Santa Fe Trail, which passed through Cimarron. Major attrac-

170

tions are the Cimarron Art Guild; the St. James Hotel, dating from 1870, where Buffalo Bill Cody organized his Wild West Shows and outlaws stayed; the Old Aztec Mill Museum; and the Philmont Scout Ranch, a 138,000-acre ranch for the Boy Scouts of America on which sits the former home of Kit Carson, which is now a museum.

Eagles Nest/Angel Fire: Vietnam Veterans Chapel The first national memorial to veterans of the war. Open daily Memorial Day through Labor Day and on weekends in fall, winter and spring.

Las Vegas: Old Town West of the Gallinas river, a showcase for Victorian homes and frontier era buildings. The Old Town Plaza, historically a focal point, is being restored.

Rough Riders Museum On Grand Avenue near Municipal Building. Town was the Roughriders reunion headquarters in 1899. 9 to 5, Monday to Friday. 9 to noon, Saturday.

Red River: 19th-Century mining town, now a well-known year-round vacation spot catering to families. Skiing, horseback, fishing; small guest ranches hidden in nearby canyons.

Taos: Blumenschein Home Ledoux Street. Home of the co-founder of Taos Society of Artists, with art and furnishings of the early 1900s. 758-0330.

D. H. Lawrence Shrine San Cristobal. Shrine is open to the public. Original cabin is used as a lodging for writers-in-residence. Several of D. H. Lawrence's paintings are on exhibit in the La Fonda hotel manager's office for $1 admission, worth the visit. 758-2211.

Governor Bent House and Museum Bent Street, north of the Plaza. Family possessions, other period pieces. 9-5 daily.

Harwood Foundation Museum and Library 25 Ledoux Street. Paintings by early Taos artists, photo archives. Spanish furniture and crafts. 758-3063.

Kit Carson Home and Museum Old Kit Carson Road, east of the Plaza. 758-4741.

Millicent Rogers Museum 4 miles north of Taos off NM 3. Turn left before blinking light and follow museum signs. Outstanding collection of Indian and Spanish arts and crafts. 758-2462.

Nicolai Fechin Institute North Pueblo Road. The Russian-born master painter carved all the wood in his house in the evenings. 758-1710.

Taos Plaza. Core of the original village, one of the few places given permission to fly the American flag both day and night.

Twining Weavers, Arroyo Seco, north of Taos on 3/64. Traditional weaving methods are practiced. 776-8367.

GHOST TOWNS

Colfax 12 miles northeast of Cimarron on U.S. 64. Coal was first discovered on this land in 1895, and the first coal mine opened here in 1901.

Elizabethtown, 5 miles north of Eagles Nest, NM 38. Founded after 1866 gold strike, former county seat lured gunfighter Clay Allison. Remnants include the old Mutz Hotel and graveyard.

Watrous 20 miles northeast of Las Vegas, NM on I-25. A Santa Fe Trail stop.

HORSE RACING

La Mesa Park One mile south of Raton on I-25. First weekend in May through the first weekend in October. P.O. Box 1147, Raton, 87740. 445-2301.

EVENTS

Annual Aspencade Red River, late September. More than 50 four-wheel-drive vehicles compete in Aspen Run Rally, along with other driving events, jeep tours. Red River Chamber of Commerce. 754-2366.

Taos Pueblo Annual San Geronimo Feast Day September 30. War and other dances, ceremonial foot races, pole climb, arts and crafts fair. 758-8626.

ENTERTAINMENT

Taos School of Music Summer Series Classical concerts, recitals, student concerts, seminars, June through early August at the Taos Community Auditorium. 776-2388.

Taos Repertory Company Performs late July through beginning of September. Performances of well-known stage plays on a revolving schedule, Tuesday through Sunday at the Taos Community Auditorium. For more information, call the Taos Art Association. 758-2052.

Taos School of Music Chamber Music Festival July and August. Most Saturdays at Taos Community Auditorium. 776-2388.

SHOPPING

This small art colony is an Eden for collectors and shoppers and a terrific place just to poke around. For serious buyers, some of the better art galleries are on the main street heading north and on the highway heading east, close to the center of town. Ledoux Street is a gem for studios. The lion's share of shops and galleries emanate from all sides of the town plaza in a two to three-block radius.

ACCOMODATIONS

The Plaza Hotel Las Vegas, 425-3591. This old-timer was built in 1882. A recent restoration left wealth of period antiques and special touches extant. Tennis, saunas, superior restaurant/lounge. Tours available at the hotel, which is centrally situated.

Sagebrush Inn Highway 64, Ranchos de Taos, 758-2254. Pool, horseback riding, swimming, tennis, restaurant and bar.

Tennis Ranch of Taos P.O. Box 707, Ski Valley Rd., Taos 87571. 2211. Resort near Taos with sauna, hot tubs, swimming and, of course, racquetball and tennis.

SOUTHEAST NEW MEXICO

Southeastern New Mexico and the part of Texas that runs south of it holds surprises and contrasts, from snowcapped peaks to desert, from historic towns to the Space Age, from irrigated fields to the empty distance of the *Llano Estacado* (Staked Plains). Carlsbad Caverns underlie part of a reef laid down by an ancient sea, and the Guadalupe Mountains are part of that same reef, which was pushed up to give Texas its four highest peaks. In the central portion is the green, mountainous homeland of the Mescalero Apache. Far to the south are Las Cruces and El Paso. This is big country, capable of absorbing as much time as you want to give it.

Carlsbad Caverns is not just another cave. To enter the caverns is to leave behind a familiar environment of sunlight and wind, of night and day, of temperatures changing with the clouds, rain, snow and sun. As you descend into a strange underground universe, you cease to hear the sounds of men, animals and machines. Your eyes adjust to the dimness, your ears to the silence. You begin to feel the awesome beauty of the limestone fantasyland, to see curtains spun of translucent stone, pillars so mighty they seem to hold up the earth. Time is eternal. You are in an alien but benign world.

The complete three-mile walk-in tour begins at the natural entrance near the visitors center and by a series of switchbacks descends quickly 200 feet (60 meters) below the surface. As natural light gradually disappears, subtle electric lighting takes over, focusing on ethereal formations. The trail then descends gradually to the lowest point, 830 feet (250 meters) below the surface, rising a little to the Big Room, which is the size of 14 football fields and as high as a 22-story building. You can take an elevator back up to the surface.

The process that made Carlsbad Caverns began 250 million years ago during the Permian Period. A limestone reef formed around the edge of a shallow sea. When the sea dried up, the reef was covered with sediment, but groundwater seeped through, dissolving the limestone and creating the caverns. Millions of years later the earth's crust buckled and pushed up one side of the reef, which became the Guadalupe Mountains, and exposed the caverns. Water continued to drip into the caverns, depositing minute crystals of limestone to create the formations seen there today.

For an experience in real spelunking, sign up for the hike into **New Cave**, 23 miles (37 km) south of the visitors center. Only 25 people at a time may take the trip, which starts with a hike up a rocky hill and goes 1½ miles inside the cavern. This cave is not lighted, and the trail is sometimes wet, slick and steep. Everyone carries a flashlight, but in the immense blackness each one is only a pinprick of feeble light. At one point during the trip, the ranger has everyone sit down and turn off his flashlight. It is for the first time in their lives that most of the people experience total blackness and almost complete silence.

Neighboring National Parks

The highway to the Caverns (U.S. Highway 62/180) continues to **Guadalupe Mountains National Park** in Texas. The

ceding
ges, riding
sunset,
w Mexico.
t, cowgirl
Artesia
d right, a
ash miner
ar
rlsbad.

two national parks are in the same range of mountains, divided only by the state line. In contrast to the Caverns on the New Mexico side, the Texas side displays the spectacular rock formations of the Permian Reef. There, a big V-shaped wedge of the reef was pushed up to form limestone crags and deep canyons. Guadalupe Mountains National Park is not developed like Carlsbad Caverns, but it does have one campground, a visitors center and miles of trails going up to the peaks and into the canyons where the geology is best exposed. In the fall, the canyons that have springs become unexpected oases of color. The Guadalupes were the last stronghold of the Mescalero Apache before they settled on their reservation 100 miles (160 km) north. The first transcontinental mail route, known as the Butterfield Trail, touched the southern tip of the Guadalupes for a brief period, and cattle and sheep ranches skirt the foothills. But for the most part, civilization flowed around the mountains, and they stand in rugged solitude.

The Mescalero Apache Reservation occupies almost a half million acres (200,000 hectares) in the Sacramento Mountains northeast of Alamogordo. Though composed of limestone like the Guadalupes, the Sacramentos have a far different character. Higher, cooler, wetter, they are covered with big stands of timber and meadows. Cattle ranching, lumber and tourism are the main occupations of these Apache. The tribal celebrations on July 3 and 4 feature powwow dancing and a rodeo at the fairgrounds in the town of Mescalero. At the northern end of the reservation, and three miles (5 km) south of the city of Ruidoso, is the Mescalero's **Inn of the Mountain Gods**, a complete luxury resort. The grounds of the Inn, situated at the base of Sierra Blanca, the tribe's sacred mountain, include a golf course, riding trails, a skeet range and a lake and stream.

Immediately north of the reservation boundary is **Ruidoso**, a year-round vacation town. With races every weekend from May through Labor Day, **Ruidoso Downs** is one of the most popular racetracks in the Southwest. The world's best quarterhorses are bought, sold and raced here. The season ends with the two richest horse

Branding cattle, New Mexico.

races in America. The finale, the **All-American Futurity**, has a purse of over $2 million. Concerts, art shows, fishing and hiking in the mountains fill the summer recreation bill. In winter nearby **Sierra Blanca Ski Area**, also owned by the Mescalero Apache, draws skiers from Texas and the Mid-west.

Where Billy the Kid Found Favor

Over the mountains north of Ruidoso is **Old Lincoln Town**. A hundred years ago this was the scene of the Lincoln County War, a localized but bloody battle involving ranchers, merchants, cowboys and politicians. Billy the Kid happened to be on the side of the good guys this time, and the courthouse where he was jailed is a state museum. Several other buildings along the main street are owned by the state and comprise a historic district. The **Wortley Hotel**, across from the courthouse, is a bed-and-breakfast inn. During the first weekend in August the citizens of Lincoln stage an outdoor drama about Billy the Kid and the Lincoln County War. Part of the celebration is a real Pony Express race from the ghost town of

White Oaks to Lincoln, with the riders carrying mail that has been especially canceled for stamp collectors.

White Sands National Monument lies along U.S. 70/82 between two mountain ranges southwest of Alamogordo. The "sand" isn't sand at all, but a 50-mile (80-km) expanse of fine gypsum eroded from the San Andres Mountains. Dunes 30 feet (nine meters) high look like the waves of a giant sea, domed by an incredibly blue sky. White Sands is a place to be young, to run and fall and roll down the dunes. The visitors center at the entrance has geological exhibits, and an eight-mile drive goes to the heart of the dunes, where there are picnic facilities. The monument is open all year, and the entrance is off U.S. 70. Surrounding White Sands are two giant military installations, Holloman Air Force Base and White Sands Missile Range.

A 20-mile (32-km) drive east of Alamogordo on U.S. 82 leads to the mountain resort village of **Cloudcroft**. The road climbs abruptly, from 4,350 feet (1,325 meters) at Alamogordo to almost 9,000 feet (2,700 meters) at Cloudcroft. Several places along the

rmations in
rlsbad
verns,
eated by
llions of
ars of
pping
estone-
dden water.

way give grand panoramic views of the White Sands below. Cloudcroft has a family-oriented ski area, and old logging roads make good cross-country ski trails. Summer visitors seek the cool, slow-paced days and chilly nights. The golf course at Cloudcroft Lodge is the highest one in the country, at 9,000 feet (2,700 meters).

Land of Black and White Dunes

Nowhere is the contrast of this region more noticeable than between the dunes of White Sands and the **Valley of Fires State Park**, directly north and almost touching it. The Valley of Fires was formed when lava flowed from a small peak near the northern end of the *malpais* (badlands) 44 miles (70 km) down the valley, solidifying for eternity into a black, tormented mass. Trails lead from the campground/picnic area onto the buckled, forbidding, but strangely beautiful lava flow.

Las Cruces took its name from a forlorn cluster of crosses that marked the place where Franciscan missionaries were killed by Apache in the early 1800s. The town was not established until after the area became a U.S. territory, but early Spanish trails passed through here. With a population of more than 45,000, it is New Mexico's third largest town. The Mesilla Valley to the north and south of it is a rich agricultural area, though desert claims the hills above the Rio Grande.

Two miles (3 km) south of Las Cruces is **La Mesilla**. Although about as old as Las Cruces, La Mesilla has remained a sleepy village while Las Cruces has developed into a modern city. Here the Gadsden Purchase was signed in 1853, fixing the continental boundary of the United States.

Twelve miles (19 km) north of Las Cruces the ruins of Fort Selden, built in 1865, are preserved as a state monument. The fort played an important role in protecting the pioneers and miners who travelled along the California Trail.

Sunland Park Race Track, 35 miles (56 km) south of Las Cruces and only five minutes from downtown El Paso, was built as close as possible to the Texas border to accommodate racing fans. Winter season lasts from early October to early May.

Yucca plant growth at White Sand National Park, near Alamogord

El Paso, Texas was originally a place where Spanish trails crossed the Rio Grande. Travellers called it *El Paso del Norte*, the Pass of the North. In 1659, a small colony was established on the south side of the river, and, in 1827, another began on the north side. After the war with Mexico when the U.S. border was set, the two colonial villages became El Paso, on the north side of the river, and **Juarez, Mexico** on the south. The two comprise an international city of well over a million people.

Cowboys and Indians

El Paso used to be a tough, gun-slinging border town, and a bit of that flavor remains in the number of cowboy boots and Stetson hats you see on the streets. Five major boot factories are located in El Paso. The annual **Sun Carnival** between Christmas and the New Year culminates in one of the oldest college football bowl games.

Traces of three Indian villages lie within 10 miles (16 km) down the Rio Grande. During the Indian Rebellion of 1680 in New Mexico, refugee Spaniards and nonhostile Indians fled to El Paso, where they established new villages. After the reconquest 12 years later, many chose to stay, and these—Ysleta del Sur, Socorro and San Elizario—are the vestiges of those settlements. Though their Indian identity has largely disappeared, each village has a mission church and other adobes reminiscent of the Indian pueblos farther north.

At least three bridges cross over to Juarez, but the Juarez exit from Interstate 10 is the best. It sweeps grandly down Avenida de las Americas about a mile to the Pronaf Center, where the street circles the finest shopping, dining and motel area in Juarez. Good buys are leather, liquor, tile, ceramics, papier-mâché and specialty food.

If you like to haggle over prices—which isn't done in the better shops—ask directions to the **Public Market**, a cacaphony of smells, sights and sounds. Daytime driving to the Pronaf Center is easy for visitors, but if you go for a night out at one of the fabulous supper clubs (Shangri La, La Fiesta or El Alcazar) you would be wiser to put your life in the hands of one of the Mexican cab drivers (they wait in droves at the border).

urch at
una
an
eblo,
st of
uquerque.

NATIONAL PARKS AND MONUMENTS

Big Bend National Park In Texas. A huge 708,000-acre mountain-and-desert park, one of the two national parks in the state. It has an interesting geologic structure and is open all year, with a full range of recreational activities including winter sports and horseback riding. For further information, write Superintendent, Big Bend National Park, TX 79834. Reservations at Chisos Mountains Lodge can be made through National Park Concessions, Inc., Big Bend National Park, TX 79834.

Chamizal National Memorial In El Paso. A park, museum and theater dedicated to the settlement of the dispute between the U.S. and Mexico over this section of borderland. Film shown in the Chamizal Theatre. 915/543-7880.

Guadalupe Mountains National Park In Texas, en route from El Paso to Carlsbad Cavern, on U.S. 62/180. In the same mountain range as Carlsbad Caverns, it has one campground, a visitors center and miles of trails going into the peaks and canyons. Horseback riding, camping and picnicking. The park includes Texas' highest point, Guadalupe Peak. 915/828-3385.

White Sands National Monument About 15 miles southwest of Alamagordo on U.S. 70 and 82. The second most popular National Park Service attraction in the state, it offers the largest deposit of shimmering gypsum in the world on a 16-mile scenic loop drive. Visitors center, open daily, tells the gypsum story. 505/899-2671.

NATIONAL FORESTS

Lincoln National Forest Borders Alamogordo, surrounds Ruidoso. Includes ski areas, camping, hiking, riding, resorts. Elevations to 11,000 feet. Ranger stations at Carlsbad: 885-4181; Cloudcroft: 682-2551; Mayhill: 687-3411; Ruidoso: 257-4095. Federal Building, Alamogordo 88310; 437-6030.

NATIONAL WILDLIFE REFUGES

Bitter Lakes 15 miles southeast of Roswell on U.S. 380. Place to catch waterfowl, birds. Winter home of crane, geese and ducks. Fishing for white bass, carp and channel catfish. P.O. Box 7, Roswell 88201. 505/622-7655.

Gruila 20 miles east of Portales on NM 88. Box 549, Muleshoe, TX 79347. 505/946-3341.

STATE PARKS

Bottomless Lakes Near Roswell. Seven small lakes, some stocked

with trout. Skin Diving, swimming, camping, riding, boating. Lots of hiking trails.

Hueco Tanks State Historical Park 24 miles east of El Paso on U.S. 62/180, then eight-mile access road. Unique rock formation with caves and cliffs covering 860 acres. Used by Indians throughout the centuries, the park contains more than 2,000 pictographs and is open for picnicking, hiking, camping. 915/859-4100.

Lea County Near Hobbs. Picnicking, camping, utility hookups, playground.

Living Desert North edge of Carlsbad, just off U.S. 285. An indoor/outdoor museum of New Mexico plants and animals: cactus, birds, animals, reptiles in their natural habitat. Day use only, no camping or recreational facilities. Instead, park offers hiking trails, rest rooms and meeting areas for large groups. Open every day.

Oliver Lee Memorial State Park South of Alamogordo on U.S. 54. A variety of rare and endangered plant species grace the entrance to Dog Canyon. Catwalk and museum near a once-massive ranching operation. Picnicking, camping, utility hookups, showers. Open daily.

Smokey Bear Historical State Park In Capitan, 21 miles north of Ruidoso. The original Smokey is buried here, where a fine museum erected in his honor also stands. Lincoln State Monument, restoration of the frontier town where Billy the Kid became legend, is 11 miles east of the park.

Valley of Fires Near Carrizozo on U.S. 380, northwest of Ruidoso. Situated amid the black, fissured rock of the Mal pais lava flow, one of the best preserved lava fields in the U.S. Interpretive trail through formations; camping/picnicking sites, drinking water, playgrounds.

NATIONAL RECREATION SITES

Aguirre Springs 22 miles east; northeast of Las Cruces on U.S. 70. 6,000-foot elevation, 35 free campsites.

Three Rivers Petroglyph 36 miles southwest of Carrizozo on U.S. 54, 5100-foot elevation, six free campsites. Hundreds of rock drawings, interpretive trail. Open every day, 24 hours.

ATTRACTIONS

Alamogordo: International Space Hall of Fame Two miles northeast of U.S. 54. Honors space pioneers, exhibits moon-rocks, satellites and has a planetarium on site. Open daily. 505/437-2840 or 1-800/545-4021.

rinity Site 70 miles north of
wn on U.S. 54. Reservation
ad. Open to public first
eekend of October each year.
rater at the site of the first
omic explosion.

arlsbad: Antique Auto Barn
½ miles south on U.S. 62-180,
out 40 antique cars on
splay, some dating from early
900s. Thurs. – Tues. 1–6.
05/885-2437.

arlsbad Fine Arts Museum In
he city library. Art and potash
xhibits and mineral displays.
01 S. Halagueno St., Hala-
ueno Park. Mon. – Sat. 10 to 6.

arlsbad Caverns 27 miles
uthwest of town on U.S. 180.
2, NM 7. Over 60 international-
 famous limestone caverns 750
et underground. Self-guided
atural entrance tour, three
iles about three hours; self-
uided elevator entrance tour,
½ miles, 45 minutes. Under-
round cafeteria. Open every
ay. Carlsbad Caverns National
ark, 3225 National Parks High-
ay, Carlsbad 88220. 505/785-
232. Bat Flights, every summer
vening at sunset through the
ntrance. New Cave, more rug-
ed than the hike through the
ain caverns, like spelunking
xpeditions undertaken by cav-
rs. Trip is somewhat strenuous.
ours daily summers, on week-
nds only during the winter.

ake Carlsbad Recreation Area
J.S. 285. Amusement rides, pic-
icking facilities, tennis, water
ports.

residents Park On the east
ank of Lake Carlsbad. 1880
intage miniature narrow-gauge
team train rides along the Pecos
River; "George Washington"
addle wheel boats cruise down
he river with an authentic pro-
ibition rum runner.

itting Bull Falls 140 miles
outhwest of Carlsbad on U.S.
85, NM 137. Waterfalls in the
Guadalupe Mountains of Lin-
oln National Forest. Picnic and
ecreation areas.

El Paso & NE Railroad Trestle
Spans a canyon just west of
town. A remnant of the spur that
logged lumber to the flatlands in
1898.

Aerial Tramway 5622-foot ride
up, panoramic view of three
states and Mexico. Daily noon to
9, June 1 through Labor Day,
limited schedule rest of year.
Alabama and McKinley Sts.,
915/566-6622.

Americana Museum Historic art
of the Americas. Civic Center,
Chamber of Commerce Bldg.

Ascarate Park City park with a
lake for boating, baseball, tennis, handball, volleyball and
golf.

Bullfight Museum 500 Alameda
in the Del Camino Motor Hotel.
Mon. – Sat. 7 a.m. to 7:30 p.m.
Sun 7 to 2:30. 915/772-2711.

Civic Center Grand Hall, theater, exhibits, conventions, you
name it. 915/541-4920.

Casas Grandes Indian pueblo
ruins more than 3000 years old,
120 miles from Juarez in heart of
Mexican cattle country.

Condova Port of Entry Entrance
to Mexico. Visas available.

U. of Texas El Paso Centennial
Museum Displays on culture and
life of Southwest and Mexico.
Daily except holidays, Sunday
afternoons. 747-5565.

El Paso Mission Tour of lower
valley sites, begins at Ysleta Mission, 14 miles east on I-10. Self
guiding, about two hours, locations well marked. Phone for
Ysleta Mission, 915/859-9848.

El Paso Museum of Art 1211
Montana Ave. Kress collection
of European masters, art, crafts,
cultural history; films, lectures,
creative workshops. Tues. –
Sat., 10 to 5, Sun. 1 to 5. 915/
541-4040.

El Paso Museum of History 15
miles southeast of El Paso on
U.S. 80 and I-10, use Americas
Ave. exit. Wed. – Sat. 9 to 5,
Sun. 1 to 5. 915/858-1928.

El Paso Tourist Information
Center On I-10. Comprehensive

literature featuring sights and
highlights of El Paso Southwest.
Tourist film upon request.
915/541-4954.

El Paso Zoological Park Ever-
green and Paisano. Animals in
natural settings. Mon. – Fri. 9:30
to 4:15. Sat. – Sun. and holidays
10 to 5. 915/541-4601.

Fort Bliss Largest air defense
center in free world, several
museums. 915/568-2121.

Fort Bliss Replica Museum
Army and Southwestern relics.
Daily 9 to 4:30. 915/568-4518.

Indian Cliffs Ranch 30 minutes
from El Paso. Horse rentals,
hayrides, trails, overnight trail
rides. 915/544-3200.

Insights Basement of the Mills
Building. Hands-on science
museum. Open afternoons 915/
542-2990.

Juarez City Market Large two-
story building open sunrise to
sunset.

Juarez Museum of Archaeology
In the Juarez Chamizal Park.
Pre-Columbian reproductions,
gardens.

Juarez Race Track Year-round
dog racing, wagering facilities,
El Paso number. 915/778-6322.

Magoffin Home 1120 Magoffin
Ave. Hacienda dating from
1875. Tours. 915/533-5147.

McKelligon Canyon 2½ miles
north on Alabama. Amphitheater
for concerts and the historical
pageant "Viva El Paso." Hiking,
camping, picnicking. Theater
phone: 915/533-1671.

Plaza Monumental Bullring,
Juarez. Fourth largest in world.
April through September.

Pronaf Center Modern shopping area in Juarez. Variety of
shops with crafts from all over
Mexico. Also museum of Mexican history, restaurants, resort
hotels, convention center.

San Elizario Presidio On famous
Camino Real Trail. A fort of the
Spanish government in the 18th
Century. 915/851-2333.

San Jacinto Plaza Original city square and park, and still a colorful focus of downtown El Paso.

Sierra del Cristo Key Anapra exit off I-10, three miles west, only a few feet from Mexican border. Pilgrimage shrine with status of Christ. Ascent takes about an hour. Use judgment before attempting.

Tigua Indian Reservation and Pueblo In suburb of Isleta. 14 miles east of El Paso. Arts and crafts center, museum, dances. Call for schedules. 915/859-3916 or 859-3917, or write, P.O. Box 17579, El Paso, TX 79917.

U.S. Army Air Defense Artillery Museum, Bldg. 5000 Pleasanton Rd. Only one of its kind in the country. 915/568-5412.

Wilderness Park Museum 8½ miles north of El Paso at the intersection of Trans-Mountain Road and Gateway South. Dioramas and displays of primitive man and Indians of the region. 915/755-4332.

Las Cruces: Amador Hotel, Amador & Water Sts. Today houses the Citizen's Bank. Former hotel contains a rare collection of area antiques and historic memorabilia, including the city's first post office.

Farmer's Market Local farmers and artisans gather to sell their goods Wednesday and Saturday mornings from early spring through late fall, at the downtown mall.

La Mesilla A one-time Mexican border town of preserved 19th Century charm and color, one mile south of Las Cruces on NM 28. Tiny plaza with quaint shops. San Albino Mission overlooking it, restaurants and historical

buildings and museums.

Playhouse Museum, 1201 N. 2nd St. Features old dolls and toys. 505/526-1207.

Pecan Orchard Five miles south of Las Cruces on NM 28. World's largest pecan grove, tours by appointment. Contact the Chamber of Commerce.

Tortugas Across highway 85 from New Mexico State Uni-

versity campus. An Indian village where Our Lady of Guadalupe Feast Day is celebrated every December 12. Indian dances and a four-mile pilgrimage to the top of "A" Mountain. After a day of fasting, pilgrims descend by torchlight. 505/526-8171.

Chaves County Historical Museum, downtown Roswell. Former home of a prominent rancher and developer, on the National Register of Historic Places.

Roswell Museum & Art Center. downtown Roswell. New Mexico's largest museum honors southwestern artists and Robert

H. Goddard, the "father o modern rocketry." Mon. – Sat. to 5, Sun. and holidays 1 to 5

Ruidoso: Lincoln, 33 miles north of Ruidoso. Focus of Lincoln County War, Billy the Kid's last jailbreak. 26 of original 44 buildings; four museums.

Lowry Ruins 9 miles west o Pleasant View on the road to Hovenweep. 1000-year-old Pueblo ruins. Open daily 8 to 6

Strater Hotel, 699 Main Ave Beautiful restoration. The Diamond Circle Theater, in the hotel, is one of the state's best period theaters, with Victorian era plays and other entertainment. Reservations recommended. 303/247-4431.

OBSERVATORIES

W. J. McDonald Observatory on Mount Locke, a 6800-foot spire near Fort Davis, Texas, to the southeast of El Paso. Operated by the University of Texas, the observatory has four reflector telescopes, including one measuring 107 inches—one of the world's largest. A visitors' information center at the bottom of the mountain offers exhibits, slide shows and general information on the walking tour. Center open Mon. – Sat., 9 to 7, Sun. 1 to 7, June 1 – Aug. 31; Mon. – Sat., 9 to 5, Sun. 1 to 5 the rest of the year. Free. 915/426-3263.

Sacramento Peak Observatory At Sunspot, near Alamagordo, NM. Open daily 8 to 5; free guided tours Sat. at 2. May 6 – Oct. 31.

HORSE RACING

Ruidoso Downs, Ruidoso. First weekend in May through Labor Day Weekend. P.O. Box 449, Ruidoso, NM 88346. 378-4431. Famous quarterhorse events include the Triple Crown (Kansas Futurity, Rainbow Futurity and

All-American Futurity, occurring in mid-June, mid-July and Labor Day, respectively), the All-American Gold Cup and the All-American Derby. The All-American Futurity, with a $2.5 million purse, is the holy roller of them all. Two major horse sales are also staged during the summer. General admission to the Downs is $2. No children under 14 or shorts are allowed. Grandstand seating is available. For reserved seat information, call 505/378-4140.

Sunland Park 45 miles south of Las Cruces. First weekend in October through the first weekend in May. 505/589-1131.

INDIAN RESERVATIONS

The Mescalero Apache Reservation is located between Ruidoso and Tularosa. The Mescalero host a four-day ceremonial every year in early July, with a dramatic Maidens' Puberty Rites Ceremonial held at dawn and a Mountain Spirits Dance performed at night around a flaming fire. Fishing, hunting, camping are popular. P.O. Box 176. Mescalero, NM 88340. 505/671-4494.

GHOST TOWNS

White Oaks, 12 miles northeast of Carrizozo on U.S. 54, NM 349. Gold mining center where Billy the Kid attempted a cattle rustling raid in 1880.

ENTERTAINMENT

The El Paso Symphony Orchestra provides a full concert season and summer pop concerts. Amateur and professional theater groups are active year round. The University of Texas at El Paso sponsors ballet and other cultural activities.

Las Cruces Symphony Orchestra, Zohn Theatre. For information, contact the Las Cruces Convention and Visitors Bureau.

Ruidoso Summer Festival Held annually, two weekends in early June. Features concerts by Southwestern symphony orchestras and distinguished guest artists from the classical world Las Vegas and Broadway. Ruidoso Summer Festival, Ruidoso 88345. 505/257-7929.

EVENTS

McKelligon Canyon Amphitheater, El Paso summer evenings. Pageant and performances.

Festival, downtown El Paso. July. Major El Paso festival of historic exhibits, ethnic foods, dance and music.

Las Cruces Whole Enchilada Fiesta, end of September–early October. Street dance, parade, contests, chile cook-off, square dancing, concerts, world's biggest enchilada. Downtown Mall and other places. Las Cruces Chamber of Commerce. 505/524-1968.

Annual Trinity Site Tour, Alamagordo, October 1. A 90-minute visit to the site of the first A-bomb explosion on the only day of the year that the site is open to the public. Annual Space Hall of Fame Induction Ceremonies. Alamagordo Chamber of Commerce. 505/437-6120.

El Paso Chilifest, Civic Center, September. The fest includes a Terlingua sanctioned cook-off, activities taking place outside of the Civic Center.

Fiesta de las Flores, El Paso. September. A weekend of carnival festivities with a Latin American flavor.

Border Folk Festival, Chamizal National Memorial, October. Weekend of folk music, dancing and crafts.

Kermezaar, El Paso Civic Center, fall. Show of the best in arts and crafts from the Southwest.

Sun Bowl, El Paso. Sports festival, November, December, January. Festivities and sports events including the annual Sun Bowl football game.

Southwest Livestock Show and Rodeo, El Paso County Coliseum, February. Livestock show, rodeo and top country and western entertainment.

Siglo de Oro Drama Festival, Chamizal, March. International Spanish drama competition.

Tigua Saint Anthony's Day Ceremony, Tigua Reservation, June 13th. Religious patron saint's day of the Tiguas—special ceremonies and dances.

SHOPPING

Juarez: Public Market is the place to haggle over prices. (Don't do it in the better shops.) A cacaphony of smells, sights, sounds.

ACCOMMODATIONS

Carrizo Lodge, two miles outside Ruidoso in the Sacramento Mountains. This resort maintains a staff of recognized artists for an in-residence art school. The school package includes meals, accommodations, classes, etc.
Adobe decor and renovated guest rooms. Drawer A, Ruidoso, NM, 88345.

Fiesta Real The ambience of Old Mexico, with arcaded walkways, patios, two good dining rooms. Juarez.

Inn of the Mountain Gods, Mescalero, NM 88340. 505/257-5141. Large, expensive resort near Ruidoso, with boating, fishing, golf, horseback riding, hunting.

Le Junta Guest Ranch, Box 139, Alto, NM 88312. 505/336-4361. In the mountains near Ruidoso. Rustic, mountain retreat with cabins, reasonable rates, horseback riding, hiking, skiing at Sierra Blanca. Cabins have fireplaces. Local clientele, lots of repeats, very casual.

The Lodge at Cloudcroft, Cloudcroft, NM 88317. 682-2566. Built at the turn of the century with quality and elegance and still adheres to those standards. Fine food and lodging. Recently renovated, golf and skiing.

Wortley Hotel, a bed and breakfast spot north of Ruidoso in Lincoln, 653-4500. Brass beds, marble top tables and oak sideboards; good ranch style cookin'. Reasonable.

SOUTHWEST NEW MEXICO

If there is a unifying theme in southwestern New Mexico, it is vastness. Most of it is made up of mountains and wilderness area, but where the Rio Grande flows there are old Spanish settlements and small farms. Points of interest here range from ghost towns to radio astronomy and modern art.

As early as 1598 the Spaniards noted how helpful the Indians were at a certain place on the Rio Grande, and when a town grew there it was named **Socorro** (help). The first church was built in 1628, but the village was abandoned during the Pueblo Revolt of 1680, and was not resettled until 1815. Socorro is in the midst of a rich mining district, and was a boom town during the last two decades of the 19th Century. When the railroad came through in 1880 it became a ranching headquarters town. The original plaza is a block off the main street, and several buildings around it are designated historic landmarks. The **New Mexico Institute of Mining and Technology** is located a few blocks west of the plaza, and the **Rock and Mineral Museum** there is worth seeing.

Birds of Different Feathers

Twenty miles (32 km) south of Socorro, on old U.S. Highway 85 (which parallels Interstate 25) is the **Bosque del Apache Wildlife Refuge** where, from November till sometime in February, thousands of waterfowl winter. Most beautiful are the snow geese with their white bodies and black-tipped wings. Sandhill cranes, a soft gray color, with a wingspan of seven feet, graze the stubble fields. The most exotic bird at Bosque del Apache is the whooping crane, the object of an experiment begun about seven years ago to try to save it from extinction. Whoopers are pure white and almost a foot taller than the sandhills, so they are easy enough to spot, even though there are only about a dozen of them to almost 10,000 of their smaller cousins.

When you go to Bosque del Apache Wildlife Refuge allow time to drive around the ponds and fields and to hike trails through the cottonwood groves.

Almost 300 kinds of birds live here, as well as foxes, bobcats, raccoons, eagles, coyotes, deer and many other kinds of wildlife. To see the waterfowl, go to the north end of the refuge to the look-out tower by 4:30. Far in the distance a dark wavy line will appear on the horizon, and soon the plaintive purr of the cranes and the continuous honk of the geese will be heard. Wave after wave comes, some flying so close overhead you can see their eyes. The sky turns from blue to rose, saffron and orange as the birds settle on their icy beds. It is cold this time of year; dress warmly and carry a thermos of something to warm up with.

West of Socorro is **Magdalena**, railhead for the Magdalena Livestock Driveway. Cattle were driven from Arizona and western New Mexico to be shipped to market. Even as late as the 1950s the trail was used occasionally. A few remnants of wooden windmills mark the famous cattle driveway.

U.S. 60 continues west across the **San Agustín Plains**, the setting for Conrad Richter's novel, *Sea of Grass*. In the middle of this ancient seafloor valley, completely encircled by mountains, is the **National Radio Astronomy Observa-**

t,
ennae at
National
dio
ronomy
servatory's
y Large
ay; and
t, open pit
per mine,
ıta Rita.

tory's **Very Large Array**. Twenty seven huge antennae mounted on a Y-shaped railroad track probe the skies, learning secrets from distant galaxies. A visitors center is at the entrance just off the highway.

The Rio Grande is dammed at **Truth or Consequences** (known as T or C), 75 miles (120 km) south of Socorro, to form **Elephant Butte Lake**. Boating, fishing and other water sports are good here. This small town on the central highlands has its share of interesting history, but it got on the map when it changed its name from Hot Springs to T or C in 1948 in response to an offer from Ralph Edwards, who had originated the radio show of that name.

Towns that Silver Built

A few miles south of T or C, State Highway 90 turns west toward the Black Range, part of **Gila National Forest** which makes up most of the southwestern part of the state. This is a scenic but slow route to Silver City, going through two old mining towns. **Hillsboro**, 17 miles (27 km) west of T or C, was the scene of a rich silver strike in the 1880s.

Ruins of the courthouse and jail remain, but most of the people who live there today are artists or retirees. A small museum has relics of the colorful days of Black Range mining, Apache attacks and cattle ranching. **Kingston**, nine miles (14 km) beyond, is almost at the edge of the forest where the road begins to climb. Its history is much the same as Hillsboro's, with silver strikes, Apache attacks and, finally, today, an eddy of quiet life and memories. Neither of these towns has motels.

If you are a rock hound take a detour south on U.S. 180 to **Rockhound State Park**, 14 miles (22 km) southeast of **Deming**. This may be the only park in the country where you can take part of it home with you—up to 15 pounds (seven kilos) of quartz, jasper, agate, amethyst and other specimens. Trails fan out from the campground and visitors center across the cactus-studded foothills of the Florida Mountains.

The border of Mexico is 35 miles (56 km) south of Deming, with **Columbus** on the American side and **Las Palomas** on the Mexican side. Both are small and don't offer much in the way of shopping or amusement, but each has an interest-

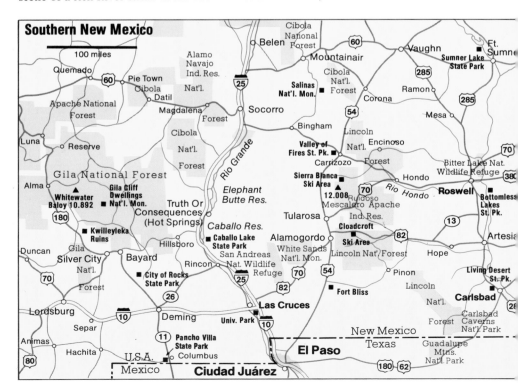

186

ing history. **Pancho Villa State Park** at Columbus commemorates much more than the revolutionary for whom it is named. In 1916 Pancho Villa led a band of rebels across the border in an attack that killed eight civilians and soldiers at Columbus and nearby Camp Furlong. This was the only time since the War of 1812 that the continental United States had been invaded by foreign troops. It is also the first time in history that air power was used in war. General John J. "Black Jack" Pershing led a pursuit party into Mexico after Pancho Villa. They were given air cover by eight little single engine places from Fort Sam Houston in Texas. Also in the park at Camp Furlong are ruins of truck ramps which are reminders that here in this forgotten border outpost mechanized warfare was born before World War I. Only a few adobe ruins remain of the camp. The campground and park are a cactus-landscaped winter hideaway.

Twenty-eight miles (45 km) north of Deming is **City of Rocks State Park and Campground**. Like a Stonehenge on the desert, boulders rise 50 and 60 feet (15 to 18 meters) high. Some look like skyscrapers, others tilt at crazy angles.

In a state where prehistoric ruins are so common, you might suppose these to be ruins, but they are the products of erosion on ancient rhyolite outcroppings. This was a favorite lookout place for Apache waiting to ambush stagecoaches on the Butterfield Trail. Camp and picnic areas are set in among the rocks and sheltered by gnarled alligator juniper trees.

A Different Kind of Ghosts

Two miles south of **Lordsburg** in the far southwestern corner of New Mexico is the classic ghost town of **Shakespeare**, owned by Rita Hill and her daughter Janaloo, who live in the general mercantile store. The ruins of Shakespeare are on their cattle ranch, which they operate. On the second Sunday of each month Rita and Janaloo don bonnets and bustles and, for a small charge, open Shakespeare to the public. The rest of the time they're too busy cowboying to have company. Rita was a movie bit player (she met her husband Frank on location), and Janaloo was a model and musician in New York before she joined her mother in the cattle

ule deer
ɔwned by
ınter at
ack Range
ountains.

and ghost town business. Both ladies are fair-skinned and genteel, almost to shyness, blending so well with the stories they tell that sometimes they are the ghosts of Shakespeare. As Rita and Janaloo will tell you as you walk down Avon Avenue, the town boomed and died through successive silver strikes and a great diamond hoax, and saw its share of hangings and brothels. It was once on the Butterfield Trail. Some of the mining promoters had read English literature, and they named it for their favorite poet.

Silver City was born of a silver boom in 1870, but, unlike most mining boom towns, it never died. It is the gateway to **Gila National Forest** and **Gila Wilderness Area** and is the largest town in this part of the state. **The Inner Loop**, a paved, hundred-mile (160-km) scenic drive (States 15, 35 and 90), goes from the edge of the Wilderness Area to Gila Cliff Dwellings National Monument. The loop returns to Silver City past lakes and farms. Several guest ranches and outfitters along here take pack and hunting trips into the Wilderness.

Six miles (10 km) out of Silver City is **Pinos Altos**, the oldest mining town in the district. The first school you see has been converted to a small museum, and across the street are the Buckhorn Restaurant and Saloon and the Opera House. In the Buckhorn, whitewashed adobe walls, heavy-beamed ceilings, carved furniture and velvet draperies add a touch of Spanish elegance. Though not the original building, the Opera House has excellent exhibits of historic photographs and Mimbres pottery, and during the summer often provides entertainment such as melodrama or old movies.

The road continues through the mountains to **Gila Cliff Dwellings National Monument**, located in a secluded canyon where prehistoric Indians lived for a thousand years. They have been gone for seven centuries. An easy trail goes to the ruins from the visitors center, and other trails begin here into the Gila Wilderness Area. A permit from the forest ranger is necessary for wilderness trips.

The Gila Wilderness was established in 1924, a half million acres (200,000 hectares) of rugged mountains through which no roads or wheeled vehicles of any kind may travel, not even fire-

New Mexico characters: left, cowboy climbs a windmill ne Grants, and right, a ranger near Lovina.

fighting equipment. A few years ago that point was made clear when some men drove into a remote canyon in a jeep, became hopelessly stuck, and were not only fined heavily, but also had to dismantle the jeep and pack out every single bolt on foot or horseback.

"Catwalking" Along a Canyon

Sixty miles (97 km) north of Silver City on U.S. 180 is the village of **Glenwood**, another headquarters for pack trips into the wilderness. There are a couple of small motels, restaurants and a district ranger station here. Near Glenwood is the **Catwalk**, remnants of a pipeline built to bring water down the canyon to a silver mill. The canyon was so narrow the pipe had to be fastened to the sheer walls, and the men who worked on it had to have the agility of cats. Today a metal mesh fence encloses the catwalk, making it safe for anyone. In some places, splashing waterfalls and quiet pools are 30 feet (nine meters) below the walk and the canyon is so narrow the sun reaches the bottom only at midday.

Three miles (five km) north of Glen-

wood a road turns toward **Mogollon**, nine miles (14 km) up in the mountains. This was the heart of a rich gold and silver district that produced millions of dollars of ore from 1875 to World War II. Relics of mines, tailings dumps and many foundations on the hills show the prominence the mining district once had. About 20 people live in Mogollon now, mostly along Main Street, which follows Silver Creek. The buildings are weathered gray, the metal rusted red. Some were built just a few years ago for a Henry Fonda movie, but they were built so well that most people can't tell the real ghosts from the new.

Catron County in west central New Mexico is the least populated part of the state—about three square miles (eight sq km) for every person. The county seat and largest town is **Reserve**, population 400. Second largest town is **Quemado**, population 200. About 30 miles (50 km) north of Quemado is the **Lightning Field**, an artwork of unbelievable magnitude. In 1970 Walter de la Maria won a commission from the Dia Art Foundation in New York City to create a work of land art that would be the essence of isolation. The land was to

ila Cliff
wellings
lational
Monument,
n the edge
f the Gila
Wilderness.

be not only the setting but also a part of the work itself. For five years de la Maria roamed the West before finding this lonely high plateau surrounded by jagged mountains on all sides.

Dazzling Lightning Field

The Lightning Field took several years to construct. It is made of 400 thin, pointed stainless-steel poles, arranged in a grid one mile by two thirds of a mile (1.6 by one km); 16 rows in one direction, 25 in the other. In the flat light of midday the poles almost disappear, but in late afternoon, early morning and even by full moonlight, light catches on the poles like spots of gold or silver shining in perfect symmetry to a diminishing point that seems to go to eternity. The poles are so precisely set that if a giant sheet of glass were laid on top, every pole would touch it.

Visitors are meant to experience the Lightning Field, not just look at it. Only six guests may go at one time, and only from June through November. You meet at the foundation's office in Quemado—175 miles (280 km) from Albuquerque—leave your car and camera there, and go by pickup to the field. An old homesteader's cabin, rustic but comfortably modernized, is your home for the next 24 hours. No one is allowed to go for less than 24 hours. Food for three meals is in the refrigerator, records are there for the stereo. The manager lives over the hill, out of sight, and after dropping off guests he disappears until the next day after lunch.

State 117 goes north from Quemado about 75 miles (120 km) to I-40 near **Grants**. There are no towns and few houses on this road, but it's a beautiful drive and two natural phenomena are noteworthy. About 30 miles (48 km) of the highway runs alongside a black and angry river of lava. Called **El Malpais National Recreation Site**, it is composed of four distinct lava flows originating around 3,000 years ago, with the last one as recent as about 500 years ago. Indian legends tell of rivers of fire in the region. A few early Indian and Spanish trails went across the southern end where the lava flow spreads out, but generally trails avoided it. The best place to see and appreciate the form and magnitude of the lava flow is at the

Mogollon ghost town

north end, 10 miles (16 km) south of I-40 at a designated viewing point and picnic area. As you drive along State 117 there are places to explore along the edges, but it is dangerous to walk very far on the lava. It shreds shoe leather in a short time.

The other point of geological interest is **La Ventana**, New Mexico's biggest natural arch, located in the sandstone bluffs that run along the east side of the lava flow. The arch is a mile or two south of the turnoff to the lava vista point.

Essence of New Mexico

At the west edge of Grants, State 53 turns south down the west side of the Malpais. More timber and grass grow on this side, and one or two dirt roads go to the edge of the flow. Signs point to the **Bandera Crater and Ice Caves**, which are privately owned, but an integral part of the Malpais. Bandera, a perfect cinder cone, was one of the sources of the lava flow. Trails go to the top of Bandera, and steps lead down into the ice caves, frozen green sheets that have been there longer than man

remembers. The trading post at the ice caves is the place to buy authentic Indian jewelry, pottery and kachina dolls.

State 53 continues to **El Morro National Monument**, 50 miles (80 km) southwest of Grants. The sandstone mesa juts up from the plateau like the prow of a ship. This was a landmark on early trails, especially since there is a pool of never-failing spring water there under an overhang. Beginning with Indian petroglyphs, hundreds of inscriptions have been carved around the base of the cliff, the oldest Spanish one made by a white man in 1605 noting the expedition of Don Juan de Oñate who was seeking the Gulf of California. On top of the mesa are ruins of a prehistoric pueblo, believed to be the ancestral home of the Zuni, whose present pueblo is 30 miles (48 km) to the west. A visitors center, camp and picnic grounds, firelight programs and the well-maintained trails over and around the mesa and bluff make this lesser-known national monument a special place to visit. This is the essence of New Mexico: space, sparkling air, mountains and the ever present signs of older civilizations.

Morro ock, a ndmark on arly trails, is ow pre-erved as l Morro ational onument.

NATIONAL FORESTS

Apache National Forest With Blue Range Wilderness, in the western portion of the state. Most of it is in Arizona. Adjoins the Gila Wilderness area and can be approached by going south from Quemado. One ranger station in Luna; 547-2611.

Gila National Forest, 2610 North Silver, Silver City, NM 88061; 388-1986. Huge southwestern New Mexico Wilderness area, includes ghost towns, towering mountains (10,900 feet), Gila Cliff Dwellings National Monument, wide range of outdoor activities including fishing, camping, hiking and riding. Guest ranches and outfitters along the road to and from Silver City for pack and hunting trips. Ranger stations at Glenwood: 539-2481; Magdalena: 538-5376; Mimbres: 534-2250; Quemado: 773-4678; Reserve: 533-6231; Silver City: 538-2771; T or C: 894-3757.

NATIONAL RECRE-ATION SITES

Datil Well, 63 miles west of Socorro on U.S. 60. 7,600-foot elevation, 22 free campsites.

El Malpais, 10 miles south of Grants on I-40 and NM 117. 6,500-foot elevation, 6 free campsites. A popular place to visit, with three prehistoric lava flows from nearby Mt. Taylor visible. Real "badland" reputation, with stories of train robberies, lost gold, etc.

NATIONAL WILDLIFE REFUGES

Bosque del Apache, 16 miles south of Socorro on I-25. P.O. Box 1246, Socorro, NM 87801. 835-1828.

Sevilleta, 15 miles north of Socorro on I-25. San Acacia, NM 87831. 864-4021.

STATE PARKS

Belen Valley, on the Rio Grande at Belen. Fishing, birdwatching, hiking and picnicking.

Caballo Lake, south of T or C off I-25. All water sports; fishing for bass, catfish and panfish; good hookups, boating, water-skiing, boat rentals, hiking trails, marina, fishing supplies.

City of Rocks State Park, between Deming and Silver City. Camping and picnicking among Stonehenge-like formations. Cactus garden, playground, solar heated facilities.

Elephant Butte Lake, north of T or C on I-25. Fishing for bass, catfish, pike, crappie. Restaurant, rental cabins, boat rentals, waterskiing.

Leasburg Dam State Park, northwest of Las Cruces on I-25, U.S. 85. Fishing, canoes, kayaks near ruins of Fort Selden State Monument, where Douglas MacArthur and his family lived for a time.

Pancho Villa State Park, south of Deming on NM 11, almost on top of the Mexican border. Commemorates Villa's 1916 raid. Beautiful desert botanical garden. Camping, picnicking, showers, water, utility hookups.

Percha Dam, south of T or C on I-25. Features fishing near the dam; camping, picnicking sites, drinking water, showers, playground, hiking trails.

ATTRACTIONS

Lightning Field, near Grants. Pointed steel poles. Reservations must be made well in advance, in writing, through the Dia Art Foundation, Box 207, Quemado, NM 87829.

Silver City: Historic district, downtown. Older homes comprise the most extensive collection of Victorian era buildings in southern New Mexico.

Kwilleylekia Ruins, 29 miles northwest on U.S. 180, NM 211. Probably the last great pueblo of the Salados Indians (1425–1575 A.D.). Ongoing excavations. By appointment only.

Memory Lane Cemetery Containing graves of latter-day luminaries like Billy the Kid's mother

and lion-killing mountain man Ben Lilly.

Pinos Altos, ghost town, 6 miles north on NM 15. Judge Roy Bean and his brother once owned a store here.

Red Rock Game Preserve, about 30 miles north of Lordsburg on NM 464. Persian gazelle and Mexican Bighorn sheep are raised here in a virtually wild state in predator-proof pastures.

Santa Rita, Hurley Mines, 11–13 miles east on U.S. 180, NM 90 Open-pit copper mine and Kennecott Copper mill and smelter Tours by reservation.

Silver City Museum, 312 W. Broadway St., downtown. Depicts the multicultural heritage of southwestern New Mexico. Closed Mondays.

Socorro: Bureau of Mines & Mineral Resources Mineral Museum, Mon. – Fri., 8 to 5. More than 9000 samples of minerals and fluorescent rocks.

The Garcia House, Illinois Brewery, Golden Crown Mill, Bursum House, Juan N. Garcia House, downtown. All built in the 1880s when Socorro was one of the wildest and wooliest of New Mexico mining towns.

San Miguel Church, north of the plaza at 403 Camino Real. One wall dates from the original 1598 mission.

Truth or Consequences: Geronimo Springs Museum, 325 Main St. Comprised of five wings containing a rock and mineral collection, Indian artifacts, art exhibits, historical and cultural exhibits. Mon. – Sat., 9 to 5.

OBSERVATORIES

Very Large Array (VLA), 52 miles west of Socorro, NM, on U.S. 60. A collection of radio telescopes, one of the most important projects of its kind in the world. A visitors center next to the complex has a display which is open to the public every day from 8:30 until the sun goes down. No admission charge. Public Education Officer, National Radio Astronomy Observatory, Box O, Socorro, NM 87801. 505/772-4255.

GHOST TOWNS

Chloride, 42 miles northwest of Truth or Consequences on I-25, NM 52. Founded after the 1881 silver strike.

Hillsboro, 32 miles southwest of Truth or Consequences on I-25 and NM 90. Founded after the 1877 gold and silver strikes which reaped around $6 million in bullion.

Kelly, 29 miles west of Socorro on U.S. 60. Founded after the 1866 lead strike which garnered more than $28 million.

Kingston, 41 miles southwest of Truth or Consequences on I-25 and NM 90. Founded after the 1882 silver strike. Actress Lillian Russell performed here. Sheba Hurst of Mark Twain's *Roughing It* is buried here.

Lake Valley, 49 miles southwest of Truth or Consequences on I-25, NM 90 and 27. Founded after 1878 silver strike. Site of the famed Bridal Chamber Mine, the richest lode in state history.

Mogollon, 75 miles northwest of Silver City, U.S. 180, NM 78. Founded after 1879 gold strike. Was Butch Cassidy's hideout in the 1890s. Well preserved.

Shakespeare, 1½ miles south of Lordsburg. The scene of the infamous 1872 diamond hoax, the town hosts guided $2 tours from 10 a.m. to 2 p.m. on the second Sunday of each month.

Steins, 19 miles southwest of Lordsburg on I-10. This is where outlaw Black Jack Ketchum executed his train robbery in 1898.

Winston, 38 miles northwest of Truth or Consequences, I-25 and NM 52. Founded 1882.

EVENTS

Annual Great American Duck Race, Deming, late August. Nearly 500 ducks, two days of craziness and speed trails leading up to the final race for the title of World's Fastest (and richest) Duck. Best-Dressed Duck Contest and the crowing of a Duck Queen at the humans-only Duck Ball. 546-2674.

Deming Rock Hound Roundup, early to mid-March. Annual gathering attracts more than 500 participants from 41 states. Guided field trips for agate, geodes, candyrock, marble and pink onyx. Also auctions and judging seminar. Deming Gem and Mineral Society. 546-2674.

Hatch Chile Festival, early September. Annual event for chile lovers. Ristras, sacks and baskets of peppers for sale. Skeet shoot, horseshoe competition, fiddlers' contest, art show, Mexican dinner and chile contest. 267-3071.

ACCOMMODATIONS

Bear Mountain Guest Ranch, Box 1163, Silver City 88062. 538-2538. This ranch is a paradise for the amateur naturalist. Birdwatching, archaeological tours, hiking, family-style meals, rustic accommodations and expert guide services make it special.

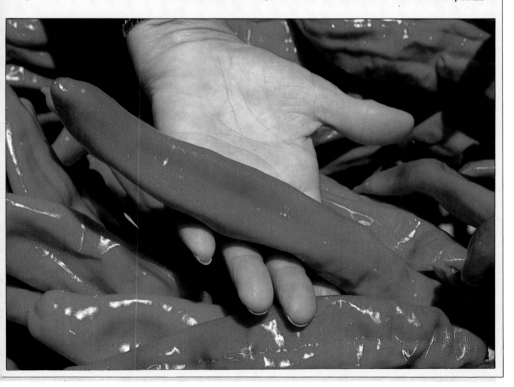

TUCSON AND THE BORDER COUNTY

Arizona's lower third lies almost entirely within the Sonoran Desert, a land mass respected by all, with the possible exception of real estate developers. The classic image of a desert—blowing sand, scorching sun and flat, waterless terrain—is found in only part of the region. The desert also includes lush mountain saddlebacks, highland firs and canyon streams. Rainfall is seasonal—toward summer's end and again at the beginning of winter—and entirely disruptive. On occasion the rain alters its schedule and dumps more water in a few days than it usually does in a year. In 1983, an unexpected torrential downpour filled every gully and *arroyo* for four days, flooding streets and highways, eroding riverbanks, washing out bridges and causing untold damages to homes and crops. Nature gave residents a sharp kick in the rear, reminding them of its power and fury.

New Kids in Town

Tucson is the major city in southern Arizona. Its first known settlement, about 1,200 years ago, included living quarters near present-day Church Avenue and Washington Street downtown; the site is now marked by a parking lot. Those first Tucsonans are today called *Hohokam*, "those who have disappeared" in the language of the Papago Indians, whose settlement at the base of a small mountain on Tucson's west side gave the city its name. It was called "Tu-uk-so-on," meaning, more or less, "settlement near a black-based mountain." Spanish-speaking newcomers, starting in the 16th Century, corrupted the Papago name to "Tuquison," which English-speaking latecomers further changed to "Tucson."

Spanish-speaking settlers established a *presidio*, whose walls protected them from Apache and others who didn't like the new kids in town. This neighborhood is now Tucson's oldest continually inhabited community; a walk around **El Presidio** reveals generations of life and work. The **Tucson Museum of Art**, El Presidio's showpiece, exhibits holdings ranging from pre-Columbian to modern cowboy. Architecture in El Presidio varies from Mexican-style homes with cactus-ribbed ceilings and patios out back to broad Midwestern-style houses with wide porches and roomy interiors. As in other downtown neighborhoods, lawyers and other young aesthetes have gentrified the more established residents out of the area. The result is a comfortable and attractive white-collar *barrio*. Kitty-corner to the art museum is **Old Town Artisans**, which carries goods crafted by Southwestern and Latin American artists. The store blends in well with its surroundings— quality standards, muted pretension and architectural integrity.

The original walled *presidio* area now serves as the backyard for downtown government buildings. One weekend every October it vibrates with **Tucson Meet Yourself**, a potpourri of music, dance and food from every cultural and ethnic group living in southern Arizona. Scottish highland dancers follow old-time fiddlers; Burmese performers are sandwiched between a *mariachi* band and Polish singers. Food booths offer delicacies as delicious as they are unpronounceable. It's a chance for locals to flash their heritage. Most Tucsonans

ceding
es, prickly
ntia
lovii cacti
home in
thwest
erts. Left,
olet" and
., Tucson
ctus
itry.

never knew that a Czechoslovakian mandolin player lives in their midst.

Controversy at Congress Street

The major east-west thoroughfare south of the government complex is **Congress Street**. In the middle of a median strip in front of the Pima County office buildings, Pancho Villa sits astride a horse. This statue—Villa riding south, knowing and confident—has been the source of a highly vocal controversy since it was given to the state by some Mexicans in 1981. Villa was a hero of the Mexican Revolution of 1910, a guerrilla bandit of the highest order. His rallying cry throughout Mexico's northwest gave hope to tens of thousands of impoverished and illiterate *campesinos*, many of whose descendants now live in the American Southwest. Villa's savagery, however, sometimes got the best of him, and survivors of his bloody raids upon innocent victims bore witness to his brutality. Their descendants also live in the Southwest, and they tried to block Villa's appearance. But the Mexican enigma remains, cocky and spirited, the pride of like-minded Tucsonans. Not even impromptu paint jobs, usually yellow and down the back, daunt him.

Another downtown landmark is **Ronstadt's Hardware Store**, founded by Federico Ronstadt who, in 1882, at the age of 14, moved from Mexico to Tucson to learn blacksmithing and the wheelwright trade. Two of his sons eventually took over the store, and starting in 1983, the next generation assumed operation. Although best known to the world for singer Linda, the Ronstadts are locally prominent for community involvement—one as head of city parks, another as chief of police, and others still scattered throughout civic and cultural groups. They still have family ties to Mexico, a situation common to many in the Southwest borderlands. Ranchers and farmers from Arizona and Mexico shop their store for horseshoes, windmills and everything in between—including Linda's records.

Two institutions, neither having much to do with the other, give the city distinct character—the **University of Arizona** and **Davis-Monthan Air Force Base**. On almost any given day, the UA will have some low-cost or free event

The San Xavier Mission, standing ta since the 18th-Century.

open to travellers—a poetry reading, football practice, a political demonstration or a movie. **The New Loft** theater south of the campus shows fare from Woody Allen to artsy foreign films. A block west of the UA is the **Arizona Heritage Center**, where the state's history is on exhibit and the **Center for Creative Photography**, a world-renowned repository for collections from the most acclaimed artistic and journalistic photographers. The Center's library serves researchers, both casual and scholarly, and its public gallery offers a view of some striking works.

Tucson's Special Sidelines

Say you had a few thousand out-of-commission airplanes—where would you put them? The Air Force decided to place its airplane graveyard at Davis-Monthan Air Force Base, where the desert atmosphere keeps corrosion to a minimum. Tours of the metallic cemetery are given twice weekly. Training for support teams for the cruise missile system is also carried out at D-M.

Hi Corbett Field, where the Cleve-

land Indians practice every spring against other cactus league teams in the majors, is also the home field for the minor league Tucson Toros. Watching the Toros square off against Pacific Coast League opponents on hot summer evenings attracts crowds.

A sign advertising the ARIZONA MOTEL wins Tucson's "best neon" competition; cruising past it on South Sixth Avenue between 28th and 29th streets on a weekend night will also expose you to youthful low-riders, whose cars are low, slow, and customized to the hilt.

A final local sight: Tucson's largest tree, a eucalyptus on West Congress Street in front of a supermarket next to the usually dry Santa Cruz River. Its circumference measures more than 19½ feet (six meters).

Driving south from Tucson on Interstate 19—the only interstate highway in the country which measures distance solely in kilometers—a white dove appears out the right window. This is the **San Xavier Mission**, a magnificent 18th-Century structure which serves the spiritual needs of many Papago living on the surrounding reservation. The

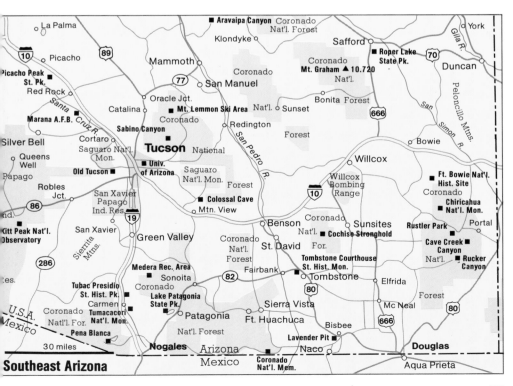

Southeast Arizona

church is maintained remarkably well, as if whitewashed daily at dawn. Public tours point out the Moorish and Byzantine features of this bedrock of Catholicism in the desert.

Most of the 8,000 Papago live further west of town on a reservation covering 3 million acres (1.2 million hectares) of cactus, mesquite and scrub. While the U.S. government recognizes their reservation only as far as Arizona's southern border, **Papaguería**—the land of the Papago—stretches into Mexico, from which many of the tribe cross freely back and forth at convenient breaks in the international fence. Papago are understandably sensitive to outsiders who approach their 75 miles (120 km) of the line for the same purpose.

Play Bingo, the Yaqui Way

Kitt Peak Observatory, at 6,875 feet (2,095 meters) in the Quinlan Mountains 52 miles (83 km) west of Tucson on land leased from the Papago carries out solar and stellar research—and has a visitors center which sells the best of Papago handicrafts at fair prices.

Yaqui Indians also have their tribal headquarters southwest of Tucson at the **Pascua Yaqui Reservation**. The Yaqui, many of whom abandoned their ancestral land in Mexico around the turn of the century after torturous treatment by the Mexican government, also have communities within Tucson and elsewhere around the state. A tribe lacking solid economic footing, the Pascua Yaqui were among the first Indians in the country to take advantage of court decisions permitting on-reservation gambling. The result is a high-stakes bingo game which nightly draws a full house to a recently constructed football-field-sized hall. These Indians, known in literature for incredible powers of perception, are now masters of a Yaqui way of bingo.

Outsiders are allowed to watch spiritual plays, ceremonial dances, and other Yaqui activities leading up to Easter Sunday with the strict proviso that no cameras, tape recorders or even paper and pencil record the proceedings. The Tucson Festival Society gives directions to interested visitors.

Nogales, Mexico, booms and busts simultaneously. Generally, the worse off the Mexican economy, the better the

As night fa on Tucson, left, the swinging country entertainer come out tc play, right.

shopping for tourists. Take advantage of this—good kitsch is hard to find these days. But, as in Agua Prieta, seek out the qualities which have attracted and repulsed so many for so long. Buy some white cheese and a fruit you've never seen before at **Futería Chihuahua**, the open-air *mercado* on the right side of Calle Obregón about six blocks into town. Yes, dine at **La Caverna** and **La Roca**, but also try **Restaurante El Mar**, the little seafood place with the shark hanging above its door on the left side on Calle Obregón about 10 blocks south of the border. Watch the eyes in the crowd surrounding a street musician from the interior. Buy candy from a snot-nosed little urchin. Climb up the stairs on the east side and look down into the city.

Stroll Canal Street and imagine the red-light district's heyday when University of Arizona fraternities packed the sidewalks. Ride a city bus to a strange neighborhood, walk around, and take a cab back to familiar terrain. Enjoy the border, but when you re-enter the United States and are asked what you're bringing back from Mexico, stifle that smile.

A Word from the Cactus

What distinguishes southern Arizona from other parts of the Southwest is its abundance and variety of cacti and all the critters which use their branches, shade and roots for homes. A cursory understanding of the desert and its mysterious life cycles makes the traveller more aware of and comfortable with the region's subtleties. At first glance a cactus is little more than a thick, thorny, green plant with its arms waving at the sky. Look closer: the root system may tell you about water storage, the direction the cactus points can serve as a compass, flowers at the top may indicate the month, the ash-like holes may be seasonal homes to birds. Insects parading up and down its crevices contribute a strong link in the food chain of nearby animals, and scrub brush near the bottom may hide the entrance to underground cottontail rabbit or iguana lizard homes.

This information can be absorbed from any of dozens of primers about the desert, or at the **Arizona-Sonora Desert Museum** in **Tucson Mountain Park** west of the city. "Museum" is a benign mis-

nomer, though, for the exhibits are changing every second of the day and night. Entertaining and educational, the ASDM displays almost all Sonoran Desert living plants and animals, from plants barely visible to the naked eye such as blue-green algae, to giant cottonwood trees, from tiny doodle bugs to the overpowering black bear. Every effort is made to duplicate the natural surroundings for each life form. A desert trek of any length from an hour to a week or longer should begin with a visit to the Desert Museum. You may not encounter a bobcat, rattler, javelina, or otter on your own journey—yes, otter live in the Sonoran Desert in the Sea of Cortez—but you'll probably be reassured knowing their habits and habitats.

ASDM's special events are scheduled to coincide with bursts of flowers, depth of snow, heat of day and clearness of night. When flowers blossom suddenly in mid-March, ASDM guides lead day trips to see the new life and explain the surrounding natural history which has shaped the annual bloom for eons. Changing plant and animal life become startlingly clear during the "one hour to Canada" drive from the base of **Mt.**

Lemmon in cactus country northeast of Tucson, up to firs and aspens near the 9,100-foot (2,800-meter) top. And finally, the Arizona-Sonora Desert Museum tells us how the Boojum—a funny-looking tree in Mexico's northwest—got its name. It seems that during a 1922 expedition near Puerto Libertad, Mexico, Godfrey Sykes was looking at distant wildlife through a telescope when a tree he'd never seen before came into view. "He gazed intently for a few minutes," his son later wrote, "and then said, 'Ho ho—a Boojum, definitely a Boojum.'" Although called *Fougueria columnaris* by botanists, the tree will forever be known to the rest of us as a Boojum, Lewis Carroll's creature of fantasy from his 1876 tale, *The Hunting of the Snark*.

Covering Cochise County

Arizona has many laws for those who choose to abide by them. Heading east from Tucson you enter what some call **The Free State of Cochise**, a land protected on all sides from conventional standards by splendid mountains, working ranches, old mining towns and the

A '46 Che

Mexican border. Historically, Cochise County has established its own code of conduct, law, and behavior. Take the Benson exit off of I-10 50 miles (80 km) east of Tucson. You'll know you're there by the huge semi in the sky, on the right side of the street, which says MARIE'S TRUCK STOP. (You won't find the cafe, however—it's been razed.) A stop at the **Singing Wind Bookshop** is in order. Singing Wind, located in an old ranch house, just north of Benson carries about the most comprehensive collections of Southwestern literature assembled anywhere, including guides for birders and hikers, history and biography, Indian detective stories and cowboy picture books.

Mormons settled **St. David**, south of Benson on U.S. Highway 80 along the San Pedro river. Visitors are welcome at their Church of Jesus Christ of Latter-Day Saints, and also at the Holy Trinity Monastery, established by Benedictines, east of town.

Tombstone, a bit farther down the road, once a mining town of some worth, was the unfortunate site of some minor gunplay in the late 1800s. Between then and now television was in-vented, and today the town spends most of its weekends recreating a history that never was. Amble down Allen Street— in Tombstone you don't walk, you amble—past the Bird Cage Theatre, the OK Corral and other mock tributes to the Earp brothers and their ilk, and you'll likely run into gunslingers per-forming shootouts on cue. After taking in Boot Hill Cemetery, you'll have com-pleted your journey to the heart of the myth of the Old West. Helldorado Days in October draws the largest crowds.

Continue east on U.S. 80, past the cutoff to Sierra Vista and Ft. Huachuca, where the U.S. Army trains spies and Mule Pass Tunnel appears at the crest of a hill. Emerging on the other side you'll begin to understand why it's often referred to as the "Time Tunnel." To-wards the bottom of the hill on your left you'll swear a picture postcard town from the turn of the century has been preserved. Gingerbread architecture, homes stacked up on canyon hillsides, a main street which winds past friendly storefronts, and a curious mix of aging hippies, small-town merchants, alcohol-ic vets, struggling artists, retired min-ers, single parents, and venture capital-

aguaro
ational
orest near
ucson.

ists. This is **Old Bisbee**, a town to which seekers of the quaint flock. Despite efforts to implant some upscale qualities ("old" and "shop" have acquired an "e" at the end on a few signs, and condo-style rentals are a-comin'), Bisbee's chief attraction is that since Phelps Dodge yanked out its mining operation in the mid-1970s, the town has been up for grabs. Old miners' homes were dirt cheap, and energetic young urban refugees and renegades settled in. Today the town is known for its artsy community, whose industrious output covers the range from works only a mother could love to impressive art, carried out with integrity and skill. **Cochise Fine Arts**, which sponsors the annual Bisbee Poetry Festival, and **Psyche's Eye** are two galleries exhibiting Bisbee works.

A Pit, a Hotel and a Gulch

By any standard the biggest attraction around is **Lavender Pit**, a 120-yard (110-meter) deep hole in the ground, 1½ mile long and ¾ mile wide (2.2 by 1.2 km). Tours of the pit, where miners dug copper for more than 75 years, and of the underground Queen Mine, give some idea of what laborers faced daily, and why during World War I the Industrial Workers of the World—the Wobblies—attracted workers to their cause. An IWW strike in 1917 proved too irksome for Phelps Dodge, which one night rounded up all Wobblies and their sympathizers, marched them at gunpoint to a baseball field, sent them off in boxcars, and let them out in the desert near Columbus, New Mexico. This infamous event in American history became known as the Bisbee Deportation, a subject about which one still speaks politely with local boosters.

The **Copper Queen Hotel**, once host to mining barons, is in good shape today, its bar convivial and its rooms comfortable. **Brewery Gulch** around the corner had it all—fine restaurants, brothels, theaters, gambling halls. That was in the early 20th Century, when copper boomed and miners caroused. Today the street is far tamer. Walk down the Gulch past **St. Elmo**—oldest of the local bars, where you can still count on a harmless slow-motion fight late at night near closing time—and on into the residential neighborhood. Restoring old homes has become a fetish

Church at Tumacacoi Arizona.

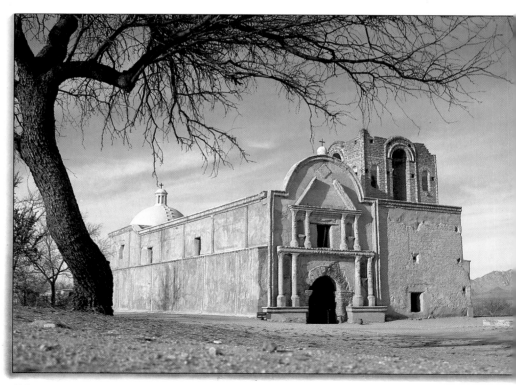

among Bisbeeites, and Brewery Gulch, or any of the canyons farther uphill, offer fine examples. The town fairly drips with ambience, most of it authentic, and its low-end economy makes for a low-profile populace. Every day you can hear conversations beginning, "I was just passing through, I didn't plan to stay...."

The 1.8 million acre (720,000 hectare) **Coronado National Forest**, 12 different mountain islands rising from the desert floor to elevations of more than 10,000 feet (3,050 meters), dominates southern Arizona's horizon. It includes primitive wilderness areas (the Galiuro Wilderness is the most inaccessible, reachable only by a fair-weather dirt road), fishing (bass at Peña Blanca Lake, trout in mountain streams in the Pinaleno range west of Safford), and travel on foot, horse, trail bike, snowmobile and 4-wheel drive as marked throughout the forest. A wide variety of easily identifiable birds has turned the forest, particularly the Chiricahua and Huachuca mountains, into a birder's paradise. Finally, to reach the spot where Apache leader Geronimo made one of his surrenders to U.S.

troops, drive about 10 miles (16 km) southeast on a dirt road from the town of Apache on U.S. 80, pass by a ranch and through a gate, and park just inside the Forest Service sign welcoming you to the Peloncillo Mountains. The precise site, determined by photographic accounts, is a quarter-mile (400-meter) walk west at a bench on a mesa.

More Border Adventures

Naco, Mexico, six miles (10 km) southwest of Bisbee, is small enough to get a sense of border towns without feeling overwhelmed. When you drive into Mexico an official will look up inquiring either with his eyes or voice where you're going. Tell him, "*aqui no más*" (just here), nod, and proceed down the road. Naco's commercial district is confined to cross-streets within three blocks of the border. Stores selling tortillas, clothes, groceries, furniture and knick-knacks welcome your business. Pesos are not necessary; bordertown merchants know the exchange rate for dollars better than most bankers. A half-mile (800 meters) or so down the road, turn left and cruise the

Border trol on zona side.

quiet residential neighborhood until you find the ruins of the old red-light district. A few former brothels are in splendid decay, with Japanese tile walls, church-like windows and cribs—the tiny rooms where prostitutes entertained—still intact outback. One of the two still-functioning brothels adjoins a decent all-night cafe, the only place where Bisbeeites and others from north of the border can get a meal after 10 p.m. A note about the brothels—they are really quite harmless bars with jarring juke-boxes and male camaraderie. (Women—at least American women—go in on occasion with no ill will in either direction.) The prostitutes are friendly, but they will leave you alone unless you want to dance or more.

Two imposing smelter stacks mark **Douglas**, the U.S. border town opposite **Agua Prieta, Mexico**. Pancho Villa fought in Agua Prieta, and long-time residents retell stories of climbing to the roof of the **Gadsden Hotel** (visit it just for the marble-columned lobby) to watch Villistas battle Mexican government troops. A trench dug along the U.S. side of the border to hide soldiers protecting America from foreign en-

croachment still exists.

Drive east along the international fence; within 10 minutes you will encounter high drama between the U.S. Border Patrol and Mexicans coming into the country. For many it is a cat and mouse game; for others, life and death. Gaping holes in the fence lead to well-worn trails and pick-up points in and around Douglas. Polite debate in Washington about immigration takes on new meaning when you encounter the situation first hand.

Where American and Mexican Cultures Meet

Spend some time walking in Agua Prieta, first along the street leading from the border with its tourist shops. Like most border towns, its culture is an overlay of the United States and Mexico. Look at the faces of *campesinos* from the interior getting off the bus, heading north. Talk with vendors and soldiers on the fringes of the plaza. Browse the sidestreet bookstore, listen to music at the record shop around the corner. Shoot pool and clink beer bottles with the unemployed, order something you can't even pronounce at the Café Central. Watch the flow of women leaving their shift at the *maquiladoras*—the assembly plants owned by U.S. corporations. Dance beneath the neon lights flooding the cavernous interior of the Santa Fe Club.

Should you find yourself in **Yuma**, a city which inspires departure, drive south to **San Luis Río Colorado, Mexico**, for its terrific Chinese restaurants and, in season, watch the *Algodoneros* ("the cotton-pickers") play minor league baseball in the Liga Norte de Sonora. Head east to Sonoyta, Mexico, on the **Camino del Diablo**, the "Devil's Highway," a road which slices through 125 miles (200 km) of organ pipe cactus forest, volcanic rock and foreboding desert. Cross back into the United States at Sonoyta, and you'll find yourself in the middle of **Organ Pipe Cactus National Monument**, a 500-square-mile (1,295-sq km) preserve filled with the unusual plant and its natural friends. The cactus, which grows in clustered "pipes" from the same roots, reaches 20 feet (six-meters) high. Its pinkish-white flower blooms in early May and reigns for eight weeks before yielding to the scorching July sun.

Left, "Cac Realty" si on Stone Avenue in Tucson; a right, gunman performs a shootout c cue at Old Tucson, Arizona.

NATIONAL PARKS AND MONUMENTS

Chiricahua National Monument, 70 miles northeast of Douglas. Extraordinary weathered-rock sculptures high in the mountains where the fabled Apache warrior Cochise used to hold sway. Enter the monument via AZ 186 or 181. The mountain road from the east (Portal) is rough, closed during the winter. Many areas in the park cannot be approached by car, only on foot or horseback. Visitors center open daily. Camping available near monument headquarters. Campers must register at the visitors center.

Coronado National Memorial, atop the Huachuca Mountains, 22 miles south of Sierra Vista, borders on Mexico. Spot where Coronado and his men first entered the U.S. in search of the Seven Cities of Cibola. Panoramic vistas. Visitors center open daily. Pageant held in April in commemoration of Coronado's expedition. Coronado National Memorial, R.R. 1, P.O. Box 126, Hereford, AZ 85615; 602/366-5515.

Fort Bowie National Historic Site Directly northwest of Chiricahua National Monument the fort was built to guard Apache Pass from raids by followers of Cochise, Geronimo and other Apache chiefs. Lonely relic sits by itself in the hills. Dirt road across the pass has some rough spots.

Organ Pipe Cactus National Monument, south of Ajo and bordering on Mexico. Rare desert flora and fauna, scenic desert to mountain drives, gateway to deep-sea fishing in the Gulf of California. Visitors center 17 miles south of the park entrance, open 8 to 5. Backcountry permits required; available at visitors center. Camping allowed, but no wood fires. Rte. 1, Box 100, Ajo, AZ 85321. 387-6849.

Saguaro National Monument, in two sections, 17 miles east and 15 miles west of Tucson. Preserves one of the state's richest stands of saguaro cactus, best seen via the Loop Drive in the Rincon Mountain (eastern) section. Visitors center at monument headquarters offers exhibits, nature walks. Open daily. Drive begins at the parking lot.

Tumacacori National Monument, 19 miles north of Nogales on I-19. Picturesque ruins of early Spanish mission now includes a modern museum and patio garden as well. Open daily 8 to 5.

NATIONAL FORESTS

Coronado National Forest Scattered among 12 areas in southern and southeastern Arizona. Collectively, these woodlands

offer a full range of activities, with riding, skiing, water sports, fishing in trout streams, big game hunting, and more. Drive from desert to pines in an hour. The Tucson to Mt. Lemmon Road, north of Tucson, is a good example. Forest encompasses Saguaro and Chiricahua National Monuments. Write Federal Building, 301 W. Congress, Tucson, AZ 85701.

STATE PARKS

Painted Rocks State Historic Park, about 25 miles northwest of Gila Bend on I-8 to Painted Rocks Road. Park preserves an exceptional collection of ancient Indian rock-art drawings and writings. Camping, water sports, hiking, fishing. 602/683-2151.

Patagonia Lake State Park, northeast of Nogales, great location for fishing and boating. Facilities include marina with dock, launch ramp, boat rentals and camper supplies. Campsites along the shore of 200-acre lake. Fishing for panfish, trout, bass, catfish. 602/287-6965.

Tombstone Courthouse State Historic Park, 219 E. Toughnut St., in beautiful downtown Tombstone. The Victorian courthouse is a museum that recaptures events of the rough-and-ready shot-'em-up days. Daily 8 to 5:30. 602/457-3311.

Tubac Presidio State Historic Park, between Tucson and Nogales on I-19, in the art colony of Tubac. One of Arizona's oldest communities, where the Spaniards made the state's first permanent European settlement in 1752. Large interpretive center with walk-through dioramas, displays and a view of the remains of the fort's main building. Thurs. – Mon. 8 to 5. 602/398-2252.

Yuma Territorial Prison State Historic Park in Yuma (4th St exit off I-8). Built by the convicts who inhabited its thick-walled stone cells. Exhibits about life in a frontier "Bastille." Open daily 8 to 5:30. 602/783-4771.

ATTRACTIONS

"A" Mountain Provides an excellent overview of Tucson, which is why it is officially called **Sentinel Peak**.

Arizona Historical Society, near the entrance of The U. of Arizona campus, Park Ave. at 949 E. 2nd St., Tucson. The history of Arizona is displayed with objects, documents, photographs and dioramas. 602/628-5774.

Arizona-Sonora Desert Museum in the Tucson Mountains, 16 miles west of Tucson. An extraordinary setting features plants and animals in displays that simulate their natural habitats. For example, you can watch otters underwater through glass panels and see vampire bats in ultra-violet light.

Cochise County Trail This 200-mile tour southeast of Tucson winds through an area riddled with relics of the Old West and the towns of Willcox, Douglas, Bisbee and Tombstone.

Cochise Stronghold, east of Tucson, 10½ miles from U.S. 666 in the scenic Dragoon Mountains and in the middle of the Coronado National Forest. This spot was for many years a hideout of the famous Apache chief.

Colossal Cave, 28 miles southeast of Tucson. One of the state's limestone wonders, offering daily tours. It was also a famous robbers' hideout; legend has it that gold is still hidden in its recesses.

Douglas, southeast of Bisbee on the Mexican border, provides an easy cross-over to Old Mexico. Douglas features the old extravagant Gadsden Hotel, which is a state historical site.

Grace H. Flandrau Planetarium, Tucson. Offers dramatic and educational theater performances on astronomy and exploration of space. 602/626-4515.

Fort Huachuca, southeast of Tucson. Once an important territorial outpost, a strategic communications base for the U.S. Army. The museum on the premises is open to the public. 602/538-2714.

Mission San Xavier del Bac, nine miles south of Tucson on San Xavier Road in the Papago Indian Reservation. Established in 1700, it is touted as one of the most architecturally beautiful missions in the Southwest. Mass is still held and historical lectures are given each day except Sunday. 602/294-2624.

Nogales, directly south of Phoenix on the Mexican border, is actually two "Twin Cities" divided by the international border and is popular for shopping and sampling the flavor of on-the-border Mexico.

Pinal Pioneer Parkway, between Phoenix and Tucson. A 250-mile loop to and from Phoenix passes valleys, farmlands, ranches, mining towns, deserts, mountains and a generous sprinkling of ghost towns. During the leg of the trip that takes you along Rte. 177/77, you see the giant open pit mine that used to be the town of Ray; the new town of Kearney; and the older towns of Hayden and Winkelman.

Pinal Pioneer Parkway Scenic Drive, Highway 89. The 40-mile stretch of the Parkway that used to be the main route between Phoenix and Tucson is a billboard-free drive through one of the state's most attractive Sonoran Desert areas. Signs identify many of the plants and cacti.

Sells, southwest of Tucson on AZ 86. Tribal headquarters for the 2,500,000-acre Papago Indian Reservations, Sells features an Arts & Crafts Center and trading posts.

Sonoita/Patagonia, south of Tucson on AZ 82. Southern Arizona's greenbelt regions, famous for the quarterhorse and cattle ranches. Patagonia houses the Museum of the Horse.

Old Tucson, in Tucson Mountain Park, 13 miles southwest of Tucson. 883-0100. A popular western movie set, open all year from 9:30 to 5.

Titan Missile Museum. Green Valley is located 25 miles south of Tucson off Interstate 19. The tour, which leaves on the hour and is by reservation, is the only public trip around an intercontinental nuclear missile. Tour is moderately strenuous; 55 stairs lead down to the bowels of the Titan. Open seven days. 602/791-2929.

Tombstone, northwest of Bisbee on U.S. 80, southeast of Tucson. "The town too tough to die" was a famous mining town. Home of the Tombstone Epitaph, the Birdcage Saloon, the Cochise County Courthouse, Boothill Cemetery, the Birdcage Theatre, Crystal Palace Bar and Wells Fargo Museum. Mock western events are frequently part of the scenery. Contact: Tombstone Tourism Association. 457-3608.

University of Arizona, Tucson. Arizona's oldest and largest university. Tucson used to be the capital of the Arizona Territory until Phoenix grabbed the title in 1877. To smooth things over, Tucson was granted the state's first university. The on-campus Arizona State Museum houses one of the finest collections of southwestern American Indian art to be found anywhere.

HORSE RACING

Douglas: Cochise County Horse Races, April and May. 364-3819.

Sonoita: Horse Races, May. 455-5585.

OBSERVATORIES

Kitt Peak National Observatory, southwest of Tucson, just inside the Papago Indian Reservation. Take State 86 to 386. This observatory has the best collection of telescopes in the world, with a large concentration of facilities for stellar and solar research. The famed McMath Solar Telescope is among the greats. Visitors Center, gift shop and exhibits open 10 to 4 daily. No admission charge. 623-5796, ext. 250.

GHOST TOWNS

Bisbee, 95 miles southeast of Tucson. "Queen of the Mining Camps." The brawling mining days of the 1880s blend with the modern city of today. Famous underground Queen Mine tours, Brewery Gulch, Copper Queen Hotel, Lavendar Pit.

Charleston, 8 miles southwest of Tombstone. In its heyday, tougher than Tombstone. Used by the U.S. Army during World War II as a training site for house-to-house combat. Only a few scattered sheets of tin and heaps of adobe rubble remain today. Park at San Pedro River bridge, walk north ½ mile to ruins.

Contention City, near Tombstone. Another of the "mill towns" where ore from Tombstone was processed. Heaps of ruin and rubble.

Courtland, 21 miles north of Douglas off U.S. 666 about 6 miles. One-time thriving mining camp named for a miner. The town's single resident does not encourage sightseers.

Dos Cabezas, AZ 186, 15 miles southeast of Willcox. Semi-ghost town where a few residents still support a small Post Office. Wells Fargo station 1885. Vacant, crumbling adobes, stage station.

Duquesne, 19 miles east of Nogales. Established around the turn of the century, this former mining center had a peak population of 1000 residents, including Westinghouse of Westinghouse Electric. Post Office from 1890.

Ehrenberg, Yuma County. Now a growing community, the only remnants left are a few old adobes and a cemetery.

Gleeson, 16 miles east of Tombstone. Even before the Spaniards arrived, Indians were mining turquoise near here. John Gleeson prospected in the 1880s. Later, Tiffany's mined the turquoise while others reaped copper, lead and zinc. Picturesque ruins, cemetery.

Harshaw, 10 miles southeast of Patagonia. Settled about 1875, this town soon boasted a newspaper, *The Bullion*, saloons, numerous stores, with 100 working mines nearby. Stone, adobe ruins, cemetery.

Hilltop, 36 miles southeast from Willcox on AZ 186. The town was first started on the west side of the mountain, and then a tunnel was put through to the east side where an even larger town was established.

Mowry, 15 miles southeast of Patagonia. Small town grown up around an old silver, lead and zinc mine purchased in the late 1850s by Sylvester Mowry, U.S. Army. Mowry's operations were aborted in 1862 when he was charged with supplying lead for Confederate bullets. He was jailed, his mine taken over by Uncle Sam. Extensive ruins.

Oro Blanco, 15 to 20 miles west of Nogales. Gold mine in operation from 1873 through 1932. Adobe ruins.

Paradise, south of I-10 on the Arizona—N. Mexico border, 6 miles northwest of Portal. Briefly active mining town dating from the early 1900s. Still home to a few oldtimers who are happy to point out the old town jail and ruins of various businesses.

Pearce, one mile off U.S. 666 from a point 29 miles south of Willcox. The old gold camp once had a population of 2000, all well

supported by the Commonwealth Mine. In its heyday, the old mine was the richest in southern Arizona. Operating store and post office, with many vacant adobes, mine and mill ruins.

Washington Camp, 20 miles south of Patagonia. Once a major service community for Duquesne, Mowry and Harshaw. Ruins. Check road conditions.

ENTERTAINMENT

Arizona Opera Company, Tucson Community Center Music Hall, Tucson. In its 12th season, the company serves both Tucson and Phoenix. 602/293-4336.

Arizona Theatre Company, Tucson Community Center Little Theatre. November through May. A professional company employing nationally recognized guest artists. Performs six plays per season; some recent offerings were *Glengarry Glen Ross, My Fair Lady, Galileo, Quilters.* 622-2823

Invisible Theatre, 1400 North First Avenue, Tucson, September through June. Performs some six plays every year. This intimate theater is experimental, local, frequently exceptional. 882-9721.

Southern Arizona Light Opera Company, Tucson Community Center Music Hall, November through May. A lighthearted experience, provided by amateurs and semi-professionals. 323-7888.

Territorial Dance Theater, Tucson Community Center Little Theatre, fall through spring. 327-1381.

Tucson Metropolitan Ballet, Tucson Community Center Music Hall, October through April. Three ballets per season, including the *Nutcracker Suite* at Christmas. Arizona's only semi-professional, resident, classical troupe. 296-0264.

Tucson Pops Orchestra, Reid Park Bandshell, summer entertainment outdoors. 791-4873.

University of Arizona Artist Series, University of Arizona Main Auditorium, September

through April. Jazz, chamber music, etc.

University of Arizona Repertory Theatre, University Theatre, summer. Three productions, with an emphasis on modern classics in musical and drama. 621-1162.

The University Theatre, University Theatre, September through April. Professional productions by the Drama Department. George Bernard Shaw, Rogers and Hart, the immortal Bard. 626-1162.

EVENTS

Sonoita Quarter Horse Show, early June. 455-5585.

Bisbee Renaissance Festival, mid to late June. 432-2141.

"Juneteenth" Festival, Tucson, mid-June. 791-4355.

World Championship Inner Tube Races, Yuma, early July. 782-2567.

Ringling Brothers Barnum & Bailey Circus, Tucson, mid-July. 791-4266.

U.S. National Championship Bicycle Race, Bisbee, late July. 432-2141.

Bisbee Poetry Festival, mid-August. 432-2141.

Old Time Fiddlers Contests, Globe, mid-August. 473-4000.

AQHA Horse Show, Douglas, late August, 364-3819.

Tombstone Wild West Days Rendezvous of gunfighters, early September. 457-2211.

PRCA Rodeo, Sonoita, early September. 455-5585.

Brewery Gulch Days, Bisbee, September.

Santa Cruz County Fair, Sonoita, mid-September. 455-5585.

Cochise County Fair, Douglas, late September. 364-3819.

Rex Allen Days & Rodeo, Willcox, early October. 384-4271.

Tombstone Helldorado Days, mid to late October. Old-time event celebrating annually Tombstone as it was in the days of the Wild West. Tombstone Tourism Association, 457-2211.

St. Francis of Assisi Celebration, San Xavier del Bac, Tucson.

Old Pueblo Gem and Mineral Show, Tucson Community Center, October.

Papago Rodeo and Fair, Sells, November.

Tucson Holiday Fair, early December. 624-2333.

Fourth Avenue Street Fair, Fourth Ave., Tucson, December.

Tumacacori Fiesta, San Jose de Tumacacori, Tucson, December.

Winterhaven Festival of Lights, Winterhaven Neighborhood, Tucson, December.

Joe Garigiola Tucson Golf Open, early January. 792-4501.

Custom Car Show, Yuma, early February. 344-3800.

Tucson Gem & Mineral Show, February. Tucson Community Center and other locations. Contact the Chamber of Commerce.

Silver Spur Rodeo & Parade, Yuma, mid-February. 738-3641.

Valentine "Heart" Ball, Bisbee, Feb. 12. 432-3543.

Fiesta de los Vaqueros Parade & Rodeo, Tucson, early March. 792-2250.

Square Dance Festival, Yuma, early March. 344-3800.

Tombstone Territorial Days, early March. 457-2211.

Shrine Circus, Tucson, mid to late March. 791-4266.

Little Britches Rodeo, Sierra Vista, early April. 458-6940.

San Xavier Festival, Tucson, April 8. 622-6911.

Fiesta de la Placita & Inter-American Arts Festival, Tucson, held in March or April, various locations throughout town. A festival blending Indian, Spanish, Mexican and American traditions, attended by 100,000

people annually. Tucson Festival Society, 622-6911.

Pima County Fair, April, Pima County Fairgrounds.

Coronado Historical Pageant, Sierra Vista. April. 458-6940.

La Vuelta de Bisbee Bike Races, late April. 432-2141.

Cingo de Mayo, May 5. Traditional Mexican celebration of Mexico's 1862 victory over France. Celebrated throughout the Southwest. Arizona Office of Tourism, 255-3618.

Rillito River Regatta, May, Rillito River.

Tombstone Wyatt Earp Days, end of May. 457-2211.

SHOPPING

Tubac, on I-19 between Tucson and Nogales, is an entire village of arts and crafts shops.

Tucson is a boutique-laden town with several interesting pockets for shoppers in need of a fix. The **Downtown Mercado**, at International Alley, off Pennington, is a peasant market with seasonal produce, crafts and ethnic foods. **Old Town Artisans**, at 186 N. Meyer Ave., is a blocklong in-town village purveying fine old and contemporary art; **El Mercado de Boutiques**, at Broadway and Wilmot is a cluster of small, elegant shops and art galleries. For antiques, uniques and all kinds of funk try **Fourth Avenue Shops** at 4th through 7th Streets, affectionately dubbed "North Beach in the Desert." The **El Presidio Gallery**, at 201 North D Court Ave. specializes in regional arts and crafts.

INDIAN RESERVATIONS

Cocopah East & West Reservations, 12 miles southwest of Yuma. Noted for beadwork. Special attraction: Heritage Art Museum, with displays of beadwork, traditional farming tools, native dress. Cocopah Tribal Council, Bin "G," Somerton, AZ 85350. 627-2102.

Fort Yuma Reservation, 185 miles southwest of Phoenix. The tribe is known for beadwork and other artifacts; reservation bor-

ders California, with headquarters in California. Attractions: Colorado River, fishing, water sports, camping. Quechan Tribal Council, P.O. Box 1352, Yuma, AZ 85364. 714/572-0213.

Pascua-Yaqui Reservation, 135 miles southwest of Phoenix, near Tucson. The tribe creates Deer Dance Statues and cultural paintings done by Indian children. Attractions: Easter Ceremonial and the September Recognition Ceremonial. Pascua-Yaqui Tribal Council, 4821 West Calle Vicam, Tucson, AZ 85706. 602/883-2838.

ACCOMMODATIONS

The Arizona Inn, 2200 East Elm, 85719. 325-1541. More expensive than the average in-town spot but replete with amenities and highly recommended.

Rancho de La Osa, Sasabe, AZ 85633. 602/823-4257. Some 200 years old, one of the last great Spanish haciendas in the U.S. Situated on the Mexican border 66 miles southwest of Tucson, this is a working cattle ranch and destination resort for horse lovers. Good food, friendly staff, heated pool, hiking, riding instruction.

Sheraton Tucson 10,000 N. Oracle Road, Tucson, AZ 85704. 602/742-7000. Again, no secret. This is an enormous complex with pool, coffee shop, dining room, golf, tennis, horseback riding, a health spa and boutiques. Expensive.

Tanque Verde Ranch, Route 8, Box 66, Tucson, AZ 85748. 602/296-6275. Old-time cattle ranch eight miles east of Tucson. Appealing rustic setting with new luxury accommodations. Riding, hiking, bird watching, tennis, golf courses nearby, swimming pools, whirlpools.

Westward Look Resort, 245 E. Ina Rd., Tucson, AZ 85704. 602/297-1151. Decor is "Southwestern modern." Resort boasts a panoramic view of the mountains. Fitness center, three swimming pools, bar and dining room overlooking the city.

In **Bisbee** try the venerable **Copper Queen Hotel**, Box CQ, Bisbee 85603. 602/432-2216. Moderate. **The Inn at Castle Rock** is a bed-and-breakfast place.

PHOENIX CITY AND ITS ENVIRONS

When Frank Lloyd Wright first saw the Salt River Valley in the late 1920s, it struck him as a "vast battleground of Titanic natural forces." Like a revelation were its "leopard spotted mountains... its great striated and stratified masses, noble and quiet," its patterns modeled on the "realism of the rattlesnake," its "nature masonry rising from the desert floor." Here, thought Wright with the zeal of someone moving in, if Arizonans could avoid the "candymakers and cactus-hunters," a civilization could be created that would "allow man to become a godlike native part of Arizona."

Even today, when candy-makers and cactus-hunters in the form of land developers have won out over Wright's visions, the settings of Phoenix is impressive. To the east soar the massive Four Peaks and the formal flank of the Superstition Mountains, while the Sierra Estrella rides the southeast horizon in dorsales of blue silk. Hemming the city north and south are lower ranges of Precambrian gneiss and schist, framing the Phoenix trademark, Camelback Mountain—a freestanding, rosy, recumbent dromedary with sedimentary head and granitic hump. Many of the mountains within town are pocked with exclusive homes, and some of the smaller formations, separating business areas from bedroom communities from tourist playgrounds, have come to function as urban room dividers. Still, geological immediacy is what gives Phoenix its own look. And by acquiring the two major mountain ranges within its borders the city of Phoenix, for all its commerce, has amassed more square footage of park than any other town in the world.

A civilization that adapted man to the Salt River Valley preceded Wright's visions by some 2,500 years. As early as 500 B.C. the Hohokam Indians developed an intricate system of canals for irrigating fields of corn, beans, squash and cotton. Remains of that system were taken over and expanded in 1868 by the Swilling Irrigation Canal Co., the first organized Anglos to stake claims in the long-deserted valley. The following year their settlement was named

Phoenix by an Englishman who saw a new civilization rising like the mythical bird from the ashes of the vanished Hohokam.

A "Dry" River

What rose from the ashes was an aggressive ranching community that catered to miners and military outposts. Canals were extended through the alluvial valley, watering fields of cotton and alfalfa, pasturage for cattle and rows of citrus to the horizon's edge. Water storage commenced on a grand scale with the construction, in 1911, of **Roosevelt Dam**, still the world's largest masonry dam, on the Salt River some 90 miles (145 km) upstream from Phoenix. Three more dams on the Salt, and two on its major tributary, the Verde, allowed a compact of agriculturalists to send water where they liked. The riverbed of the Salt became the driest place in Phoenix, while all available water was deflected through the stems of plants and the gullets of mammals, including the human being.

Because of its dry air and temperate winter climate, asthmatic and tubercular patients came to Phoenix as soon as ranchers had made enough of a community to receive visitors. Medical centers for pulmonary diseases sprang up soon after the turn of the century, to treat what locals referred to as Arizona tenors. Now that the Southwest seemed safe as well as glamorous, the outskirts of Phoenix also bloomed with that Arizona specialty, the desert dude ranch. What became the Santa Fe Railroad already reached Phoenix in the 1880s, and air service began in the late 1920s. It was discovered that Eastern dudes, usually arriving by train, would pay handsomely for the chance to ride horses, eat T-bones grilled over mesquite fires, dance Put-Your-Little-Foot to guitars and accordians, and wear exotic pants called blue jeans. Dude ranches from rustic to lavish numbered in the hundreds and succumbed only recently to urbanization and more extravagant tastes in entertainment. The extremes of dude ranch living still survive in obscure corners. **The Wigwam**, in Litchfield Park west of Phoenix, begun as a corporate retreat by the Goodyear Corporation in the late 1920s and now a quiet contemporary resort, retains the leather-and-copper-flecked interiors of

receding
ages,
Mansion
lub,"
rigley
ouse; and
ft, Sun City
ea closing
on
rmlands.

adobe plush. Perpetuating the actual way of life is **Saguaro Lake Ranch**, just south of Stewart Mountain Dam, where Arizona's oldest continually operating dude ranch preserves the mission furniture and cactus skeleton decor of the 1930s as if under a bell jar.

The Phoenician Golden Age

With a slack economy to begin with, Phoenix hardly noticed the Depression, living off its own agriculture and catering to those tourists who had kept their money. The great monument to that period is the **Arizona Biltmore.** Built just before the stock market crash, it sailed in splendor through the bleakest of times. It is to the Biltmore that Phoenix owes the arrival in the valley of Frank Lloyd Wright. The hotel was originally designed by a former student of Wright who found himself in trouble and summoned the master for help. Wright probably gave more help than required, for the result was a masterpiece of textile block construction from Wright's middle period. Gutted by fire in 1973, the interior was refurnished with furniture and textile designs from all periods of Wright's career. The visitor who enters no other building in Phoenix should make it to 24th Street and Missouri to inspect the Arizona Biltmore. It was through working on the hotel, meanwhile, that Wright was moved to establish **Taliesin West**, the winter quarters of his architectural school, in the desert west of Phoenix. From that elegant perch he remained an architectural contributor, ideological gadfly and the valley's most interesting citizen until his death in 1959.

Residents with long memories recall the 1930s as a Phoenician golden age. Those who couldn't afford the Biltmore found it too snobbish anyway and frequented a lively downtown that was still Spanish-American in flavor. In summer, when temperatures climbed over 120°F (50°C) and daytime highs did not dip below the hundreds for months, locals complained less of the heat than they boasted of trick ways to stay cool. It was common sport to be pulled on an aquaplane along the canals, holding a rope from a car. Outdoor dances were popular, and some families even slept outdoors, in backyard gazebos and screened porches.

Big Surf.

216

If Phoenix was insulated from the Depression, it was transformed forever by World War II. The open desert was ideal for aviation training, and all Phoenix became a kind of extension of Luke Air Force Base. Aviation equipment companies moved into the valley, and even the cotton fields turned out silk for parachutes. It is less known that Phoenix had concentration camps for German prisoners of war, and many of the prisoners, as susceptible to the desert as anyone else, remained in the area after the War and melted into the social fabric.

Arrival of the Air Conditioner

Besides popularizing the area with young people who otherwise would never have seen it, the military revolutionized Phoenician life with a device called air-conditioning. The city had previously seen minor use of the evaporative or "swamp" cooler, but what it now discovered was genuine refrigeration. Suddenly Phoenix was a year-round possibility for those who couldn't stand the heat. With the end of the War and the beginning of air-conditioning,

the great migration was on.

Chronicles of urban sprawl are as deadening to those looking back as they are, at the time, exhilarating to the chamber of commerce and disruptive to those caught in its path. Camelback Mountain, at whose feet lay the most elegant dude ranches, was swamped by suburbia. To the east greater Phoenix engulfed the once isolated communities of Scottsdale, Tempe, Mesa and finally Apache Junction, at the base of the Superstition Mountains some 25 miles (40 km) from Phoenix city limits. Development leapt to the west when **Sun City**, America's first fully planned retirement community, was pitched by the Del Webb Corporation in 1960. More recently, cactus forest to the north of Phoenix has been bulldozed for a realtors' bonanza, and Phoenix and Scottsdale have competed in annexing the area under the pretext that they are only trying to control development. Expansion has taken such forms as trailer parks to the east, tract housing to the west, and walled-in mazes of simulated adobe ranchettes in the newly populated areas to the northeast.

Attending bloat is the classic decline

Washington Street, Phoenix, in days gone by.

in health. With the advent of peripheral shopping malls, downtown businesses collapsed, prosperity dropped, and the crime rate soared. Small-scaled buildings with Spanish tracery were felled for slab-style office buildings, many of which stand half-empty years after construction. Lateral growth doomed the trolley system, and the automobile took over. The city's mountains, lovely as they are, trap the pollutants in chronic winter inversions, and at the height of the tourist season its redeeming backdrop recedes through a scrim of particulates. Phoenix is now America's ninth largest city, and when the mountains disappear it may well be its ninth ugliest.

The Valley of the Sun

Many Phoenicians, particularly those who predate the end of World War II, lament the urbanization of the Salt River Valley. But it is important to remember that the forces that transformed Phoenix were, like the mythical bird, self-generated. Whatever freedom and individualism meant to the framers of the Constitution, they have been interpreted locally as the right to do whatever one wants with any property one can get one's hand on. Zoning, pollution control, even a minimal sign ordinance, have been seen as socialism rather than social responsibility, and symbolic of the Phoenician viewpoint is the hilltop mansion of Barry Goldwater, from which the apostle of free enterprise can survey the prosperity through the binoculars mounted on his desk. The migration of Snowbelt retirees, ironically living in rule-bound planned communities, only fueled a conservatism already entrenched. The more recent influx of career-oriented young people to the microchip industry has so altered the population that the average resident within city limits, astonishingly, is *younger* than the national average, and the ideological balance may even tip. But brakes are a little late. The Salt River Valley is now known to the outside world by its Chamber of Commerce nickname, the Valley of the Sun, while jaded locals call it the Valley of the Schmun, Phoenicia, the Valley of Celestial Heat, and familiarly just the Valley.

Still, Phoenix draws millions of visitors annually, and the past is their least

Rawhide, a stagecoach stop town during the 1880s.

concern. They even overlook the most interesting historical remnants—the canals that were first plotted two and a half millenia ago by the Hohokam and today are lined by smooth-topped banks some 10 feet (three meters) wide. Slicing the city at rakish angles, the canals provide welcome refuge from city traffic for strollers, joggers and bicyclists, a hidden system of transportation for those making their way without combustion. Though alfalfa fields and orange groves have given way to residential areas, irrigation near the canals is still accomplished by opening the floodgates once a month and letting water steep on lawns overnight. Periodically the canals are drained for repairs, revealing such surprises as shopping carts, Schwinns, and the occasional missing person.

Those interested in the original canal-diggers may visit several excavation sites near the Salt River, as well as those in the path of the Papago Freeway, a long-planned crosstown expressway held up, in part, by frantic archaeologists. The area's most impressive pre-Columbian survivor is the freestanding four-story pueblo at **Casa Grande**

National Monument, 50 miles (80 km) south of Phoenix near Coolidge. A permanent collection of traditional Indian art plus changing shows of contemporary work are displayed at the **Heard Museum**, a mission-style building just east of Central Avenue on Monte Vista.

Desert Drives

Visitors, traditionally, have come largely for the surrounding scenery. Of the desert drives outside of Phoenix, by far the most spectacular is the **Apache Trail**. One must endure the drive 25 miles (40 km) eastward through trailer parks and roadside businesses to **Apache Junction**, where the western flank of the Superstition Mountains rises like a crumbling mansard roof. The road from there to Roosevelt Dam weaves through 50 miles (80 km) of volcanic ash spewed 35 to 15 million years ago and settled into rhyolite and tuff swirling like brains. Here and there, lakes of the dammed Salt River form blue calms in the riot of cactus and disordered stone. The Superstition Mountains themselves are protected by Wilderness status, and offer labyrin-

l Arabian
orse Show,
cottsdale.

thine trails for hiking, riding and back-packing. The well-named Superstitions are also the setting of the legendary Lost Dutchman Mine, with its attendant lore of skulduggery and strange disappearances. Inasmuch as the Superstitions do not contain gold-bearing formations, one may assume that the stories are tall, and that any disappearances may be traced to an improper regard for the desert itself.

Another fine drive, with fewer maddening turns and less preliminary clutter, is west on Shea Boulevard to State Highway 87, then north toward **Payson**, leading one through saguaro forest, past the majestic **Four Peaks**, through slopes of granite boulders, into uplands of chaparral. Those preferring to sample the desert without fighting traffic may take the trails up **Camelback Mountain** and **Squaw Peak** from parks at their base, or the network of easier hiking trails in **South Mountain Park**.

And for those preferring man untrammeled by nature, there are the sumptuous new resorts north of Scottsdale and the three mountainside **Pointe** resorts on the north and south edges of Phoenix. Gone is any pretense of dude ranch culture, and the only reference to cactus may be worked into the macrame in the lobby. Offering golf, tennis, saunas, pools with underwater bar stools, French restaurants, nightclubs, discos, refrigerated suites and a clientele armored in credit cards, these are not desert hideaways but total-concept luxury resort complexes. One has to admire that the creators have Thought of Everything, but the traveller could be anywhere. Those with the means and the wish to remember they are in Phoenix, not Cancun, are advised to stick to the older places that have survived—**Camelback Inn**, **The Royal Palms**, **The Arizona Biltmore**, the **Wigwam** in Litchfield Park—or to seek modest digs and save their money for more local vices.

Chief among these is shopping, a Phoenician specialty ever since **Scottsdale** grew from a ranching crossroad to a gift shop maelstrom in the late 1950s. Jammed side by side are card shops, candle shops, brass shops, leather shops, gem shops, kitchen shops and optical shops, plus the tightest phalanx of art galleries between Santa Fe and Carmel. Some are stocked with desert

Paradise Valley golf course; the Phoenix area appeals to those who seek a relaxed life style.

sunsets and weeping clowns, but several are noted for quality: **O'Brien's Art Emporium** for good desert realism, **Period Gallery West** for paintings in the Russell and Remington tradition, **Gallery 10** for ancient and current Native American art, the **Elaine Horwich** and **Marilyn Butler galleries** for contemporary art, and the **Suzanne Brown Gallery** for the trendiest in hip and hype. Giving Scottsdale stiff competition is the **Borgata**, a shopping center on Scottsdale Road south of Lincoln Drive, built to resemble an Italian walled city. The Disneyesque exterior gives way to courtyards of splashing fountains.

The Cultural Scene

With a population explosion on top of a ranching tradition, Phoenix cannot be called culturally mature. Phoenix did build a glittering **Symphony Hall** at its new downtown convention plaza, and Scottsdale has a **Center for the Arts** in an impressively planned park. The Phoenix Symphony Orchestra is improving in quality, but adventurous conductors collide with recalcitrant audiences and conservative board members.

Community theater is lively, if uneven, and Phoenix seems a last stand for national touring companies. The **Phoenix Art Museum**, at Central Avenue and McDowell Road, supplements an obscure permanent collection with splendid visiting shows and owns a choice group of recent Mexican works. Phoenix's cultural community despairs, conceding that Tucson, with the help of its arts-oriented University of Arizona, is the state's cultural capital.

Sports enthusiasts have it better. Golf, tennis and swimming are practicable all year, while spectators have Arizona State University's Sun Devils in football, the Phoenix Suns in basketball, and such national events as the **Phoenix Open** in golf. Cynical desert rats, in fact, claim that the quietest time to visit the desert is on New Year's Day, when everyone who owns a jeep, a trail bike or a gun is glued to nonstop football on TV.

It seems unproductive to seek in Phoenix what other cities offer more lavishly, but in one area Phoenix is unmatched. Architecture buffs are in luck, for works from the middle and late periods of Frank Lloyd Wright, America's protean architect, are spread joyously through the valley. Besides a half-dozen homes, unlisted as a service to their inhabitants, must viewing are the previously mentioned Arizona Biltmore, **First Christian Church** on North Seventh Avenue, **Grady Gammage Auditorium** in Tempe, and—above all—**Taliesin West**, Wright's architectural school on Shea Boulevard, where students conduct guided tours hourly during workdays. For contrast one can visit the studio of **Paolo Soleri**, on Doubletree Road in Paradise Valley. A student of Wright, Soleri broke away to design futuristic cities that pack residents into monumental hives while leaving the landscape intact. Scale models of his visions are sure to provide visions of your own, of allure or of fright.

Surrounded by volcanism, Phoenix itself is spreading like lava. Still dramatic in its setting, it is a classically American disharmony of the scenic, the vulgar and the hidden treasure. It is also probably the major pulse point for taking the Southwestern temperature. And for those wishing to bake every such consideration from their systems, Phoenix has what it has always had—plenty of hot dry sun.

r all its
an sprawl,
oenix
inity
vides
oitats for
untain
atures like
Citellus eticaudus,
round
iirrel.

ATTRACTIONS

Ahwatukee "House of the Future," 11218 Beaver Tail Dr., 85044. 602/957-0800. Designed by the Frank Lloyd Wright Foundation, this unique house showcases the present state-of-the-art in technology, ecology and sociology. Open Tuesday through Sunday.

All Western Stables, 10220 S. Central Avenue, Phoenix. 602/276-5862. South Mountain riding. Rent by the hour or day. Hay rides, steak rides and breakfast rides.

Amusements Unlimited, 48th Street and I-10, entrance on Frontage Road, Phoenix. 894-9581. Family recreation center featuring miniature golf, formula racing, go-carts, bumper cars, arcade, skeetball and fountain displays.

Apache Lake Marina and Resort, northeast of Apache Junction, east of Phoenix. 602/467-2511. Destination site in the Superstition Mountains, with restaurant, bar, motel, houseboats, boat rentals, horseback riding, swimming, boating and wilderness trails.

Apache Trail, AZ 88 northeast of Phoenix. Beginning at Apache Junction, 34 miles east of Phoenix, this world-famous trail winds through rugged mountain scenery to Globe.

Arizona Mineral Resource Museum, State Fairgrounds, Phoenix. 602/255-3791. Largest and finest array of minerals and ores from Arizona. Also a limited number of specimens from other states and nations. Admission free.

The Arizona Museum, 1002 W. Van Buren Street, Phoenix. 602/253-2734. 2,000 years of Arizona history in the original adobe building of the first Phoenix museum. Wednesday through Sunday, 11 a.m. through 4 p.m. Donations only.

Arizona Soaring/Estrella Sailport, Tempe, 602/568-2318. Take I-10 east exit at 162A. In Maricopa, follow sign on left hand side. Demonstration rides, lessons and aerobatics.

Arizona Veterans Memorial Coliseum, 1826 W. McDowell Road, Phoenix. 602/252-6771. 14,000-seat indoor multipurpose arena hosting State Fair Arizona. Professional basketball, hockey, tennis, circus, ice shows, conventions, concerts, agricultural events.

Arizona Wranglers USFL Pro Football Club, 2200 N. Central Avenue, Ste. 107, Phoenix. 253-7777. Home games are held at Sun Devil Stadium in Tempe. For tickets, call 602/254-6464.

Arcosanti, Cordes Junction, on I-17 north of Phoenix, 632-7135

or 948-6145. Ecologically sound, energy efficient "City of the Future," designed by Paolo Soleri. Open 9 to 5 daily. Tours hourly.

Big Surf, 1500 N. Hayden Road, Tempe, AZ. 602/947-2478. Arizona's "ocean." Swimming, raft riding, 300-foot twisting surf slide, new rampage water toboggan ride, Polynesian atmosphere. March 12 through the end of September.

Black Canyon Trap and Skeet, Phoenix. 602/582-0300. World's largest combination shooting range. Camping facilities available. Open Wednesday through Friday 1 p.m. to 10 p.m., Saturday and Sunday 10 a.m. to 6 p.m.

Camelback Mountain, between Phoenix and Scottsdale north of Camelback Road.

Canyon Lake Marina, 2265 E. Sahuaro Drive, Phoenix. 602/867-8597. Located in the Superstition Wilderness, Canyon Lake Marina has boat rentals available, plus scenic lake tours through canyons formed millions of years ago.

Central Arizona Museum of History, 1242 N. Central Avenue, Phoenix. 602/255-4479. Features the history of Arizona and Central Arizona. Exhibits include an old-time general store, pharmacy, toy store. Admission free.

Copperstate Rodeo Productions, 16601 E. Guadalupe Rd., Gilbert, southeast of Phoenix. 602/883-5085. Rodeo at the Grand Canyon. Evening performances, professional cowboys. Rodeo museum and cowboy center. Group rates available.

Cosanti Foundation, 6433 Doubletree Road, Scottsdale. 602/948-6145. Noted architect and environmentalist Paolo Soleri's studios and workshops. Windbells made and sold here. Open seven days, 9 to 5.

Desert Botanical Garden, Galvin Parkway, Papago Park, Phoenix. 602/941-1217. More than 12,000 plants from arid lands. Classes, workshops, lectures, tours, exhibits and field trips available. Open daily 8 a.m. to sunset. Admission charge.

Encanto Park, 15th Avenue and Encanto Boulevard, Phoenix. Central Phoenix park with a full variety of recreational facilities.

Fountain Hills World's Highest Fountain, 14 miles east of Scottsdale Road on Shea Boulevard. Rises 560 feet in the air from a sparkling 28-acre lake.

Gila River Indian Arts & Crafts Center, 25 miles south of Phoenix, on I-10 at Exit 175. 602/963-3981. Authentic crafts museum and restaurant. Group rates and banquet facilities.

Glendale Historical Society, 7035 N. 56th Avenue, Glendale. 602/937-7836. The society collects artifacts for a future museum. It is currently involved with public exhibits and oral history.

Heard Museum, 22 E. Monte Vista Road, Phoenix. 602/252-8848. Collection of anthropology and primitive arts with focus on the prehistory and history of the Southwest as well as contemporary Indian culture. Admission charge.

Heritage Square, 6th Street and Monroe, Phoenix. 602/262-5071. Victorian architecture, including the 1894 Rosson House.

Legend City Amusement Park, 1200 W. Washington Street, Tempe, AZ. 602/275-8553. Family amusement park featuring over 25 rides, attractions, numerous shops and concession stands.

Malibu Grand Prix Entertainment Center, 1616 N. Hayden Road, Tempe, AZ. 602/941-2437. Race formula cars around challenging road course. Family amusement center, noon to 11 p.m. daily. Group rates.

Mesa Museum, 53 N. MacDonald St., Mesa, east of Phoenix. 834-2230. The museum features participation exhibits, including gold panning, ancient Hohokam tools and an 1890's jail cell. Six changing exhibits each year. 10 a.m. to 4 p.m., Tuesday through Saturday. Free.

Mystery Castle, 800 E. Mineral Road, Phoenix. 602/268-1581. Tours of the castle Tuesday through Sunday, 10 to 5. Closed July 1 to October 1.

North Mountain Stables, 12633 N. 7th Street, Phoenix. 602/993-8430. Riding stables, steak fries and hayrides.

Phoenix Art Museum, 1625 N. Central Avenue, Phoenix. 602/257-1222. Permanent collection includes Renaissance, 18th-Century French, American, Western Mexican and Chinese costumes. 10 a.m. to 5 p.m., Tuesday through Saturday; Wednesday until 9 p.m.; 1 to 5 p.m. Sunday. Entry fee voluntary.

Phoenix Giants Baseball, Phoenix Municipal Stadium, 56th Street and E. Van Buren Street, Phoenix. 602/275-4488. Spring training begins in March, league games in April.

Phoenix Greyhound Park, 3801 E. Washington Street at 40th Street, Phoenix. 602/273-7181. Year-round greyhound racing with pari-mutuel wagering. Clubhouse dining. First race 7:30 p.m.

Phoenix Suns National Basketball Association, Veterans Memorial Coliseum, 1826 W. McDowell Road, Phoenix. 602/263-SUNS. Tickets for all games available at Diamond's Box Office locations, the Suns Office and the Coliseum Box Office.

Phoenix Trap & Skeet Club, Litchfield Park, due west of Phoenix. 602/935-2691. Second largest club in U.S. 48 trap fields. Ten skeet fields and lighted fields for night shooting.

Phoenix Zoo, 5810 E. Van Buren Street, Phoenix. 602/273-1341. 1,000 animals, 125 acres, guided safari train tours, children's zoo. Arizona exhibit. Group rates available. Open 9 to 5.

Pioneer Arizona Museum, Black Canyon Stage, Phoenix. 602/993-0212. The trail to Pioneer. Located at Pioneer Road exit and I-17. A living history of Arizona in the 1880s. Admission charge; age five and under free. 9 a.m. to 4:30 p.m. Tuesday through Sunday. Closed when it rains.

The Pointe Resort Hole in the Wall Riding Stables, 7677 N. 16th Street, Phoenix. 602/997-2626. Trail rides in the 2700-acre Phoenix Mountain Preserve, hayrides, desert steak fries, moonlit rides, riding lessons.

Ponderosa and South Mountain Stables, 10215 S. Central Avenue, Phoenix. 602/268-1261 or 276-8131. Open daily. Horses for rent. Breakfast rides, group rides, steak fries. Reservations.

Pueblo Grande Museum, 4619 E. Washington Street, Phoenix. 602/275-3452. Hohokam ruins thought to have been occupied 200 B.C. to 1400 A.D. Exhibits 9 a.m. to 4.45 p.m., Monday through Saturday; 1-4.45 p.m. on Sunday. Admission 50 cents for those six years and over.

Rawhide, 23023 N. Scottsdale Road, Scottsdale. 602/992-6111.

An escape to the nostalgia of the early West. Rides, shops, shootouts, critters roaming the streets.

Roosevelt (Theodore) Dam, 79 miles from Phoenix on the Apache Trail. One of the first Federal reclamation projects, the 273-foot-high dam forms a lake 25 miles in length.

Salt River Project History Center, 1521 Project Drive, Tempe, 602/273-2208. Prehistoric Indian artifacts, exhibits depicting the construction of Roosevelt Dam and the electric power history of SRP. Admission free. 9 a.m. to 4 p.m. Monday through Friday.

Scottsdale Historical Society, 3939 Civic Center Plaza, Scottsdale. 602/945-6650. A rotating display of Scottsdale artifacts is located in the Chamber of Commerce building—the Red Schoolhouse on the Scottsdale Mall. Admission free. 8:30 a.m. to 5 p.m., Monday to Friday.

Squaw Peak Park, 2701 Squaw Peak Drive, approach from Lincoln Drive, Phoenix. Desert-mountain wilderness area with riding and hiking trails.

State Capitol Museum, 1700 W. Washington Street, Phoenix. 602/255-4581. The original Arizona Capitol building was completed in 1901. Restoration has returned the building to its original visual condition. Weekdays, 8 a.m. to 5 p.m. Free.

Superstition Mountains, east of Mesa. Majestic cliffs rising above the valley. Site of the legendary "Lost Dutchman" gold mine.

Taliesin West, 108th Street and E. Shea Boulevard, Scottsdale. 602/948-6670. The western architectural school and the winter office and home of the late Frank Lloyd Wright.

Tempe Historical Museum, Southern Avenue and Rural Road, Tempe Community Center. 602/966-7902. History of Tempe presented through exhibits of furniture, clothing, toys, tools, photographs, documents, period rooms, post office, chuckwagon and fire engine. Admission free. 9 a.m. to 5 p.m., Tuesday to Saturday.

Tenderfoot Prospectors Inc., 6702 E. Coronado Road, Scottsdale. 602/946-1071. Full and half-day gold panning tours.

Turf Soaring School, Pleasant Valley Airport, 8902 W. Carefree Highway. Phoenix. 602/582-3621. Glider rides and lessons available, by individual or by the group.

Wax Museum: Josephine Tussaud's, 5555 E. Van Buren Street, Phoenix. 602/273-1368.

EVENTS

Spring Amphitheater Concerts, Mesa, early June through mid-July and mid-September through mid-November. 834-2198.

Mexican Fiesta Days, Peoria, mid-September. 979-3720.

Billy Moore Days Western Celebration, Avondale, mid-October. 932-2260.

Phoenix Greek Festival, mid-October. 264-7926.

Grand Prix Go-Cart Races, Coolidge, October, 723-3009.

Arizona State Fair, Phoenix, late October to early November.

Phoenix Ice Follies, late January. 252-6771.

Phoenix Open Golf Tournament, late January. 263-0757.

Apache Junction Lost Dutchman Days, late January. 982-3141.

Parada del Sol Parade & Rodeo, Scottsdale, early February. Parada includes a street dance, rodeo and the longest horse-drawn parade in the world. Scottsdale Chamber of Commerce, 945-8481.

All Arabian Horse Show & Desert Pageant, Scottsdale, mid-February. 997-5505.

Valley of the Sun Open Horseshoe Tournament, Mesa, mid-February. 985-1525.

Indian Fair, Heard Museum, Phoenix, mid to late February. 252-8848.

Arizona Horseshow, Phoenix, Feb. 14-20. 252-6771.

Desert Botanical Garden Cactus Show, Phoenix, late February. 941-1217.

Annual National Culinary Arts Festival, Scottsdale, mid to late February. 994-ARTS.

Fiesta del Sol Rodeo, Apache Junction, December, 982-6081.

Fiesta Bowl Parade, Phoenix, end of December. One of the ten largest parades in the country, featuring floats, horse units, bands, etc.

Tempe Annual Fiesta Bowl, One of the nation's top bowl games, viewed by more than 75,000 spectators in addition to a national television audience. Early January. 952-1280.

Arizona National Livestock Show, Arizona State Fairgrounds and Coliseum, Phoenix. Cattle, sheep, hog and horse shows. Junior auctions. Trade show. PRCA Turquoise Circuit Rodeo Championship Finals. First week in January. 258-8568.

Chandler Spring Festival, early March. 963-4571.

Coolidge Cotton Festival, early March. 723-3009.

Phoenix Jaycees Rodeo of Rodeos Parade, early to mid-March. 264-4808.

Maricopa County Fair, Phoenix, mid-March. 267-1996.

South Mountain Festival of Arts, Phoenix, late March. 963-7742.

Pioneer Days, Peoria, late March. 979-3601.

Spring Arts Festival, Scottsdale, late March. 994-ARTS.

Old Town Tempe Festival of the Arts, Tempe, April. 967-4877.

Cave Creek Fiesta Days, early April. 488-3381.

Outdoor Jazz Festival, Scottsdale, early May. 994-ARTS.

ENTERTAINMENT

Celebrity Theatre A 2700-seat arena theater with revolving stage. 267-1600.

Gammage Center for the Performing Arts, Tempe. Frank Lloyd Wright's acoustically perfect housing for cultural events is on the Arizona State University campus. 965-3434.

Phoenix Symphony Orchestra, Performs at the Phoenix Civic Plaza Convention Center and Symphony Hall, October through May. Classical and pop concerts with world class guest artists. 264-4754.

Scottsdale Symphony Orchestra, Scottsdale. Year-round performances of symphony, pops and youth orchestra. 945-8071.

Sundome Center for the Performing Arts, Sun City West. A new showplace for celebrity concerts, Broadway shows, dance, international symphonies. Seats 7200. 975-1900.

Winterstock Regional Theater, Mesa. Legitimate professional theater "truck and bus troupe" carries portable stage, sets, lights and actors to 80 performances in various facilities throughout the state. Reasonably priced tickets. 964-1171.

SHOPPING

The Borgata in Scottsdale—which is itself a notorious gift-shop ghetto—is presently considered one of the premier shopping centers in the entire United States. 6166 N. Scottsdale Road. 998-1822.

Try Old Scottsdale, with its Old West atmosphere, 100-plus gift shops, art galleries and restaurants. 947-4961.

The Biltmore Fashion Park, in Phoenix. 955-8400. A shameless concentration of opulent shopping palaces: imagine I. Magnin, Saks Fifth Avenue, Gucci, Polo/Ralph Lauren and others, all in roughly the same place.

Spanish Village, Carefree. 488-9644. Reminiscent of Old Spain with patios, fountains, gardens.

INDIAN RESERVATIONS

Papago Reservation, 136 miles south of Phoenix. A large southern reservation whose tribe produces basketry and pottery. Within it are the Kitt Peak National Observatory, rodeo and fair, Papago Village Solar Power Project at Schuchuli (the world's first totally electric village), Ventana Cave, Forteleza Ruins, Mission San Xavier Del Bac. Papago Tribal Council, P.O. Box 837, Sells, AZ 85634. 602/383-2221.

Salt River Reservation, 15 miles northeast of Phoenix adjacent to Scottsdale. Known for basketry and pottery, the tribe lives close to the Salt River. Tubing, camping and picnicking. Salt River Pima-Maricopa Tribal Council, Rte. 1, Box 216, Scottsdale, AZ 85256. 601/949-7234.

Ak-Chin Reservation A small reservation 56 miles south of Phoenix. The tribe is noted for its fine basketry and successful farming enterprise. The St. Francis Church Feast is held on October 4 and the tribal election is held in conjunction with a special barbecue on the second Saturday in January. Ak-Chin Indian Community, Rte. 2, P.O. Box 27, Maricopa, AZ 85239. 602/568-2227.

Gila River Reservation, 40 miles south of Phoenix. Noted for Pima Basketry and Maricopa Pottery, the reservation is the homeland of the Pima and Maricopa. Attractions: Gila River Arts and Crafts Center, Gila Heritage Village and Museum, Firebird Lake and Water Sports Marina, Mul-Cha-Tha ("The Gathering of the People"), Rodeo and Miss Gila River Pageant in April and the St. John's Mission Fair in March. Gila River Indian Community, P.O. Box 97, Sacaton, AZ 85247; 602/963-4323 or 562-3311.

ACCOMMODATIONS

The Arizona Biltmore, 24th Street and Missouri, Phoenix 85002; 602/955-6600 or 800/228-3000. Telex 165709. Huge place with 502 units, architecture inspired by Frank Lloyd Wright.

The Camelback Inn (Marriott's) 5402 E. Lincoln Drive, Scottsdale 85252. 602/948-1700 or 800/228-9290. Telex 910 9501198.

Carefree Inn, Carefree, AZ 85331. 602/448-3551; 800/528-0294. Huge 10,000-acre resort 45 minutes north of Phoenix in ghost-town country.

John Gardiner's Tennis Ranch, 5700 E. Mcdonald Drive, Scottsdale, 85283. 602/948-2100.

The Pointe at Squaw Peak, 7677 N. 16th St., Phoenix 85020. 602/997-2626 or 800/528-0428. Telex 948-2844.

The Royal Palms Inn, 5200 E. Camelback Road, Phoenix 85018. 602/840-3610. 32-acre resort with 55 units, two miles from Scottsdale. Also a plush older spot that was a private estate prior to 1948.

Saguaro Lake Guest Ranch, 13020 Bush Highway, Mesa, AZ 85205. 602/984-2194. The oldest continually operating guest ranch in Arizona offers guided horseback riding and birdwatching.

The Wigwam, Litchfield Park, AZ 85340. 602/935-3811. A slice of tradition 15 miles west of Phoenix in Litchfield, on a grand scale with concomitant prices.

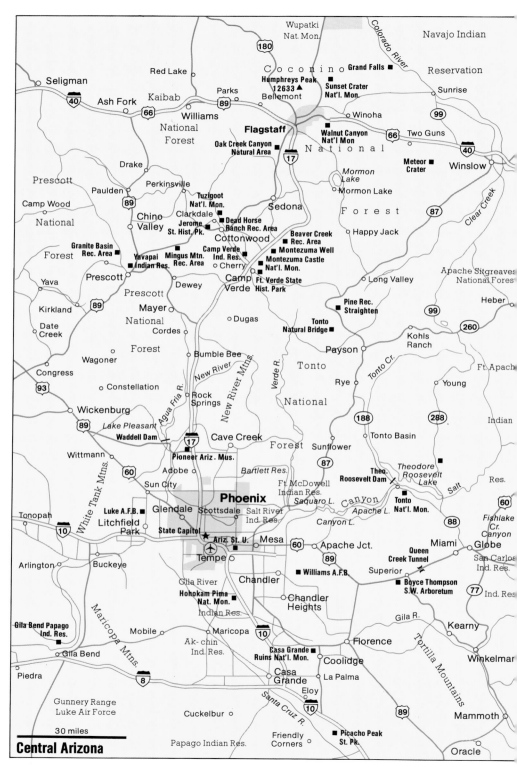

Central Arizona

30 miles

CENTRAL ARIZONA

To understand the scenic richness and variety of human settlement that sends the visitor looping through central Arizona, one must first get a grip on its geology. In the north, one stands on the southern edge of the Colorado Plateau, a mile in the air, surrounded by ponderosa pines and Douglas firs or the prismatic barrens of old seabeds. The Plateau ends abruptly to the south, where the Mogollon Rim drops 2,000 feet (600 meters) in an escarpment that runs nearly the width of Arizona and is cut by some of the state's most memorable canyons. From the Rim's base rise the central highlands, a band of tight mountains some 80 miles (130 km) wide, enclosing narrow ranching valleys and bristling with a chaparral of small oaks and leathery scrub. More recent volcanic upheavals provide the kind of mining that feeds on geological crack-ups. Southward, the land drops more sanely, ranges keep their distance, and one enters the rich cactus forest of the Sonoran Desert. Elevations remain high in eastern Arizona, but where the land declines southwest toward the Colorado River delta, there is too little rainfall even for cactus to make much of a show. The eye, undistracted, is drawn over greasewood and saltbush to mountains that wander the horizon like lost battleships, and one feels on the brink of the surreal.

Offers of a Highway

The straightest shot through this labyrinth is on Interstate 17 from Flagstaff to Tucson. The road bends through the high forests and follows lava flows down the **Mogollon Rim**. The first interesting exits driving from Flagstaff occur at **Montezuma Well**, a grand limestone sink, and **Montezuma Castle National Monument**, with well-preserved cliff dwellings from the Anasazi period. After crossing the idyllic Verde Valley, the road climbs toward a cluster of service stations called Cordes Junction. By exiting to the east and following a mile-long dirt road that parallels I-17 northward, one arrives at **Arcosanti**, where futurist architect

receding ages, redawn at ainted desert nvokes onder. elow, cliff wellings at Montezuma astle National Monument.

Paolo Soleri is building an experimental community that will pack its citizens into hive-like domes while preserving the surrounding terrain. Arcosanti is open daily for inspection, and offers tours by Soleri's students. Beyond Cordes Junction, I-17 crests a yucca-spiked volcanic plateau whose **Sunset Point Rest Area**, with shaded picnic tables, educational displays and a panorama of the Bradshaw Mountains, may be the finest institution of its kind.

The highway soon descends toward the **Sonoran Desert**, and the first saguaro cacti burst from the black rock. The horizon flattens and may even disappear as I-17 swings through Phoenix and changes its name to I-10. Cotton and alfalfa fields line the highway for the next 50 miles (80 km). Beyond Eloy, there is a last dramatic moment as I-10 passes between Newman Peak and the spire of **Picacho Peak**. Here the adventurous motorist is encouraged to pause for a two-hour diversion. Picacho Peak looks unclimbable, but a trail leads from a small state park to a saddle, around the back of the mountain, along guardrails and over metallic gangplanks, to deliver the hiker

safe and amazed to the summit. On clear days the vistas reach into Mexico, and the remaining 40-mile (64-km) run into Tucson lies spread out below. But for all its sideshows, I-17 smothers geology, reduces cactus to a khaki blur, and funnels you through mid-Arizona in the dullest way possible.

A more vivid alternative begins at **Petrified Forest National Park**, 115 miles (185 km) east of Flagstaff. The surrounding **Painted Desert**, a strange landscape of Triassic volcanic ash, spreads in wrinkled undulations of mauve, liver and rust. The same volcanic ash has preserved ancient pines by replacing their cells with silica, so that their cross sections shine in blues and reds that glow from a dark mahogany. The Petrified Forest is one of the few natural wonders ideally visited in the rain, which heightens the agatized colors.

State Highway 77 south from Holbrook leads to Show Low, on the edge of the Fort Apache Indian Reservation. The elevation is still high and logging is the principal industry, but the area is rapidly filling with vacation homes for residents of Phoenix and Tucson. **The Sunrise Ski Area** lies nearby, and sum-

Arcosanti, Paolo Soleri's creation, is open for da tours.

mer offers fishing, golf and very popular relief from the desert heat.

Difficult Decision at Show Low

From Show Low, one is faced with an agonizing choice, for both routes south are spectacular. State 260 proceeds west along the Mogollon Rim, offering immense views to the south before it takes the plunge. Near Kohl's Ranch, a small sign indicates a mile-long dirt road to the cabin where **Zane Grey** wrote many of his novels and which is open to the public. Hiking trails lead in both directions along the bottom of the Mogollon Rim. State 260 reaches State 87 at Payson, where you can turn south for an eventful ride into Phoenix. To the west stretch the **Mazatzal Mountains**, with Wilderness status and an intricate network of hiking trails. The road dives into canyons lined with sycamores, climbs through fields of gigantic granite boulders, descends into saguaro forest backed by the sawtooth mass of Four Peaks, crosses the Verde River on the Fort McDowell Indian Reservation and ushers you into Phoenix.

The alternative from Show Low, U.S. Highway 60, drops off the Mogollon Rim and then dodges and weaves to the brink of the **Salt River Canyon**. For sheer breadth this may be Arizona's most impressive gorge after the Grand Canyon, a gaping vee with switchbacks that ply both sides, through pines and past weathered limestone. **The Salt River** itself frays upstream into minor tributaries and dies downstream behind four dams before its dry run through Phoenix.

Beyond the Salt River Canyon, the highway reaches **Globe** and **Miami**, contiguous copper-mining towns surrounded by open pits so deep and round, and tailings so mountainous and square that one is also impressed—or at least stunned—by the works of man. The Arizona copper industry has been in decline for some years, a fact reflected in these towns, but some mines are still operational and offer tours.

After a switchbacking, tunneled descent of these mineral-rich mountains, just east of Superior, U.S. 60 passes the **Boyce Thompson Southwestern Arboretum**, with 1,500 species of trees and plants from around the world—

etrified log
ne
rified
est
ional
k.

nearly a complete inventory of, the world's desert vegetation. The arboretum features seasonal displays and is open daily to the public. U.S. 60 continues along the turreted south flank of the Superstition Mountains and on into Phoenix. But a turn southward at Florence Junction allows you to play out your exploration toward Tucson. U.S. 89 is the old road between Phoenix and Tucson, and now that urbanites are speeding back and forth on I-10, it is little-travelled and delightful. It soon leads past the little town of **Florence**, best known as the home of the Arizona State Penitentiary, but also distinguished by a number of fine buildings from the Territorial period, including a flamboyant courthouse built in 1891. One old-timer maintains that if the Florence city fathers hadn't torn down the old buildings because they were ashamed of them, Florence could have been "another Santa Fe."

Pinal Pioneer Parkway

South of Florence, U.S. 89 becomes the Pinal Pioneer Parkway—the road, otherwise unimproved, is graced with sheltered picnic tables, and many of the plants of this dense cactus forest are identified with discreet signs. At one of the rest stops, a cast-iron silhouette of a saddled, riderless horse is dedicated to the 1940s' Western star Tom Mix, who died nearby in a flash flood while shooting a film. At Oracle Junction, one can continue into Tucson. But in order to keep avoiding cities, turn east on State 77 to the pleasant town of **Oracle**, under the northern extremity of the Catalina Mountains. Twenty miles (32 km) beyond Oracle is the turnoff to **Aravaipa Canyon**, with one of the few perennial streams through the desert ranges. Aravaipa can only be visited on foot and has Wilderness protection.

Those wishing to take the old road from Phoenix to Tucson as an alternative to I-10 may connect with it by taking U.S. 60 east to Florence Junction and turning south, or by taking I-10 as far as the turnoff to Coolidge, then proceeding east to Florence. The latter route takes you past **Casa Grande Ruins National Monument**, a freestanding four-story adobe building that is almost the only remnant of the prehistoric Salado Culture.

Meteor Crater, whose rim rises near 200 feet above the ground is near Winslow, Arizona.

If one prefers to explore central Arizona on the west side of I-17, the sights are at least as impressive—and certainly better known. Leaving south from Flagstaff on Alternate 89, the road ambles innocently through ponderosa forest, until suddenly the bottom drops out: one is at the brink of **Oak Creek Canyon**. A set of switchbacks materializes from nowhere, and drops you into a deciduous canyon cut from the same sandstones, limestones and shales that form the upper strata of the Grand Canyon. But here, despite cliffs that range from 1,500 to 2,500 feet (450 to 760 meters) in vibrant creams and cayennes, the narrowness and the vegetation create more a sense of intimacy than one of grandeur.

At the mouth of the canyon, one emerges at **Sedona**, once a small Western town. Unfortunately, its radiant setting has been overtaken by the most thoughtless kind of development, zoning controls are baffled by a county line that runs through the middle of the valley, and the eye that would feast on beauty must look above ground level. A redeeming creation is **Tlaquepaque**, a walled-in shopping area built in true Mexican colonial style, set in a dazzling sycamore grove and blessed with Sedona's least abrasive gift shops.

As Alternate 89 proceeds southwest, keep a sharp watch to the north, where new permutations of red keep playing on the Mogollon Rim. At the **Verde River** are the small towns of Cottonwood and Clarkdale, between which lies **Tuzigoot National Monument**, with hilltop ruins of the Sinagua Culture. The Verde Valley is a haven for wildlife, and a walk by the river may lead to heron rookeries and the nesting grounds of great horned owls.

The Town that Almost Died

Beyond the Verde River, the road climbs toward **Jerome**, possibly the only American town situated like one of the hill towns of Italy or Spain. But the houses are mostly wooden and are propped up on stilts where the ground drops from beneath them: some on the ridge tops show only one story from the street, but reveal two more stories beneath entrance level once one is inside. Jerome was founded in 1876 as a company town for the Phelps Dodge

sa Grande g House), lt of reinforced y in the rly 14th ntury.

copper mines. When the mines closed in 1953, the town almost died, but, in recent years, has been restored as a center for shops galleries and museums. Three major fires ran through the wooden structures, yet the architectural style remains coherent—partly because stiff zoning favors patching up old buildings over raising new ones and because the town, for all its dependence on visitors, lacks overnight accommodations.

From Jerome, the road finishes its trip over **Mingus Mountain**, crosses the ranchlands of **Chino Valley**, and enters **Prescott** through a granite dell. Prescott was proclaimed the first territorial capital of Arizona in 1864 and is full of splendid Victorian houses and historic public buildings. The history buff should visit **Sharlott Hall**, a museum that recreates the feel of Territorial Arizona in a series of restored buildings, and the tippler should pay homage to **Whiskey Row**, as old and as seasoned a tavern as the Southwest possesses. U.S. 89 offers one more town of note to the Southwest, the dude-ranching capital of **Wickenburg**. Also dating from Territorial days, Wickenburg is less fully preserved, but is surrounded by horsy resorts that have stayed alive with the help of batallions of tennis courts. From Wickenburg, one can head on the continuation of U.S. 89 to Phoenix, or veer farther west, below the little-visited **Harquahala Mountains**, toward the Colorado River.

Where Weekend Revelers Flock

Two further north-to-south crossings of central Arizona are possible, along the state's boundaries. In the east, U.S. 666 stays in little-populated high country where forestry is the leading industry. In the west, State 95 parallels the Colorado River from **Davis Dam** to **Parker**, then heads straight south to Yuma. "River" no longer seems an honest word for the succession of reservoirs and wide sluices that this stretch of the Colorado has become, and, while "waterworks" has been proposed, our language really needs a new noun. Whatever it is, it is lined with resorts, instant cities and trailer parks, and is converged upon during the summer by thousands of weekend revelers from Phoenix and Los Angeles. Its most famous attraction is the **London Bridge**, brought over by the developer of **Havasu City** to call attention to his real estate. That the Colorado River has not just been tamed but Thamed may seem a last absurdity, but those who go to laugh at the bridge may be surprised— for its graceful, solid arches match in integrity the wild volcanic ranges in the background, revealing the essential shabbiness of the developments in between. After leaving the Colorado River at Park, State 95 passes the **Kofa National Wildlife Refuge**. The Kofa Mountains are among the most remote in Arizona, harbor one of the last stands of desert mountain sheep and offer some of the most adventurous back country for hiking and camping in the state.

If Arizona's Anglo history is brief, its native American history reaches back into myth, and its visible geology to the Precambrian. A serious exploration presupposes time to follow the whims and arabesques suggested by the road map, rather than the north-south strands arranged for convenience here. Central Arizona is a geological, historical and environmental labyrinth, but you are guaranteed your way out, bearing gifts.

Left, Davis Dam at the Colorado River and right, sunst snowstorm the Mazat. Mountains

NATIONAL PARKS AND MONUMENTS

Casa Grande Ruins National Monument, 50 miles south of Phoenix, near Coolidge. An outstanding example of a Hohokam apartment-watchtower of the 12th to 14th centuries. Thought to be a prehistoric observatory of sorts. Open daily 7 a.m. to 6 p.m. Coolidge, AZ 85228. 723-3172.

Montezuma Castle National Monument, near Camp Verde on I-17. Five-story cameo-like cliff dwelling. Montezuma Well, nearby, has smaller ruins. Visitors center. Monument and Well open daily. Camp Verde, Az 86322. 567-3322.

Tonto National Monument, east of Roosevelt Dam on the Apache Trail. Very well preserved prehistoric cliff dwellings. Visitors center *cum* museum with Indian artifacts, open every day. Ranger-conducted tours to more remote cliff dwellings are available. P.O. Box 707, Roosevelt, AZ 85545. 467-2241.

Tuzigoot National Monument. A pre-Columbian pueblo ruin two miles east of Clarkdale. Visitors center and museum with pottery, shell beads and bracelets. Open every day. Box 68, Clarkdale, AZ 86324; 634-5564.

Walnut Canyon National Monument, just outside of Flagstaff. Four hundred tiny cliff dwellings. Paved trail passes some dwellings, another trail follows the canyon rim. Visitors center, museum. Open daily; trails may be closed by snow and ice in winter. Route 1, Box 25, Flagstaff, AZ 86001. 526-3367.

NATIONAL FORESTS

Apache-Sitgreaves National Forests Two adjoining sections, currently administered as one. Over two million acres that include prime fishing lakes, the Mogollon Rim, pine forests, scenic roads like the Coronado Trail, good big game hunting, wilderness pack trips, camping, boating, horseback riding. Apache-Sitgreaves National Forests, P.O. Box 640, Springerville, AZ 85938. 333-4301.

Coconino National Forest, 2323 E. Greenlaw Lane, Flagstaff, AZ 86001. In central Arizona adjacent to Flagstaff. Considered by many to be the state's finest woodland region. Wooded plateaus cut by deep gorges, the Mogollon Rim, winter skiing, state's highest elevation, Oak Creek Canyon, resorts, campgrounds, motor trips, horseback riding, full range of offerings.

Prescott National Forest, in two parts surrounding the Prescott Valley area of Central Arizona. Great variety of terrain and elevation includes Horsethief Basin, Mingus Mountain, Thumb Butte, Granite Mountain; the "ghost town" of Jerome; excellent autumn hunting; pack and hiking trips. One of the state's most popular year-round forest regions. 344 S. Cortez, P.O. Box 2549, Prescott, AZ 86302.

STATE PARKS

Alamo Lake State Park, on Bill Williams River 38 miles north of Wenden. A 4900-acre park featuring a 500-acre lake for fishing and water sports. Also, rock hunting and wild burro herds. 669-2088.

Buckskin Mountain State Park, 11 miles north of Parker on Rt. 95, on the Colorado River. Well-developed area comprising 1676 acres of fertile ground for water sports, camping. 667-3231.

Dead Horse Ranch State Park, in the Verde Valley north of Cottonwood off U.S. 89A. A wildlife sanctuary with birdwatching, pond and river fishing, tree-lined walking trails, picnicking, camping, riding, 634-5283.

Fort Verde State Historic Park, two miles east of I-17 at Camp Verde. Century-old military base with museum and officers' homes open to the public. Museum open every day from 8 to 5:30. 567-3275.

Lake Havasu State Park Large, 13,000 recreational spot on the Colorado River (AZ 95) covering no less than 45 miles of shoreline. Boating, fishing, swimming, horseback riding,

camping; accommodations at Pittsburg Point. 855-7851.

Lost Dutchman State Park, five miles northeast of Apache Junction on AZ 88. Legendary lost gold mine is supposed to be in the Superstition Mountains rising behind the park. Camping, picnicking, nature trails lined with desert plants link up with the Forest Service paths into the wilderness area. 982-4485.

Lyman Lake State Park, 11 miles south of St. Johns off U.S. 666. More than 160 acres of lake and campgrounds near the headwaters of the Colorado River. In warmer months, water sports are popular. In cooler ones, fishermen go after walleye pike, channel catfish and bass. 337-4441.

McFarland State Historic Park, downtown Florence. An authentic slice of pioneer days in the town's "old town" with original adobes among the best of their type in Arizona. Chief landmark is the restored first Pinal County Courthouse, which is now a museum. The Pinal County Visitors Center, at 8th and Pinal in the restored Jacob Souter House, is a focal point for information. 868-5216.

Picacho Peak State Park, off I-10. Hiking and camping in a 3400-acre desert mountain park between Phoenix and Tucson. Park was the scene of the only Civil War battle fought in Arizona. 466-3183.

Roper Lake State Park, six miles south of Safford in eastern Arizona. Thirty-acre lake in the hills near two major highways, U.S. 666 and 70, is a favorite for boating, fishing for catfish, bass, bluegill. Campsites close to shore. 428-6760.

Bedrock City, north of Flagstaff en route to the Grand Canyon. Home of the Flintstones. Snap a picture with Fred and Barney.

Boyce Thompson Southwestern Arboretum, between Florence Junction and Superior, on the return leg of the Apache Trail (U.S. 60). This famous sanctuary of plant life features the world's great collection of desert plants. More than two miles of easy walking trails wind through the outdoor displays. A state park. 689-2811.

Coronado Trail, in the extreme eastern part of the state, U.S. 666 between Clifton and Alpine. Scenic trail said to have been followed by Coronado in his search for Cibola.

Deer Farm, Williams, 25 miles west of Flagstaff on I-40. Children's paradise of pigmy goats. Llamas, kangaroos, monkeys, miniature donkeys, peacocks; deer eat from your hand. 8 a.m. to dusk summers, 9 a.m. to dusk rest of the year. Closed February and winter Tuesdays. 635-2357.

Kingman, west of Flagstaff on I-40, is known as the Gateway to the Colorado River recreation area. Sights include the Mojave Museum of History and Arts (753-3195) and the Kingman Locomotive Park.

London Bridge, Lake Havasu City, on the Colorado River and near the California border. Famed bridge transplanted here.

Meteor Crater, 45 miles southeast of Flagstaff, is the best-preserved meteoric crater on Earth and is huge: three miles in circumference, 570 feet deep, more than 4000 feet from rim to rim. It is used as a training site for U.S. astronauts.

Mogollon Rim runs east-west to the east of and roughly between Flagstaff and Phoenix. Steep drops and rises in altitude where Spanish conquistadors sought the gold of the fabled Seven Cities of Cibola. Full of lodges, fishing spots, recreational areas. Parts of the rim border Apache Reservation.

Museum of Northern Arizona, 3 miles north of Flagstaff on U.S. 180. Dedicated to preserving, exhibiting and researching the natural and cultural history of the Colorado Plateau, which encompasses northern Arizona and the Four Corners area. Displays deal with natural history, Indian arts and crafts. Hopi and Navajo shows held in July. Small admission charge. 774-5211.

Oak Creek Canyon, south of Flagstaff on U.S. 89A. A favorite spot for anglers and waders, with trout-filled waters and colorful sandstone formations lining the highway. Twenty miles down the road the highway reaches Slide Rock, a natural water slide. Bring a bathing suit.

Pioneer's Historical Museum, Flagstaff. Houses the most complete collection of early pioneer artifacts ever assembled.

Prescott Territorial Capital, southwest of Flagstaff on U.S. 89. Historic gold-mining town and site of Arizona's first capital. The first rodeo in the world took place here, and frontier-type events are held at various times throughout the year.

Salt River Canyon, on U.S. 60 north of Globe. Spectacular gorge with scenic approaches and lookout points.

San Francisco Peaks, seven miles due north of Flagstaff. Home of the Hopi kachinas and the Snow Bowl Ski Resort.

Sedona, southeast of Flagstaff on U.S. 89. A thriving mecca for art lovers and collectors drawn to the community by the profusion of artists and art galleries. **Tlaquepaque** is a rambling shopping village styled after Old Mexico and can be recognized by the bell tower which rises above Sedona's tallest trees.

Tortilla Flat, AZ 88, northeast of Apache Junction, 996-8066. A historic remnant of an old Western town (population six). Gift store, post office, riding stable, restaurant, saloon, hotel.

Williams, 23 miles west of Flagstaff on I-40. Home of the Bill Williams Mountain Men, who perpetuate the memory of rugged mountain men of frontier days.

HORSE RACING

Flagstaff: Fort Tuthill Horse Races, early July. 779-6631.

Prescott: Prescott Downs Horse Races, late May through September. 445-0220.

OBSERVATORIES

Lowell Observatory, on the campus at Northern Arizona University, Flagstaff. Founded in 1894 by Dr. Percival Lowell, this world-famous observatory discovered the planet Pluto in 1930 and has since contributed extensive data on the solar system and its evolution. Guided tours are conducted at 1:30 weekdays only; during the summer, visitors' nights are held on Friday. On the top of Mars Hill, it's right in the city. 774-4505.

EVENTS

Coconino Combined Event Horse Trials, Flagstaff, early June. 774-3411.

Territorial Days, Prescott, early June. 445-2000.

Flagstaff Appaloosa Horse Show, mid-June. 774-7422.

Pine Country Rodeo, Flagstaff, mid to late June. 774-4505.

Payson Country Music Festival, mid-June. 474-4515.

Flagstaff Festival of the Arts, mid-June through beginning of August. A six-week celebration of the arts featuring artists and musicians from all over the country. Flagstaff Chamber of Commerce. 774-4505.

Flagstaff Festival of Native American Arts, mid-June through early August. 779-5944.

San Juan Fiesta Days, St. Johns, late June. 337-4390.

Flagstaff, Native American Dancing & Outdoor Market, early July. 774-5211; 779-5944.

Whiteriver Indian Celebration, early July. 338-4617.

Hopi Indian Show, Flagstaff, early July. 774-5211.

Prescott Frontier Days, early July. Arizona's territorial capital comes alive each year with activities, including parade, rodeo and contests in the Plaza. Attended by more than 85,000 annually. 445-2000.

Payson Gospel Music Festival, early July. 478-4218.

Snowflake Pioneer Days, late July. 536-4412.

St. Johns Pioneer Days, late July. 337-2000.

Prescott Bluegrass Festival, late July. 445-2000.

Ham Radio Operators' Festival, Flagstaff, end of July. 779-6631.

Payson Loggers' Sawdust Festival, end of July. A contest between men and women of the logging industry throughout the States. 474-4515.

Navajo Indian Show, Flagstaff, end of July through early August. 774-5211.

Smoki Ceremonials & Snake Dance, Prescott, early August. 445-1230.

Visual Arts Display, Flagstaff, mid-August through mid-September. 779-5944.

World's Oldest Continuous Rodeo, Payson, mid or late August. The world's first rodeo of record, this three-day event has been held continuously since 1884. 474-4515.

Coconino County Fair, Flagstaff, early September. 779-6631.

Bill Williams Mountain Men's Rodeo, Williams, early September. This three-day celebration includes a rodeo and parade featuring the Bill Williams Mountain Men. Williams Chamber of Commerce. 635-2041.

Square Dance Festival, Payson, early September. 474-4515.

Apache County Fair, St. Johns, mid-September. 337-2695.

Northern Arizona Logger's Festival, Flagstaff, mid-September. 779-6631.

Northern Gila County Fair, Pine, mid-September. 474-2359.

Yavapai County Fair, Prescott, late September. 445-7820.

Gila County Fair, Globe, late September. 425-7611.

State Fiddler's Championship, Payson, late September. This is a popular two-day event featuring entertainment and competition to determine the state fiddling champion. 474-4515.

Visual Arts Display, Flagstaff, late September through early November. 779-5944.

Quarter Horse Show, Prescott, end of September through early October. 445-7820.

October Art Fest, Payson, early October. 474-4515.

Copper Country Square Dance Festival, Globe, mid-October. 425-8431.

London Bridge Fifty and Ninety Mile Waterski Marathon, Lake Havasu City, late October. 453-7722.

Rodeo Weekend, Parker, late October. 669-2174.

Arizona Mule Days, Globe, late October. 425-4495.

Four Corners States Bluegrass Music Finals, Wickenburg, November. Three-day competition and festival to determine the regional champion in varying bluegrass categories. Wickenburg Chamber, 684-5479.

Lake Havasu City Sailing Federation Cruise, early January. 602/855-4115.

Iceberg Derby Sailboat Races, Lake Havasu City, late January. 855-4115.

Hashknife Pony Express Ride, Holbrook, February. 524-6558.

Quartzsite Pow-wow, Gem & Mineral Show, Quartzsite, early February. The single largest tourist attraction in the state, with attendance of 850,000 to 1 million annually. Quartzite Improvement Center, 927-6325.

Wickenburg Gold Rush Days & Rodeo, mid-February. 684-5479.

Alpine Winter Carnival, Alpine, mid-February. 339-4754.

O'Odham Tash Indian Pow-wow and Rodeo, Casa Grande, mid-February. Highlights include a parade, rodeos, ceremonial dances, an all-Indian basketball tournament, choosing of the "O'Odham" queen. Casa Grande Chamber, 836-2125.

Pinetop Winter Carnival, early March. 336-4290.

Sunrise Winterfest, McNary. early March. 334-2122.

La Paz County Fair and Miss Parker Pageant, Parker, mid-March. 669-8100.

St. Patrick's Day Parade & Celebration, Sedona, mid-March. 282-7722.

Waterski Marathon, Lake Havasu City, mid-March. 855-4115.

Mining Country Arts & Crafts Fair & Bicycle Race, Miami, early April. 473-3871.

Spring Art Festival, Lake Havasu City, early April. 855-4115.

Desert Regatta, Lake Havasu City, early April. 855-4115.

Copper Dust Stampede, Globe, early April. 425-4495.

Jim Thompson Rodeo, Florence, mid-April. 868-5873.

Pioneer Days, Kearny, late April. 363-5554.

All Police Rodeo, Prescott, late April. 778-1967.

Yavapai County Sheriff Posse Roping, Prescott, May. 445-5713.

Bill Williams Rendezvous Days, Williams, end of May. 635-2041.

GHOST TOWNS

Cochran, 16 miles east of Florence on Kelvin Highway, north on dirt road to Gila River. Once the site of a railroad depot, now only a few buildings remain.

Congress, approximately two miles from Congress Junction. Site of a rich gold mine. Ruins of old cabins and rubble strewn flats, old cemetery well maintained. Mine and adjacent buildings closed to the public.

Goldfield, five miles from Apache Junction on AZ 88. Mining town in the 1890s. Four of the original mine shafts, stopes and timbers can be seen.

Goldroad, 23 miles southwest of Kingman. Gold first discovered by John Moss and party around 1864. A new strike was made by Joe Jerez in 1902.

Harrisburg, approximately eight miles south of Wenden. First town in this part of the desert.

Jerome, 33 miles northeast of Prescott. Established 1876, this famous copper camp hit a peak population of 15,000 about 1929 and its main mine produced some $500 million in ore before closing in 1952.

Kofa, 24 miles on U.S. 95 from a point 28 miles south of Quartzsite on U.S. 60/70. Site of the rich King of Arizona gold mine discovered 1896.

La Paz, eight miles north of Ehrenberg. Flourished for seven years as a gold center and river port. Between 1862 and 1873, the town had more than 5000 residents. The central portion is being reconstructed; the public may view the excavations.

McCabe, 2½ miles west of Rte. 69 at Humboldt, via yard of Iron King Mine. Mining and milling town dating from late 19th Century.

McMillen, near U.S. 60 about 10 miles northeast of Globe. Supported by the celebrated Stonewall Jackson Mine discovered in 1876.

Mineral Park, about 15 miles northwest of Kingman near Duval Copper Mine. Was one of the county's important early towns and the county seat from 1877 till 1887. Still populated.

Oatman, 32 miles southwest of Kingman. Gold mining town active 1900 through 1942. Many buildings and picturesque ruins.

Signal, on Big Sandy Road, 60 miles northwest of Wickenburg, eight miles south of Wickieup on U.S. 93, and another 12 miles west on a dirt road. Established late in 1870s as milling town for

ore from McCrackin and Signal mines, this center was prosperous for many years.

Stanton, six miles east of Arrowhead Station on U.S. 89, 42 miles southwest of Prescott. Active mining camp in late 1800s.

Tiger, northeast of Wickenburg, near Wagoner on Hassayampa Creek. Said to have been the first silver mine of import discovered in northern Arizona.

Vulture Mine, 12 miles west of Wickenburg on Vulture Mine Road. Gold and silver discovered by Henry Wickenburg in 1863. The mine gave up $200 million before the government closed it in 1942.

Walker, six miles south on AZ 69 from a point four miles east of Prescott. Mill and mine ruins from late 1800s.

Weaver or Weaverville, northeast of Wickenburg, two miles beyond Stanton. A very picturesque town named after Pauline Weaver, a guide whose party accidentally discovered a rich gold trove.

INDIAN RESERVATIONS

Camp Verde Reservation The tribe is known for basketmaking. Attractions: Indian Ruins; Yavapai-Apache Information Center, just off the Blank Canyon Freeway with a Tribal Museum and Arts & Crafts; Montezuma Castle National Monument, Montezuma Well, hunting, hiking and fishing. Yavapai-Apache Indian Community, P.O. Box 1188, Camp Verde, AZ 86322. 602/567-3649.

Colorado River Reservation Known for basketry, beadwork and wall clocks. The reservation fronts approximately 100 miles of river on both sides of the Colorado; Lake Moovala is the scene of speed boat races, All-Indian Rodeo, Indian Day Celebration, Arts & Crafts Center and Museum, hunting (dove and quail), fishing, water sports. Colorado River Indian Tribes, Rte. 1, Box 23-B, Parker, AZ 85344. 602/669-9211.

Fort Apache Reservation A huge reservation with a number of attractions, such as the Apache Sunrise Resort, Annual Rodeo and Fair on Labor Day Weekend, ceremonials, camping, fishing, horseback riding and hiking. Noted for "Burden Baskets" and beadwork. White Mountain Apache Tribe, P.O. Box 700, Whiteriver, AZ 85941. 602/338-4346.

Fort McDowell Reservation, 36 miles northeast of Phoenix in Maricopa County. Basketry, also manufactures jojoba bean oil for retail sale. Camping, fishing and inner tubing. Mojave-Apache Tribal Council, P.O. Box 17779, Fountain Hills, AZ 85268. 990-0995.

San Carlos Reservation, adjacent to Fort Apache. Basketry, beadwork and peridot jewelry. The San Carlos Lake provides fishing, camping and hunting. The Indians mine and manufacture peridot jewelry and jojoba bean oil and hold ceremonials, rodeo and fair. San Carlos Apache Tribal Council, P.O. Box 0, San Carlos, AZ 85550. 475-2361.

Tonto-Apache Reservation Noted for basketry and beadwork. Hiking and picnicking. Tonto-Apache Tribal Council, P.O. Box 1440, Payson, AZ 85541. 474-5000.

Yavapai-Prescott Reservation Known for its basketry. Picnicking and hiking. Yavapai-Prescott Tribal Council, P.O. Box 348, Prescott, AZ 86302. 445-8790.

ACCOMMODATIONS

Poco Diablo Resort, Box 1709, Sedona, AZ 86336. 602/282-7333. One mile south of Sedona near Oak Creek Canyon.

The Wickenburg Inn Tennis & Guest Ranch, P.O. Box P, Wickenburg, AZ 85358, 602/684-7811 or 800/528-4227. A 4700-acre wildlife preserve with tennis, riding, home cooking, pool, clinics, Spanish style casitas.

Rancho de los Caballeros, Wickenburg, AZ 85358. 602/684-5484. A working ranch off U.S. 60 and 70, it offers riding, trap and skeet range, square dancing golf and swimming.

LAS VEGAS,
A NEON CITY

Reputedly Lady Luck's favorite piece of real estate, Las Vegas is a neon valley of round-the-clock risk-taking, and endless extravagance. This mecca for schemers, dreamers and pleasure seekers, a fantasyland for adults who never want to grow up, attracts over 12 million people annually, all of them eager to suspend disbelief and immerse themselves in glittering illusions.

The ultimate extrovert, Las Vegas pulls out all the stops to entertain you and to keep you spending your money. The casinos and hotels range from flash to class, the food and entertainment from budget to gourmet. There is something here for the most jaded visitor and much here for the wide-eyed novice. The town's slogan is "No one does it better," and it's true. She may at times annoy you with her flamboyance, and upset you with her showy promises, but in the end, Las Vegas will have you right where she wants you, dazzled by her extravagance and ready to throw your luck in with her.

Las Vegas is improbably centered in a desert valley ringed by treeless mountains. The sky seems endless, especially to big-city eyes. Gaming and glitter in the middle of nowhere creates a fantasyland atmosphere.

The history of Las Vegas is as colorful as one of her casinos. The earliest people in the area were Anglo traders travelling from Sante Fe to California on the old Spanish Trail. They discovered Las Vegas to be a natural oasis of refreshing springs and grassy fields. "Las Vegas" means "The Meadows" in Spanish.

Although explorers like Jedediah Smith and Captain John C. Fremont noted this oasis in their travels, the area remained largely uninhabited until 1855, when Brigham Young sent a band of 30 Mormon men to Las Vegas to mine for lead in the mountains and to convert the Indians. They did not stay long, discouraged by their lack of success in converting the Indians and in smelting the ore they found here. (They could not have known it then, but the unsatisfactory lead was silver.)

When the fabled Comstock Lode, a rich vein of gold and silver, was discov-ered in 1849, Nevada came into her own. Boom towns sprang up all around Las Vegas. Nevada was recognized as a territory in 1861 and as a state in 1864, because the Union needed the wealth of the Comstock Lode to win the Civil War.

In time, the area around the abandoned Mormon settlement became the property of a succession of ranches. They provided a way station for California-bound travellers. One of these ranchers, Helen Stewart, is an example of the strong-willed, self-sufficient pioneer women of the Old West. She remained on the ranch, a lone woman with several young children, after her husband was mysteriously shot and killed there. She supervised the 1,800-acre (738-hectare) ranch, cooked meals for travellers, and offered lodging for boarders until the coming of the railroad.

In 1902, Helen Stewart sold her property to the San Pedro, Salt Lake and Los Angeles Railroad, forerunner of the Union Pacific. The railroad had come to link the West with the East, and Las Vegas was to be a division point depot. The town was born on May 15,

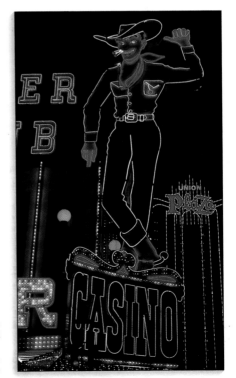

1905, when the railroad auctioned off some 1,200 lots to high-bidding speculators. In two days, all the lots were sold and a boom town of tents and shacks soon appeared on the scene.

Las Vegas remained a railroad company town, small and sleepy, until the 1930s when the construction of the Boulder (Hoover) Dam brought in workers from all over the country. In 1931, gambling was legalized in Nevada to funnel much-needed revenue into the state. Liberal marriage and divorce laws were also enacted in 1931, and Las Vegas became a capital for six-week residents awaiting a Nevada divorce.

A Never-Never Land

Las Vegas is an easy town to navigate. Most of the gambling activity is concentrated in two main areas: the famed Las Vegas Strip and the downtown area on Fremont Street. The Strip (officially known as Las Vegas Boulevard South) begins at Sahara Avenue with the Sahara Hotel and runs south to the Hacienda Hotel, almost to the airport.

The downtown area is about three

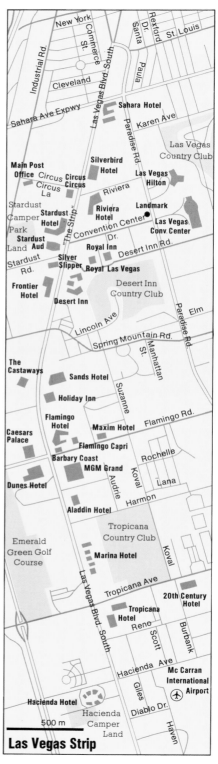

The bells to █ at any hour █ the Wedding Chapel, The Strip.

miles (five km) north of the Strip area. A third area is building up just off the Strip along Convention Center Drive. It includes the 63-acre (25-hectare) Las Vegas Hilton, almost a self-contained community, and the hexagonal tower of the Landmark Hotel.

The Strip is a special effect come to life. Where else would you find a colonnaded palace (Caesar's), a circus big top (Circus-Circus), a blue pagoda (Imperial Palace) and a Mississippi River steamboat (Holiday Inn Center Strip) sharing the same stretch of highway? Not to mention all the other hotels, motels, casinos, fountains, statues, coffee shops, gas stations, wedding chapels, souvenir stands, and shopping centers?

The hotels themselves are part of the visual excitement. They are sheathed in lights, reflective glass and marble. The latest trend is towards blindingly brilliant illuminated covered entrances called *portes cochéres.* Your hometown hotel never looked like this!

The city that never sleeps is also the place where nothing ever remains the same. Las Vegas properties are constantly doing face-lifting, renovating, adding on towers and making other structural changes. It is an unwritten law here that you are only as good as your latest superlative. Even McDonald's, that bastion of Middle America, has been swept up with Las Vegas Fever, adding glittering neon tubing to the familiar golden arches.

Caesar's Palace and Grand Hotels

Some of the Strip hotels are self-contained attractions. There's **Caesar's Palace**, a rather grandiose structure that sits on several city blocks of prime Strip frontage. Lavish fountains, reproductions of classic statuary and impressive 50-foot (15-meter) high cypress trees set off the grillwork exterior of this huge hotel. At night Caesar's is theatrically bathed in blue-green light. Also part of the "empire" is an arcaded automatic People Mover and the geodesic-domed Omnimax Theatre. Only in Las Vegas, folks!

Another world-famous hotel is the **MGM Grand**, worth a detour to see. The casino itself is bigger than a football field. The MGM stands on what is known as The Golden Corner of the

amingo
tel Casino,
ere
tunes are
ade and
st.

Strip—Las Vegas Boulevard South at Flamingo. Other golden corner occupants are the Dunes Hotel, the Flamingo Hilton and the Barbary Coast.

The **Flamingo Hilton**'s history is decidedly more interesting than the corporate ones of the MGM and Caesar's. The original Flamingo was built in 1946 by one Benjamin "Bugsy" Siegel, described by newspapers of the day as "an Eastern gambler." The story is that Bugsy built the Flamingo to impress his California mistress, Virginia Hill. He spared no expense in creating a posh resort with an elegant palm-lined casino and large outdoor swimming pool. The Flamingo's grand opening had all the trappings of a Hollywood premiere, with many of that town's celebrities in attendance. Unfortunately for Bugsy, he overlooked one small detail. He neglected to repay a loan he had obtained from his investors, a cheery New York City gang known as Murder, Inc. Siegel was gunned down in his mistress' Beverly Hills home one year after he opened his Fabulous Flamingo.

Siegel's gruesome slaying added a note of titillating notoriety to little Las Vegas. Sightseers came to town wanting to play in the casino a gangster had built. The underworld overtones became part of the Las Vegas mystique.

A construction boom of luxurious ranch-style resort hotels followed the success of the Flamingo. Las Vegas launched a national publicity blitz promoting the desert oasis as "the gambling and entertainment capital of the world." Leggy showgirls were a fixture in every publicity shot (and there were thousands) telegraphed around the world.

Other colorful early characters include the gambler known as Nick the Greek, hotelmen Del Webb, Benny Binion and Kirk Kerkorian, and of course, the reclusive Howard Hughes. Hughes arrived in Las Vegas in 1967, taking up residence in a suite of rooms at the Desert Inn. By the time he left town in 1970, he had purchased the Sands Desert Inn, Castaways, Silver Slipper, Frontier and the Landmark hotels, along with a country club, television station, airport, ranch, mining claims and parcels of vacant land. The Las Vegas properties, along with Harolds Club in Reno, are today part of the Summa Corporation. Many regard

Casinos like the Oasis (left) and the Westward (right) provide a paradise for gamblers.

the Hughes takeover of the Las Vegas casinos as a watershed in the town's history. Early Las Vegas entrepreneurs were freewheeling types who operated their establishments with a certain carefree abandon. Howard Hughes turned over the management of his casinos to "the guys in the three-piece suits from back East." In Las Vegas, "the good old days" refers to the period preceeding inflation and corporate ownership.

Trial Marriages

All up and down the Strip are establishments where couples come to try a gamble of another sort—marriage. The marriage business is drawing people to Las Vegas in larger numbers each year, according to the Las Vegas News Bureau. Couples can be wed (or "hitched," as one chapel sign puts it) at any hour, providing they have a license from the Marriage Bureau. The bureau is located downtown and is conveniently open from 8 a.m. to midnight Monday through Thursday and from 8 a.m. Friday through 12 midnight Sunday, including holidays. There's no blood test or waiting period. Las Vegas wedding chapels run the gamut from the barely picturesque to the outright garish. **The Little Church of the West** is a historic building by Las Vegas standards, dating back to 1942.

Frills and Fancies on Downtown

Downtown Las Vegas is not without its own special excitement. Unlike the Strip, which had miles of empty desert on which to build sprawling resort hotels, the downtown gambling area was limited to the five blocks of Fremont Street in the town's commercial center. You'll find 12 major casinos, dozens of slot machine "joints" and souvenir shops literally wall to wall with storefront businesses. This close proximity allows the action to spill out of the casinos and onto the sidewalks, creating a carnival-like atmosphere. While the Strip is ablaze with color, Downtown is alive with sound. Everywhere you go you hear sirens announcing slot machine jackpots and barkers hawking food bars, free slot machine pulls and other gimmicks.

The oldest and newest in promotional

advertising is very much in evidence on Fremont Street. **Vegas Vic** is a huge, illuminated cowboy figure who has been waving to passers-by from his perch high above the **Pioneer Club** since the early 1950s. (At one time, Vegas Vic had a voice which drawled, "Howdy, podner" 24 hours a day. "They silenced that thing," says one longtime resident. "It was a mercy.") Across the street from Vic is another illumination called **Vegas Vicky**, perpetually kicking one leg up at Vic. **Sassy Sally's**, a slot machine emporium, has positioned a trio of mechanized, talking animal figures at the entrance. The center figure is a dance hall pig who calls out to pedestrians in Mae West-like tones.

High technology is represented on Fremont Street with the **Golden Nugget**'s state of the art computerized marquee, which spells out messages and flashes pictures.

Downtown is also home of the **Fabulous Four Corners**, the intersection of Fremont and Casino Center Boulevard. The lights of the Golden Nugget, Horseshoe, Four Queens and Fremont hotels combine to make this the most brilliantly illuminated intersection in

the world. Nevada Power Company estimates that the average monthly electric bill for downtown hotels exceeds $350,000. The average Strip resort hotel spends about $5,000 a day on electricity, mostly for air-conditioning and heat.

Years ago, the downtown area was known as **Glitter Gulch**. The merchants ran a contest to find a more sophisticated name for the district and "Casino Center" was the winner. Nonetheless, the old names are still in use— Downtown, Glitter Gulch, or simply Fremont Street.

Downtown has changed considerably in recent years. Fremont Street, always a great place to gamble, did not have hotel accommodations until recently. Today the Golden Nugget, Four Queens, Union Plaza and the Mint are among major casinos with hotel space and gourmet dining rooms as fine as any on the Strip. In addition, the Downtown area now has its own mini-convention facility, the **Cashman Field Center**, which opened in 1982 at a site moments away from Glitter Gulch.

As a rule, it costs less to gamble at Downtown than on the Strip. Stakes are

Fountain spray from Caesar's Palace, T Strip.

lower and it is still possible to find nickel slots and 25¢ craps tables. Some people think Downtown dealers are friendlier and more tolerant too. Downtown casinos are said to have loose slots, machines that have been adjusted to pay out up to 90 percent of the money that is deposited in them. The volume of slot enthusiasts is so high that frequent payoffs are good promotions for the casino because they bring in more traffic. There is no skill involved in playing the slots, so they are often a tourist's first foray into casino gambling. The attraction of hitting a jackpot keeps casinos humming incessantly with the noise of machines in action. The newest versions are dollar carousels, which collect and pay out in dollars. They are very popular, and may mean the demise of the standard casino machine.

This is not to say that the high rollers or big shooters do not frequent the Downtown area. **Binion's Horseshoe** is a downtown property known for its players. (A player in Las Vegas parlance is someone who plays for very high stakes as opposed to a grind, who makes small bets.)

Gambling or Gaming?

There is no place on earth where a little knowledge is more of a dangerous thing than in a casino. They don't call this place "Lost Wages" for nothing. It will be worth your while to study some of the many books available on casino gambling and to learn gaming etiquette and strategies.

Several casinos offer seminars in blackjack (or "21"), craps and baccarat. It is a mistake to assume that you can rely on the assistance of the dealer, however. Although some dealers can be very helpful, you must remember that they are all employees of the casino and in most cases are forbidden to take interest in the activity around them.

It is generally acknowledged that baccarat, blackjack and craps offer the lowest house odds. Because of the way most people play, however, the return to the house is 19 percent on craps and baccarat and 21 percent on blackjack. The lowest return to the house, only 7 percent, is from bingo. Roulette returns 27 percent to the house, keno 28 percent, and the "Wheel of Fortune" or "Big Six" 51 percent.

Is there a pattern here? Yes, The games in which you can exercise some control generally present you with better opportunities to win. " An intelligent craps player can do well," says a casino executive. "The problem is that so few people bother to understand the complicated betting involved in craps."

Dealers, who receive low salaries from casinos and therefore are very dependent on tips from customers, will appreciate tip (or toke, as it is called here). The custom here is to make a bet for the dealer, usually half the size of your own. Dealers are required to tap a casino chip against the table or employ some other signal to indicate to the pit boss (or supervisor) that he is pocketing his tip.

All of the casinos serve complimentary drinks. If you are gambling and have not been served by a cocktail waitress, ask a dealer to summon one for you. You should tip her with cash or a casino chip.

The nonstop activity of Nevada casinos resulted in over $2.6 billion in gross gaming revenues for the state in 1982. The industry is carefully monitored by the Nevada Gaming Commission. (The state prefers the term "gaming" to "gambling.") The Gaming Commission is an effective policeman. The casinos have to be honest—cheating could result in the loss of a casino license worth millions of dollars.

The Strip offers a parade of entertainment nightly. There are big-name performers appearing in the major showrooms and world-famous production shows like the *Lido de Paris* at the **Stardust** and the *Folies Bergere* at the **Tropicana**. The trend has been toward mounting Broadway musicals in the showrooms of the **Desert Inn** and the **Sands**.

If your heart is set on seeing a particular performer, it is best to book a room at the hotel where he or she is performing, since showrooms give preferential treatment to hotel guests. You should make a reservation the day of the show with the hotel guest-relations coordinator or the bellcap. Show admission is by reservation, not ticket. You will have a choice of a dinner show (with a minimum price) or a cocktail show. There is usually a two- or four-drink minimum at a cocktail show. Be forewarned that the evening could get

Vegas is a
bright by d
(left) and b
night (righ

pricey—your showroom tab will be subject to a 10 percent entertainment tax and a 5¾ percent state sales tax, plus gratuities. In true Las Vegas style, the maitre d' who seats you will be much more considerate in selecting a table for you if you palm him a tip when you first enter the showroom (anywhere from $5 to $20).

If you do not have a reservation for a show, you will be allowed to wait in the "no reservations" line. It is akin to flying standby.

The bare-breasted beauties in the chorus line are no longer the wicked attractions they once were back in the early 1950s, when production shows made their debut on the Strip. Audiences are more wordly now and more demanding. These days the special effects are the stars of the show. The MGM's *Jubilee* presents a recreation of the sinking of the Titanic and the fall of the temple from the Biblical tale of Samson and Delilah.

A local favorite is the production of *Beyond Belief* at the **Frontier**. It is a lavish showcase for the incredible illusions of magic stars Siegfried and Roy.

Las Vegas casinos have been plying customers with inexpensive, bountiful food buffets since the early 1950s. Prices keep nudging up toward reality, but food is still a bargain here. You can find 99¢ steak-and-egg breakfasts and all-you-can-eat lunch and dinner buffets which may or may not include champagne. Sunday brunches at the MGM and Caesar's Palace are events in themselves. Every hotel also has a 24-hour coffee shop, where you may have everything from the proverbial cup to a full course dinner. If you're keno buffs, you can relax and play a game or two in hotel coffee shops while you eat. In addition, each major hotel has several restaurants, one of which is designated the gourmet room. These restaurants are carefully decorated showpieces. Dine in a Kismet-inspired tented pleasure palace (**Sultan's Table** at the Dunes), or in a pretty Japanese setting with running streams (**Benihana Village** at the Las Vegas Hilton) or amid the glory that was Caesar's (**Baacchanal** in Caesar's Palace). Other rooms have a New York flair, European elegance or garden-like charm. The meals here are generally memorable for the expense as well as the setting.

ACTION OUTDOORS

For complete information on Nevada's state parks and facilities, write the Nevada Division of State Parks, Capitol Complex, Carson City, NV 89710.

Lake Mead National Recreation Area extends north from Davis Dam 115 miles along the Colorado River to the Grand Canyon National Park embracing both Lake Mead and Lake Mojave (See Info—Grand Canyon). At its southernmost point, Lake Mead is backed up by the **Hoover Dam**. Constructed to generate electricity and to control flooding it was claimed to be the "eighth engineering wonder of the world." The dam can be viewed from both sides of Black Canyon, while a more spectacular panorama can be seen from helicopter rides originating at the Golden Strike Inn four miles west on U.S. 93. Elevators also carry passengers down to the powerplant for a daily guided tour. Hoover Dam can be approached from Boulder City, which lies a short distance from the northern end of U.S. 95. U.S. 93 runs northeast from Kingman on I-40 and provides a more scenic route cutting through Lake Mead National Recreation Area.

Toiyabe National Forest, northwest of Las Vegas. Includes the fifth highest mountain in the state, Mt. Charleston. Picnic sites, campground, small commercial development, 35 miles north of the city on U.S. 95, turn west at Kyle or Lee Canyons. U.S. Forest Service Campgrounds are available, as well as an abundance of private RV parks. For information, call the U.S. Forest Service, 702/385-6255. Area also offers skiing at Lee Canyon Ski Area; an 80-percent intermediate area with two lifts and a 1,000-foot vertical range. See Info—The Great Outdoors, page 82.

ATTRACTIONS

Calamity Jane's Ice Cream House and Coca-Cola Museum, Sam's Town Hotel, Gambling Hall and Bowling Center, 5111 Boulder Highway. 10 a.m. to 11:30 a.m. every day. Old-fashioned ice cream parlor, memorabilia. 702/454-8021 for party reservations.

Imperial Palace Auto Collection, 3535 Las Vegas Blvd. South. Large privately-owned automobile collection. 9:30 a.m. to 11:30 p.m. daily.

Las Vegas Art Museum, 3333 W. Washington in Lorenzi Park. 702/647-4300.

The Liberace Museum, 1775 E. Tropicana Ave. 10 to 5:30 every day. 702/798-5595.

Lost City Museum, Overton. North on I-15 to 169 toward the Valley of Fire. Impressive collection of early Pueblo culture. Daily 8.30 to 4.30. 702/397-2193.

Mount Charleston, 40-minute drive from the heart of town north on U.S. 95, turn west at Kyle or Lee canyons. Pine forests, ski areas—a refreshing change from the desert.

Museum of Natural History, on U. of Nevada campus, 4505 S. Maryland Parkway. Southwestern Indian culture, fine collection of silver, more. 9 to 5 Mon. through Fri. 702/739-3381.

Nevada State Museum in Lorenzi Park, 700 Twin Lakes Dr. Part of Nevada State Museum system. History, archaeology, anthropology, animal and plant life. 7 to 4:30, Wed. through Sun. 702/385-0115.

Old Mormon Fort, 908 Las Vegas Blvd. North. History exhibit, replica of frontier Mormon living room. Call Cultural Focus. 702/382-7198.

Old Nevada, down the road from Red Rock and Spring Mountain Ranch. A "recreated" Nevada boom town.

Planetarium, on the campus of Clark County Community College, 3200 E. Cheyenne Ave. in North Las Vegas. Shows at 6:30 and 8 p.m. 702/643-6060.

Red Rock Canyon/Spring Mountain Ranch, West Charleston Boulevard for 17 miles to new visitors center *cum* museum on Nevada Route 159 and 13-mile scenic drive. Hiking, exploring, limited camping. 702/363-1921. 528-acre ranch is five miles further west, tours available. Call 702/875-4141.

Southern Nevada Museum, Boulder Highway between Henderson and Boulder City. 8 to 5:30 daily. Indoor and outdoor exhibits focus on the history of southern Nevada. 702/565-0907.

Tour of Death Valley. Full-day round trip, toward Los Angeles on I-15, to Arden/Blue Diamond exit on Nevada Rte. 160. At Pahrump, turn west for California and follow signs to Death Valley. Back by way of Beatty, to ghost town of Rhyolite.

EVENTS

Helldorado Days, Las Vegas Convention Center, June. This annual professional rodeo and celebration has been an important Las Vegas tradition for nearly half a century.

Jaycees State Fair, August. Five days of festivities include a carnival, races, booths and special show.

Frontier 500, late August or early September. Based at the

Frontier Hotel, off-road racers take a grueling two-day journey to Reno. 702/734-0110.

Mint Trapshooting Tournament, September. This nationally-known event takes place at the Mint Gun Club in Las Vegas.

Jerry Lewis Muscular Distrophy Association Telethon, early September, Caesars Palace. 702/731-7110.

Las Vegas Boat and Ski Races, September. From Boulder Beach water-skiers race in 50- and 75-mile Lake Mead marathons. 702/293-2034.

Las Vegas Pro-Celebrity Classic, September. Inaugural of golf's richest tournament occurred 1983, with a $1 million-plus purse. All the game's top players and many celebrities. For information and tickets, call 702/382-6616.

San Gennaro Feast, mid to late September. Italian celebration with bands, dancing, food and celebrities. Dunes Hotel. 702/369-5501.

Pahrump Harvest Festival Fair and Rodeo, Pahrump, September. Parade, rodeo, dance, farmers' market. 702/727-5800.

The Gamblernationals Las Vegas Speedrome, late September. National Hot Rod Association/Winston World Championship. 702/644-1482.

Tropicana Sports Car Olympics, Tropicana Hotel, late September to early October. Rally, autocross, funkhana and *concours d'elegance* open to the public. 702/873-1926.

Caesar's Palace Grand Prix Late September or early October. Four-day event features top drivers. Call 702/731-7865 or 800/634-6681.

Boulder City Art in the Park Festival, early October. Government and Bicentennial Parks, Boulder City. 702/293-2034.

North Las Vegas Fairshow and Nevada Championship Balloon Races, late October. 702/642-1944.

Imperial Palace Antique Auto Run, October. Classic cars race

58 miles from the Imperial Palace to Red Rock Canyon and back. 702/731-3311.

Showboat Invitational Bowling Tournament, January. The $150,000 tourney is the oldest stop on the PBA tour and one of the most rewarding—$27,000 went to the 1982 winner. The Showboat Hotel hosts another pro-bowling tournament in July. 385-9123.

Parade of Lights, December. Christmas lights on Lake Mead; a flotilla of local boats makes a nighttime run between Lake Mead Marina and Boulder Beach.

New Year's Fireworks Show, New Year's Eve. At the Union Plaza, 702/386-2110.

Desert Inn LPGA Golf Tournament, April. The best players on the women's pro golf tour visit for a four-day Pro-Am with guest celebrities at the Desert Inn Country Club. 702/733-4444.

Boulder City Spring Jamboree, Boulder City, April. Local citizens celebrate spring's arrival with races, tournaments, barbecue and the Black Canyon Juried Art Show. Boulder City Chamber of Commerce. 702/293-2034.

Alan King Tennis Classic, April. This Caesar's Palace event features top men and women pros as well as a celebrity tournament. 702/731-7222.

World Series of Poker, Binion's Horseshoe, April. The granddaddy of high-stakes poker showdowns has been held at this Las Vegas hotspot each spring since 1970. 702/382-1600.

Moapa Valley Art Show, Overton, April. This annual art show and sale is one of Nevada's largest.

Henderson Industrial Days, Henderson, April. Nevada's youngest city (Henderson was established in 1941) throws a five-day celebration. Contact: Henderson Chamber of Commerce. 702/565-8951.

Mint 400, the Mint Hotel, April. The hotel hosts the toughest and richest off-road race in America, featuring a pre-race inspection

of cars and drivers on downtown's Fremont Street.

Military Appreciation Day, North Las Vegas, May. The people of North Las Vegas join those at Nellis Air Force Base for a day of golf, feasting and merriment. Contact: North Las Vegas Chamber of Commerce. 702/642-9595.

SHOPPING

The Miracle Mile is not famous for good buys, although most large hotels have their own shopping malls and the place is replete with souvenirs of all kinds. Some of the best shopping here may be the delicious chocolates available at **See's Candy** and **Ethel M's,** whose chocolates are manufactured in Henderson, just outside of Las Vegas. Particularly recommended: the liqueur-filled cordials. **Boulevard Mall** is the "granny" of shopping malls, one of the few in the country with valet parking and multiple taxi lanes. This is a one-story mecca with a domed center area for meeting and watching. **Fashion Show** is a classy mall on the Strip — Saks, Nieman-Marcus, Bullock's and Goldwater's lurk here, interspersed with some interesting boutiques and a host of jewelry stores.

ACCOMMODATIONS

Desert Inn (702/733-4444). A local favorite for upscale contemporary decor and atmosphere, known to natives as "DI." Small and understated by Las Vegas standards.

El Morocco Motel, 2975 Las Vegas Boulevard South. 702/735-7145. Better-than-average motel conveniently located on the Strip.

Gold Nugget, East Fremont. 702/385-7111. Presently known to be the "class act" downtown.

The Frontier, Las Vegas Boulevard South. 702/734-0110. Centrally located on the Strip.

La Concha Motel, 2955 Las Vegas Boulevard South. 702/735-1255. Another favored motel on the Strip. The lobby is shaped like a conch shell, hence the name.

INDIAN TRIBES

There are over 50 Indian reservations in the Southwest, each representing more or less a distinct group. The Apache have four different reservations, scattered from the Fort Apache and San Carlos Apache in Central Arizona, the Mescalero Apache in Southern New Mexico to the Jicarilla in Northwestern New Mexico. The Navajo have by far the largest reservation, spanning the entire northeastern corner of Arizona, a slice of southern Colorado and a slice of New Mexico, with the Hopi reservation taking up a large chunk in the middle. The Papago and Pima live south of Phoenix and Tucson respectively, and the 21 Pueblo are scattered among the urban cities and Hispanic villages of the northern Rio Grande in New Mexico. These are the largest and most culturally intact Native American groups in the Southwest, and are the ones covered in this section.

Smaller tribes include the Havasupi, who have the distinction of living in the Grand Canyon, the Ute of southern Utah, the Paiute in northern Arizona, and the Walapai, Hualapai, Mohave, Yavapai, Chemehuevi, Yuma, Cocopa, Maricopa and Yaqui Indians, all living in parts of western Arizona. Many of these western Arizona tribes have friends and relatives in Mexico—the border created between the United States and Mexico was not theirs.

Though these tribes are as diverse as, say, various European cultures, they have in common their status as Native Americans and their struggle to maintain their traditions in the face of an almost overwhelming Anglo culture. Southwest Indians raised on the reservation have a cadence and rhythm to their speech that are distinct and unique ways of using words and concepts in English, which is a second language for many. With the exception of the Navajo, each piece in this section is written by an Indian, and it is hoped that some of these rhythms and attitudes come through in the writing and will give the reader some small insight into the cultures.

THE PUEBLO

Although details may vary from pueblo to pueblo, the story of the Creation of the Universe begins with a single Mind which "thought" the entire Universe into existence. Once the Creation had been completed, the people and animals found themselves in a dimness full of running water which was the First World, the Blue World. They journeyed upward, into the Red World, then up to the Yellow World, which was the Third World where they rested before climbing upward into the White World, which was full of flowers and grass and beautiful running water. Many wanted to remain there because it was a paradise, but the people had been told that theirs must be the Fifth World, the one we know now, because it would be necessary to live in a certain way, and this could be accomplished only by travelling there.

The animals, insects and plants had some discussions and decided they must accompany their brethren, the human beings, into the Fifth World. But when the people and creatures arrived at the opening into the Fifth World, they found the hole was blocked by a large stone. The people tried but were unable to move the stone. The Badger People began digging with their long claws and managed to loosen the stone. But it was one of the Antelope People who decided to butt the stone with his head. Antelope took a run at the stone. The stone moved only a little. He hit it again and the stone moved a little more. The fourth time he struck it with his head, the stone flew out of the hole and Antelope led all the people and creatures into the Present World.

The Present World of the Pueblo Indian people is comprised of 19 separate Pueblo tribes in New Mexico, and the Hopi Pueblo tribe in northeastern Arizona. Although the Pueblo people share similar religious beliefs which reveal a common world view, vast linguistic differences distinguish each pueblo from the other.

From the very beginning, the Fifth or Present World presented human beings with a great many challenges and difficulties. But

Preceding pages, Navajo woman sheepherder goes on horseback to better watch over her flock. Left, Jose Toledo, famous artist of the Jemez Pueblo.

it is precisely by these struggles that the people were to realize their spirituality and humanity and, most important, their place with all other living beings in the Universe. Thus the Pueblo view of the world emphasizes the interdependence of human beings and animals, the lowliest insects, and the plants and trees. Pueblo clans further recognize this familial relationship by calling themselves, say, the Badger Clan or the Corn Clan. Each animal, each plant, each tree that the people might take on to satisfy human needs has always been prayed to and asked to give itself to the people.

Voluntary Sacrifices

Among the Keresan-speaking Pueblo, for instance, the deer which is brought home by the hunter is placed in the center of the home, and treated as a guest of honor. Turquoise is draped on the dead animal's neck and antlers, and family and guests approach the deer to "feed" it ceremonially by placing pinches of blessed corn meal on its nose. No part of the deer's body is wasted or in any way dishonored. The hunter must participate in the Deer Dance rituals, and "dance" the soul of the deer back to the mountains where the people believe the soul will be re-born into another deer, who will remember the love and respect of the humans and thus choose to once again give its life to the hunter.

The Southwest land the Pueblo people call "Mother" is a beautiful but unpredictable land where extremes of drought or winter cold have made human survival a great challenge. In the thousands of years the Pueblo people have lived in the Southwest they have met the challenge, but only with the grace of the spirits of all living beings and the love of Mother Earth. The Pueblo people are by necessity among the greatest skywatchers. Ancient Pueblo observatories where winter sun symbols were inscribed on sandstone and special windows allowed sunlight to illuminate the petroglyphs only on the day of the winter solstice, have been found throughout the Southwest. In a land where the sky determines what the fortunes of Pueblo farming will be, religious devotion to watching cloud formations, winds, the positions of the sun and the moon and the tracking of Venus, Jupiter and Mars, gave the Pueblo people the intricate information necessary for successful agriculture.

When the Spanish invaders arrived at Zuni Pueblo in 1540, they found neat, prosperous fields full of corn, beans, squash, melons and cotton, which was woven into cloth. The Spaniards taxed the agriculture and, gradually, the Pueblo people got fed up. The agricultural output was barely enough to feed the people of each pueblo. So, in 1680, the people organized a military and reconnaissance maneuver which is still to be marveled at because of the great distances between the pueblos. The Pueblo staged a great revolt, in which Spanish priests, soldiers and settlers were slaughtered and the survivors driven out of Pueblo country to El Paso del Norte. For some eight years, the Pueblo again enjoyed life without the invaders. Then, in 1692, the Spanish returned, and, according to one theory, factionalism between the Pueblo prevented another military victory for the Pueblo. At any rate, the Spaniards who returned were more cautious in their dealings with the Pueblo.

Eventually, even the King of Spain realized that he was dealing with sovereign governmental entities, and Pueblo leaders were acknowledged as sovereign powers by a silver-headed cane each. Grants of land from the King of Spain to each of the pueblos were forthcoming.

Pueblo Rituals and Art:
Appeasing the Spirits

Today, as long ago, what you may see at any given pueblo is not nearly so important as what you do not see—what you will never be permitted to see. The closest an outside person may come is attending a Pueblo dance, which is actually only part of a longer religious ritual. Certain ritual dances at pueblo are now off-limits to visitors due to years of bad manners on the part of prying ethnologists and camera-toting tourists. Dances which are still accessible to visitors are important religious acts, regardless of the apparent informality of the Pueblo onlookers. Thus tape recorders and cameras are in extreme bad taste.

Among the ceremonies open to the public is Taos Pueblo's San Geronimo Festival (on September 29 and 30 each fall). For centuries, this event has included an intertribal trade fair. On display are cottonwood drums and undecorated micaceous pottery, a gleaming pinkish ware with occasional smoke spots, as is beadwork on moccasins that are traded for by other Indians.

In Santa Clara Canyon each July, the Puye Cliff Ceremonial, a thrilling weekend event, takes place high atop the mesa. A modest craft show accompanies traditional dances performed against a backdrop of stone and adobe ruins. Puye, which is part of the Pajarito Plateau, is a majestic place to see a pair of Eagle dancers, wearing white feathered headdresses.

Indian dances are propitiations to the spirit world for blessings and they often are combined with Christian feast days. On Christmas Eve in the Catholic church of San Felipe Pueblo, the spirits of the animal kingdom pay homage to the Christ Child as dancers representing deer or buffalo, and elaborately dressed women dancers, enter the church after midnight mass. In hushed closeness, onlookers await the arrival of the procession. No one is supposed to be abroad to see the dancers come from their *kiva*. Buffalo dancers, wearing the dark fur and horned headdress of the buffalo, with their exposed skin darkened, stomp on the floor. Deer dancers bent over their sticks,

hand. The men wear short white embroidered kilts with long bold sashes, armbands and moccasins and they too carry pine boughs. The entry of two long files of dancers into the plaza is pageantry at its finest, but the purpose is sacred—to raise the spirits of rain and fertility, to stamp the earth, to beat the drum and chant and raise the vibrations of the earth to insure a fine harvest.

Zuni Pueblo holds its Shalako Ceremonial in late November or early December; it is among the most spectacular Indian celebrations. The all-night event centers upon the coming of 12-foot (3½-meter) Shalakos and their retinues who bless new or renovated homes. In the yet-to-be-completed houses, pits are dug to enable the tall Shalako to enter and dance. The extremely costly cos-

headdresses bedecked with antlers, move more lightly.

The Corn Dance is held at various times on the different pueblos. Santo Domingo holds it on August 4th, the feast of Saint Dominic, in an open-air extravaganza involving 500 dancers from age two to age 80. Each barefoot woman dancer has a blue stepped tablita painted on her glossy black hair to symbolize a mountain with an indication of rain. She wears a one-shouldered manta—a woven sash—the best family jewelry, and she holds a pine bough in each

Eagle dancers doing their own thing. Their mimicry of the bird goes beyond the external; they become eagles in spirit.

tumes are draped over a wooden framework, which includes pulleys to move parts like a puppeteer.

Complex social relationship grow out of this Pueblo view of the world in which the well-being of all living creatures is tied to the well-being of every individual person or animal. In this way, much of what might appear to be mere day-to-day comings and goings between neighbors and families is actually a part of a greater whole, even a spiritual and religious whole. Although the current fashion trends in Pueblo silverwork, pottery, baskets or Hopi "kachina dolls" invariably gain the most attention, the most powerful manifestation of all of the Pueblo is still this vision of Wholeness.

THE NAVAJO

Their own name for themselves is *Dinneh*—The People. The White men called them Navajo. They came a long way to settle down in the American Southwest. Of Athapascan stock, they originally lived somewhere in the forests of northwestern Canada. They drifted down into the Four Corners area in small groups of skin-clad hunters. By 1400 A.D., they were well-established in their new homeland. It is a land of ever-changing colors, of yellow deserts, blood-red mesas and canyons, green fir and aspen-covered highlands and silvery expanses of sage overspread by a turquoise sky. This beautiful land was sacred to them because it had been created by the Holy Ones for The People to live in. The People had to pass through four previous worlds before emerging into this, the Fifth World of White Radiance.

In the beginning, they knew how to hunt and little else. They wore a loincloth of animal skin or, in the case of women, an apron, also of animal skin, or a fringed skirt of plant fibers. In colder weather, they wore blankets made from the fur and hide of animals. Among the weapons they brought with them from the north were the lance, a sinew-backed bow and a hide shield.

Nomadic and warlike, they used these weapons to raid the villages of their Pueblo Indian neighbors who had lived in the land since the dawn of human history. They took from the peaceful Pueblo not only many useful things that were new to them, but also women who taught them how to plant corn and squash, how to weave and how to make pottery. The Navajo were good learners. In time, they became even better weavers than their Pueblo teachers. Much later they learned from the Spaniards how to ride and how to raise sheep and, still later, how to become silversmiths.

Nomads No More

Planting and sheepherding turned the roving nomads into sedentary herdsmen with a settled home at whose core was the beautiful Canyon de Chelly. In 1851, the American Army built Fort Defiance, especially to "defy" and control the Navajo. In 1863, Kit Carson was sent to subdue them altogether and to remove The People. Carson waged a cruel war: he did not hunt down the small groups of Navajo hidden in the depths of their canyons, but made war instead upon their crops and their sheep. Livestock was killed, the corn supplies burned. Winter came and saw the Indians cooped up in their canyon caves, where they starved and froze to death. At last, they surrendered.

They were made to go on the Long Walk to Bosque Redondo, 350 miles (563 km) away. What they encountered at their destination was worse than the march itself. They were forced to make do in a flat, inhospitable land, with nothing to drink but alkali water, which made them sick. They had no materials to build shelters and lived, like gophers in earth holes. They never had enough to eat as their crops withered in the hostile soil. Out of 8,000 Navajo, 1,500 died. After four years, the government relented and let the survivors go back to their homeland. This time, they did not mind the five weeks' walk despite its hardship.

The People made a new start under the most unfavorable conditions. That the Navajo are flourishing now as the largest of all tribes in the country is a tribute to their hardiness and resilience, but, after more than a hundred years, the Long Walk still haunts tribal memories.

Home life revolves around the hogan— the Navajo house. The earliest type was the "forked stick" hogan made of three crotched poles interlaced at the top, covered with sticks and plastered over with earth. In the center of the sunken floor was the firepit and at the top the smoke hole. The hogan was well-suited to the country—cool in summer and snugly warm in winter. Inside, people slept with their feet toward the fire like so many spokes of a wheel. Modern hogans are octagonal log cabins with a domed roof through which the stovepipe rises. Many have electric lights, refrigerators and, very important, a color TV set. They are much roomier than the old-style hogan, but still preserve its original design.

If a Navajo died inside the hogan, an opening was made in the back of the dwelling through which to remove the body. The hogan and everything in it were burned, and from then on, the place was shunned for fear of the *achindee*, the ghosts of the dead who hover around the spot where they died. Witches and witchcraft are likewise feared.

Not observing certain taboos can arouse the anger of powerful supernaturals. Navajo life, in fact, is so regulated by taboo that a man cannot possibly obey all the restrictions expected of him. Rather, he may honor the most serious ones and, in time of misfortune, determine what he has done to displease the supernaturals and then rectify his error.

In that case, it is time to have a "Sing," for which one must procure the help of a medicine man, the *Hatàli*, or chanter, who can bring evil under ritual control. His knowledge is not gained easily. Before a Sing, he spends days in fasting, taking sweat

paintings are small and can be finished by one man in an hour or two. Others may be 20 feet long, requiring the help of several assistants. The patient who is "sung over" sits in the center of the painting, where his living body becomes part of the sacred altar. When the ritual is over, patient and painting are symbolically united as the medicine man, having dipped his fingers into a liquid and then into the sand painting, transfers some of the painting to the patient's body, giving him some of its power. Finally the painting will be destroyed, the sand scattered in

baths and communing with the powers. He searches for the cause of evil through "listening" or "trembling." His whole body shakes, his trembling hands wander, hesitate, hover over a patch or cornmeal until, finally the finger traces upon it some ancient design that indicates the cause of the disease and the appropriate ritual to exorcise it.

The sand painting, this tracing of an ancient design, can last several days. If the Sing is done right, the song chanted beautifully and perfectly, the sand painting as it should be, then all will be well. Some sand

Navajo Indian checks condition of his horse by looking at its teeth and gums, on reservation near Hubbell Trading Post.

all the sacred directions. Thus, the designs seen on the plywood "sand paintings" sold as curios, or on certain rugs, have their roots in Navajo religious symbolism.

The Holy People's Family Tree

Navajo religion is complex, its teachings, legends, songs and rituals beautifully haunting and poetical. The Navajo believe in the Holy People, powerful and mysterious, who can travel on the wind, on a sunbeam or on a thunderbolt. At the head of these supernaturals stands Changing Woman, the Earth Mother, forever young, beautiful, gift-giving, watching over the people's well-being. Changing Woman was found by First

Man and First Woman as a baby, lying in a supernaturally created cradleboard on top of a sacred mountain. Within four days, Changing Woman grew to maturity. It was She who taught humans how to propitiate and live in harmony with the forces of nature. She built the first hogan out of turquoise and shell. The Navajos' chief ritual, Blessing Way, came to them from Changing Woman and other Holy People. Changing Woman was impregnated by the rays of the Sun and gave birth to the Hero Twins, who killed many evil monsters and enemies of mankind, but she suffered Old Age and Death to exist because they have their part in the scheme of human existence.

Religion was an integral part of daily life and, for many traditional Navajo, still is

Of the sun's rays have I made the back.
Of clouds have I made the blanket.
Of the rainbow have I made the head bow.

Coming of age is the occasion for many rituals, which in the case of girls were very elaborate. The time of a girl's "First Bleed" is a proud moment for her, and she hurries to tell her parents, who joyfully spread the news. The event is celebrated by a ceremony called *Kinaalda*.

The girl has her hair washed in yucca suds. For three days, wearing her best jewelry, she grinds corn on the old family metate. Each day, she undergoes a "molding" rite. Lying on a blanket, she is kneaded and "shaped" by a favorite friend or relative to make her as beautiful as Changing Woman. Every dawn,

today. Men go into the fields singing corn-growing songs, weavers make a spirit path thread in their rugs, while hide-curers put a turquoise bead on their tanning poles to keep their joints limber. When a woman has a hard time giving birth, her female relatives and friends loosen their hair to "untie" the baby. A chanter might be summoned to coax the baby along with an eagle-feather fan. Twins are a cause for great joy because they are a sign of Holy People's blessing. The father himself makes the cradleboard. When the baby is placed in it, a special song is chanted:

I have made a baby board for you, my child.
May you grow to a great old age.

the girl races toward the East, each time a little faster. Others are allowed to run with her but are careful not to pass her so that they do not grow old before she does. On the fourth day, older women make a big cake from the corn which the girl has ground, sometimes as big as six feet across. When the cake is ready, after racing for the last time, the girl distributes it to all the guests. After that she is considered a woman, ready to marry and to start a family of her own.

Navajo cultures are as intrigue as they are old; left, hogan at Monument Valley preserves original design of such dwellings, and right, sand painting is still practiced.

Religious symbolism has influenced Navajo art, which is rich, beautiful and economically important. Wherever there is a Navajo woman, there is a loom. Originally only blankets were woven. The famous Navajo rug was an invention of white traders after the coming of the railroads and tourists. The traders didn't take long to find out that travellers from the East had little use for blankets worn like ponchos. So they called them rugs and gave birth to a new industry.

Different regions of the Navajo reservation developed their own characteristic styles—Ganado Reds, geometric Two Gray Hills, figural Shiprock Yeis, to name a few. Fine Navajo rugs are a good investment, provided one does not fall for cheap Mexican imitations. Women also weave fine

built machines at the huge tribal sawmill. He might be a newspaper editor on the *Navajo Times*, or a professor at the Navajo Community College—all glass and steel but built in the shape of a traditional hogan. The modern Navajo man or woman shares some of the advantages and all the frustrations, problems and anxieties of their White fellow Americans.

With a population of almost 150,000, the Navajo are the largest of all tribes. Their reservation is bigger than New Hampshire, Connecticut, Vermont and Rhode Island combined. It contains energy resources, including oil, coal, uranium, and timber, that bring in money, but also wrenching changes—pollution, dependency on outside forces, a certain amount of industrialization,

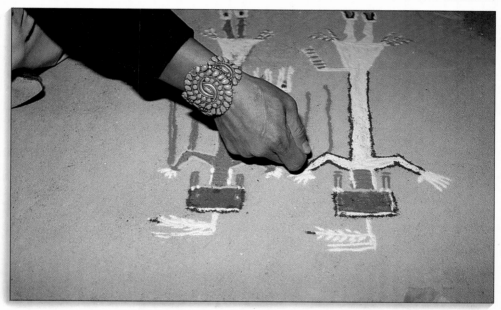

baskets, while men excel in creating some of the best silver and turquoise work to be found in all the Southwest. At the tribal capital of Window Rock, one may visit the Navajo Arts and Crafts Center, but rugs, baskets and jewelry are also sold in innumerable shops throughout the general area.

"Progress," the Giant Bulldozer

The modern Navajo, who does not choose to live the traditional life in the hogan, might be a lawyer, an electrician, a policewoman, a telephone operator. He might operate one of the giant cranes at the nearby strip mine or operate one of the complicated Japanese-

the relocation of people whose homes happen to be in the way.

In spite of all the natural resources, poverty is still pervasive, housing and health care substandard. Schools do not prepare students for the problems they will face in a White, technological world. Religion and language fight for survival against the inroads of an alien culture which is not better, but more powerful. But the young people are not discouraged. They are proud to be Indians, to be Navajo.

As one of them said: "We have survived the Spaniards, the missionaries and the Long Walk. We still walk in beauty. We will still be here, still be Navajo, a hundred years from now."

THE HOPI

Approaching Hopi country from any direction may be a bleak or nondescript experience for some travellers, but once having met and mingled with its inhabitants, a visitor generally comes away from the experience with anything but bleak or nondescript impressions. If Hopi people were inclined to describe themselves, which they are not, they would say they aspire to be industrious, hospitable and helpful. Tradition and custom mandate such attitudes and behavior. Today these qualities are very much in evidence among those of earlier generations raised and taught in a simpler cultural milieu. Modern influences tend to neutralize this natural elan with a certain wariness and sophistication which is most clearly evident among the young.

Hopi country can be most loosely described as high desert dry country, supporting little else beside the tenacious Hopi (some travellers have compared the terrain to that of the moon!). They manage to cajole the most wondrous yield of cultivated farm products out of it, most notably corn in infinite variety. Hopi country is comprised of 11 distinct villages lined northeast-northwest along a 35-mile (56-km) perimeter of Black Mesa in northeastern Arizona. These villages, some settled for centuries and others founded as recently as 1910, are home to 10,000 people who are, closely knit by tradition, blood, and custom, but distinctively separate linguistically and politically.

Speech patterns and vocabulary differ from village to village within the same general language structure, providing natural boundaries. These differences also provide a great deal of chauvinistic interplay with words among residents of each village. The traditional governing system also encourages a certain distance between villages, politically, though these differences are not easily discernible except to those familiar with Hopi society.

The Kinship System

The kinship system, which is still intact, provides the unity which allows free intercourse between villages in all the important functions of communal living: family rela-

A modern Hopi youth, who chooses to live away from his parents' traditional hogan, faces the danger of cultural alienation.

tionships, rites and ceremonies. It may be straining, but only a little, to say that most Hopi growing up and living on the reservation know, if they know nothing else, who they are and where they came from. A Hopi will first give you the name of his village home, and if prodded further, he will most likely tell you his clan affiliation and Hopi name.

The kinship system, in which lineage passes through the female line, serves as a philosophy based on familial and spiritual unity. All children of maternal sisters and paternal brothers, for instance, become brothers and sisters, enjoying common parent-figures, although in lesser degrees of intimacy beyond the immediate family. Paternal sisters and maternal brothers are aunts and uncles, but within the second generation, only the uncle's children are named nephews and nieces. The aunt's children fall into relationship patterns dictated by clan formulas.

Superimposed over the biological kinship structure is the clan structure. The clan system sees people within a single relational universe, that of brother and sister. The clan line is also matrilineal.

Legendary tales, closely guarded by hereditary caretakers within each clan unit, recount the extensive prehistoric migrations of one ancestral group after another over a vast area of the southwestern United States, southern California, and Mexico. Storytellers can identify landmarks as far south as Central New Mexico, southern Colorado and Utah. Mythic tales of creation provide the basis for a system of beliefs and practices so complete and advanced as to mesmerize generations of scholars throughout the world.

Ritual and Ceremony

The traveller will find Hopi people naturally open and friendly in the privacy of their home, though somewhat distant in public, social and ceremonial gatherings—unless of course the traveller has "Hopi friends." It is not uncommon to find at least one Pahaana (white man) among the participants at wedding, natal and Kachina ceremonial preparation parties.

Hopi are particularly sensitive to the aesthetic tastes of the travelling public, whether these tastes be for art, services or showmanship such as the dancing Kachinas, which have become such a magnetic attraction for countless outsiders. Ritual and ceremony may be the most distinctive aspects of Hopi culture today. A serious issue among Hopi is how best they can preserve Hopi ways which are rapidly changing because of pressures, both within and without, created by modern living and technology. There is no doubt that Hopi do not want to let go of all the "old" ways of doing. These ways have enabled them to survive the shattering elemental and fateful whimsy so characteristic of the land they are bound to occupy, a land that is as much a part of their identity as their villages and clans. The spectre of losing tradition and custom to modern technology and life-styles hovers constantly over the

her, bearing appropriate gifts," he said. (Even second-generation Hopi born this century might be hard put to know that the right gift for him to bring is a load of wood, symbol of hearth and home.)

Young people sitting around that table in that modern house were quite surprised and fascinated to hear this, as no one had really explained these things to them. Their only experience with weddings consisted of the mixture of Western and Hopi ceremonial activities which has become the modern Hopi wedding: at most, a two-day affair replete with an abundance of foods from the traditional pantry as well as the supermarket, wrapped gifts mingling with the native foodstuffs customarily given to the bride's and groom's families, table decor contrast-

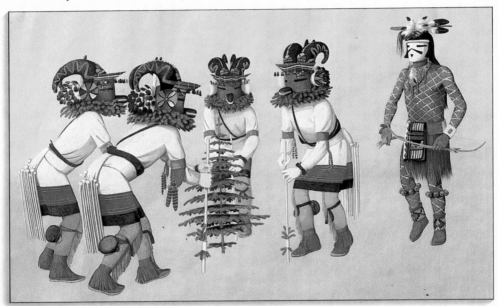

activities which serve to perpetuate those very traditions.

The modern Hopi wedding was being discussed around the breakfast table recently in a Hopi home. One man remarked at the sheer spectacle of the marshaling of a caravan of automobiles to escort the new bride home at the culmination of wedding festivities. He counted 20 odd trucks, each loaded down with gifts to be distributed among the bride's relatives. He was obviously saddened at the blatant ignorance displayed by the two sets of relatives about the original significance of the bridal homecoming. "The bride goes back to her mother's house alone to await her new husband's pleasure. When he decides to accept her as a bride he will follow

ing with makeshift outdoor open fires for cooking. So it goes. And so it goes in other rites which are still vital, such as natal rites and passage into ceremonial societies. It is this innovative mixing of the old and new which separates one generation from the other, because, if the truth be told, these hybrids have an ambience of their own, an appealing vitality not to be dismissed.

This attractive mixture of the old and new can also be seen during one of the many summer weekends on which Kachina or

Ceremonial dances may be the most distinctive aspect to Hopi culture; left, painting shows Bighorn Dance, ca 1930. Right, 19th-Century Hopi girls in butterfly hairdo.

other dances are sponsored. Less than a generation ago, Kachinas were first introduced to the Hopi child as spiritual beings who come to this world from the Spirit Home, which may refer to either an opening in the floor of a ceremonial room called the *kiva* or to a shrine on the San Francisco Peaks near Flagstaff, Arizona, which is a "secret opening."

Kachina Dances

Kachinas are most commonly presented in the dances which are held indoors, in *Kivas*, and outdoors, in village plazas, depending on the time of year. These colorful masked beings represent elements, qualities, and inhabitants of the universe; at times, they

some families. When all the relatives have gathered, there may be a fleet of five to 10 vehicles, mostly trucks, in front of each house in that village. Even though these autos may have come loaded with provisions and supplies from the supermarkets of the urban centers, the preparation of traditional feast foods is not abandoned. It is within this backdrop to the drama of the dance where many a Pahaana has found a fascinating niche.

The atmosphere in a village during dance day is a fascinating mixture of the modern and the past, appreciated most by those who have experienced the speed with which time changes everything. Corn, the symbolic Mother to the Hopi, is the most visible traditional food, secular and sacred, for this

may be cast, in their spiritual state, in specific roles for various purposes, some didactic and others inspirational.

Kachina dances are very much taken as a matter of course; there is at least one in each village each year. The Kachina and Kachina dancing act as a magnet to a new breed of Hopi urban dwellers a generation or two removed from reservation upbringing, who return as spectators and participants.

An upcoming dance mobilizes, as nothing else can, all the combined resources of a village. It is not unusual for Hopi to travel from Los Angeles, San Francisco, Denver or Oklahoma City for these events; coming in from Tucson, Phoenix and even Salt Lake City can be a weekly or monthly habit with

occasion, as it is for most ceremonial observances. Visitors are well warned to expect to see and eat corn in some form of cookery all day.

The ceremony is a series of dances, usually seven or eight in all, performed at intervals of two hours during the day, with 30-minute intermissions, beginning about midmorning and ending at sundown. The staging of the Kachina Dance is an example of the refined sense of the dramatic which is also another trademark of Hopi, and also of the other Pueblo peoples of the Southwest. Aside from the obvious impression that the Kachinas present a colorful spectacle, they represent the most visible evidence of the Hopi creative talents in the performing arts.

THE APACHE

Like most other Southwest Native Americans, the Apache dispute the anthropological theory that they migrated to North America across the Bering Strait. An elderly San Carlos Apache tells the story handed down for centuries: "Our ancestors tell us that we were created in the area where we now live. In the beginning, there was no living person upon Mother Earth, only supernatural beings. When our people were created, there were wicked creatures who killed them. During this time, the White Painted Lady gave birth to twin sons. One of these sons went to his father, Sun, and returned to Mother Earth dressed in proper Apache clothing, carrying a bow and arrows and leading several horses. After he taught our people how to use these things, he helped kill the evil creatures. Mother Earth then became a good place to live for our people." All Apache have a creation story similar to this one.

Before contact with the Spaniards during the middle to late 1500s, the Apache intermingled freely among themselves and the Navajo. The Apache, like the Navajo, are of the Athapascan-speaking family and have no written history or language. The Apache called themselves the People, but to others they were the Enemy.

The land the Apache roamed, hunting and gathering for livelihood, encompassed present-day Arizona, New Mexico and northern Mexico. While they were, in essence, one family, each group had its own hunting territory and did not encroach on that of its neighbors. The relatively peaceful, nomadic life the Apache led was one day drastically altered by the intrusion of outsiders into the Apache domain: Spaniards, Mexicans and finally the Anglos.

Anglo and Spanish Colonization

When Coronado made his expedition into the Southwest, he unwittingly introduced a new mode of travel to the Apache, which they would adopt and use more than any other Southwestern tribe. The horse became a beast of burden, a source of food and a reliable form of transportation that enabled the Apache to expand their geographical range far beyond their original territories.

Apache reaction to Spanish and Anglo colonization took the form of raiding and warfare, which was so effective that twice the intruders were temporarily driven out for as long as a decade. Southern Arizona was one of the last areas of the Southwest to be settled by the Spanish and Americans. Contrary to popular belief, Apache raiding did not include wanton destruction; it was to steal livestock.

When the Gadsden Purchase was made in 1853, all of Arizona came under the control of the United States of America. This, and the discovery of gold in western Apache territory 10 years later, brought an influx of Anglo settlers and prospectors. The Arizona

Territory Legislature officially decided that the only way to control the Apache was to exterminate them. The Department of the Interior in Washington disagreed with this policy, and the Territory lacked the means to carry out the extermination. This fact, together with the slaughter of 75 unarmed Apache women and children near Tucson by a mob of outraged citizens and a group of Papago Indians, led to the implementation of the so-called Peace Policy.

This policy called for the rounding up of

The Puberty Ceremony is performed at Apache reservations by grotesque masked Mountain Spirit dancers, such as those seen above left and right.

266

all Apache and confining them to reservations, where they would have to make a living by growing crops and raising livestock. This plan required the removal of some tribes from their homelands. The removals were met with surprisingly mixed feelings by the Apache. Some had become weary of the hardships of war and preferred to settle down in peace. Others, however, waited for a chance to escape. Two of those who bolted were Geronimo and Victorio. But by 1890, the Apache wars were over.

Today, the remaining Apache tribes of performed within a single block of time during the year.

The awesome and colorful masked Mountain Spirit dancers, or *gans*, still perform at the puberty rites of the San Carlos, White Mountain and Mescalero tribes. (The Jicarilla Apache have not used the dancers as part of their ceremonies since the introduction of the vaccination program on their reservation. The Jicarilla leaders decreed that anyone who had been vaccinated could not participate as a Mountain Spirit dancer, and the result was the disqualification of nearly

Arizona and New Mexico have been significantly Anglicized. Many of the old tribal ways are gone. Present-day Apache are struggling to become economically self-sufficient by using modern technologies, and in the past decade, there has been a shift from a livestock to a wage economy. Some very important aspects of Apache culture are intact, however, and they pertain to religion, mythology and craftsmanship.

Ceremony and Crafts

The Apache Puberty Ceremony can be seen several times a year on the San Carlos, White Mountain and Jicarilla reservations. The Mescalero Apache ceremonies are all all Jicarilla youth.)

The ceremony for a girl, if she and her family want and can afford it, is usually held after she has had her first menstruation. The girl, who will be entering womanhood upon completion of the ceremony, will need four general qualities—strength, patience, good luck and wisdom—to help her during her lifetime. These qualities are possessed by the White Painted Lady and are acquired by the girl during the four-day ceremony when the White Painted Lady resides in her body.

Certain crafts are still made on Apache reservations. The most notable of these are **weave baskets and pretty beadwork, made for use in ceremonies or for sale on the reservations.**

THE PAPAGO AND THE PIMA

They hear her last name spoken. It makes no response in the memory. It brings no places or other names to mind. So, they ask her, "Where are you from?"

"I'm from Casa Grande."

The information that this place-name carries imparts that it is off the reservation; that the place is a cotton-farming area; that most Papago who now live there came from someplace else. And so they ask, "Where were your parents really from?"

"They are from the other side. They are from Quitovac."

"Ah, yes. The place where they do that rain ceremony. Yes, that is an old place. The people on this side used to do that ceremony but they quit. I don't know why they quit. Yes, I know who you are. My mother is from that side too. She used to go to the ceremony every year. She probably knows your family. She is probably related to you. All the people from down there are related to each other. Yes, I know exactly who you are."

She now has a place associated with her name. A place that is an old Papago settlement, one that is rich in history and culture. She is now put in a perspective that has a universal meaning for all Papago.

The family names are important, but the place where one is from is even more important. The village where a Papago comes from can be a village that may have running water but no electricity. It can be a place where their grandmother still fills large containers of water so that when the pump stops pumping because the electricity has stopped for whatever reason, the family will still have water in the house. It can be a place where neighbors are the whole extended family or where the entire village is made up of a whole extended family.

The village may be any number of small villages dotting the Sonoran Desert where the Papago reservation is found. The reservation is comprised of over 2½ million acres (1 million hectares) for a population of fewer than 18,000 people. The village may be one of any number that have such unassuming names as *Si:l Naggia* (Saddle Hanging), *Hawan Naggia* (Crow Hanging) or *Hodai Son Wo'o* (Rock Basin Tank), or even *Gogs Mek* (Dog Burnt) and *Kaij Mek* (Seed Burnt).

A person can be from any one of these

Left, elder of the Elmer Campus Papago tribe in San Xavier, Arizona.

villages, or he might be from Sells, which has, in the past decade, become the melting-pot village. Papago who make up the community of Sells (named after an Indian Commissioner) are from someplace else. Most of them have come for a specific reason. Some have come for job opportunities with the Bureau of Indian Affairs; others have come for the "HUD housing," which has in past years become prevalent on all reservation communities.

Sells is a quasi-urbanized sprawl that nestles below the sacred mountain, *Waw Giwulk* or *Baboquivari*, the home of the Protector of the Papago people. Despite the non-traditional housing, many Papago call this place home, the place where one is from. But the entire reservation is home as well, since all of it was the aboriginal land of the Papago. The people still use the Papago names of those areas that did not become part of the reservation proper and so maintain their special connection to them. To the east of the reservation lies the metropolis of Tucson, whose name is a bastardization of *Cuk Son* (Black base mountain). To the west, there is the mining town of Ajo (the Spanish name given because of the abundance of wild garlic in the area); the Papago called this area, *Moik Wahia* (Soft Well), for the nice wells there. To the south (on the American-Mexican border), there is Sonoyta, called *Son Oidag* (Spring Field) and inside Mexico, where a majority of the aboriginal land became a part of Mexico, there is Poso Verde, called *Ce:dagi Wahia* (Green Well).

A Papago may live in a place like Sells, where there are red-brick buildings with ocotilla fences. A place where the sounds on a summer night are the murmuring of swamp coolers, soft voices, the laughter of children and the blaring of music from radios and TVs. A Papago can live in a village where the buildings are soft mud adobe with ocotilla fences. Where the sounds are of desert creatures, the soft voices of people and the laughter of children. A place where, in the distance, the sound of country western music plays on a radio. Either place is home.

From the Pimas' Point of View

In another place approximately 50 miles north of the Papagos' home lies the Pima reservation. Here, another dialogue of memories begins. An old Pima man is talking: "People used to like to work together. When the wheat was ready, all the people would come together to harvest. They would cut the wheat down by hand. They would wait for a windy day or night and they would all get together and throw the wheat up in the air so that the little grass and things would blow out. A night that had a full moon and the wind was blowing was the best time. The people would work all night. That is how they used to do things."

Less than 10,000 Pima Indians reside in a little over 3,000 acres (1,214 hectares). The reservation is called the Gila River Indian Reservation, a reserve shared with a few hundred Maricopa Indians. The Maricopa Indians belong to the linguistic family called Yuman and are not related to the Pima in any way.

From all evidence, archaeological and anthropological, the Pima and Papago Indians were, at one time, the same. They are said to be descendents of Hohokam, or as they are called by the people, the *Hukukam*, "the ones that have gone now." Linguistically the two groups are very closely related. Their languages are mutually intelligible, and socially the two tribes resemble one another. Many of their rituals, stories and songs are similar. The only distinction that separates them is, again, place, the area where one is from.

Desert People and River People

The Pima and Papago distinguish one another by placing in front of their tribal name the geographic feature that refers to the place they are from. The Papago, who live in the desert, call themselves the *Tohono O'odham* (Desert People). The Pima, who have traditionally lived along the banks of rivers in the valley of south central Arizona call themselves, *Akimel O'odham* (River People).

The "River People," the Pima, are well-documented by the Spaniards and later by the Anglos as having had a truly rich, agrarian society. The sight of hundreds of Pima throwing wheat into the wind on a moonlit night was once a common one, but this scene, as the old Pima recalls, is no more. With the coming of the Anglos, the fight for domination over the water of the Gila River became a major part of the history of the Pima people.

The people are still called River People even though the river which winds through their reservation no longer carries water. The floor of the river is now cracked and dusty, a home only to lizards, horned toads and rattlesnakes. There is no traditional farming, only that which uses water brought from other places in concrete canals or pumped from deep within the ground. But this place along the dry river is home. The other lands that make up the reservation, like the one along the Salt River, are only a small part of what was once the aboriginal land of the Pima. The Salt River Reservation butts against the condominiums of Scottsdale. Another tiny segment (shared with the Papago) is called, ironically, *Aki Cin* (River Mouth).

The Pima and Papago Indians were more open to the religious and cultural influences of the Spanish missionaries than any other Southwestern tribe. Though they were probably attracted more by Spanish cattle than religion, there was in fact more demand for missions than the Jesuits could provide. This early acculturation process was hastened by a common enemy—raiding Apache. It only continued when U.S. troops arrived. Their forts were a welcome refuge from the Apache, and the Papago formed a standing army to help the government troops.

After centuries of battling Mexican and Anglo-European cattle ranchers for water holes, many Papago began raising cattle themselves, a tradition which continues to this day. By the 1930s, most Pima worked off the reservation, in Tucson and Phoenix. This move was largely forced upon them when Anglo settlers dug irrigation canals which took all of their water.

The Pima, and to a lesser extent the Papago, are the most acculturated Native American tribes in the Southwest. Since the time of their earliest recorded contacts with whites, the Pima especially have been looked upon as friendly Indians. During the mid 19th-Century Gold Rush in California, the Pima sold provisions to the white gold diggers and escorted them through Apache territory. At the time of the Apache wars (1861–1886), a large number of the Pima served as scouts for the U.S. Army. Such close contacts with white culture resulted in disintegration of aboriginal culture. Although both tribes have retained their native language and a few ritual ceremonies, and Papago woven baskets are still believed to be among the finest made, their life-styles and beliefs do not differ greatly from their Anglo and Hispanic neighbors.

Smiling-woman exemplifies her tribe whom the white men have regarded as "friendly Indians" since the mid 19th-Century.

GUIDE IN BRIEF

Travel Advisories

Most visitors, upon entering the United States, must have a passport and visitor's visa, and if they are from (or have passed through) an infected area, a health record. Canadian citizens entering from the Western Hemisphere need not have a visa or a passport. Neither do Mexican citizens who possess a border pass.

At the Nevada, Oregon and Mexican borders, the State Department of Food and Agriculture inspects all produce, plant materials and wild animals to see if they are admissable under current quarantine regulations. To avoid a lengthy inspection, do not bring any agricultural products into the region.

The use of American-dollar traveller's checks is advised. When lost or stolen, most traveller's checks can be replaced and they are as acceptable as cash in most stores, restaurants and hotels. Banks will readily cash large amounts of traveller's checks.

In most states, a sales tax is added to retail goods. You're a genius if you can understand the logic behind the tax laws; most people simply memorize them. There is a tax on books, for instance, but no tax on magazines. If you buy a hamburger and eat it in the restaurant they will tax you, but if you eat the hamburger in your car they cannot tax you. If you fail to make sense of these laws, you will be in the same boat as the natives.

Getting Acquainted

Climate

Catryna Ten Eyck Seymour, in her book *Enjoying the Southwest*, recounts the fable of a cowboy who decided to go for a swim on a scorching day. He took his clothes off and dove into a stream. As he jumped, a drought dried up the stream, but then a flash flood came along just in time for the cowboy to land safely in the water. As he came up for air, a wind rose from the northeast and froze the water. "The cowboy would surely have drowned if the sun had not quickly reappeared and evaporated the stream," Seymour writes. "The only mishap from the experience was that the cowboy got a bad sunburn before he was able to get his clothes back on again."

The Southwest is full of surprises. *Sunset Books*, which issued a pictorial entitled *The Beautiful Southwest*, remarks on the jacket that one of the editors, in the process of some back-road scouting, encountered a cyclone, a sandstorm and a blizzard, all in the same day. Unlike the cowboy fable, this is no legend. In the Southwest, mountain can rather abruptly melt into plain, forest into desert. Snow appears on the tops of mountains even as the thermometer in the desert registers 110 in the shade—if you can find any shade. The horizon is so distant that it is not uncommon to see rainclouds pouring showers on some vicinity off in Never Never Land, while where you are it is as dry as a bone. Sudden, eruptive flash floods and hailstorms are seasonal occurrences.

Generally, though—and this is the great weather paradox of the Southwest—sunshine is a given. Vast portions of the area are in the "Sun Belt" region. Freak storms notwithstanding, this is a land of sparse rainfall, as surrounding mountains dispel the promise of precipitation emanating from the Pacific Ocean and the Gulf of Mexico. Summer is the rainy season, during which precipitation descends in the form of highly localized, flash storms that appear suddenly, often accompanied by thunder and lightning. In Arizona, rainfall patterns tend to produce steady rains in the winter and thundershowers in August and the first half of September. Winter's wet season is brief, leaving traces mostly in the form of snow at the high elevations, with some rain in low-lying areas. Generally, as altitudes rise, rainfall increases, accounting for the relatively lush greenery in more mountainous sections.

Wide temperature swings are also caused by abrupt shifts in altitude. The rule of thumb is that every 1,000 feet of added elevation creates a temperature change the equivalent of travelling 300 miles north or south. Thus, driving from the lowest to the highest points in Arizona is roughly comparable to travelling north/south from Key West to the northern part of Hudson Bay in Canada. The prevailing low humidity of the Southwest as a whole also accounts for wide day-to-night temperature swings. Hot 110-degree days in the desert summers are tempered both by low humidity and the fact that the thermometer unfailingly drops dramatically at night. The mountains of the north and some in the south get snow in winter, creating good skiing in places like Taos, and Sierra Blanca, NM and Flagstaff, AZ. Most southern sections, with some exceptions, get little snow, hardly ever more than a slight dusting. Winds may sometimes be brisk, but like the region's rain showers, dominate only briefly. The Southwest as a whole spans half a dozen different climate or life zones, blessing the region with a certain diversity. But within that diversity lies consistency. By and large, sunny skies, low humidity, and little moisture provide a consistent picture which is amazing considering the sheer size of the indomitable Southwest. With this in mind, here are some specifics reported by individual states within the region:

Arizona: As a whole, Arizona receives 80 percent of available sunshine annually. Annual rainfall averages 12.55 inches. Wind velocity for most cities is under eight m.p.h. Northern regions average around 73 percent sunshine; southern sections around 90 percent. Annual number of clear days is 222; another 85 are only partly cloudy. Desert cities (in Arizona and elsewhere) generally receive more sun than the overall state average. Phoenix, which houses about one-third of Arizona's entire population, is hot and dry, registering annually 86 percent sunshine; average temperatures skyrocket into the 100s in summer, down into the high 30s in the dead of winter. About seven meager inches of rainfall splatter on the streets of Phoenix each year. To the north some 142 miles, Flagstaff registers highs in the mid-70s to the low 80s in summer, while at the opposite extreme, overnight lows in winter may swoop down to the mid-teens. Annual precipitation in Flagstaff averages 84.4 inches, with a great deal of it falling in July, August and December.

Grand Canyon: At its hottest, the south rim of the Grand Canyon is 80 or 90 degrees F around the rim, rising into the 100s at the bottom of the canyon. Flash thunderstorms are common. Generally, the weather is more comfortable in the spring and fall "off-seasons."

New Mexico: Every part of the state receives at least 70 percent sunshine year-round, with July and August thunderstorms providing most of the precipitation. December-to-March snowfalls vary from two inches, in the lower Rio Grande Valley, to 300 inches or more in the north central mountains. Albuquerque registers highs in summer in the low 90s; winter lows in January sink to the high 20s. Only 59 miles to the northeast, and with a somewhat higher elevation, Santa Fe reports July highs in the mid-80s and January lows of 18 degrees. Temperatures may occasionally hit 100 degrees in summer, but more typically range from the 80s and 90s in lower elevations to the 70s and 80s higher up. The mountains will usually be from 20 to 40 degrees cooler on any given day. Winter temperatures range from the 50s to the 70s in the south, from the 40s to the 60s in the north. Above 7500 feet a considerable amount of snow falls.

Utah: Utah's parks region generally follows the stated pattern—sunny days, cooler nights, little precipitation. Occasional summer days register highs well into the 100s which make hiking inadvisable in the noonday sun. For instance, the Arches National Park registers consistent summer temperatures of 110 or 115, dropping to the mid-70s at night. At Natural Bridges National Monument, temperatures are cooler than at Arches, with brief thunderstorms common, especially in summer. Bryce Canyon, at a high elevation, is much cooler, with temperatures in July and August in the 70s and 80s falling to a brisk mid-40s overnight. Zion visitors encounter an occasional 115, more typically high 90s in the summer, with temperatures dropping at night to the 50s and 60s. Thunderstorms, usually of brief duration, may occur in any of these parks. Generally, visitors can count on warm to hot dry days and should prepare for nights requiring heavier clothing.

Las Vegas: June through September, daytime temperatures rarely register below 100 degrees. Spring and fall seasons are relatively short, with temperatures in the 70s. Daytime temperatures in

the winter range generally in the 50s and 60s, with January and February nights near freezing. High summer temperatures allow for much indoor activity.

El Paso: Daytime summer temperatures frequently rise above 90 degrees but only occasionally above 100. Summer nights are usually cool, in the 60s. When temperatures are high, the relative humidity is usually low. Winters are mild; days register 55-60 degrees, dropping at night below freezing about half the time in December and January. The nearby Rio Grande Valley is noticeably cooler at all times. Rainfall is slight. Much of it occurs from July through September in the form of the flash thunderstorms typical of the Southwest. Touches of snow fall in winter, just enough to dust the earth. El Paso experiences dust and sandstorms, most frequently in March and April, which greatly reduce visibility.

Clothing

Jeans are practically a uniform in much of the Southwest, with notable exceptions. Las Vegas has a mode very much unto itself ("Jackets please, gentlemen"), with dressing up more the norm for dining, gambling and shows, although casual wear is perfectly acceptable for streetwear. Be sure to bring light wraps for the cooler evenings in spring and fall, something heavier for the winter. The Santa Fe Opera, as well as symphonies and like events in the Southwest's handful of larger cities, call for something dressier. In the Southwest, though, "dressier" can frequently mean anything from black tie to merely "more interesting": This is the land of the self-proclaimed individualist, the concha belt, the rhinestone cowboy, with tongue firmly planted in cheek. When on an evening out, a vivid imagination can frequently substitute for the traditional.

One realizes that blue jeans are not just a trend, but makes sense in a dry, dusty land where good clothes will only get dirty. The cowboy uniform is another case in point: The hat protects one's face from the everpresent sun and the boot is a wonderful foil for dust and rocks. If you are planning to hike or go camping, be sure to take along a good pair of hard-soled hiking shoes or boots (tennis shoes won't do it) and enough layers of clothing to take care of any and all of the various weather options (rain, snow if applicable, sudden drops or rises in temperature). Native clothing in much of the Southwest reflects a strong Indian/Spanish heritage. Beads and turquoise jewelry look good here; heavy sweaters feel good much of the time.

Some public places—restaurants, stores, movies—in Arizona keep their air conditioning so high in summer that denizens are always getting colds from shock. Carry a sweater if you go into an Arizona building in the summer. And keep a towel or piece of cloth over the steering wheel if you expect to be able to touch it when you get out. But rules are few: wear what you like to wear, preferably in layers. Here is a generalized month-by-month calendar that should be helpful for most parts of the Southwest:

January: coats, sweaters, ski jackets, woolies and warmies.

February: about the same, with a few days of "false spring." Wear layers and peel as needed.

March: "Only a fool would predict March."

April: Beginning to warm up and green up. Bring sweaters, all-weather coats and jackets, lighter weight slacks and suits.

May: Summer almost here but not quite. You'll want a sweater or light wrap for evenings or mountains. And bear in mind that springtime can be fickle.

June: Summer is here. Usually the hottest and driest month of the year, but you'll still need a sweater some evenings, at least in the north and the mountains.

July: Deep summer. Daytime temperatures can climb, but usually the summer thundershower season begins during July, which act as a giant air conditioner, dropping temperatures suddenly in the afternoon or evening.

August: About the same as July.

September: Days often continue to be warm, but there's a tang in the air that says fall is coming in. Thundershowers persist.

October: Crisp, golden days. Fall has come. Leaves are brilliant.

November: Sunny and crisp but chilly, sometimes even with snow.

December: Always sees some snow. Even on a cold day if you are in the sun and out of the wind you will be warm, but take heavy clothing anyway.

Time Zones

Miraculously, almost all of this spacious region runs on Mountain Standard Time, with the sole exception of Las Vegas, which sits in the Pacific Standard Time zone, and is one hour earlier than Mountain. From New York and other eastern cities, Mountain Time is two hours earlier; air travellers pick up two hours flying West, lose them on the eastward bound flights. All of the Southwest except Arizona has Daylight Savings Time from May through October. "Spring ahead, fall back": set clocks and watches an hour ahead in spring, an hour back in the fall. Arizona, in effect, is on Pacific Savings Time during summer.

Tipping

As in other parts of the country, Southwestern service personnel rely on tips for a large part of their income, and tipping is expected in a variety of situations. The accepted rate for baggage handlers at the airport is 25 cents to 50 cents per bag (most resorts and cities call for the high end). For hotel bellboys, 25 cents a bag is the usual tip (again, a more posh milieu may command 50 cents) but use common sense; if there are a lot of bags and he or she is exceptionally pleasant and helpful, by all means feel free to leave extra. For overnight hotel stays, it is not necessary to tip the chambermaid; for longer stays, the rule of thumb is to leave a minimum tip of $1 a day. A doorman expects to be tipped for help unloading your car or for other services; 50 cents to $1, depending on the service, should cover it.

In most instances, 15 to 20 percent, depending on the quality of service rendered, is the going rule for tipping. In resorts like Las Vegas, and in larger cities, taxi drivers tend to expect 20 percent. Sometimes tips are included on restaurant bills when more than six dine together. Tipping—at meals especially—is, of course, a personal decision. Particularly good service may warrant a larger tip, while, given particularly bad or surly service, it is not unheard of to express displeasure by leaving a very small tip or none at all.

On charters and package tours, conductors and drivers usually receive a tip; check whether this is already figured into the cost. The accepted rate is $5 to $10 for the group as a whole.

Crowds

You wanted to see it, right? The Grand Canyon, right? And so did everyone else! One obvious solution to the crowd problem is to concentrate on less-frequented sights—the Southwest has many—and avoid the hot spots. But if this is to be your one Big Trip to Arizona for a while, it would be silly not to get a glimpse of one of the world's natural wonders simply because there might be a few other people there. On the other hand, crowds can be extremely annoying.

Summers are generally the worst. Spring and fall, on the other hand, hold forth promise of good—if sometimes brisk—weather, fewer people, and (this is the best part) cheaper prices. Hotels and motels, especially, offer substantial discounts during low season, so this may be a major consideration. If you must tread the well-trodden path at high season, prepare for the other treaders. Get to campgrounds as early as possible to be assured of a space. If staying at a hotel or motel, make a reservation, if feasible, or arrive well before dinner. Above all, accept the fact of other people. They are part of the deal.

Liquor laws

Liquor sales and laws vary according to which Southwestern state you're in, the most dramatic differences being encountered in Utah, where practices pertaining to alcohol consumption are affected by the state's Mormon heritage. The legal drinking age is 21 in Arizona, New Mexico, Utah, Nevada and Colorado, where 18-year-olds can buy 3.2 liquor, on sale at most supermarkets. In Texas, it's 18. Colorado, New Mexico, and Texas do not permit package sales on Sunday. In Arizona, liquor stores are open from noon until 1 a.m.; in New Mexico, from noon until 2 a.m., by local option.

State laws also vary on the manner in which liquor is sold. In Arizona and Las Vegas state law permits sale of liquor by the bottle and by the drink in any licensed establishment. In New Mexico, bottled liquor is sold in drug, grocery and liquor stores and purveyed by the drink in bars or other licensed establishments. In Texas, it is sold by the package in package stores and by the drink in any licensed establishment. In Colorado, you can find bottled liquor in liquor and most drug stores, which usually also sell by the drink, with some restrictions. In Utah, packaged liquor is sold in state liquor stores, restaurants, hotels and private clubs.

It should be noted that Colorado's drunk driving laws are among the strictest in the country. Jail sentences for DUI (driving under the influence of alcohol) are mandatory for residents and visitors alike. Recent public awareness of the perils of driving under the influence of alcohol countrywide has made police officers more alert to the problem, with the result that other Southwestern states also have strict ordinances against drunk driving. It is also illegal in most places to carry liquor around with you or to drink it in your vehicle.

Utah: The State of Utah puts out a free guide that gives everything you need to know about their seemingly odd approach to modern man's addiction. The booklet, available from the Salt Lake Valley Convention and Visitors Bureau, Salt Palace, Suite 200, 100 South West Temple, Salt Lake City, UT 84101 (801/521-2822) lists private clubs, restaurants and others who sell liquor.

All Utah liquor sales are made through state licensed stores. You must be 21 and cash is preferred, as most stores do not accept checks or plastic. All package agencies (where liquor is not consumed on the premises) are closed Sundays and holidays.

Many restaurants and hotels are licensed to sell mini-bottles and "splits" of wine. This is the procedure by which you purchase the liquor personally, then return to the table to order mixer or "setups." Liquor purchased at a restaurant store must be ingested on the premises with your meal.

The so-called "private clubs" serve cocktails. Some have two-week memberships available for visiting guests who are sponsored by a member. Many restaurants and private clubs do sell liquor on Sunday. Beer is available at most restaurants, grocery and drug stores seven days a week.

Public Holidays

Many public holidays no longer fall on the exact day of the commemorated event, but on the closest Monday to it, in order, to provide a three-day weekend for businesses and employees. Important exceptions are Christmas, Thanksgiv-ing, Election Day, and Independence Day (Fourth of July). During many of the holidays listed below, state, local and federal agencies may be closed, along with local banks, post offices and some other businesses. Except for major holidays like Christmas and Thanksgiving, convenience stores generally stay open to provide essentials.

New Year's Day: January 1
Martin Luther King, Jr.'s Birthday: January 15
Abraham Lincoln's/George Washington's birth-day (President's day): third Monday in February.
Texas Independence Day: March 2 (Texas only)
Good Friday
Easter Sunday
San Jacinto Day: April 21 (Texas)
El Cinco de Mayo: May 5 (Mexican festival, with assorted celebrations in Arizona and New Mexico)
Memorial Day for veterans of all wars: last Monday in May
Emancipation Day: June 19 (Texas)
Independence Day: July 4
Pioneer Day: July 24 (Utah only)
Lyndon B. Johnson's birthday: August 27 (Texas)
Labor Day: first Monday in September
Columbus Day: second Monday in October
General election day: first Tuesday after the first Monday in November of even-numbered years (liquor stores are closed).
Veteran's Day: November 11
Thanksgiving Day: fourth Thursday in November
Christmas Day: December 25

Tourist Information

Chambers of Commerce

Cities and resorts throughout the Southwest generally have Chambers of Commerce to provide free information of all kinds about the area. Accommodations, dining, shopping, medical facilities, points of interest, business and other general information are areas in which they can be of assistance. The fastest way to telephone chambers is generally, again, to simply dial for information and ask for the number of the local Chamber of Commerce. Listed below are chambers and/or visitors bureaus in most of the tourist centers within the area:

Arizona

Arizona Office of Tourism
3507 North Central Avenue
Suite 506
Phoenix, AZ 85012
(602)255-3618

Apache Junction Chamber of Commerce, P.O. Box 1747, Apache Junction, AZ 85220. 602/982-3141.

Benson Chamber of Commerce, P.O. Drawer AQ, Benson, AZ 85602. 602/586-2842.

Bisbee Chamber of Commerce, P.O. Drawer BA, Bisbee, AZ. 602/432-2141.

Camp Verde Chamber of Commerce, P.O. Box 1665, Camp Verde, AZ 86322. 602/567-9294.

Casa Grande Chamber of Commerce, P.O. Box 464, Casa Grande, AZ 85222. 602/836-2125.

Clarkdale-Verde Valley Chamber of Commerce, 1010 S. Main St., Cottonwood, 86326. 602/634-7593.

Cochise Visitor Center, 151 West Maley, Willcox, AZ 85643. 602/384-4271.

Douglas Chamber of Commerce, P.O. Drawer F., Douglas, AZ 85607. 602/364-2477.

Flagstaff Chamber of Commerce, 101 W. Santa Fe, Flagstaff, AZ 86001. 602/774-4505.

Globe Chamber of Commerce, P.O. Box 2539, Globe, AZ 85501. 602/425-4495.

Grand Canyon Chamber of Commerce, P.O. Box 3007, Grand Canyon, AZ 86023. 602/638-2681.

Holbrook-Petrified Forest Chamber of Commerce, 324 Navajo Blvd., Holbrook, AZ 86025. 602/524-6558.

Jerome Chamber of Commerce, P.O. Box 788, Jerome, AZ 86331. 602/634-5716.

Kearny Chamber of Commerce, P.O. Box 206, Kearny, AZ 85237. 602/363-5501.

Kingman Chamber of Commerce, P.O. Box 1150, Kingman, AZ 86402. 602/753-6106.

Miami Chamber of Commerce, 410 Live Oak St., Miami, AZ 85539. 602/473-3871.

Nogales-Santa Cruz County Chamber of Commerce, Kino Park, Nogales, AZ 85621. 602/287-3685.

Page Chamber of Commerce, P.O. Box 727, Page, AZ 86040. 602/645-2741.

The Papago Tribe, P.O. Box 837, Sells, AZ 85634. 602/383-2221.

Phoenix & Valley of the Sun Convention & Visitors Bureau, 4455 E. Camelback Road, Suite 146, Phoenix, AZ 85018. 602/952-8687. Reservations: 800/528-6149.

Pinal County Visitor's Center, P.O. Box 967, Florence, AZ 85232. 602/868-4331.

Prescott Chamber of Commerce, P.O. Box 1147, Prescott, AZ 86302. 602/445-2000.

Scottsdale Chamber of Commerce, P.O. Box 129, Scottsdale, AZ 85252. 602/945-8481.

Sedona-Oak Creek Chamber of Commerce, P.O. Box 478, Sedona, AZ 86336. 602/282-7722.

Seligman Chamber of Commerce, P.O. Box 426, Seligman, AZ 86337. 602/422-3352.

Tempe Chamber of Commerce, 504 E. Southern Ave., Tempe, AZ 85282. 602/967-7891.

Tombstone Tourism Association, P.O. Box 67, Tombstone, AZ 85638. 602/457-2211.

Tucson Convention & Visitors Bureau, P.O. Box 3028, Tucson AZ 85702. 602/624-1817.

Verde Valley Chamber of Commerce, 1010 S. Main St., Cottonwood, AZ 86326. 602/634-7593.

Willcox Chamber of Commerce, 1500 N. Circle I Drive, Willcox, AZ 85643. 602/384-2272.

Williams Chamber of Commerce, P.O. Box 235, Williams, AZ 86046. 602/635-2041.

Winslow Chamber of Commerce, P.O. Box 460, Winslow, AZ 86047. 602/289-2434.

Yuma County Chamber of Commerce, P.O. Box 230, Yuma, AZ 85364. 602/782-2567.

Yuma Convention Bureau, P.O. Box 6468, Yuma, AZ 85364. 602/344-3800.

New Mexico

New Mexico State Tourism and Travel Department Bataan Building, Santa Fe, NM 87503 505/827-6230.

Alamogordo Chamber of Commerce. P.O. Box 518, Alamogordo, NM 88310. 505/437-6120.

Albuquerque Convention & Visitors Bureau, P.O. Box 26866, Albuquerque, NM 87125. 505/243-3696.

Albuquerque Hispano Chamber of Commerce, 407 Rio Grande Blvd. NW, Suite 2, Albuquerque, NM 87104. 505/842-9003.

Aztec Chamber of Commerce, 125 North Main, Aztec, NM 87410. 505/334-9551.

Bloomfield Chamber of Commerce, P.O. Box 1570, Bloomfield, NM 87413. 505/632-9248.

Carlsbad Convention & Visitors Bureau, P.O. Box 910, Carlsbad, NM 88220. 505/887-6516.

Cloudcroft Chamber of Commerce, P.O. Box 125, Cloudcroft, NM 88317. 505/682-2733.

Clovis Chamber of Commerce, P.O. Drawer C, Clovis, NM 88101. 505/763-3435.

Deming Chamber of Commerce, P.O. Box 8, Deming, NM 88030. 505/546-2674.

Eagle Nest/Angel Fire Chamber of Commerce, P.O. Box 322, NM 87718. 505/377-2243.

Espanola Chamber of Commerce, 417 Big Rock Center, Espanola, NM 87532. 505/753-2831.

Farmington Chamber of Commerce, P.O. Box 267, Farmington, NM 87401. 505/325-0279.

Gallup Chamber of Commerce, P.O. Box 1395, Gallup, NM 87301. 505/722-2228.

Grants Chamber of Commerce, P.O. Box 297, Grants, NM 87020. 505/287-4802.

Las Cruces Convention and Visitors Bureau, 311 N. Downtown Mall, Las Cruces, NM 88001. 505/524-8521.

Las Cruces Chamber of Commerce, P.O. Drawer 519, Las Cruces, NM 88001, 505/524-1968.

Las Vegas Chamber of Commerce, P.O. Box 148, Las Vegas, NM 87701. 505/425-8631.

Las Vegas Hispano Chamber of Commerce, 131 Bridge, Las Vegas, NM 87701. 505/454-1930.

Lordsburg Chamber of Commerce, P.O. Box 699, Lordsburg, NM 88045. 505/542-9864.

Los Alamos/White Rock Chamber of Commerce. P.O. Box 888. Los Alamos, NM 87544. 505/-662-8105

New Mexico State Assn. of Hispano Chambers of Commerce, 131 Bridge, Las Vegas, NM 87701. 505/454-1930.

Raton Chamber of Commerce, P.O. Box 1211, Raton, NM 87740. 505/445-3689.

Roswell Convention & Visitors Bureau, P.O. Drawer 70, Roswell, NM 88201. 505/623-5695.

Ruidoso Chamber of Commerce, P.O. Box 698, Ruidoso, NM 88345. 505/257-7395.

Santa Fe Convention and Visitors Bureau, P.O. Box 1928QP, Santa Fe, NM 87501. 505/983-7317.

Santa Fe Hispano Chamber of Commerce, P.O. Box 4206, Santa Fe, NM 87502. 505/988-4597.

Silver City Chamber of Commerce, 1103 North Hudson, Silver City, NM 88061. 505/538-3785.

Socorro Chamber of Commerce, P.O. Box 743, Socorro, NM 87801. 505/835-0424.

Taos County Chamber of Commerce, P.O. Drawer 1, Taos, NM 87571. 505/758-3873.

Truth or Consequences (T or C) Chamber of Commerce, P.O. Box 31, T or C, NM 87901. 505/894-3536.

Tucumcari Chamber of Commerce, Drawer E, Tucumcari, NM 88401. 505/461-1694.

Colorado

Cortez, Chamber of Commerce, Cortez, CO 81321. 303/565-3414.

Durango Chamber of Commerce, Box 2587, Durango, Co 81301. 303/247-0314.

Mesa Verde Company, Box 277, 109 South Main, Mancos, Colorado 81328. 303/529-4421.

Utah

Utah Travel Council
Council Hall/Capitol Hill
Salt Lake City, UT 84114
801/533-5681
(*Note: The Utah Travel Council has divided Utah into recreation areas which can be contacted separately for information on specific regions. Due to the specialized service this offers the visitor, we are listing the specified regions instead of pertinent Chambers of Commerce. Utah also has an impressive network of visitor information centers—in towns, on the highways, and in every national park and monument in the state*)

Canyonlands Region, P.O. Box 490 Dept. CB, Monticello, UT 84535. 801/587-2231.

Castle Country (includes Green River, Goblin Valley, part of Capitol Reef National Park), P.O. Box 1037, Price, UT 84501.

Color Country (includes Bryce Canyon, Lake Powell, Zion, Grand Canyon North Rim), P.O. Box 220, Cedar City, UT 84720. 801/586-4022.

Garfield County Information Center, Panguitch, UT 84759.

Kane County Travel Council, P.O. Box 1230, Kanab, UT 84741. 801/644-5033.

Washington County Travel Information Center, 185 East St. George Boulevard, St. George, UT 84770.

Panoramaland (includes Capitol Reef National Park, Big Rock Candy Mountain) P.O. Box 788, Richfield, UT 84701. 801/896-8545.

El Paso, Texas

El Paso Chamber of Commerce, 10 Civic Center Plaza, El Paso, Tx 79987, 915/544-7880.

Las Vegas, Nevada

Las Vegas Convention and Visitors Authority, 3150 Paradise Road. Excellent, free map. 702/733-2323.

Greater Las Vegas Chamber of Commerce, 2301 East Sahara Avenue, Las Vegas, NV 89104. 702/457-4664.

Bureau Land Management

The U.S. BLM has jurisdiction over backpacking, river running, rockhounding, camping, and wilderness areas and also provides maps:
Arizona: BLM, 2400 Valley National Bank Center, Phoenix 85073.
New Mexico: BLM, P.O. Box 1449, Santa Fe 87504; 505/988-6000.
Utah: BLM University Club Building, Room 1500, 136 East South Temple, Salt Lake City 84111; 801/524-5348

Transportation

Within the Southwest region, travellers have several options of moving about.

By Air

Several domestic carriers offer regular commuter service to the major airports of the Southwest. When contemplating a trip to this area, it is a good idea to consult a map or a reliable travel agent and pinpoint a destination most appropriate to individual travel plans. One proven method is to fly into one city, rent a car for travel within the area, ending up in another Southwestern city offering flights home. Deregulation, together with the recent woes of individual airline companies, have resulted in fluctuating routes and schedules and total chaos in pricing. Most larger travel agencies are now computerized to the extent that the most up-to-date information on package deals, and discounts is available to the traveller.

Phoenix is a major hub for air travel coming into Arizona from out-of-state, and it is also a logical mecca for embarking on sightseeing in the area. Phoenix Sky Harbor International Airport is served by *American Airlines, Continental, Delta, Eastern, Northwest Orient, Pacific Southwest, Southwest Airlines, TWA, United, USAir* and *Western.* The airport is also served by *CP Air Holidays,* a commercial airline charter operating out of Vancouver which flies to and from Canada, the South Pacific, Mexico and the United Kingdom. Phoenix offers ground connections to Flagstaff, Prescott and Sedona; Sky Harbor Transportation operates an airport shuttle within the city's metropolitan area. Other choices of limousine service are extensive; some are highly plush and therefore rather expensive.

From Phoenix, it is also possible to connect with in-state flight companies who operate scenic "flight-seeing" tours via chartered plane or helicopter to places like the Grand Canyon, Lake Powell and Monument Valley (Navajo Indian Reservation.) Gambling junkets to Las Vegas are also available. 1-800-221-5596 in-state — which is useful for booking just about everything, from air tours to accommodations, car rentals, bus tours, or even mule rides into the Grand Canyon.

The **Grand Canyon** (South Rim) has its own small airport, with regular flights from Phoenix and Las Vegas. The strip is served by Air Cortez. Air LA, Air Nevada, Las Vegas Airlines, Republic and Scenic Airlines. An airport bus to Grand Canyon village is available.

Las Vegas' McCarran International Airport was the 15th busiest airport in the United States in 1983, serving 10,350,000 arriving and departing passengers. Demand is growing; the airport is scheduled to triple in size by the year 2000. In addition to the lure of gambling and nightlife, Las Vegas, on the western rim of the Southwestern region, offers proximity to Lake Mead and the Grand Canyon, as well as quick highway access to southern Utah. Airlines flying into McCarran International are Air Nevada, American, Continental, Delta, Eastern, Golden Pacific, Havasu, Northwest Orient, Ozark, Pacific Coast, Pacific Southwest, Pan Am, TWA, United and Western. Limousine and taxi service is available round-the-clock. Las Vegas is a designated port of entry with authorization to clear foreign aircraft and cargo shipments. Both McCarran and North Las Vegas Air Terminal service private aviation.

Salt Lake City, Utah, is not within the circums cribed Southwestern area for the purposes of this guide, but it does provide access to the geologically rich area in the southern part of Utah which includes Canyonlands, Bryce Canyon and Zion National Parks, et al. Airlines flying into Salt Lake International Airport are American, Continental Delta, Eastern, Sky West, Transwestern, TWA, United, Western and Wien Air Alaska. Charter air taxi service from Salt Lake connects with local airports in Cedar City and St. George, which are close to Zion and Bryce Canyon. Air taxi to this area is also available from Las Vegas. Bus lines offer connections within the park region; however, good bus tours to the parks are considered sparse compared with the generally good ground service available in other parts of the state. Because of the flexibility automobile travel offers, and the general remoteness of the Canyonlands portion, most travellers to this area choose the car as the most feasible means of transport. Major car rental agencies are situated in St. George and Cedar City.

Colorado's Mesa Verde section is accessible by air through connecting flights from Denver, Phoenix and Albuquerque that wind up in smaller airports at either Durango or Cortez. Durango is served by Continental and Sun West; Cortez by Pioneer and Trans-Colorado. Major car rental agencies are situated in both.

Albuquerque International, an adobe structure that speaks for the New Mexico artistic heritage, is New Mexico's major airstrip, served by American West, American, Continental, Delta, Eastern, Mesa Airshuttle, Pacific Southwest, Ross Aviation, TWA, United and Western. From there, smaller commuter flights hook up with other cities in the region. Good bus shuttle connections are available to Santa Fe, as well as air transport via Pioneer.

El Paso International Airport is a gateway to **Mexico** and offers access into southern New Mexico. Airways of New Mexico, American, American West, Continental, Eastern, Southwest and Western all fly into this Texas destination.

Tucson, Arizona's second International Airport, handles American, Continental, Eastern, Golden Airways, Pacific Southwest, Royal American, Sierra Vista Aviation, Sun West, Texasamerican, TWA, United, USAir and Western flights.

Virtually all of the major airports in the Southwest offer from adequate to very good facilities for the elderly and handicapped, as well as regional commuter flights for short hops to landing strips in smaller Southwestern cities.

Most airlines can be contacted by toll-free numbers. The numbers, though, vary depending on where the call is placed. Call 1-800-555-1212 to obtain toll free number of particular airline. In addition, toll-free calls can now be placed to car rental agencies, limo/bus operators, major hotel/motel systems, some state tourist boards and major tour operators.

By Train

Amtrak provides inter-city service through large portions of the Southwest. The Southwest Limited, from Los Angeles to Chicago, stops at the New Mexican cities of Raton, Las Vegas, Lamy, Albuquerque and Gallup, then goes through Arizona—Winslow, Flagstaff, Phoenix, Seligman and Kingman—before moving on to California and L.A. The Lamy stop offers connections to Santa Fe; from Albuquerque, a Trailways bus provides links to El Paso, with through-ticketing available through Amtrak; from Flagstaff, bus tours can be gotten to the Grand Canyon; and travellers can connect by bus to Las Vegas through Amtrak's Kingman, Arizona, stop.

The Desert Wind route goes from Denver to Las Vegas, with an intermediate stop at Salt Lake City. The Pioneer offers a Chicago to Salt Lake route via Denver. The Sunset Limited links Lordsburg and Deming, New Mexico, with El Paso, Texas, on its run from Los Angeles to New Orleans.

The Amtrak way is the slow, leisurely way, designed for travellers who have plenty of time to enjoy the scenery. In general, pricing is competitive with airline travel to the same destinations, although, again, it is advisable to make inquiries and "shop around." For specific information on rail service to the Southwest, call Amtrak's toll-free number, 800-872-7245 from anywhere in the Continental United States. And, by all means, consult your travel agent: many handle AMTRAK reservations.

By Bus

Both major bus companies—Trailways and Greyhound—as well as a slew of smaller charter companies, provide an impressive network of ground travel throughout the Southwest. Gray Line offers a variety of sightseeing tours on a daily basis, although there may be seasonal variations in specific areas. Greyhound and Trailways offer daily service to many towns and cities. Depend on good bus service to the most important destinations. Beyond that, routes tend to fluctuate, and it is wise to check in advance with local bus companies or Chambers of Commerce. For information on booking group charters through Greyhound, call 800-528-0447. For Trailways Charter information, call 1-800-555-1212 for the toll-free number in your area.

Driving

The automobile is by far the most popular means of travel within the Southwest, and for this reason it is also an important way to get to the area. Taxis are expensive; buses and trains are notoriously slow and in some areas, like southern Utah, practically nonexistent. Car rentals are plentiful. Vast stretches of territory within the Southwest are sparsely inhabited; yet, it is uncommon to find a town or city that is not served by good roads. The popularity of camping is still another incentive to rely on automobile travel. It is still the quickest and most carefree way to see as much of this area as possible in a relatively short space of time. If a traveller adheres to the time-honored adage "when in Rome do as the Romans do," the car is a logical choice.

Main arteries within the area are generally the quickest, if not always the most entertaining, ways of getting from Point A to Point B. Several interstate highways crisscross the Southwest. Interstate 25 travels in a vertical path through Colorado, linking Denver with northern New Mexico, where it enters Raton, winds through Santa Fe and Albuquerque, and continues south to Las Cruces, NM, where it merges into I-10 on its journey to El Paso, Texas. At Albuquerque, I-25 crosses the east-west I-40, which follows the U.S. Highway 66 of song and fable and connects Tucumcari, in eastern New Mexico, with Gallup, NM and Flagstaff, Arizona before striking off into California's Mojave Desert. Westward from Las Cruces, Interstate 10 becomes a more southerly east-west route than I-40. At Tucson, it adopts a brief northward path toward Phoenix before heading straight west for California and Los Angeles. Still further south, I-8 carves out the southernmost major Arizona byway, winding up in San Diego, CA. U.S. 70, which joins I-10 in southwest New Mexico, separates from it at Lordsburg, NM, offering a faster lane to Phoenix.

I-17, or the Black Canyon Highway, as it is sometimes called, is a north-south throughway emanating from Phoenix, north toward Sedona and Flagstaff, where it crosses I-40. Interstate 15 travels in a southwesterly pattern through Utah and on to Las Vegas, Nevada. Interstate 70 is an east-west road through central Utah which provides connections to the Canyonlands, Moab, et al and eventually winds up in Denver, Colorado. Interstate 19, another north-south road, pokes southward from Tucson to Nogales and Mexico.

Of course, it would be impossible to see most of the Southwest's natural wonders without venturing off Interstate highways. A good road map (and much of the information in this guide) will help you get to major attractions, such as national parks and monuments. Even off the beaten path, the network of roads is generally very good. Nevertheless, there are exceptions, so when ferreting through out-of-the-way regions, it makes good sense to use a modicum of caution. Consult with maps and park authorities whenever possible and be aware of the weather. Mountain passes in the northern parts of the Southwest may be closed on account of snow as late as April or May. Some roads to Indian ruins, such as the entry to Mesa Verde, are paved and in good shape regardless of season or weather changes. Others require a bit of foresight, for example, plenty of gas, since there are no services once you get on the road. These out-of-the-way landmarks are often among the most fascinating, so it pays to be a Boy Scout: in other words, be prepared. Some examples of scenic, unpaved stretches with no alternatives: the road to Chaco Canyon, in New Mexico; the Burr Trail, from Utah State Highway 24 at Notom to Boulder and the road over Boulder Mountain, from Utah State 24 at Torrey, also to Boulder, both of which are passable to all vehicles in summers, but inquire about conditions. Utah State 12, between Escalante and Boulder, is possibly the most spectacular of the little-travelled paved roads in the Southwest.

Other variations on the speedy-but-sometimes-boring Interstate Highway theme are abundant in the Southwest. For example, New Mexico State 14 between Santa Fe and Albuquerque offers glimpses of ghost towns in varying degrees of decay. There are many others which unfold as you consider the areas of many attractions. Again, allow for the extra time it takes to travel the longer and more winding roads.

In the beginning, there were State Highway departments. They kept track of the rules and cheerfully dispensed information on such diverse subjects as drunk driving laws, weather and driving conditions. Sometimes they dispensed maps. They still do. Contact:

Arizona Department of Transportation, 206 South 17th Avenue, Phoenix, AZ 85002; Arizona Department of Safety, 2310 North 20th Avenue, Phoenix 85009; Road and weather information: 602/262-8261. Highway Patrol: 602/262-8011.

New Mexico Highway Department Public Information Office, 1120 Cerrillos Road, Santa Fe 87503, 505/827-5100.

Utah Department of Transportation, 4501 South 2700 West, Salt Lake City, UT 84119, 801/965-4000; 532-6000 for recorded road report. Write Aeronautical Operations Division, 135

North 2400 West, Salt Lake City 84116; for airport director and aeronautical charts and regulations, phone 801/533-5057.

Some of the best state maps are issued free of charge by state agencies. They are usually quite detailed and frequently offer additional useful information, such as mileage charts, emergency telephone numbers and the like. For an excellent map of New Mexico, write the New Mexico State Tourism and Travel, Bataan Memorial Building, Santa Fe. NM87503, or telephone (505) 827-6230. The Arizona Office of Tourism at 3507 North Central Avenue, Suite 506, Phoenix, AZ 85012, telephone (602) 255-3618, also provides a true beauty compliments of *Arizona Highways Magazine.* Nevada's State Department of Transportation, Room 206, 1263 South Stewart Street, Carson City, NV89712, offers both a good state map and an aeronautical chart for flying Nevada's friendly skies. For Utah's map, contact the Utah Department of Transportation (see address, above). The good old days when every gasoline station came equipped with neat rows of maps are gone; however, maps can still be found here by the pump on occasion, notably at Amoco stations. For seat-of-the-pants travellers, the old standby, the *Rand McNally Road Atlas of the U.S., Canada and Mexico* retails for $5.95 in most bookstores, drugstores and Seven Elevens. These stores usually carry their own state map, also issued by Rand McNally, for around $2.00.

The American Automobile Association (AAA) is worth joining (annual membership $33), if only for the emergency road service offered by this organization. AAA tour books and road maps are issued to members free and are a useful bonus. The individual state maps are excellent guides, almost on a par with those issued by the state agencies, while AAA's map of the entire Western region is quite handy and not commonly available anywhere else. The tour books are a storehouse of information on · accommodations, restaurants, attractions and just about anything you can imagine. But you have to join: AAA's goodies are no longer available to nonmembers at any price.

In the Southwest, driving conditions vary depending upon whether you are in the mountains or the desert. In the mountains, it is useful to remember that altitude causes temperatures to drop dramatically, so be prepared for cooler weather, even in an area loosely lumped into the "Sun Belt." Southern Utah, much of New Mexico, and the northern third of Arizona are places you can expect wintry conditions. Also, rules for high altitude apply: drinking alcohol and smoking cigarettes will have a greater effect than they do at sea level or lower elevations. Mountain routes over passes may be snowy in every season except summer, so check for road closings, which are rare but not unheard of. In snowy weather, vehicles should be suitably equipped with snow tires or chains and ice scraper. Make sure the defroster and heater work. Also, be prepared for the longer amount of time it takes to traverse an equal distance through the winding roads of the mountains.

Check tires carefully before long stretches of desert driving. Heat builds pressure, so have them at or slightly below normal air pressure. The desert's arid climate makes carrying extra water—both for thirsty travellers and equally thirsty vehicles—one of the essentials. If off paved roads, carry at least one gallon per person. Try 2½ and five:gallon plastic containers or "collapsible" jugs favored by hikers. A little food doesn't hurt either—not every town has service stations, and some tend to close early. Keep an eye on the gas tank—it's a good idea to have a bit more than you think you need. This is a vast region.

Flash storms can occur during the rainy season, generally summer into fall. During this season drivers should stay out of dry arroyos (drainage points, or "dips"). In other words, use common sense; keep to high ground and be aware of weather conditions while travelling. Dust storms are also indigenous to the desert, and are especially fierce on I-10 in Arizona between Casa Grande and Eloy. Radio stations 550, 620 and 910 in Arizona broadcast a dust storm alert; elsewhere, stay tuned to local air waves for information on possible rain or dust storms. If a storm should occur, travellers are advised to pull vehicles off the road as far as possible and wait it out. Leave your lights on so another person following suit doesn't ram you and your car.

The rural character of much of this area is manifested by flocks of sheep or herds of cattle, notably in northern New Mexico, which usually only adds to the fun, but will certainly slow you down. An alternate route which is not through open grazing range may be the answer for travellers in a hurry. Also, be aware that road delays do occur at times in southern New Mexico, part of which is hard by a missile range (noted on most maps).

A gasoline credit card or two can be a real plus when travelling through this area; without it, cash may dwindle rather rapidly. Gas stations encountered frequently that issue cards are Phillips 66, Chevron, Texaco and Shell (Conoco). Bear in mind that these days, most gas stations also honor major credit cards.

A word of caution which may save your life: If you should have car trouble on a back road, or become lost, do not strike out on foot, even with water. A car, visible from the air and, presumably, on a road, is easier to spot than a mere mortal and it affords shelter from the weather. Wait to be found rather than pursue your rescuers.

A word on hitchhiking: while no out-and-out dangerous areas have been identified, it is important to always—always—be careful. If possible, find an alternative. In southern Utah, it is especially difficult to hitchhike, since the major highways don't offer good access. And this lightly populated region offers little bus, train or airline service. So, even if you're tight on cash, consider renting a car in Las Vegas NV, Grand Junction CO, Flagstaff AZ or Salt Lake City. Pay by the week and try to get unlimited mileage free. Who knows? You might take your late-model rental car places you'd never go on your own.

Down Mexico Way: Short trips across the border into Mexico are widely encouraged in that no travel permits are required as long as you are going for less than 24 hours and less than 15 miles into the country. A one-day car insurance policy should be obtained prior to crossing as U.S. auto insurance is not valid in Mexico. One-day policies are easy to get and can be arranged through a reliable Mexican insurance company, AAA (members only) and some state automobile associations. Companies like Sanborn's, Palms and Overland International, to mention just a few, with offices in many Southwestern border cities, offer insurance, and they cheerfully answer questions regarding your trip into Mexico. For a one-day trip the cost is negligible, but it goes up rather dramatically if you stay on. Border towns and duty free areas are only too happy to have your U.S. currency. Elsewhere, money can be converted easily into pesos at banks and foreign exchange offices. Major credit cards are honored throughout Mexico. Aliens must carry their registration cards; naturalized citizens should carry certificates. Travellers are currently permitted to carry $300 worth of merchandise back duty-free. For more than a one-day trip, it is helpful to have more complete information and travel tips, available from a Mexican consulate or Mexican Government Tourism Office in any Southwestern state.

Car Rentals

For many travellers, renting a car is the answer to ground travel in the Southwest. Automobile rentals are plentiful in major tourist centers, major and even smaller cities and at most airports. The competition makes the range, both in rates and types of cars available, a wide one. Even smaller airports tend to have Hertz and Avis represented. Larger centers also offer Budget (Sears) and National, as well as other lesser-known rental companies. Frequently, smaller local rental companies, both at airports and in towns and cities, offer better rates than the better-known agencies; it is best to do some comparisons. But be sure to check insurance coverage provisions before signing anything.

Most automobile rental agencies require you to be at least 21 years old and to hold a valid driver's license and a major credit card before they will rent you a car. Some will take a cash deposit, sometimes as high as $500, in lieu of a credit card (best not to rely on this if you are definitely planning car rental.) Foreign travellers may need to produce an international driver's license or a license from their own country. Liability is not automatically included in the terms of your lease, so advertised rates usually do not include additional fees for insurance. You should also check with your airline, bus or rail agent, or travel agent for special package deals that provide rental cars at reduced rates.

Minimum ages for drivers: Arizona 18, 16 with parents' consent. New Mexico, Colorado, Utah 16. Texas, 16 with approved driver education course, 18 without.

Drivers must abide by state traffic laws. And, each state being a separate entity in this regard, laws will vary. For more complete information on car rentals and laws in particular states, please contact State Highway departments.

Taxi Service

Taxis are plentiful in major destination cities in the Southwest, and frequently in smaller cities as well. At least 15 cities in New Mexico, for example, have one or more taxi services available. Rates fluctuate widely. In New Mexico, prices range from 80 cents to $2.50 minimum (from the first eighth of a mile to transportation within city limits) and from 60 to 80 cents for each additional mile. Arizona taxis are particularly prone to rate swings, as pricing is deregulated, meaning that rates (which must be posted) are up to the driver. Phoenix offers at least three taxi services for the Valley and surrounding areas. The minimum fare is 85 cents. A one-mile trip costs about $1.70, 90 cents for each additional mile. In other words, not cheap. Taxi service is also available from airports outside of major towns and cities, and tends to be expensive. A cab ride from Santa Fe Municipal Airport into town, for instance, may cost as much as $12.00. Cabs are frequently posted at airports, train and bus terminals, and major hotels; otherwise, order by telephone.

Accommodations

State Tourism Offices (read Tourist Information notes of this guide in brief) provide accommodations listings in their standard packets, as do Chambers of Commerce. Many of these lists provide a scale of pricing, as well as little dots or symbols to pinpoint specific amenities offered by various establishments.

AAA tourbooks are handy. The Automobile Association of America maintains its own system of quality-rating that is known to be as reliable as anything else, and is one technique for finding places to stay quickly and painlessly. Tour Books include information on pricing, telephone numbers, and a wealth of information designed to help you decide where to stay.

Another time-honored system for banking reliability involves chain operations. Quality is not totally guaranteed, but certain standards go with the territory. Furthermore, if you are planning extensive travelling around, often hotel/motel chains will wire ahead at your next destination and make a reservation for you. Holidays Inns, Ramada Inns, Hilton, Sheraton, Howard Johnson's and Marriott are all names with the appeal of the familiar. Best Western is another respected and reliable grouping. Prices fluctuate madly, even within chains, so there is no predicting them. Off-season pricing is radically different, in many cases, from on-season. Especially during off-season, and even during high season don't be hesitant to shop around for the best prices.

Phoenix, for example, is notorious for extravagant price differentials for the same basic amenities.

If you are travelling with the aid of a travel agent, ask about accommodations in the places you are going to. Chances are, the agent will have at least a good list. Better yet, he or she may have first-hand knowledge, always an invaluable tool. The Info sections concluding each Places chapter of this book offer some suggestions in the respective areas. You do well to call and check with resorts and hotels for the possibility of off-season closures. Most of the time, you do even better to reserve well in advance if possible, especially in the region's desert country, as motels are in fairly short supply. Moab, Torrey, Bryce and Springdale for example, are prime towns with proximity to respective parks and monuments.

Note: It's nice to have a credit card while travelling, more so if your travel plan includes numerous overnight stays at hotels/motels.

Communications

Postal Services

Post office hours may vary in central, big-city branches and smaller cities and towns. Hotel or motel personnel will answer questions about post office hours nearest you. If you do not know where you will be staying in any particular town, you can receive mail by having it addressed to you, care of General Delivery, at the main post office in that town. You must pick up General Delivery mail in person. For simply mailing letters or postcards, hotels frequently have stamps available with a mailbox nearby. Inquire at the desk wherever you are staying.

Telegrams and Telex

Western Union and International Telephone and Telegraph (ITT) will take telegram and telex messages by phone. Check the local phone directory or call local information for the toll-free numbers of their offices.

Telephones

The telephone is often the quickest way to get information, even if you need to deal with the vagaries of a pay phone. Hotels or motels with telephones in the room are a good way to sidestep the Phone Booth Blues.

The fastest way to get assistance for a telephone/communications problem that arises in the Southwest is to dial "0" for operator on any phone. If the operator cannot be of direct assistance, he/she will probably be able to connect you with the proper party. Another indispensible all-purpose number, particularly if some jerk has ripped entire pages out of the telephone directory in the booth, is that for information assistance;

for information within any state, dial 1-555-1212; out of state, dial 1, the state's area code, then 555-1212. For information on toll-free numbers, dial 1-800-555-1212.

Make use of toll-free numbers whenever possible; for personal calls, especially, take advantage of lower long-distance rates after 5 p.m. and on weekends. Rates are often lower on holidays, but phone lines are frequently so congested on holidays like Christmas, Thanksgiving, Mother's Day, etc., it may be difficult to get a call through.

News Media

Television and Radio

All major Southwestern cities can be counted upon to have affiliations with major national networks, local stations and a vast offering of cable television hookups. It is now almost standard for decent motels and hotels to include television in the price of a room. Television listings can be found in most local newspapers on a daily basis; it is standard for Sunday newspapers to have special weekly guides. Information on radio programming is also available in the newspapers. Many of the state maps mentioned in the Transportation section (under Driving) of this guide in brief list major radio stations within the given state so that travellers can find them easily while driving in a car. In mountain areas, television signals may be blocked making it impossible to tune into your favorite show. On the other hand, listening to the radio in less densely populated areas like the Southwest can be fun, particularly at night. The relatively few signals makes it possible to locate far-distant stations in cities and towns you have probably never been to. Local radio stations are also the sine qua non for things like weather and road conditions, which are reported on a continuous—usually hourly—basis, in places where it counts, that is , ski areas, flood and dust storm locales, etc. Stay tuned.

Newspapers and Magazines

Any decent-sized city and most resorts in the Southwest print at least one newspaper of their own. In the case of resorts, the newspaper is usually a weekly. Most of these periodicals give an excellent idea of what is happening on any given week, offering the most current information on movies, shows, art gallery openings and the like. Many resorts also currently publish magazines of the glossy, full-color variety; these tend to appear and disappear with amazing regularity, are usually published roughly from bi-monthly to bi-annually, and can be found on local newsstands, in drugstores and supermarkets. Regardless of the unpredictable nature of this revolving media "scene," it's worth a look to get a good flavor for where you are.

Information, ranging from general blurbs to extensive lists, on specific stations, publications, etc. is frequently available from Chambers of Commerce (see addresses and phone number above) or in the Yellow Pages section of your friendly telephone directory.

Newspaper in Arizona include,

Bisbee:*Bisbee Daily Review*;
Casa Grande:*Casa Grande Dispatch*;
Chandler: *The Chandler Arizonan*;
Douglas: *The Daily Dispatch*;
Flagstaff: *The Arizona Daily Sun*;
Kingman: *The Kingman Daily Miner*;
Mesa: *Tribune*;
Nogales: *Herald*;
Phoenix: *The Arizona Republic* and
    The Phoenix Gazette;
Prescott: *Courier*;
Scottsdale: *Scottsdale Daily Progress*;
Sierra Vista: *Daily Herald-Dispatch*;
Sun City: *Daily News-Sun*;
Tempe: *News*;
Tucson: *Tucson Newspapers Inc.*,
    Tucson Citizen,
    The Arizona Daily Star, and
    The Daily Territorial;
Yuma: *The Yuma Daily Sun*.

In New Mexico,

Alamogordo: *Alamogordo Daily News;*
Albuquerque: Albuquerque Publishing Co.,
    Albuquerque Journal, and
    The Albuquerque Tribune;
Artesia: *Artesia Daily Press*;
Carlsbad: *Carlsbad Current-Argus*;
Clovis: *Clovis News-Journal*;
Deming: *Deming Headlight*;
Farmington: *Farmington Daily Times*;
Gallup: *Gallup Independent*;
Grants: *Grants Daily Beacon*;
Hobbs: *Hobbs Daily News-Sun*;
Las Cruces: *Las Cruces Sun-News*;
Las Vegas: *Optic*;
Los Alamos: *Los Alamos Monitor*;
Lovington: *Lovington Daily Leader*;
Portales: *Portales News-Tribune*;
Raton: *Raton Range*;
Roswell: *Roswell Daily Record*;
Santa Fe: *The New Mexican*;
Silver City: *Press & Independent*.

In Utah,

St George: *Spectrum*;
Salt Lake City: Newspaper Agency Corp., and
    The Salt Lake Tribune.

In Nevada,

Las Vegas: *Las Vegas Sun*, and
    Las Vegas Review-Journal;
North Las Vegas: *The Valley Times*.

In El Paso,

El Paso: *The El Paso Times*,

El Paso Herald-Post, and
El Continental (Spanish).

Health and Emergencies

Sunburn

Anyone who has ever gone skiing on a warm sunny day knows that the "glow" acquired by the upturned face is not all nice warm color. It glows, all right. And it burns. A beautiful day rafting on the river can have a similar effect, only not just on the face. In the glare of constant sunlight, the reflection caused by both snow and water can create an intense experience. The sunglasses you wear to protect your eyes from the sun cut down on the cosmetic benefits too. Owl face!

One of the basics, of course, is to use common sense. If you are not well-oiled by a good sunscreen, preferably one containing PABA, cover up as much as possible. Sunglasses that cut out the unseen rays that blithely penetrate cheaper lenses may cost more, but they protect your eyes more thoroughly.

The elderly and ill, small children and infants, and people with fair skin are especially vulnerable to the sun. Excessive pain or redness and certainly blistering or numb skin areas, indicate a need for professional medical treatment. Minor sunburn can be soothed by taking a cool bath.

Insects and Pests

In all fairness, the Southwest is generally a pretty safe place. With this in mind, here is a brief rundown on what to watch out for and how to guard against it (them), especially when camping or otherwise intimately connected with the great outdoors.

Rattlesnakes, coral snakes: They exist in the Southwest, although not in great abundance. There are three varieties of rattler and one coral; rattlesnake bites have been recorded. According to writer Ed Abbey, only 3 percent of rattlesnake bites are fatal, and these are mainly from bites inflicted on small children, whose bodies are simply too small to withstand the venom. Rattlesnakes have heat sensors that can tell how big something is and don't want to waste precious venom on you if you are too large to eat. They will bite, therefore, only if surprised. Obvious precautions are the best: Try to walk in the open, proceed with caution and slowly in the rocks, make noise in grass or shake a stick—like a saguaro stake—ahead of you, do not step too close to dark places or dense, overgrown areas where a snake might lurk, shake out bedding or clothing that has been lying on the ground, wear sturdy hiking boots and watch where they take you. Snakes like to lie on the pavement at night because of the heat, so use a flashlight if you are walking on a desert highway after dark. Snake bite kits are good psychological protection, but there is some controversy over how effective they really are.

If bit, apply a tourniquet lightly above the bite, in the direction of the heart; kill the snake if possible so the species can be identified and the proper anti-toxin used and get thee to a doctor. If that's not possible, stay still and wait for the venom to run its course, with fair assurance that it won't be fatal. Snakes, by the way, do not crawl into sleeping bags. Millions of GIs were trained in the Mojave Desert during World War II, and it never happened once.

Gila monster: a lizard, the only poisonous Southwestern variety on record. It is big and menacing, with a thick tail, but don't worry about it. Gilas are easily recognized and rarely encountered in the ordinary course of events.

Insects: Bees and bumblebees exist in general abundance, which should be of major concern to those allergic to the sting and not of particular concern to others. The kissing bug is an unusual-looking black bug with an unpleasant bite. There are stinging fire ants and some varieties of wasp. While these bugs may not be exactly friendly, they are not normally dangerous. Black widow spiders and scorpions could be more of a problem if encountered. Scorpions are nocturnal, so use a flashlight if you walk barefoot in the dark. They do crawl into things, so shake out clothes and bedding and check shoes in the morning. There are many species, many of them non-serious. The bite of the tarantula is no worse than that of the generic spider and the only danger is they like to hang out in outhouses and the like and can carry secondary infections. Withal, there are few reports of serious situations arising from insect or spider bites within this region.

Plague is a rare disease, but it is encountered, if infrequently, in the Southwest. It can be carried by the bite of a flea which has fed on a plague-infected animal such as a prairie dog. New Mexico (northern New Mexico is the only area of significant occurrence) reports an average of 5-10 cases annually. Precautions like not handling sick or dead animals, especially rodents and rabbits, using flea powder on a pet (more effective than a collar), keeping camp free of open-air garbage, and keeping covered up when hiking through areas where that are a lot of fleas are all good ways to avoid the possibility of plague. Once contracted, plague is curable provided early treatment is given. Warning signs are high fever, definite feeling of sickness, and a painful lump or swelling in the groin area, under the arms or in the neck.

Small, unseen, dangerous things in water: Never drink water out of creeks downstream from grazing land or near human activity. Giardia is a particularly small and particularly virile micro-organism that is not usually life-threatening but can easily ruin a trip with the uncivilized things it does to your gastrointestinal system. It and its not as easily identified brethren sometimes subsist on the waters of the Great Outdoors. Spring water flowing directly from rock formations, on the other hand, can be extermely pure and a joy to drink.

It is possible to have giardia and not even know it. If you have symptoms—loss of appetite, cramping, diarrhea, bloating, nausea—you can be cured by a visit to the doctor and a week or two of the right medication. Water can be treated for giardia; the best way is to boil it for at least one minute, at high altitudes three to five minutes for an additional margin of safety.

Pack rats: Celebrated in story and fable, they may make off with something or another at your campsite, leaving a relic of plant life or some other replacements. More amusing than dangerous.

Cactus: To avoid being stuck, it is best not to bushwhack through cactus country. Stay on the trail. Wear long pants, if possible. Some people may have allergies to one of the several prickly varieties of this beautiful but potentially annoying succulent. Information centers in park areas usually have information on fauna which is very helpful. Watch out for the variety of cactus affectionately known as "heel plug," the kind that covers the ground with its dense growths and especially be wary when riding a bicycle. Heel plugs are hell on wheels.

Miscellaneous note: Arizona has a Cactus Patrol to catch cactus rustlers. This is a serious business; if you see someone in the act of digging up cactus call 602/255-4373.

Hypothermia: Remember that at high elevations, one drink is the rough equivalent of two. If you are already susceptible to alcohol or if you are driving, take it easy. In cold weather, use common sense: dress warmly, watch the weather, watch for your own personal body signals. Under certain conditions, the combination of alcohol and the cold, thin air can produce hypothermia. Hypothermia occurs when the body temperature falls below 95 degrees F. People engaged in outdoor sports are susceptible to hypothermia, especially if they get wet. An overdose of alcohol doesn't help. Symptoms to watch for are disorientation, drowsiness and sometimes increased urination. The best thing to do is get to the hospital, but if that isn't possible, blankets and extra clothing should be piled on for warmth. Don't use hot water or electric heaters and don't rub the skin. The elderly should be especially carefully not to get too cold.

Emergencies

Arizona

Emergency: 911
Highway Patrol: 602/262-8011.
Phoenix: Call the operator or Crime Stop, 262-6151. Ambulance, 264-2881; Fire, 253-1191.

New Mexico

State Police
    Santa Fe: 505/827-2551
    Las Vegas: 505/425-6771
    Roswell: 505/622-7200

Las Cruces: 505/522-2202
Albuquerque: 505/842-3082
Gallup: 505/863-9353
Española: 505/752-2277
Alamagordo: 505/437-1313
Clovis: 505-763-3426
Farmington: 505/325-7547
Socorro: 505/835-0741
Hobbs: 505/392-5588
Taos: 505/758-8878
Raton: 505/445-5571

Emergency medical help in event of accidents:
Toll free, 24 hours a day, call New Mexico
Medical Crisis Center, Poison/Drug Informa-
tion Center. 1-800-432-6866.

Citizen Band (CB) Radio operators: Project
Medic is a volunteer emergency CB Network
for reporting accidents to the Medical Crisis
Center. To report an accident, request that a
nearby base station relay the report by the
above (800) number to the Center.

Utah

Highway Patrol
Cedar City: 801/586-9445
Kanab: 801/644-2478
Moab: 801/259-5612
Monticello: 801/587-2662
Richfield: 801/896-6471
St. George: 801/673-9651

(*Area hospitals are located in Beaver, Cedar City,
Moab, Monticello, Panguitch, Richfield, and St.
George.*)

El Paso

Dial 911 for Police or Emergency Medical Service. Medical and health-care facilities and services available in El Paso are among the best in
the Southwest. There are 14 hospitals, eight of
which provide 24-hour emergency service.

Las Vegas

Highway Patrol: Dial "0" for Operator and ask
for ZENITH 1-2000.

Colorado

Call 911 for fire, police, ambulance. Poison control, all areas: 1-800/332-3073. Local numbers are
listed on the inside front cover of local directories.
In a pinch, dial "0" and stay on the line; if that's
impossible, give the Operator the street address
and community where help is needed.

Food

—by Ronald Johnson

To travellers from Maine to Tokyo daily dining
in the Southwest will be as outlandish and colorful
as are its huge striped canyons and mesas standing

red against a turquoise sky. A single plate may call
forth both red and green chiles, both yellow and
blue cornmeals, a dark brown mound of beans
with snowy sour cream, a crisp pile of shredded
lettuce, an improbably neon-green whip called
guacamole with salty fried chips of tortilla stuck in
like banners, and a particolor sauce of red
tomatoes, green chiles and coriander, and white
onion, to top off everything. It will be full of sass
and spice, it will offer a platter of texture and
contrast, and it will be unforgettable.

And like the desert itself, it is addictive. All
natives keep a pot of beans on the stove and every
day eat some dish with tortillas and chiles. The
locals say anyone who eats this food for a month
will eat it the rest of his life—and with some
reason. Exiles poke around Fortnum & Mason's
looking for canned tortillas and carry chile powder
in their jewel cases. Elizabeth Taylor ordered 10
gallons of chile sent to her in Rome, to fortify her
during the long filming of Cleopatra.

While in the Southwest, eat as much as you like
of chile, and if you like it very much, poke around
for a good cookbook and look for bags of local
ground chile, dried chiles from a redolent bin,
masa harina for putting *tamales* together, blue
cornmeal, canned green chiles and *tomatillos*, and
certainly as many hand-patted tortillas as you can
safely smuggle away.

Colorful centers like Santa Fe, Taos and
Phoenix offer everything from pasta parlors to
novelle cuisine. Albuquerque even has a *dim sum*
cafe worth notice. But nice as these are, stick to
the real stuff: go find a bowl of *posole*, taste the
ever-rarer blue cornmeal tortilla, check out the
carne adovada, pick up a *taco* or *burrito* for a
hand-held lunch, and feast on beans, beans,
beans.

In even the smallest town, ask the gas station
attendant, or anyone on a streetcorner, and you'll
be given a frank, friendly opinion on the best table
in town. There are usually at least two—
sometimes not very pretty or without a license for
beer (in which case you should inquire about
bringing your own in, in a brown paper bag)—
and both of them will offer some special dish.

As recently as D.H. Lawrence's stay in Taos,
the local Indians could be seen on their lands
patting tortillas, toasting squash blossoms over
glowing coals, candying whole pumpkins with a
dust of sugar and cinnamon and turning a haunch
on the spit, while brushing it with twigs of wild
sage, marjoram, and crushed juniper berries.

The first convenience foods and appliances took
hold quietly and swept the country like prairie
fire. The Pueblo sported blenders and powdered
and canned evaporated milk, like everyone else.
Old fragrant ways of the seasons were ignored—
the time for bread to bake, even the slow grinding
of corn on stone *metates*. It looked like a complete
ancient cuisine was going to simply fade away into
a sunset of store-bought bread, jello and soda
pop.

Luckily the last years have brought a new push
for tried resources and true food.

The newer cookbooks explain how to broil
beaver tails, with only salt and pepper—"until
rough hide peels off easily"—these are "delicious

served with refried beans or garbanzo soup." You can learn how to stuff a wild turkey with piñon nut stuffing, bake a prairie dog, and how to make beef jerky, venison pemmican, and jackrabbit stew. The Pima have a "peelings fry" of crisply deep-fried carrot and potato skins, better than any chip in the supermarket. From the Pueblo you find a way to take an unripe pumpkin and turn it into a savory stew with corn, onions, green chiles, garlic and butter. The Hopi tell how to make blue marbles and Hopi hush puppies, from their fine blue cornmeal.

On feast days or family occasions such as births and weddings, it is common to find sunflower and pumpkin seeds, the old dried "leather" beans and squash, hulled piñon nuts with gathered wild celery, mint and marjoram, rabbit and venison coaxed into stews, coffee from sunflower and lemonade from squawbush, a bouquet of wild greens, early sprouts and late pollen from cattails. Any visitor should be counted lucky to be invited to such a feast.

Most open affairs for visitors offer only a simple stew of red or green chiles, with either lamb or beef. There will also be "fry bread" spread with beans and cheese and lettuce—or with dribbled honey, for dessert. These are all a delight to sample, but introductions are in order if you want to taste the real thing.

Two of the specialties you might sample, depending on the time of year and whether or not a *fiesta* is brewing, are pueblo bread and *piki*. Pueblo bread is a crusty round loaf with a dense texture that lasts for days. It is always baked in the large outside ovens of stone and adobe you see dotting the grounds. These are called *hornos* and resemble giant beehives. Part of the savor of the loaf comes from the fires of juniper or piñon laid in, and their crackling crust is a result of a radiant heat no home oven can duplicate.

The best time to see *hornos* curling out their delectable smoke into the clear air, and turning out loaves, is two or three days before a *fiesta*, when the women of almost every household bake 30 to 50 pounds of bread. The entire village fills with the fragrance of bread baking and wood smoke. Frequently when driving down the road one sees a "Bread for Sale" sign and if all else fails there is usually one woman selling bread at the Indian market on the Plaza in Santa Fe. (This one is wrapped in plastic, to satisfy health authorities.)

Lucky are those who can taste rare *piki*, a tissue-thin bread baked on special stones. It dates back from time immemorial, and each family has its own *piki* stone handed down from mother to daughter. The stones are heated by a fire carefully laid underneath, then spread from time to time with cooked brains to give a glassy sheen. A thin batter is made of blue cornmeal, and ashes of sage (or other plants, depending on the tribe) mixed with water are then strained. The ash is said to preserve the blue color of the meal. The *piki* maker slowly smears a sheet of batter with a sweeping motion of her hand over the hot stone (dipping it immediately back into the batter to cool off!). In a minute or two the edges begin to curl, the sheet can be lifted off and folded up into rolls. For some festivities *piki* may also be colored pink by the addition of coxcomb, or yellow with safflower.

About the only hope of tasting *piki* is the Hopi-owned restaurant on Second Mesa, in New Mexico, operated in conjunction with a motel, museum and arts-and-crafts center. But Indian women also prepare it at various state fairs and Indian crafts and dance exhibitions throughout New Mexico and Arizona.

The yearly crop of Indian blue corn produces a blue-gray meal when ground, is one of the best kept culinary secrets in the world. If you are not able to sample it at the hand of its proprietors, at least make sure to order blue tortillas in some form or other while you are in the Southwest. (New Mexico is better for this than Arizona.) Blue may seem an odd color for food at first, but one crunch into a simple *taco* made with a blue tortilla will be enough to convince anyone of its superiority in both taste and texture.

Every season in the desert country seems to have a charm of its own, but autumn here is most people's hands-down favorite. The green chiles will have turned a brilliant scarlet. They are to be seen everywhere for sale, often along with strings of particolored corn and knobby white ropes of garlic. Orange pumpkins blaze against the pink adobe, the cottonwoods turn a rattling yellow, and everywhere blue smoke begins to sift up from the roofs where the first piñon fires are being laid.

Whatever time of year, anyone travelling to Arizona and New Mexico for the first time will need a whole new glossary to read the menu. The first and most basic lesson will come into play when you have ordered at random from the entrée section at a restaurant and your waiter inquires: "Red or Green?"

You will have overlooked it, though it is always listed on the menu as a choice of chile sauce. And except for dishes by nature either solely red or green, which only the natives know, these same natives always specify a color with their order. My tactic is to order two things, so when the question comes I can act like a local and say: "Oh, a green *taco* and the *enchilada* red." It seems to work.

Local food, no matter how you order, will be based on the trio of corn, beans and chile. However these three are interchanged—harmonious as they are—to make a new tune on the tongue.

Corn will come in the form of a tortilla, a bread for all occasions. It may appear as a distant cousin of fresh bread, hot and steaming from a basket, asking to be slathered with butter. It may be quickly fried to a softness, then stuffed and sauced into an *enchilada*, or it may be crisped into a saucer or envelope shape to become either a *tostada* or *taco*. (The *tostada* is sometimes also called a *chalupa*.)

On special days you might uncover a stew of *cabrito* (young goat), Mama Something's home-made *tamales*, *carne adovado* (the ultimate in homegrown red chile at its purest and hottest), or some elusive *quesadilla*, a stuffed and battered fried green chile, or a cactus appetizer.

The pinto bean (so called because it is speckled over like a pinto horse) seems to have more flavor than any other bean. They are most always served "refried." This means they are cooked, then mashed into hot oil and fried till they have a slightly crispy crust. Unless they come with a topping already, they are meant to be doused with *salsa* and eaten with crisp, fried tortilla chips. Ideally refried beans should also have sour cream melting into their hotness, but your beans may be so fine they don't need anything.

They will never tell you, but in most places something known to the kitchen as "spanish rice" will be included as a filler. As this is never much good but for pushing around a plate, always request a double order of beans rather than the rice.

Chile permeates everything. There is some green chile in that bowl of *salsa*, and probably a little red thrown in as the beans cook. Either the red or green will constitute a sauce for the beef-or chicken-filled *enchilada, tostada* or *taco*. It will spark up whatever *hors d'oeuvres* or soup you might summon. It will be inescapable, pervasive, and food will never seem the same again.

For breakfast you will find *huevos rancheros* offered everywhere. These "ranch eggs" are either poached or fried, laid on a tortilla, then sauced liberally with chile (usually red, here) then sprinkled with cheese and shreds of crisp lettuce.

Posole—called hominy in other parts of the country—is corn kernels which have been leached with lime, puffed up, then dried or frozen. These are then stewed into a soup with pork and chicken, red or green chiles, fragrant coriander and oregano, garlic and onion, and often garnished with crisp fried strips of tortilla, with a cut lime for you to squeeze in if you wish.

At cocktail hour, another specialty to seek out is a snack called *nachos*. These are triangles of crisp tortilla with melted cheese on top, to be dribbled with fresh *salsa* or doused with mashed beans, chile powder, garlic, or little pickled chiles called *jalapeños*. From the simplest to the most elaborate these are always welcome with a frosty glass of beer or a *margarita*.

With all this spiciness beer is always in order, rather than wine, for wine simply loses all its nuance set against brash chile. American beer is rather bland and tasteless, but most good places will have a selection of robust Mexican beers which will be a delight.

The cocktail called *margarita* is a refreshing (though deadly after two) frozen mixture of lime juice, tequila and Triple Sec. Those who prefer their toddy simple should order the best chilled tequila the bartender recommends, with lime and salt. The wedge of lime is held between the forefinger and thumb, salt is placed at the base of the thumb, and before and after a swig of tequila these are tasted to quench the fire.

After a hot spicy dinner only the simplest dessert seems possible. A light refreshing fruit ice is the best, but if *nantillas* is on the menu sample that. *Nantillas* is a cousin to the custard known everywhere as Floating Island, but here the egg whites are stirred in rather than left floating on top. It is given a refreshing zing of cinnamon dusted on top and is a comforting way to quench any lingering chile on the tastebuds.

Many places also serve a basket of *sopapillas* after a meal. These are deep-fried squares of biscuit dough which puff up into "pillows," and are meant to be slit open and filled with honey. In some fancy restaurants they are also filled with a fruit and nut cream or with jam. Some think they sit a little heavy, but many people dote on them.

You may wonder how your stomach will bear up under this unfamiliar onslaught of spice and fire. Since many of the dishes are hot enough to sear the tongue of a novice, it may be wise to start slowly and work up to the real stuff. Green chiles are almost always milder than red—though they can be quite hot too.

The chile is a curious plant that can bear hot and mild pods on the same plant, and one field may be hotter than the next according to soil or slope. At the same time nutritionists advise us that chile is one of the finest natural digestives in the world. The best advice is to remember that a number of fried and even refried foods are involved here: fat porks and *sopapillas*, all manner of tortilla dishes, not to mention the absorbent bean. This is what causes indigestion, not the chile.

But even when spiced for the most timid taste, the foods of the Southwest are as much a reason to visit (and revisit!) as the Grand Canyon, Picture Rock, the Indian ceremonies and the beautiful adobe clusters of Santa Fe and Taos. Enjoy, enjoy.

Accompanying the Southwest's home-style cooking of native ethnic origins is a polyglut hodgepodge of just about every kind of cuisine imaginable. French, Italian, Oriental, Continental, and good old American entrées—from colonial to gooey Western barbecue—fill the rosters of dining spots from Las Vegas to Tucumcari. The Southwest, for better or for worse, is also a thriving franchiseville, with McDonald's, Wendy's and Taco Bell lining highways and byways with golden arches and other insignias, serving up a monotone style of microwave-based cooking that is anything but native.

Restaurants Listing

Arizona

Arizona lays a tentative claim to truly regional cuisine. Many natives feel the state's best food—including Mexican—is imported from somewhere else.

Avanti at two locations in Phoenix. 2728 E. Thomas Road, 956-0900 or 955-9977; 3102 N. Scottsdale Road, Scottsdale, 949-8333 or 941-9926. Northern Italian food featuring mussels, veal, pasta, fresh fish and seafood. Unusual decor in black, white and silver with columned mirrors, blown glass globes with candles and posters by Southwestern artist Georgia O'Keeffe. A fine place to *be*. Moderately expensive.

Different Pointe of View Restaurant at the Pointe Resort, 11111 N. 7th Street. Three-story complex perched on a hill overlooking all of Phoenix. Cocktails outdoors, subdued art deco interior, haute cuisine and equally haute prices. One of the best.

Durants 2611 N. Central Ave., Phoenix, 264-5967. Good American food, steaks, chops that are well-prepared, reasonably priced and generously portioned. The decor is Middle-American plush. A favorite with locals, who often stand five-deep at the bar.

El Chorro Lodge 5550 E. Lincoln Drive, Scottsdale, 948-5170. Breakfast, lunch and dinner served in an old rambling house with adobe walls and a scant two rooms to let. The restaurant is a complex consisting of seven rooms with juniper log-burning fireplaces, a bar full of gifts to the owner and a large terrace for dining in good weather. The only place in town that still captures the feel of the old dude ranches. Simple American food, well prepared and amply portioned with rack of lamb and chateaubriand specialties of the house.

Golden Rule Cafe 808 E. Jefferson, Phoenix, 262-9256. Soul food, wonderfully prepared and heaping. Chicken fried steak, chicken in gravy, beans, black-eyed peas. Smoking, drinking, and swearing not permitted. No checks—you report what you ate to the cashier who fixes you with a gaze you wouldn't lie to.

Katz' Delicatessen and Sandwich Shop 5144 N. Central, Phoenix. Nothing more or less than the best kosher deli in the Valley. Cafe atmosphere. Inexpensive.

Kroenauer's Prescott, continental food featuring French and Austrian. Highly recommended by at least one discriminating native. And expensive.

Lawrence and Beulah's Sunflower Store Sunflower, on AZ 87 between Payson and Mesa. A highway favorite, a truck stop loaded with cards, signs and Western art. Colorful clientele and Mexican food, with green chile burritos, enchilada style, a must. Cheap. And there's no competition for miles.

The Orangerie At the Arizona Biltmore. Decor by Frank Lloyd Wright in a dining room that began as the hotel's solarium in 1929—surely the most beautiful dining room in the state. Very high cuisine, complete with multi-tiered dessert wagon. Pianist on duty. Expensive.

The Owl Sedona, a local tradition. Rustic, good continental food, moderately priced, with owls worked through the decor.

Rene's Tlaquepaque, Sedona. Fine French food, elegant setting. Moderately expensive.

Rosita's Place 1914 E. Buckeye Road, Phoenix, 262-9372. Far and away the best Mexican food in the Valley, with daily stews (cocidos), mole poblano (chicken in mole sauce) and other dishes unavailable elsewhere. Unpretentious cafe atmosphere. Cheap. The food is more savory than the neighborhood, so stay alert.

Also recommended in Tucson are **Irv's Deli**, for those who hanker after pickles and pastrami, and for gourmets the **White Dove** at the Sheraton El Conquistador and the **Tack Room**. The city has numerous cafes which serve Sonoran-style Mexican food (as opposed to the Tex-Mex or New Mexico variety). Sonoran is marked by abundant use of cheeses, huge, thin flour tortillas, and restrained use of chiles. The best of these eateries are usually found on the city's west and south sides and include **Mi Nidito**, **Micha's**, **Cora's Cafe**

and **El Minuto**. Southside restaurants with great chimichangas are **El Dorado** and **Arturo's**. Other Phoenix highlights are **Ninth & Ash** and **Fung Lum's Mexican-Chinese Restaurant**.

New Mexico

Casa Cordova Arroyo Seco, outside of Taos en route to Taos Ski Valley, 505/776-2200, 758-3560. Continental and New Mexican cuisine, expensive and worth it. The Casa offers quiet seclusion, the atmosphere of an old adobe hacienda. Good wine list.

The Compound 653 Canyon Road, Santa Fe, 505/982-4353. Elegant hot-spot serving award-winning French, American, and Continental cuisine. Open for lunch and dinner.

El Farol Restaurant & Bar 802 Canyon Road, Santa Fe, 505/983-9912. Another popular Santa Fe spot, an intimate bistro with a take-it-as-it-is New Mexican flavor. Open for dinner from 5.30 on.

La Placita Old Town Plaza NW, Albuquerque, 505/247-2204. Good New Mexican food served in an 18th-Century adobe hacienda. Sopapillas reportedly originated here. Also good are the enchiladas, chile rellenos, salsa verde or rojo (green and red sauce), carne adovado, posole. American food is also available. The New Mexican entrées are good examples of regional dishes that have evolved through centuries of mixing, sharing and utilizing crops that thrive in the area.

La Posta In La Mesilla, two miles south of Las Cruces, 505/524-3524. In an old adobe building that was once a stagecoach stop on the Butterfield Trail. Superb New Mexican food. Popular.

Mexican Pete's on the Turquoise Trail, Highway 14, between Santa Fe and Albuquerque. Good honest New Mexican food, hot and tasty. Nothing fancy.

Owl Bar and Cafe San Antonio, 15 miles southeast of Socorro, 505/835-9946. This is an out-of-the-way place that nevertheless has been discovered. Atmosphere is early greasy spoon; the air is blue with greasy smoke, the tables are draped in oilcloth and the decor leaves much to be desired. But it has the best green chile hamburgers in the world. Really.

Rancho de Chimayo In Chimayo on the High Road to Taos northeast of Santa Fe, 351-4444. This place has been recommended by so many people it's got to be good. Make reservations. Specialities are blue margaritas, flautas, enchiladas, carne adovado. The restaurant, ensconced in an old Spanish hacienda, has been in the same capable family hands for years. Dining on a large outdoor portal and terraces in summer and fall. Adobe, fireplaces, everything it ought to be.

Tinnie's a chain of restaurants throughout New Mexico known for purveying steak, seafood, chops, quail, trout and the like in lavishly restored historical sites. Tinnie's Double Eagle, in La Mesilla, is on the Plaza. Tinnie's Maria Teresa in Albuquerque, Tinnie's Legal Tender, south of Santa Fe in Lamy, Tinnie's Silver Dollar in Tinnie, Tinnie's Palace in Raton, and any other Tinnie's that may have cropped up by the time you read this all follow the same pattern and all are popular with diners. Make reservations.

Also recommended in Santa Fe are: **Josie's**, a couple of blocks from the Plaza. Small and a favorite with locals for lunch, they have the distinction of serving blue tortillas and a very fine posole. The **Pink Adobe** has a specialty called *Steak Dunigan* with a splendid green chile sauce. **La Tertulia**, in addition to the good local cuisine, has Spanish decor in an old convent. New, but with reportedly fine and innovative cooking are **The Fresco**, **Santa Cafe** and **Comme Chez Vous**.

Utah

A few bright spots in a desert landscape include:

Francisca's Central and Third East, Monticello. Good Mexican food in an area of generally dismal cuisine. Cantina atmosphere. Inexpensive.

La Buena Vida Cantina Caineville (on the eastern edge of Capitol Reef National Park). Fantastic Mexican food, very cheap, Michelob on draught (remember, this is Utah). (We understand that celebrities like Roger Mudd and Robert Redford eat here.) Specialties include the Machaca burrito, made with dried, shredded beef. Atmospherically, this is a small, simple oasis surrounded by big cottonwoods.

Las Vegas

Las Vegas' taste in restaurants is supremely eclectic. Naturally, they cater to the late-night— and all-night—crowds there, so that one need never go hungry, at any hour. Most of the fine restaurants are located in the hotels. Some current local favorites are the **Quarterdeck** at the Mint Hotel for seafood and **Hugo's Cellar** at the Four Queens for generous servings of good steaks, seafood, duck, lamb. Both are downtown.

Each hotel has a gourmet room. Probably the finest of these is the **Palace Court** at Caesar's Palace, which used to open its doors only to VIP guests of this famous Strip hotel. The Court is now available to anyone with an expense-account budget, but worth it for the ambience, service and cuisine.

Two excellent French restaurant off the strip: **Pamplemousse**, in a small cottage at 400 E. Sahara (down the street from the Sahara Hotel), 733-2066; and **Andre's**, at 401 S. Sixth St., off Las Vegas Boulevard near the business district, has the feel of a French country inn, 385-5016. Reservations recommended at both.

Shopping

(This article only discusses the items which are worthy mementoes to bring back from your trip. For a listing of where to get them, please read short notes on "shopping" in the respective **Info** sections of this book.)

Indian arts and crafts, retailed both on and off the pueblos and reservations, are immensely attractive to visitors to Arizona and New Mexico, as fine handcrafted Indian works have real artistic value. Some of the better Indian trading posts (for example, Hubbell's Trading Post) are good places to view and buy these goods, although a great deal of Indian art has inevitably filtered into shopping arenas in Southwestern cities as well. (See also listings of Indian pueblos and reservations in the Info sections.)

The Southwest is a burgeoning mecca for arts and crafts browsing in general. Small, seductive shops in major cities or art centers like Santa Fe, Taos and Sedona purvey luscious specimens of handmade pottery, weavings, clothing and jewelry. These shops are frequently clustered in plaza or other pockets of art-conscious areas; the wares they display tend to embody the Southwestern style, which is a sort of melding of American casual with Spanish and Indian influences.

The work of Southwestern painters is clearly in evidence in these same towns and cities, where regional art is freely displayed in lobbies, restaurants, bars and the like. Some of these artists have become very much in demand, and collectors flock to the better art galleries, in Santa Fe, Taos and elsewhere, to buy up their work before the price goes still higher. Indian artists create traditional paintings, mostly watercolors, some oils. They are marked by a starkness and simplicity in style and by dramatic use of color. Navajo, and some Hopi, works dominate.

Superior examples of basketry are crafted by the Hopi, Pima, and the Papago. Hopi Kachina dolls, representing some of the more than 250 masked supernatural beings in the Hopi religion, are highly sought after. Sizes vary from eight to some 14 inches high; the dolls are carved from cottonwood roots. Prices vary too; the tag depends on the degree of workmanship and the quality of materials used rather than on the size. These dolls are a collector's item, and for those serious about collecting, there are several good books available on the subject.

Silver and turquoise are the chief components of the Indian-crafted jewelry. Distinctive Arizona forms are Hopi overlay and Navajo cast and hand-stamped works. The Apache make peridot jewelry.

Navajo rugs are justly famous. Also look for rare Hopi-made kilts, sashes and shawls.

Tours and Attractions

The **Info** section, found at the end of each "Places" chapter of this book, is designed to give you easy access to specific information on the tours and attractions available in a particular region. They cover the practical information in brief, as well as virtually everything else you might want to know about the American Southwest, and are categorized as follows:

National Parks

These are administered by the Department of the Interior and the National Park Service. They tend to be recreationally oriented, often created around areas of outstanding beauty and interest, and often including designated Wilderness Areas where motorized vehicles are not allowed. There is an admission fee to National Parks, but for a one-time fee the Golden Eagle Passport provides free entry or substantial discounts on all National Parks and Monuments in the United States for a year. Senior citizen discounts are available to those 62 years or above who get a free Golden Age Passport.

Arizona boasts more National Park Service areas than any other state in the union. For more information on them, contact the U.S. National Park Service, Southern Arizona Group, 1115 North 1st ST., Phoenix, AZ 85004, tel. 602/261-4956.

For more information on New Mexico National Parks and Monuments, contact the National Park Service, Southwest Region Office, P.O. Box 728, Santa Fe, NM 87501, tel. 505/988-6375.

National Forests

These are administered by the Department of Agriculture and the U.S. Forest Service. They are multi-purpose areas, frequently commodity oriented, with timbering, mining, livestock grazing and ski areas common within their borders. National Forest campgrounds are generally more primitive than National Park campgrounds, and fees to enter them are usually less. There is no fee to enter the National Forest itself.

For more information on Arizona National Forests find the nearest city on a map, call information and ask for the number of the U.S. Forest Service. This will work for New Mexico as well. Or contact the U.S. Forest Service Office, 517 Gold Avenue SW, Albuquerque, NM 87102, tel. 505/766-2444. Ranger stations offer information as well. For country maps in New Mexico contact the New Mexico Highway Department, 1120 Cerrillos, Santa Fe, NM 87503, tel. 505/983-0452.

States Parks

The quality of these parks is unpredictable, and they range from small urban parks to thousands of acres offering camping and a variety of recreational activities. The New Mexico State Park Division compiles a free descriptive listing of more than 40 New Mexico state parks. Contact the New Mexico State Park & Recreation Division, National Resources Department, 141 East De Vargas, Santa Fe, NM 87503, tel. 505/827-7465. Complete information concerning state park regulations, boating laws and boat safety equipment requirements is also available from the same office. In Arizona State Historic Parks are open from 8 to 5:30 daily, all others are open at all times; there is a 15-day limit on camping. For general information contact Arizona State Parks, 1688 West Adams, Phoenix, AZ 85007, tel. 602/255-4174.

Attractions

Attractions are high points in the categories of museums, zoos, landmarks, hot springs, etc. Phone numbers and hours are up-to-date at time of print, but, in these changing times, they are not cast in stone.

Ghost Towns

Abandoned mining centers, otherwise known as Ghost Towns, dot the mountainous areas of the Southwest. Visitors are asked to observe and respect all posted signs, leave all gates as they are, and not remove anything in order to preserve these remnants of Arizona's colorful past. In desert regions flash floods and road washouts are a possibility, so whenever possible inquire locally about conditions.

Most of the New Mexico ghost towns are actually inhabited. A $1.50 booklet called "Listen to the Wind" can be obtained through *New Mexico Magazine*, Room 165, Bataan Building, Santa Fe, NM 87503, tel. 505/827-2642. A special ghost town map ($2.25) is available from Maps by Cowling, 6313 Cuesta Northwest, Albuquerque, NM 87120, tel. 505/898-6790.

Festivals, Events and Entertainment

Annual events in the Southwest comprise a formidable crazyquilt. The range includes Indian events; western events like rodeos and Frontier Days; scores of gems and mineral shows; horse shows and horse racing; hot air balloon shows and races; arts and crafts festivals, sports events; commemorative festivals and more.

Again, continuing events of particular regional significance are listed in the **Info** sections of the book. The listings offer highlights, but are not intended to be complete — nor is it a foregone conclusion that all events listed will be held in successive years. Contact local Chamber of Commerce or the phone numbers provided for the most accurate up-to-date information.

In general, winter is a frenetic season in the southernmost regions and also Las Vegas, with dozens of events jammed into a crowded calender. Things tone down a bit during the summer, when suddenly the northern areas spring to life.

On the cultural side, orchestras, chamber music and the like are listed separately under "Entertainment" in the **Info**.

Gambling has become synonymous with Las Vegas' nightlife entertainment. Here is a listing of the major centrally located gambling halls and hotel/casinos. Call 1-800/555-1212 for toll-free phone numbers.

Aladdin: 736-0111.
Ambassador: 733-7777.
Barbary Coast: 737-7111.

Bingo Palace: 876-8223.
Binion's Horseshoe: 382-1600.
Caesar's Palace: 731-7222.
California: 385-1222.
Castaways: 731-5252.
Circus Circus: 734-0410.
Del Webb's Mint: 385-7440
Desert Inn: 733-4444
Dunes: 737-4110
El Cortez: 385-5200.
Eldorado, Henderson: 564-1811.
El Rancho: 796-2222.
Flamingo Hilton: 733-3111.
Four Queens: 385-4011.
Fremont: 385-3232.
Frontier: 734-0110.
Golden Gate: 382-3510.
Golden Nugget: 385-7111.
Hacienda: 739-8911.
Holiday: 369-5000.
Imperial Palace: 731-3311.
Landmark: 733-1110.
Las Vegas Club: 385-1664.
Las Vegas Hilton: 732-5111.
Las Vegas Inn: 731-3222.
Marina: 739-1500.
Maxim: 731-4300.
MGM Grand: 739-4222.
Nevada Palace: 458-8810.
Riviera: 734-5110.
Sahara: 737-2111.
Sam's Town: 456-7777.
Sands: 733-5000.
Showboat: 385-9123.
Silver City: 732-4152.
Silver Nugget: 399-1111.
Silver Slipper: 734-1212.
Stardust: 732-6111.
Sundance: 382-6111.
Tropicana: 739-2222.
Union Plaza: 386-2110.
Vegas World: 382-2000.

Gambling, however, is not confined to Las Vegas. Laughlin, Nevada, near Davis Dam and across from Bullhead City, Arizona, is said to have much better odds and is a town that is comprised solely of a collection of casinos. You get there in a ferry across the Colorado River and each casino has its own ferry. Some of these include:

Searchlight Nugget: 297-1201.
Colorado Belle, Laughlin: 298-2425.
Edgewater, Laughlin: 298-2453.
Nevada Club, Laughlin: 298-2512.
Pioneer, Laughlin: 298-2442.
Regency, Laughlin: 298-2439.
Riverside Resort, Laughlin: 298-2535.
Goldstrike Inn, Hoover Dam: 293-5000.
Exchange Club, Beatty: 553-2368.

The *Nevada Vacation Tours and Recreation Guide* published by the State's Department of Tourism, has a more comprehensive listing.

Business Assistance

The Southwest is a growing area, with certain kinds of manufacturing, mining, energy resources and tourism comprising the leading growth areas. For businesses considering relocating, inquiries are generally encouraged. New Mexico, with a concentration of energy resources, agriculture and food processing, research and development, arts and crafts and tourism, has experienced economic growth since the mid-1970s. The Economic Development Division of New Mexico's Commerce and Industry Department provides information and assistance to businesses seeking to trade or relocate in the state and can be contacted at the Bataan Building, Santa Fe, NM 87503, 505/827-6200. In Arizona write Office of Economic Planning and Development, State Capitol, West Wing, Phoenix, AZ 85007, 602/255-5371. In Utah, write the Utah Division of Industrial Development, 200 South Main Street, Suite 620, Salt Lake City, Utah 84101, 801/533-5325. For information on possibilities in Colorado write the state's Division of Commerce and Development, State Office of Tourism, 1313 Sherman Street, Denver, CO 80203. More specifically, in southern Colorado, Cortez and Durango are growing communities, with Durango in particular currently experiencing optimism about the future and an influx of new residents from other areas. See pages 277-279 for their respective Chambers of Commerce. Those interested in inquiring about El Paso as a potential site for manufacturing are encouraged to write the El Paso Industrial Development Corporation, 9 Civic Center Plaza, El Paso, TX 79901, 915/532-8281. In Las Vegas, the economy depends heavily on tourism; for assistance and knowledgeable information, write Nevada Development Authority, P.O. Box 11128, McCarran International Airport, Las Vegas, NV 89111.

Recommended Readings

Abbey, Edward. *Abbey's Road*. New York: E. P. Dutton, 1979. A personal odyssey. Abbey writes with vitality and immediacy about his experience of the Southwest.
Abbey, Edward. *Desert Solitaire*. New York: McGraw-Hill, 1968. A summer spent at Arches. Prophetic, compelling, much about Abbey's direct experience with weather, dangers, plants, animals, you name it.
Other notable books by Abbey: *Down the River, The Hidden Canyon, The Journey Home, The Monkey Wrench Gang*.
Armstrong, Ruth. *New Mexico, From Arrowhead to Atom*. New York: A.S. Barnes and Co., 1969. A straightforward history of New Mexico.
Arnold, Elliott. *The Time of the Gringo*. New York: Alfred A. Knopf, 1953. A modern

classic, dealing with the American occupation of New Mexico.

Bailey, L.R. *The Long Walk: A History of the Navajo Wars, 1846-68*. Pasadena, CA: Western Lore, 1964.

Bandelier, Adolph. *The Delight Makers*. New York: Dodd, Mead & Co., 1942. Fiction set in a prehistoric Indian pueblo. Bandelier is a well-known archaeologist.

Beck, Warren A. *New Mexico: A History of Four Centuries*. Norman: University of Oklahoma Press, 1979.

Broder, Patricia Janis. *The American West: The Modern Vision*. New York: New Graphic Society, 1984.

Brown, Dee. *Bury My Heart at Wounded Knee*. New York: Holt, Rinehart & Winston, 1971. A famous history that has had great impact on American attitudes. Documents the tragic story from the point of view of the American Indian.

Butchart, Harvey. *Grand Canyon Treks*. Glendale, CA: La Siesta Press, 1976. Guidebooks detail the inner canyon and extended canyon routes.

Dent, Huntley. *The Feast of Santa Fe: Cooking of The American Southwest*. New York: Simon and Schuster, 1985. Excellent discussion of the history and traditions of this cuisine. Delicious recipes.

Dobie, J. Frank. *Apache Gold & Yaqui Silver*. New York: Little, Brown, 1939. Dobie is a storyteller at heart; many of his books approach the Southwest through its folklore and tales of lost mines and buried treasure.

Dobie, J. Frank. *Guide to Life and Literature of the Southwest*. Austin: University of Texas Press, 1943.

Fergusson, Erna. *Dancing Gods*. New York: Alfred A. Knopf, 1941. Comprehensive treatment of Indian ceremonials.

Fergusson, Erna. *New Mexico: A Pageant of Three Peoples*. New York: Alfred A. Knopf, 1964. Well-researched history focussing on the peoples of the Southwest.

Fletcher, Colin. *The Man Who Walked Through Time*. New York: Knopf, 1968. Account of a journey through the Grand Canyon.

Fradkin, Philip L. *A River No More*. New York: Knopf, 1981. A cogent, critical study of the uses and misuses of the Colorado River. This book that has been widely acknowledged for its outspokenness.

Hibben, Frank C. *Kiva Art of the Anasazi*. Las Vegas: KC Publications, 1975.

Hillerman, Anthony Grove. *The Blessing Way*. New York: Harper and Row, 1970. Listed among the Notable Books of 1970 by the American Library Association and received an Honorable Mention Award, Mystery Writers of America.

Hillerman. *Listening Woman*. New York: Harper and Row, 1977. This mystery made the New York Times "Best Books of the Year" list and the ALA Notable Books List.

Horgan, Paul. *The Centuries of Santa Fe*. New York: Dutton, 1956. A charming history. Horgan is a prolific writer who has written novels as well as books on the Southwest.

Horgan. *The Great River*. New York: Rinehart, 1954. Comprehensive, two-volume history of the Rio Grande. A prize-winner.

Kluckhohn, Clyde. *Beyond the Rainbow*. Boston: Christopher Publishing House. 1933. Kluckhohn is an anthropologist who brings that viewpoint to his writings on the Southwest and Indian culture.

Kluckhohn, Clyde and Leighton, Dorothea. *The Navajo*. Cambridge: Harvard U. Press, 1974.

Krutch, Joseph Wood. *Grand Canyon*. Garden City, NY: Doubleday, 1958. Krutch is a well-known Southwestern author who writes gracefully on the desert environment, geology, man's involvement with nature.

Krutch. *The Great Chain of Life*. New York: Houghton, 1977.

Leydet, Francois. *Time and the River Flowing: Grand Canyon*. New York: Ballantine Books, 1968. Color pictorial plus extensive text, quotes from well-known Southwestern writers. Composed with an eye for beauty and a feel for ecology.

Mails, Thomas E. *The People Called Apache*. Englewood Cliffs, NJ: Prentice-Hall, 1974.

Miller, Tom. *On the Border: Portraits of America's Southwestern Frontier*. New York: Harper & Row, 1981. People, problems and folklore of the U.S./Mexican border.

Nichols, John. *The Last Beautiful Days of Autumn*. New York: Holt, Rhinehart and Winston, 1982.

Pike, Donald G. and Muench, David. *Anasazi, Ancient People of the Rock*. New York: Crown Publications, 1974. Important pictorial/essay history for those with an interest in the Anasazi.

Pillsbury, Dorothy. *Adobe Doorways*. Santa Fe: Lightning Tree Press, 1983. Collections of essays; intimate, insightful articles about old Santa Fe.

Scully, Vincent. *Pueblo: Mountain, Village, Dance*. New York: The Viking Press, 1972. Scully, an art professor at Yale, writes intelligently about Indian art, culture, dance, architecture.

Seymour, Catryna Ten Eyck. *Enjoying the Southwest*. New York: Lippincott, 1973. Useful and colorful travelogue with personal touches.

Silberstand, Edwin. *The Winner's Guide to Casino Gambling*. New York: New American Library, 1981. For the serious gambler. Great detail about the rules and strategies of each game, interesting reading on the history and contemporary management of casinos.

Silko, Leslie Marmon. *Ceremony*. New York: Signet, 1977.

Simmons, Marc. *New Mexico: A History*. New York: W.W. Norton & Co., 1977. Well-written history coming out of the bi-centennial.

Steiner, Stark. *Dark and Dashing Horsemen*. New York: Harper & Row, 1981.

Sterling, E. M. *Western Trips & Trails*. Boulder: Pruett Publishing Company, 1981. Camping and vacationing in nine states, with tips on weather, camping, hikes, etc.

Sunset Books. *Ghost Towns of the West*. Menlo Park, CA: Lane Magazine and Book Co., 1971. Pictorial including Southwestern ghost towns, among others.

ART/PHOTO CREDITS

154	Richard Erdoes	206	Suzi Barnes	266	Richard Erdoes
155L	Ellis Armstrong	207	Buddy Mays	267	Richard Erdoes
155R	Richard Erdoes	208	Allen Grazer	268	Suzi Barnes
156	Buddy Mays	212-213	Terrence Moore	271	C. Allan Morgan
157	Buddy Mays	214	Terrence Moore		
160-161	Buddy Mays	216	Terrence Moore		
162	Ellis Armstrong	217	Courtesy of Colorado	End	Vautier-de Nanxe
163	Buddy Mays		Historical Society	paper,	
164	Ellis Armstrong	218	Terrence Moore	back	
165	Richard Erdoes	219	Terrence Moore	Book	
166	Buddy Mays	220	Terrence Moore	spine	Terrence Moore (Mission)
167	Buddy Mays	221	C. Allan Morgan	(top to	Buddy Mays (ranger)
168	Ellis Armstrong	222	Terrence Moore	bottom)	Vautier-de Nanxe (arch)
169	Ellis Armstrong	225	Terrence Moore		C. Allan Morgan (cactus)
172-173	Buddy Mays	226-227	Kathleen N. Cook		
174	Buddy Mays	229	Terrence Moore		
175	Buddy Mays	230	Terrence Moore	Back	Vautier-de Nanxe
176	Buddy Mays	231	C. Allan Morgan	cover	(excursions)
177	Maxine Lundberg	232	C. Allan Morgan		Vautier-de Nanxe
178	Vautier-de Nanxe	233	Terrence Moore		(canyons)
179	Terrence Moore	234	Terrence Moore		Lee Marmon
180	Buddy Mays	235	Kathleen N. Cook		(Indians)
182	Terrence Moore	240	Dallas & John Heaton		Vautier-de Nanxe
184	Karl Kernberger	241	Dallas & John Heaton		(deserts)
185	Ellis Armstrong	242	Vautier-de Nanxe		Karl Kernberger
187	Buddy Mays	243	Dallas & John Heaton		(signals)
188L	Buddy Mays	244	Vautier-de Nanxe		Dallas & John Heaton
188R	Buddy Mays	245	Vautier-de Nanxe		(neon)
189	Buddy Mays	246	Dallas & John Heaton		Richard Erdoes
190	Ellis Armstrong	247	Dallas & John Heaton		(pueblos)
191	Richard Erdoes	248	Vautier-de Nanxe		Buddy Mays
193	Terrence Moore	249	Vautier-de Nanxe		(beasts)
194-195	Vautier-de Nanxe	250	Dallas & John Heaton		Terrence Moore
196	Terrence Moore	252-253	Richard Erdoes		(cowgirls)
197	Sam Curtis	254	Richard Erdoes		Vautier-de Nanxe
198	C. Allan Morgan	257	Lee Marmon		(rodeos)
200	Suzi Barnes	259	Ronnie Pinsler		Richard Erdoes
201	Terrence Moore	260	Terrence Moore		(slopes)
202	Terrence Moore	261	Richard Erdoes		Buddy Mays
203	David Ryan	262	Vautier-de Nanxe		(gems)
204	C. Allan Morgan	264	Vautier-de Nanxe		Vautier-de Nanxe
205	Terrence Moore	265	Richard Erdoes		(whitewater)

300